Homeland Calling

Homeland Calling
Exile Patriotism & the Balkan Wars

Paul Hockenos

CORNELL UNIVERSITY PRESS

Ithaca & London

First published 2003 by Cornell University Press

Printed in the United States of America

Library of Congress Cataloging-in-Publication Data

Hockenos, Paul, 1963–
    Homeland calling : exile patriotism and the Balkan wars / Paul Hockenos.
        p. cm.
Includes bibliographical references and index.
    ISBN 0-8014-4158-7 (cloth)
    1. Yugoslavia—Politics and government—1980-1992. 2. Yugoslav War, 1991–1995—Causes. 3. Yugoslavs—Foreign countries. 4. Nationalism—Serbia and Montenegro. I. Title.
    DR1309.H63 2003
    949.703—dc21
                                            2003010042

Cornell University Press strives to use environmentally responsible suppliers and materials to the fullest extent possible in the publishing of its books. Such materials include vegetable-based, low-VOC inks and acid-free papers that are recycled, totally chlorine-free, or partly composed of nonwood fibers. For further information, visit our website at www.cornellpress.cornell.edu.

Cloth printing   10 9 8 7 6 5 4 3 2 1

To Anne and Warren

Exiles, émigrés, refugees and expatriates uprooted from their lands must make do in new surroundings, and the creativity as well as the sadness that can be seen in what they do is one of the experiences that has still to find its chroniclers.

EDWARD SAID, *Reflections on Exile and Other Essays*

Contents

Preface

For those closely following events in southeastern Europe during the 1990s, the specter of the region's national diasporas presented one of the more opaque variables in the conflicts that ripped Yugoslavia apart. Exile figures, such as Croatia's defense minister, Gojko Šušak, and Yugoslavia's 1992 prime minister, Milan Panić, had assumed key positions of power. But from the proximity of the front lines it was impossible to determine whether the likes of either Šušak, an arch right-wing former pizza baker from Canada, or Panić, a California pharmaceuticals tycoon, accurately represented their people's greater diasporas or, indeed, anyone other than themselves.

Ample evidence indicated that overseas ethnic communities had mobilized to aid nationalist political factions well before the shooting started. The money trails led not only from the underworlds in Buenos Aires and Geneva but also from suburban neighborhoods, church groups, and folk dancing societies in the model democracies of the West. But how, exactly, and through what transnational networks did these diverse actors bankroll their causes? Equally ambiguous was the background of these borderless organizations and their leaders, despite the fact that they had agitated in our midst for decades. The untamed propaganda aside, no one could evaluate with any degree of certainty the real impact the diasporas were having on the Balkan conflicts, such as their roles in the rampant arms smuggling and the financing of electoral campaigns. Did nationalist politicians control the purse strings of the diasporas? Or was it the other way around, that the political forces in the homeland were spurred on by militant exiles? The regional protagonists charged that multimillion-dollar émigré lobbies swayed the foreign policies of the United States, Germany, and Great Britain. Rumors were rife, but facts were scarce.

As a journalist covering the Balkan wars, and then as an official of the Organization for Security and Cooperation in Europe Mission to Bosnia and Herzegovina, I pondered these questions and probed others who knew more. Many sources possessed fragments of a much larger, more elaborate story that spanned decades and continents. But no one person offered anything close to a comprehensive account, nor had any single researcher tried to piece those fragments together and, critically, endeavor to travel through the diasporas to hear the story as told by the émigré activists.

Originally this was a book I wanted to read, not necessarily write. But curiosity is a powerful motivator. And once I embarked on the project I quickly picked up a few essential lessons concerning diasporas. They are insular communities, highly suspicious of outsiders who poke into their affairs. "Are you a friend of Croatia's or are you critical?" one Canadian Croat searchingly responded to my request for an interview. Before anyone from Ontario's Croat community agreed to meet me, a flurry of telephone calls between Zagreb, Toronto, and Široki Brijeg settled the issue: it would be contractor John Zdunić, one of the Toronto area's wealthiest ethnic Croats. Presumably these discussions determined what should and should not be divulged. And Zdunić let me know when I pushed too far. In response to a question about the Croat diaspora's campaign to arm the home country, Zdunić snapped that this was a "family matter"—and thus no business of mine. I learned that diasporas resemble families in more ways than one.

Joe and Shirley DioGuardi, the self-appointed first couple of the Albanian diaspora, conducted a thorough web search before they ascertained that my previous publications treating Albanian issues were sound enough to warrant an interview appointment. In person, they continued to quiz me: Did I work for another lobby? Who had I already spoken with? Was my surname Greek? "You can't imagine how much trouble those Greeks have given me," Joe DioGuardi explained, when I informed him that this was not the case.

During the two years that I traveled through the Balkans, Western Europe, and North America in search of the diaspora story, most of the people I aspired to interview met with me, though often reluctantly at first. I promised my interlocutors that I wished to understand their actions and motivations, and that I would present them as accurately as I could, even if I disagreed profoundly with their politics, which was often the case. In the pages that follow I have tried to honor that pledge. Some interviewees began with egregiously self-serving, one-sided narratives of their involvement in world events in the twentieth century. Others lied blatantly. Still others proved remarkably candid, so convinced of the righteousness of their campaigns that they reasoned that any genuinely nonpartisan person of average intelligence could not help but buy their arguments. There were those, such as the former radical Croat leader Marin Sopta and the Milošević loyalist Radmila Milentijević, who surely suspected that a liberal-minded Western journalist was not going to sympathize with their positions. Nevertheless, they and others like them spoke with me at length, and for that they won my respect.

There were people who declined to be interviewed for this book. Djurdja Šušak, the late minister's widow and former official herself in Croatia's Defense Ministry, refused to speak to me, as she did to other chroniclers of the recent past. In this, I feel, she does her late husband a disservice. The Herzegovina's Croat Franciscans in Široki Brijeg's hilltop monastery were among the least forthcoming. One husky brother, bearded and clad in brown cassock and leather sandals, responded to my polite inquiries by blocking the seminary door with his considerable girth. Nosy journalists, he informed me in a mixture of broken German and body language that could not be misinterpreted, entered the walled grounds of the Assumption of the Blessed Virgin Mary at their own physical peril.

Most, though, told their stories willingly, and I profited in many ways from their renditions of lives so steeped in history. Only a fraction of those I interviewed appear in these chapters. I thank them all for being so generous with their time and thoughts.

I owe my gratitude to many people who contributed to the completion of this project. I thank the German Marshall Fund of the United States and the Journalisten-Kolleg at the Freie Universität Berlin for fellowship grants to conduct research. I also owe a debt to the ever helpful staffs of the Skidmore College library, the Staatsbibliothek Berlin on Potsdamerstrasse, the Deutsche Bundespressearchiv and the Nacionalna i Šveuciliša Biblioteka in Zagreb. The following people read portions of the manuscript during different stages of its development: Dragan Kremer, Mark Thompson, Marcus Cox, Dejan Jović, Dardan Gashi, Fabian Schmidt, Dejan Djokić, Jack Seymour, Anne Crookall Hockenos, Klaus Buchenau, Joe Knowles, Susan Bernofsky, Bob Van Meter, and Beate Andrees. I thank them for their comments and critiques, which have made this a better book. I also acknowledge my soulmates at the European Stability Initiative and in particular Gerald Knaus. Of course, any of the project's shortcomings are mine. Last, I pay respects to my first-rate agent, Cecelia A. Cancellaro of Idea Architects, and my commissioning editor at Cornell University Press, Roger Haydon.

PAUL HOCKENOS

Berlin

Author's Note

With topics Balkan it is impossible to please everyone on issues of style, terminology, and spelling. I have made my choices out of the desire to be as clear, consistent, and respectful as possible. Sometimes these priorities conflict with one another. I offer apologies if my choices unintentionally offend my subjects in any way.

The place names are infamously debatable, especially when people of rival ethnicities, who inhabit (or claim) the location in question, know these same cities, mountain chains, and rivers by different names. When writing about Kosovo I have chosen to use Serbian names rather than Albanian simply because they are more widely known and tend to be used on most (non-Albanian) maps. I use the standard "Kosovo" rather than the Albanian "Kosova" for this reason. However, when quoting an Albanian source that specifically uses "Kosova" I have retained that spelling. For the sake of simplicity I often refer to Bosnia and Herzegovina as "Bosnia," and to the Croats, Muslims, or Serbs of Bosnia and Herzegovina as "Bosnian Croats," "Bosnian Muslims," or "Bosnian Serbs." I try to make it apparent when I am writing specifically about Croats from Herzegovina, as I do quite often in the early chapters. Similarly I sometimes refer to Kosovar Albanians as "Kosovars." In most cases the context should make the subjects' ethnicity clear. In cases when the home territory of an Albanian subject may be questionable, I usually use "ethnic Albanian" to signify an Albanian not from Albania proper.

Regarding the names of émigré figures, I have employed the Serbo-Croatian letters with diacriticals to all names that have not been anglicized. Many émigrés with names that end in the typical Slavic "ić" (pronounced "ich") have chosen to add an "h" to their anglicized surnames, as did Michael Djordjevich (born Miroslav Djordjević). Others such as Milan Panić have not, and though they omit the acute accent when in North America, they continue to pronounce their surnames as their parents did in the Old Country. Still others such as Gojko Šušak dropped the diacriticals from their names and changed the pronunciation. Gojko Šušak (pronounced "shoe-shock") became Garry Susak and pronounced his name as a native English speaker would. There is no rule.

Potentially confusing are my references to Yugoslavia's secret services and armies. The Uprava Državne Bezbednosti (Management of State Security), or UDBA, was the Yugoslav secret service from 1946 to 1954, which kept a close eye on diaspora activities and occasionally assassinated prominent émigrés. In 1954 it became the Služba Državne Bezbednosti (Service of State Security), or SDB. Many émigrés continued to refer to the organization by the acronym UDBA throughout the Cold War, which itself is indicative of the exile mind-set. I leave their quotes intact. Further, Yugoslavia's armed forces during the era of socialist Yugoslavia, the Jugoslovenska Narodna Armija (Yugoslav People's Army), or JNA, became the Vojska Jugoslavije (Army of Yugoslavia) in 1992. I refer to the latter simply as the Yugoslav army.

I have chosen to reference sources sparingly, particularly on standard accounts of the recent or distant past such as the siege of Sarajevo, the history of the Ustashe, or the importance of 1389 for the Serbs. I am deeply indebted to many fine colleagues whose painstaking efforts to chronicle the regional conflicts of the 1990s have produced a bedrock for others in the field. The books of Christopher Bennett, Roger Cohen, Laura Silber and Allan Little, Mark Thompson, Misha Glenny, and Tim Judah, among others, were never far from my reach. For historical accounts stretching further back in time I tried to rely on the academic canon. I cite sources only when quoting directly or referring to an issue original to that work. The selected bibliography includes those works indispensable to each part of the book, as well as other, more obscure sources that might be of interest to other researchers in the field. Works cited in the notes do not appear in the bibliography. All direct and indirect quotations that are not cited come from the interviews I conducted between 1999 and 2002.

Introduction

In the Balkans every Croat or Slovene, Serb or Macedonian, is acutely aware that fractured generations of his ethnic kinsmen reside on alien shores.

Few are the families in the former Yugoslavia that never had an uncle, at the very least, who sent part of his paycheck or Christmas parcels back from Germany, Sweden, Australia, or even the United States. Some of these relatives never returned to their places of birth, building new lives in better-off, faraway countries. From the cracking apartment blocs and stony mountains of the Balkans, these wayward cousins are viewed with a mixture of pride and melancholy, resentment and awe. Some émigrés, as is well known, are fabulously rich, even millionaires among them. Yet their dislocated lives testify to tragic collisions with history. They are objects of envy for their wealth, and of suspicion for their acquired New World ways, as well as for their checkered pasts. The diaspora represents the best and worst of the nation: tycoons, basketball stars, congressmen, war criminals, gangsters.

In times of crisis they flee, and when they return, if they do, they bring back to the homeland perceptions and plans transformed by their odysseys. These expatriate kin, though estranged in time and place, their native tongues now heavy with accent, have continued to remain part of the nation. For them, and for their countrymen, the primordial pull of ancestry forges a timeless bond, indubitably stronger than the acquired legal credentials of foreign citizenship. Nevertheless, the vast new distance between their worlds cannot be easily masked.

Hail a taxi in Belgrade or Sarajevo, and almost inevitably you will encounter a cabbie who can chat in broken Swiss or Schwabian German. These men were among the millions of "Yugoslavs" who, along with Turks, Italians, and Greeks, bolstered Western Europe's undermanned work force during the latter decades of the Cold War. The migrant workers bunked together in stark hostels, accepting the menial jobs that the Germans and Swiss turned down. On their return they built up whole towns in central Bosnia, the Herzegovina, and Kosovo with houses that bear a homemade resemblance to those in Alpine villages. These *gastarbeiter*, or guest workers, changed the face of postwar Western Europe and, in turn, transformed socialist Yugoslavia into a country more prosperous and less provincial than its less fortunate Eastern bloc neighbors.

Older diaspora communities—disparate groups with histories that intersect and clash—had made their homes outside Yugoslavia long before these itinerant workers strolled through the Iron Curtain. World War II political exiles fell into their own unenviable category, viewed inside Yugoslavia as either sinister right-wing provocateurs or persecuted heroes, depending on the viewers' family background. These banished souls comprised the detritus of the communists' battlefield foes and ideological nemeses, chased from their places of birth as Tito's Partisans and the Soviet Red Army swept across the country. The mixed bag of clergy and officer corps, ordinary soldiers and implacable fascists, fled as far away as Australia, South Africa, and North and South America, where they vigilantly nursed dreams of a return triumphant.

Yugoslavia's postwar regime vilified the political exiles as counterrevolutionaries, a reactionary "sixth column" that schemed to overthrow the socialist state. Apparently Tito took these exilic fantasies as seriously as the exiles did. A package from the wrong great-uncle in Toronto could result in a visit from the police, whether the package contained a few folded sheets of royalist propaganda or not. On the margins of the Cold War, Tito's agents waged running battles with the exile agitators in North America, Australia, and Western Europe, infiltrating their back-street organizations and assassinating their leaders. The caricature of the unrepentant, plotting exile was sometimes apt, even if the Yugoslav state vastly exaggerated their power and reach. The image of the neofascist émigré was a transparent ruse to discredit all anticommunist opposition coming from abroad. As long as the Cold War status quo prevailed, such factions posed no threat to Yugoslavia. Only after the socialist state imploded did these defiant visions became viable, abetted with remarkable zeal by the same communist guard that had once persecuted the exiles so vigorously.

While the Yugoslav regime perpetuated an image of the perfidious diaspora, a concurrent mythology existed of the self-made émigré, the one who had made it big in the West. For poor people from small countries, learning that their countrymen had their own companies in Canada or had patented an international invention spoke to the worth of their nation, and thus to their own worth. They believed that if their co-nationals could make it as

U.S. industrialists or, more likely, restaurant owners in Germany, then they could, too, if only given the chance. After 1965, when Yugoslavia liberalized its emigration policies, another wave of migrants were given that chance. Millionaires aside, the large diaspora communities in Chicago or Cleveland, for example, were proudly touted as integral constituencies of those cities. Indeed, some of their forefathers, immigrants from the nineteenth and early twentieth centuries, toiled in steel and textile mills to help build these Midwestern metropolises.

One afternoon the director of Croatia's Cultural Heritage Foundation, a state-run agency responsible for links with the diaspora, escorted me around the organization's voluminous cube-shaped building in central Zagreb, Croatia's capital city. The walls were lined with grainy, blown-up portraits from turn-of-the century Croatian-American clubs depicting football stars wearing old leather helmets and other proud-looking men and women with Americanized Croatian surnames. These people are members of the Croat family, too, he noted; they are both part of the homeland and separated from it. Croatia's accomplished native sons stand as real-life documentation of their nation's resourcefulness. The exhibition implied that the cruel course of history may have swept the émigrés abroad, but, no less calamitous, it thwarted the potential of those condemned to stay.

The tradition of sanctuary has its own mystique. In the Balkans, war, tyranny, and political persecution have sent waves of refugees abroad in search of safe haven. High-minded, brave, and foolhardy men have returned to shape the destinies of their countries, for better or for worse. During the final decades of the Ottoman Empire, Albania's intellectuals reconstituted themselves abroad in Romania, Italy, and even the United States to assert the rights of their subjugated nation. A long line of Serb royalty that began with the legendary founder of the Karadjordjević dynasty, Black George, relied on European exile bases in times of trouble. The notorious Ustashe, Croatia's homegrown fascists, assumed power from exile and then fled again after World War II, establishing new bases in Spain, Argentina, West Germany, and the United States. More recently, in the 1980s and 1990s, Kosovar Albanians, fleeing the heavy hand of the Serbian regime, sought political asylum in Europe and North America by the hundreds of thousands. Undoubtedly Serbia's leadership had not imagined that these same refugees would labor so resolutely and effectively from abroad to wrest their homeland from Serb rule.

Another case was the "brain drainers" of the 1990s, the educated young people who abandoned their dysfunctional states to apply their professional skills abroad. More than two hundred thousand Serbs fled Slobodan Milošević's Serbia during that decade. Naturally, upon arriving in the West, they encountered the resident Serb diaspora. Recalling that time, they remember how shocked they were to find these communities so locked in bygone times, passionately committed to traditions they had never known. In fact, by the late 1980s, those in the mother country and those in the diaspora recognized each other largely through the filters of myth and legend. Decades of disparate socialization, conflicting propaganda, and limited travel possibilities had obstructed a healthy exchange of ideas and experiences. Living worlds apart, they had grown further apart.

Nevertheless, with the collapse of communism in Eastern Europe, suddenly all that was impossible seemed possible. The peoples of Yugoslavia, as elsewhere in Eastern Europe, hoped that their diasporas might contribute guidance and, more pointedly, financial succor for the transitions out of socialism. Nationalist currents in the homeland, including the Orthodox and Catholic churches, had been in close touch with diaspora communities for decades and considered them key allies in their plans for the future. They did not have to beckon twice. Many émigré groups and individual patriots had never taken their eyes off their ancestral homes, and indeed some had been planning their return for decades. In fact, many were already on their way. Their homecomings defied whatever vague expectations may have been in the air.

Perhaps some optimists imagined that one of their own brethren might come to resemble Eastern Europe's most renowned émigré, the Hungarian billionaire investor and philanthropist George Soros. In the 1980s his private organization funneled millions of dollars into communist-ruled central Europe to fund grassroots democratic and liberal anticommunist opposition groups. When the walls tumbled, Soros redoubled his efforts to anchor civil society in the newly democratic states. His crowning achievement was the Central European University. The spanking new facility in Budapest, stocked with visiting Ivy League professors, doles out scholarships to Central Europe's best and brightest, providing sterling liberal educations for the region's future leaders.

But Soros proved to be one of a kind. As a news correspondent in the early 1990s I toured central and southeastern Europe and crossed paths with handfuls of returnees, some with overt political agendas. Others were after quick fortunes of one kind or another. In the Baltics, scores of former expatriates returned to land top governmental positions. Also, after decades of hibernation, exiled royalty too were shaking the sleep out of their eyes. Yugoslavia's Prince Alexander, the heir to the Karadjordjević dynasty, took a renewed interest in the throne his father had fled in 1941. In Romania, Albania, and Bulgaria, as well, forgotten monarchs inquired longingly about confiscated property and voided titles.

In socialist Yugoslavia Serbia's new leader, Slobodan Milošević, had the Serb diaspora in his sights even before the Berlin Wall fell. In the late 1980s, as an early overture to the diaspora, Milošević relaxed some of the more draconian restrictions on the visitation rights of political exiles. A few years later he hatched a giant investment scheme to milk the diaspora for long-term loans, purportedly to modernize Serbian industry. As it turned out, the monies financed Serbia's territorial wars, something most of the diaspora investors, had they known about it in the first place, probably would not have objected to.

But the historical date of June 28, 1989, the Serbs' revered St. Vitus Day, marked a veritable sea change in Serbia's relations with the diaspora. At Serbia's invitation, thousands of émigré Serbs joined the estimated one million pilgrims who descended on Kosovo's legendary Field of the Blackbirds to celebrate the six hundredth anniversary of the Serbian kingdom's defeat at the hands of the Ottoman army. Émigré patriots from as far away as Melbourne and Seattle cheered Milošević to the skies as he ushered in a decade of war. Among the flushed Americans in the crowd were Maryland Congresswoman Helen Delich Bentley and a New York City university dean, Radmila Milentijević. So awestruck were the two Serbian Americans by the extravaganza that they volunteered to act as international spokespersons for the new Serb leader.

Several months later Croatian TV broadcast its own surreal scenes. Boisterous contingents of Croat émigrés landed at Zagreb's Pleso Airport, their red, blue, and white Croatian flags flying high. Until that day many of the travelers' names had topped official black lists: the infamous "politicals" banned from entering Yugoslavia. They were visiting a relatively new friend, the Partisan general-turned-nationalist dissident Franjo Tudjman, Croatia's future president. Tudjman had boldly reached out to the diaspora during exploratory trips to North America and Europe in the late 1980s. The right-wing émigrés took his promises of political power literally and lined the front rows at the first convention of his nationalist party, the Croatian Democratic Community. Speaking to the euphoric returnees, Tudjman outlined a program that would steer Croatia through a turbulent decade. His foresight was remarkable: years in advance Tudjman had intuited that these men would be instrumental to his plans.

Elsewhere in Yugoslavia in the early 1990s, in the republics of Slovenia, Bosnia and Herzegovina, and Macedonia, émigrés were also returning to their homelands. The wealthy Muslim businessman Adil Zulfikarpašić returned from Switzerland to help found the leading party of the Bosnian Muslims, the Party for Democratic Action (SDA). In the nasty diplomatic tussle over Macedonian statehood, Slavic Macedonians from Canada and Australia took up the fight on behalf of their fledgling nation.[1] To be sure, the powerful Greek diaspora, already well established in the West, weighed in forcefully against the Macedonian republic's bid for independence, not the last time during the 1990s that Athens would meddle in the affairs of the former Yugoslavia.

In stark contrast, in Serbia's southern province of Kosovo, joyous home-comings were out of the question. The Serbian republic had been steadily tightening screws on the 1.7 million ethnic Albanians in Kosovo who consti-tuted a 9 to 1 majority over their Kosovar Serb neighbors. Since the late 1960s ethnic Albanians had been exiting their homeland, first at a trickle and then en masse. In 1990 the entire ethnic Albanian membership of the Kosovar parliament packed its bags and headed into exile, followed shortly thereafter by a renegade government that would operate from abroad until 1999. The exiled prime minister Bujar Bukoshi, from bases in Slovenia and then southern Germany, raised more than $100 million to fund Kosovo's schools and hospitals, the pillars of the ethnic Albanians' parallel state. But when a decade of peaceful resistance failed to win the Kosovar Albanians their freedom, a guerrilla movement emerged from the drab gastarbeiter clubs in Switzerland and Germany that would try to do so by force.

A year or so after the émigrés' trumpeted returns, the former Yugoslavia stood on the brink of the bloodiest European conflict since 1945. The naive, fleeting hope that the diasporas might help guide their beloved homelands into the Western fold—toward multicultural democracies like the ones in which they had thrived—perished without a trace. Contrary to some interpretations, it was not the diasporas that precipitated the wars that engulfed the Balkans. One variation on the diaspora myth contends that the "other" diasporas, those of rival nations acting from behind the scenes in Western capitals, pulled the strings that triggered the disintegra-tion of Yugoslavia. That is not the case. Responsibility for the wars in the former Yugoslavia lies firmly with the citizenry there and their nationalist leaders. Nevertheless, at critical junctures the diasporas contributed deci-sively to the conflicts. Tudjman's supporters bankrolled his upstart party's first campaign in 1990, helping to catapult it into power. In Serbia, Croatia, and later Kosovo, shadowy diaspora figures returned from abroad to take up ministerial positions in the new governments. When the patria required it, the diaspora sent arms, soldiers, even generals to the frontlines. Home-land Calling, for example, was the worldwide diaspora fund set up to fi-nance Kosovo's guerrilla army. In Western countries diasporas organized ethnic lobbies that campaigned for their causes. Much to their discredit, only rarely did the diasporas use their resources to bolster the frail demo-cratic forces that offered the only alternative to the madness of unchecked nationalism.

At the same time, when examining the roles played by nonresident com-munities in the Balkan conflicts, it is unfair to speak in overly broad terms about "the diasporas." The entire Croat diaspora did not finance Tudjman nor did every Serbian American cheer Milošević. To the contrary, these are heterogeneous ethnic communities that span classes, generations, and continents. The reactions of Croatian Americans or Serbian Australians, for example, were as diverse as the patchwork diasporas from which they hailed. Many émigrés consciously chose to remain separate from the nostalgic or militant exile groups. Dissenting voices in diasporas, however, tend to be muffled by the willful, mobilized actors in their communities who push their own agendas to the fore. In the wild world of diaspora politics, eccentric and usually wealthy diaspora individuals pretend to speak in the name of the entire diaspora, the national cause, and even the mother country. These are exalted claims by individuals and groups that were neither elected by diaspora constituencies nor appointed by states. The membership of even the biggest associations is shockingly small, a mere sliver of the diaspora as a whole. In crucial instances diaspora figures or organizations that had the greatest impact belonged to their respective community's radical fringe.

Individual personalities tend to loom large in organized diasporas, and the transnational Balkan communities are no exception. Among émigrés, the political is intensely personal. This book traces the life stories of the leading diaspora figures from the former Yugoslavia, people who sought, through their engagement in the affairs of the homeland, to influence the course of events in the Balkans. Sometimes they succeeded; at other times their efforts to intervene failed in spectacular fashion. A degree of hubris and folly characterized almost all of them. The stories of a Serbian American chemical magnate, a Croatian Canadian pizza maker, and an exiled Albanian urologist would seem to have little that binds them. But as different as these men and women are, taken together their experiences shed light on the nature of diasporas, on exile politics, and on the recent wars in the Balkans.

The issues before us beg certain questions. For example, what is a diaspora? The generic definition is that a diaspora comprises those members of a common ethnic-national group living outside the borders of their native home territory. The two key criteria are ethnicity and foreign residency. But this shorthand definition raises other questions: Are workers who are living abroad temporarily, such as the gastarbeiter, part of the diaspora? Are refugees who receive safe haven during conflicts also diaspora? And what about ethnic minorities living in neighboring countries, such as the ethnic Croats in Hungary and Austria? There is also the problem of ethnicity. Do children of mixed marriages still qualify as "ethnic Serbs" or "ethnic Macedonians"? Do the second, third, or fourth generations of immigrant families count? Must one speak the native language to be considered part of a diaspora?

These questions have no simple answers, but they help to explain the gross discrepancies in numbers provided by, and for, diasporas. Croatian president Tudjman, for example, claimed that as many Croats live outside of the country as do in Croatia (nearly four million). Yet when the Croat diaspora received voting rights in 1995, the state could locate only four hundred thousand Croat citizens residing abroad—formal citizenship being required to cast a ballot. Moreover, three hundred thousand of those eligible "diaspora Croats" lived next door in Bosnia and Herzegovina.

For my purposes, I employ an elastic definition by which the diaspora includes immigrant families and their subsequent generations, gastarbeiter, exile communities, expatriates, and refugees. Ultimately a diaspora is made up of individuals who identify themselves, and are accepted, as its members. An American with Greek ancestry is a member of the Greek diaspora if he feels that he is and if he participates in the diaspora community. Whether he understands Greek is irrelevant. All diaspora constituents somehow divide their loyalties between their adopted homes and their ancestral homeland. These individuals keep one eye trained on their home country and can be moved to act on its behalf, particularly in times of crisis. They may pay dues to one of the many diaspora associations or may subscribe to émigré periodicals. At the very least they usually attend religious services at their national churches, follow events in the Old World, and communicate regularly with relatives in the homeland. In these ways they keep alive emotional ties with the Old Country and, through the institutions of the diaspora, sustain a degree of cohesion in the community. Without these institutions, such as periodicals, associations, lobby groups, churches, and websites, there would be no diasporas at all, only people of different ethnicity scattered across the globe.

The word *diaspora* has Greek roots. It derives from the Greek verb *speiro* (to sow or to scatter) and the preposition *dia* (over). But the origins of its contemporary use lie deep in Jewish tradition. "Babylonian exile" refers to the expulsion of the Jews from Jerusalem in the sixth century B.C. King Nebuchadnezzar, according to the Old Testament, exiled the Jews to Babylon where they languished in captivity. Thereafter the Jewish people dispersed to other foreign lands, compelled to live as outsiders in a hostile, alien world. Babylonian exile connotes forcible expulsion, persecution, and enslavement, and implies the prospect of return. By definition, those in exile are to cultivate their native traditions and culture in preparation for a return to the Promised Land.

More recently, however, in the lively discourse that has arisen around the notion of global diasporas, the Babylonian "victim typology" is deemed inadequate to make sense of today's heterogeneous transnational communities.[2] It discounts other kinds of migrations such as economic emigration or voluntary expatriation. It also precludes the possibility, not to mention the desirability, of partial or full assimilation. The Babylonian model presents the narrowest possible identity for diaspora groups. In reality, even the most loyal exile patriots have other facets to their characters. In this age of globalization, diasporas defined so strictly by the bonds of nation and state appear sadly anachronistic. Theoretically, in a democratic, transnational world, the model of Babylonian exile should become obsolete—certainly the benefits of its doing so seem clear.

But this is not the reality. As unsavory as this paradigm may be, it reflects tellingly on one pivotal strain of Balkan exile—those whose activities defined Cold War–era diaspora politics, namely, World War II and postwar era political exiles. It was these "ideological deviants," pushed out of the young socialist state in the war's aftermath, whose declared love for their lost homeland and loathing of the communist dictator Tito would dictate the terms of their political engagement for decades. The conditions of their emigration, indeed their own Babylonian exile, set the tenor for Balkan diaspora politics during the Cold War and beyond.

These political exiles bore the telltale scars of battlefield defeat, expulsion, and flight, although they were neither enslaved nor, for the most part, persecuted in their new residencies. Over the long Cold War decades they put down roots, and some even became rich. Michael Djordjevich, for example, the Serbian American who, in the 1990s, founded Serbia's biggest lobby group, is a successful California insurance executive. But Djordjevich's family and their ilk did not choose their fate; it was imposed on them by conquering armies. Fleeing their occupied, war-ravaged countries, they escaped first to Western Europe and usually ended up in one of the teeming refugee camps in Italy, Austria, or Germany. From there they fanned out to other continents, arriving traumatized and penniless in uncomprehending societies.

Even the established diaspora communities in these countries rarely welcomed the postwar exiles. The prewar diaspora communities tended to include simple working-class immigrants, many with rural backgrounds, most intent on blending in, and contributing to, their adopted states. The new émigrés, on the other hand, included Yugoslavia's disinherited bourgeois. In contrast to the diaspora "old timers," they were often educated and urban: families associated with deposed royal houses, the military elite, and banned political movements. Abandoned by the Western powers, they started off with nothing, even a notch lower on the ladder than former commoners from their own country.

"Exile," writes the Palestinian critic Edward Said, "can produce rancor and regret, as well as a sharpened vision. What has been left behind can either be mourned, or it can be used to provide a different set of lenses. Since almost by definition exile and memory go together, it is what one remembers of the past that determines how one sees the future."[3]

It was rancor and regret, not sharpened vision, that colored the political movements, organizations, émigré literature, and insular micro-societies that the diaspora newcomers created for themselves in the West in the 1950s and 1960s. They lived in disoriented time-warped worlds, their present overdetermined by their past. Like a stagnant swamp, these communities bred infectious cultures of paranoia, hatred, and far-fetched theories of conspiracy. The inhabitants remained wedded to the brittle nationalistic ideologies that, as young men, they had been prepared to die for in the trenches. In the Serb diaspora, royalist organizations dreamed of restoring the Karadjordjević monarchy in Yugoslavia. The interwar Albanian political spectrum reconstituted itself almost intact in Turkey, Western Europe, and North America. Among diaspora Croats, well into the 1980s groups like the Croatian Liberation Movement and the Croatian National Resistance kindled fantasies of a resurgent neofascist state. These kinds of movements, fiercely bitter and screaming for revenge, elbowed aside the benevolent societies and cultural clubs of the old-timer immigrants, introducing a qualitatively new phenomenon in their adopted domiciles.

In the early postwar decades these professional exiles believed, with religious conviction, that the demise of communism was imminent and that they would return victorious, perhaps behind U.S. army tanks. After all, it was Washington that spoke in grandiose terms of a rollback of Soviet forces in Eastern Europe, even if it had struck up a cautious friendship with the maverick communist Tito, an act utterly inexplicable to the émigrés. The myriad of postwar diaspora organizations shared one critical common denominator: pathological anticommunism. Theirs was the loudest, shrillest version of the West's rallying cry against world communism. Significantly, the conservative right in the United States actively encouraged these illiberal movements in order to fan domestic anticommunism. The Central Intelligence Agency pumped millions of dollars into the Captive Nations[4] societies and even funded covert guerrilla invasions of Albanian exiles into Albania in the early 1950s. The right-wing of the U.S. Republican Party, in particular, courted the votes and campaign contributions of Eastern European immigrants, blessing their causes and legitimizing their operations. Thus when democracy did come to captive Europe, its Western diasporas were ill equipped to advance it, a state of affairs for which America's cold warriors must bear some of the blame.

The motifs of Babylonian exile surface repeatedly in the stories of the Croat, Albanian, and Serb diasporas. One such prototypical exile was Gojko Šušak, a Bosnian Croat émigré who, after several decades in Canada, moved to Croatia to become President Tudjman's powerful right-hand man. In Canada Šušak and his coterie had circulated in a seamy underground of militant ultranationalist splinter groups. These men never established roots in

Canada's multiethnic society but dwelled in the subcultural enclaves they had carved out for themselves. Late into the night at their private clubs, they fantasized about returning together to an independent Croatia. The Croatia they mapped out in their publications covered the Croatian republic and half of Bosnia and Herzegovina, stretching all the way to the River Drina, just as it had in the 1940s.

Šušak's circle piqued Tudjman's interest because of its political coordinates, not despite them. During his trips to Canada in the late 1980s the future Croatian president understood that this segment of the diaspora would work for him—and would also fortify his movement ideologically. A key component of Tudjman's Croatian National Policy was the concept of "Iseljena Hrvatska." Roughly translated as "exiled Croatia," it implied that all ethnic Croats living outside Croatia proper were in fact political exiles, Croats forcibly expelled or in some way pressured to leave against their will. They *belonged* in Croatia. His messianic plan was to repatriate the diaspora Croats to Croatia, to those parts of the country where non-Croat ethnic minorities lived. Tudjman's vision of an ethnic Greater Croatia relied on Iseljena Hrvatska. The first wave of repatriation included Šušak and his like, whom Tudjman promised positions in the national administration. Šušak was named the first minister of return and immigration, the man responsible for restocking the Croatian state. In other words, he would oversee the shifting of ethnic populations to manufacture a more ethnically compact nation. As Croatia's powerful defense minister from 1992 to 1998, he would pursue Tudjman's demographic project by other means.

The Babylonian–Iseljena Hrvatska paradigm fits for some diaspora players but not for others. Even at its best, however, the lion's share of diaspora politics exhibits shades of Babylon. With their sights set squarely on the homeland, the politically oriented diaspora organizations tend to flaunt an emotional, defensive brand of nationalism. They take principled stands heedless of the repercussions this could have in the home country. Diaspora "politicians" evade accountability to constituencies—both in the diaspora and in the homeland. Their ultra-patriotism may stem, in part, from the nagging feelings of guilt many émigrés endure for leading better lives than their relatives and countrymen in the Old World. Moreover, the émigrés no longer live cheek-by-jowl with the other ethnic groups that comprise part of their native land's citizenry. In the homeland decades of coexistence have often smoothed over old resentments, whereas in the diaspora they festered. And, not to ignore the obvious, diasporas are ethnic groupings that champion the interests of one ethnic group—their own. Other ethnicities either fail to appear on their radar screen at all or do so as arch enemies.

Finally, diaspora activists often come off as arrogant and condescending. Brows knit together, they shake their heads at the chaotic political free-for-alls and mired economies in their home countries. The émigrés, of course, having already proven themselves in Western countries with market economies, obviously possess a unique knowledge of Western ways and of their homeland. Who better to take charge? Given the opportunity to do so, however, seldom has their know-how yielded constructive results.

If one prominent émigré defies the exile stereotype it is Milan Panić, the Serbian American pharmaceuticals manufacturer who served as the Yugoslav prime minister in 1992. Panić, a teenage courier for the communist Partisans, defected from Yugoslavia in the 1950s. On his arrival in the United States, he discarded his Yugoslav passport, stopped speaking Serbian, and declined any association with the diaspora or with Yugoslavia. Panić became an American—an enormously successful, wealthy American. When Yugoslavia opened up slowly to foreign business in the 1980s, Panić spotted a unique opportunity to expand his operations into southeastern Europe. At first Panić saw the new reformer Slobodan Milošević as being on the right track. But Panić soon ran afoul of the Serbian president and turned on him with all his considerable energy. As prime minister and then a candidate against Milošević in the 1992 race for the Serbian presidency, the fiery millionaire launched the first serious challenge to Milošević within Serbia.

But even Panić, so atypical among the diaspora protagonists, stumbled into the same thicket as other returnees. He had lost touch with his country of birth. Time and again he displayed a shocking naïveté about the region and the complexities of Balkan politics. And his pompous style put off even potential allies. Yugoslavia, he learned the hard way, could not be run like a California-based multinational corporation.

In Yugoslavia Panić was out of his depth. In the West, however, diaspora groups exhibited canny insider knowledge of the political systems of their adopted countries and how to use them to their advantage. In the United States, diaspora groups, benefiting from the Jewish and Greek experiences, set up Washington-based lobby groups complete with their own political action committees. As war raged in the mountains of Bosnia, in Washington the émigrés waged fierce battles for congressional influence, for influence over U.S. public opinion, and for media coverage. Lawmakers in the United States listened closely to the lobbyists, especially those bearing generous gifts for their campaigns. But the Washington channel proved to be a two-way street. American policymakers, through their diaspora associations, sent strong messages back to the Balkans.

Despite the close ties between the Serb diaspora and the established Greek lobby, it was the Albanians who surged ahead first with a well-funded, professional lobby run by the gregarious former U.S. congressman Joe DioGuardi. The Albanians' multimillion-dollar lobby and fund-raising campaigns dwarfed those of the other Balkan diaspora groups, which had no equivalent reinforcements like the influx of Kosovar Albanians that streamed into the West during the 1990s. Fresh from the "occupied" homeland, seething with anger and intent on return, the Kosovar Albanians turned their ire into concrete action. In addition to financing the U.S. lobbies, their resources kept Kosovo afloat for nearly ten years. Through remittances and organized fund-raising, the Kosovar Albanian diaspora paid for Kosovo's education, social welfare, and health care systems, and ultimately not one but two guerrilla armies.

The diasporas largely relied on the legal forums of democratic states to agitate for their causes. But at critical junctures U.S.–based diaspora associations and their international networks pursued goals in direct conflict with the foreign policy priorities of those democracies—and of democracy in general. In past eras the public engagement of U.S.–based ethnic groups in open contempt of U.S. policy would surely have provoked cries of disloyalty. In the 1990s, however, no one blinked. So strong was the call of their homeland that at times it appeared to elevate the émigrés above the law. In violation of international sanctions, all sides used transnational networks to funnel arms, and money for arms and frontline supplies.

It was their compatriots in the homeland, those who should have benefited enormously from the émigrés' knowledge and experience, who suffered the greatest injustice. According to Polish exile and writer Eva Hoffman: "It may often be easier to live in exile with a fantasy of paradise than to suffer the inevitable ambiguities and compromises of cultivating actual, earthly places."[5] These wise words notwithstanding, ultimately, in the former Yugoslavia, it was the nature of the émigrés' fantasies, not their compromises, that caused the greatest suffering.

PART I

Croatia: Prodigal Sons

He spared nothing to achieve the Croatian dream.

Croatian president FRANJO TUDJMAN eulogizing Croatian defense minister, GOJKO ŠUŠAK (1945–1998)

CHAPTER ONE

Picnic in Mississauga

cross the arid mountain villages and cement-poured towns of
western Herzegovina, the deserted streets and silent coffee
bars signaled ominously that all was not well. In Čapljina, a
town of thirty-thousand Bosnian Croats,* only the deep peal of St. Franjo's
church bells shattered the mid-day stillness. In countless windows throughout the town, candles drew the eye to adjacent photos of a smiling man
in his mid-fifties with an angular jaw and bushy beetle eyebrows. Čapljina's
eerie quiet and manifestations of grieving on May 7, 1998, were duplicated
across the hardscrabble West Herzegovina, the historical stronghold of fer-
vent Bosnian Croat nationalists. In neighboring Croatia proper, the day had
been declared an official day of mourning. Televisions everywhere were
tuned to the live funeral ceremonies being broadcast from Zagreb's Mirogoj
Cemetery, where Herzegovina native, Croatia's longtime defense minister,
Gojko Šušak, was being laid to rest with full military honors.

Šušak's death, after a long battle with lung cancer, was hardly unexpected. But it shook the Bosnian Croats nevertheless. Through three-and-
a-half years of war in Bosnia and two years of an internationally sponsored
peace process, the Croats of Čapljina, West Mostar, and Široki Brijeg had
come to rely on Šušak as their patron in the Croatian government, as
someone who understood and shared their fierce passion to break away
from Bosnia and join Croatia. Even after the signing of the 1995 Dayton
peace agreement, which reaffirmed the internationally recognized borders
of Bosnia and Herzegovina, the Bosnian Croats hoped that their dream was
not lost. But with news of Šušak's passing, a pall of uncertainty descended
over the region. "Everyone was upset because he was from West Herzegovina. He was our man," explains Sanja, a thirty-year-old economist from
Čapljina. "We felt lost. What will become of us now? we wondered. It was

---

* The state of Bosnia and Herzegovina is made up of two adjacent territories, Bosnia to the
north and Herzegovina in the south. According to the 1991 census, Bosnia and Herzegovina had
a population of 4,355,000. Thirty-one percent declared themselves Serbs; 44 percent, Muslims;
and 17 percent, Croats. The remainder declared themselves Yugoslavs or another nationality. Of
the roughly 740,000 ethnic Croats in the country, about 200,000 lived in western Herzegovina
before the war. The remainder lived in Bosnia. For simplicity's sake I refer to all ethnic Croats in
Bosnia and Herzegovina as "Bosnian Croats."

the only topic of conversation. He was always the person who protected our interests."

And in Croatia, the state-loyal media strove to surpass one another in tributes to the man, who, as defense minister since 1991, had led the government's fight against the Serb rebellion in Croatia. It was Šušak, reported the daily *Večernji List*,[1] who had forged a battle-ready Croatian army that "completed the liberation of the homeland in a few glorious days, in spectacular operations which are already being studied in military academies." The paper called Šušak "the favorite minister" of Croatian president Franjo Tudjman.

In a condolence telegram to Šušak's wife and three children, Tudjman referred to the late minister's twenty-year exile in Canada, where, he claimed, Šušak had worked tirelessly for the Croat cause. The president described his right-hand man as a patriot and hero:

> The years he spent abroad were dedicated to achieving the age-old Croatian dream—the establishment of a self-sufficient, independent, sovereign, and democratic Croatia. Upon returning to his homeland, Gojko performed the most important duties for the Croatian Democratic Community and the Croatian government, during the most difficult period of creating our country and during the Homeland War.[2]

It was no accident that Tudjman referred to Šušak's "homeland" as Croatia, although Šušak's birthplace, Široki Brijeg, lies in the neighboring state of Bosnia and Herzegovina.

Even in the West, some had viewed Šušak as a trusted ally, a "can do" man with first-rate anticommunist credentials. To the former U.S. secretary of defense William Perry, one of President Clinton's Balkan troubleshooters, Šušak counted as a personal friend as well. "Gojko Šušak's death is . . . a great loss for Croatia," Perry said at the funeral, flanked by Croatia's military brass. Quoting Shakespeare he added: "Now there goes a man, we shall never see his like again." Perry, a pivotal figure in securing the U.S. go-ahead to build up the Croatian army, was the highest-profile foreign guest attending the ceremony. He described his late counterpart, a man with no military experience prior to 1991, as a visionary in military matters, and said that Šušak's legacy was an army that would one day be a valued participant in Western security organizations.

In Bosnia and Croatia Šušak's legacy, like many chapters in the turbulent decade, is a bitterly contested subject. If Bosnian Croats in West Mostar consider Šušak to have been their long-lost son and political sponsor, Bosnian Muslims in artillery-scarred East Mostar, across the make-shift wire footbridge strung over the River Neretva, believe Šušak to have been nothing less than a war criminal, Zagreb's point man in the bloody 1993–94 war between Bosnian Croats and Bosnian Muslims. Only under heavy diplomatic pressure, largely from the United States and Germany, did the Croat leadership reluctantly back down from its aim to annex—through force of arms—large swaths of Bosnia and Herzegovina.

During the conflict it was no secret that on the Croat side the chain of military command, as well as the pipeline for arms and ammunition, ran across Croatia-Bosnia state lines straight from Šušak's ministry on Zagreb's Krešimir Square to the headquarters of the Bosnian Croat militia in West Mostar. The master plan to ethnically cleanse chunks of Bosnia and Herzegovina and link them with Croatia, a plan Tudjman and Šušak grandly referred to as Croatian National Policy, succeeded in part: many of the targeted valleys and urban centers in Bosnia and Herzegovina are now completely free of Muslims and Serbs. In central Bosnia the multicultural fabric that had been woven through centuries of coexistence was ruthlessly ripped apart. Šušak and President Tudjman (who died a year after Šušak in December 1999) had been under investigation by the International Tribunal for Crimes in the former Yugoslavia for their roles in Bosnia, but they both passed away before the court could pass verdict on their conduct. In early 2001 the tribunal's chief prosecutor, Carla Del Ponte, confirmed that the Tudjman investigation was nearing an end when Tudjman died. "Were he not dead," she said, "he would have been one of The Hague tribunal indictees."[3] The same, one can safely assume, is true of Šušak.

That Gojko Šušak returned to Croatia after twenty years in Canada is more than a curious footnote to the past decade of Balkan wars. The "pizza man" (as Croatia's liberal journalists mockingly dubbed the former co-owner of Tops Pizza in Ottawa) became the most influential of the Croat émigrés from North America, Australia, South America, and Europe to take a hand in shaping independent Croatia. Within the tight inner circle around Croatia's autocratic president, Šušak was the dominant figure in the so-called Herzegovina lobby, a clique of ministers and advisers who guarded the regime's extreme right wing. While this particular stripe of nationalism had long had adherents in regional pockets in Croatia and Bosnia, the trumpeted return of right-wing émigrés and the well-funded blitz victory of their party of choice, the Croatian Democratic Community (HDZ), ushered these ideas squarely into the mainstream. This headstrong Croatia-first nationalism would help propel Croatia toward war, first with its own Serb minority and then in Bosnia.

In the diaspora, in contrast to the story Šušak spun—and the one most of the Croatian press[4] lapped up uncritically—Šušak was distinguished neither as a prominent businessman nor a high-profile émigré leader. His credentials for the position of minister of defense were transparently thin. But the lanky chain-smoker from Široki Brijeg was one of a tight circle of Ontario-based expatriates who did have certain assets. Even in the late 1980s, before Yugoslavia's breakup, the dissident nationalist historian and World War II Partisan general Franjo Tudjman recognized that these connections could be crucial for his own future political career when socialist Yugoslavia began to unravel, as he was certain it would. For one, the Herzegovinian background of Šušak and his allies was key to securing the allegiance of the tough-minded, clannish Croats of southwestern Herzegovina, who were typically suspicious of urban city slickers from far-off Zagreb. Tudjman's own shifting picture of Greater Croatia included, at the very least, Croatia proper plus western Herzegovina. On this issue the loyalty of Šušak and the right-wing diaspora was beyond question, unlike that of the vast number of ordinary Croats who had never harbored fraternal feelings for the Herzegovina. In fact, many turned up their noses at the mountain folk and cigarette smugglers from the south.

Furthermore, as a member of the far-right wing of the Croat diaspora, Šušak and his associates lent irrefutable nationalist legitimacy to Tudjman, the gray-haired ex-communist general with the disarming smile. During World War II the multinational Partisan forces under Josip Broz, known by his nom de guerre as Tito, waged a brutal guerrilla war against the Italian- and German-backed Croatian regime, which was run by indigenous fascists known as the Ustashe. A central plank of Tudjman's political program was that Croat communists and Croat nationalists should shelve their historical differences and fight together for a free, independent Croatia. Tudjman heralded the burying of this historical hatchet as Croatia's "national reconciliation." Alone, the Partisan general constituted only half the equation. Finally, and perhaps most critically, the diaspora spelled money. The one to two million Croats abroad, from Buenos Aires to Sydney and from Los Angeles to Munich, represented a veritable jackpot for the Croat politician who could win them over.

Making inroads into the diaspora, particularly to the nationalist Croats in Canada and the United States, had been on Franjo Tudjman's personal agenda at least since 1987, when he traveled to Ontario for the first time. The idea alone was daring. It was well known that these émigré communities were thoroughly infiltrated by informers from a variety of national security services and that any contact with them was guaranteed to catch the eye of the Yugoslav authorities. For decades, Yugoslav propaganda had singled out the Croat diaspora as the incarnation of evil, as being comprised of fanatic fascist terrorists bent on destroying the socialist state. The *Ustaška emigracija*, the propaganda declared, labored assiduously from its bases around the world to return the "genocidal Ustashe regime" to power. The Yugoslav leadership seemed convinced of its own hyperbole. Hired hitmen from Yugoslavia's secret police periodically assassinated prominent Croat émigrés, as well as radical activists from the Serb and Albanian diasporas.

While the Tito-era propaganda distorted the complex and varied nature of the Croat diaspora, there were indeed marginal, loosely organized, ultra-nationalist currents that professed ideologies uncomfortably close to those of the fascist Ustashe. During the 1970s, in North America, Australia, and Western Europe, these splinter groups carried out "revolutionary strikes" against the Tito regime abroad through the sensational hijackings of jumbo jets, embassy bombings, and cold-blooded assassinations that made international headlines. At the time, in the late 1980s, Tudjman could not possibly have predicted the kind of welcome that this nationalist diaspora would give an ex-Partisan general, even one whose political convictions had come full circle over the last forty years.

Tudjman ended a decorated military career in Belgrade in the late 1950s to take up the directorship of the newly established Institute for the History of the Workers Movement in Zagreb. By 1967 he had been fired for nationalism, and he served brief jail terms in the 1970s and again in the early 1980s. Among the retired general's excesses in socialist Yugoslavia was the content of his historical research, which played down the crimes that Croat fascists committed during World War II, as well as the number of people killed in Croat concentration camps. Employing dubious historical methods, Tudjman's books appear as ideologically driven tracts intent on exonerating the Croat nation from World War II atrocities. In socialist Yugoslavia this was pure heresy.

The circumstances under which a dissident Croat nationalist of Tudjman's stature managed to get the Yugoslav authorities to issue him a passport in 1987 has been the subject of intense speculation in Croatia. But by the latter half of the 1980s, political tremors were shaking the very foundation of socialist Yugoslavia, and pressures from within the country as well as those reverberating across the international stage were forcing changes that were inconceivable only one year earlier. In 1987 Yugoslavia's most famous dissident, Milovan Djilas, was granted permission to travel abroad. Djilas was Montenegrin, and perhaps as a quid pro quo to show even-handedness the Croat Tudjman was allowed the same privilege.

According to the Croat Canadian businessman John (Ivica) Zdunić, Toronto's Croat émigré community picked up the tab for the historian's travel and accommodations just as it would for other visiting speakers. Zdunić was familiar with the books Tudjman had written during the past two decades and wanted to offer the historian the chance to speak in public, an opportunity he was denied in Croatia.

Yet, interestingly, Tudjman was the first such figure to receive an invitation and, at that time, a relative unknown among the diaspora Croats, one character of many in the nationalist revival movement of the late 1960s and early 1970s known as the Croatian Spring. Tito crushed the movement decisively with the arrest and imprisonment of its leading voices. During the prison terms of the Croatian Spring protagonists, diaspora groups picketed in front of Yugoslav embassies on their behalf and dutifully passed the hat around to help out the dissidents' families. Old photographs from Canadian newspapers show Tudjman's face on a picket sign wielded by émigré protesters in front of the Yugoslav embassy in Canada's capital city, Ottawa. From the blurred black-and-white newspaper clippings, it is impossible to pick out Gojko Šušak among the demonstrators, although he could well have been there, perhaps with one of his brothers.

Other observers, however, see in Tudjman's moves in the late 1980s the unmistakable fingerprints of Croatia's security services. Investigative reports in the independent Croatian media[5] present some evidence, although not overwhelming, that patrons high in the Croatian communist party and in the republican intelligence services, both of which had potent nationalist factions, handpicked Tudjman to push the nationalist envelope at a time when a man named Slobodan Milošević was doing just that from the halls of power in Serbia. The centralized Yugoslav state was looking more vulnerable every day in the late 1980s, and these pro-Croatia currents in the republic's administration, so the theory goes, sensed big changes in the wind. Rather than crack down on reformers, an option increasingly untenable for a variety of reasons, the national communists tried to accommodate the flow of history, or even control it, by pulling strings from behind the scenes. It was a strategy of pure self-interest designed to protect their positions during the upcoming political upheavals. Former officials high in the socialist republic's interior ministry, such as Josip Manolić, claim that they organized Tudjman's visits abroad, right down to buying his plane tickets.[6] These very officials were later among the founders and leaders of Tudjman's new party, the HDZ.

There is little doubt that the secret services had their eye on events—and a hand in the process. Without at least their tacit approval, Tudjman would never have received a passport. Knowing the men who ran Croatia at that time also helped. As Partisan officers they had fought side by side, and even after Tudjman's break with communism their personal friendships crossed party lines. (During his stints in prison, Tudjman received special treatment as a Yugoslav war hero, enjoying privileges not shared by his fellow political prisoners.) Yet several uncomfortable questions remain. Why did Tudjman, among the dozen or so Croat dissidents, receive traveling papers first? And who tipped Tudjman off that it was the right time to apply for travel, and so brazenly to start out in Ontario, a right-wing bastion of the Croat diaspora? Whatever the background dealings may have been, Tudjman was no puppet of the Yugoslav secret services, as the Croatian media reports imply. His loyalty was to a nationalist program that had been evolving in his thoughts and historical work for several decades. Whatever role the secret services may have played, the events that were to unfold in the years ahead assumed a direction and momentum that even the most farsighted operatives could not have foreseen.

In June 1987 Tudjman's first destination was Toronto, to the home of an old friend John (Zlatko) Čaldarević, a respected émigré businessman. Čaldarević had met Tudjman in the early 1960s in Zagreb. Ever since Čaldarević left Yugoslavia in 1968, he had corresponded with Tudjman and helped him some financially. "At first I thought he was coming just for a visit, to relax," recollects Čaldarević thirteen years later, today the owner of a small company that exports Canadian herring to European markets. A spiffy dresser and rapid-fire talker in his early seventies, Čaldarević is president of the Zagreb Patriotic Chapter of the Croatian Fraternal Union of America, the oldest and largest Croat émigré body in the world, an organization founded in Pittsburgh in 1894. Čaldarević takes pains to stress that the union is "non-political."[7] In other words, he wants to underscore that it never directly backed Tudjman or his party, the HDZ.

Once in Canada, Tudjman's plans caught Čaldarević off guard. "He started meeting with people, with extremists, without telling me," says Čaldarević, who describes himself as a moderate, close to the interwar Croatian Peasants Party, a party associated with parliamentary democracy in the 1920s and 1930s. People such as Marin Sopta, North America's president of the militant Croatian National Resistance (Hrvatski Narodni Otpor), known to insiders simply as Otpor (Croatian for "resistance") showed up uninvited—and most unwelcome—in Čaldarević's living room. Otpor, banned at the time in Germany for terrorist activities, was a conspiratorial ultra-nationalist group that operated in a murky gray zone between legitimate émigré functions and a thuggish underworld. As vigorously as its leaders tried to distance the organization from the acts of the so-called renegade elements that hijacked international flights and served prison sentences for extortion, the organization's unflattering track record spoke for itself. Otpor embraced a radical nationalist ideology that differed only marginally from that of Croatia's World War II fascists.

In Ottawa, a four-hour drive east of Toronto, Tudjman was introduced to Sopta's close friend and fellow émigré, Gojko Šušak. By then, Šušak had sold his share in the take-out pizza shop and had started up a small painting business, G&G Décor, with a friend. Šušak, whom his neighbors knew as Garry Susak, held minor positions in émigré community organizations, jobs such as part-time teacher in the Croatian language school in Ottawa and branch president of the Croatian National Congress, a worldwide umbrella organization for Croat émigré groups. Within the local émigré community, he had the reputation of a nationalist hothead. Šušak bragged that his father had fought with the Ustashe and, like Sopta, had stridently promoted "revolutionary tactics" to spring Croatia from Yugoslavia's grip. In the pizza shop, copies of Otpor's strident periodical were for sale along with similar literature.

"I advised Tudjman not to meet these people, not to go to these places," says Čaldarević, referring to Sopta, Šušak, and the radical friars at the Croat Franciscans' community center in Norval, twenty-five miles north of Toronto. "I said if someone takes a picture of you beneath a Pavelić [the World War II Croatian fascist leader] photograph you'll end up in jail again." But Čaldarević's protests were to no avail: "He went and did what he wanted."

The world of the Croat diaspora that Tudjman stepped into was a cob-webbed attic full of abandoned and discredited ideas from the past century of Croatian history. It was a world unto itself, shaped by diverse waves of immigration, antiquated currents of political thought, and disparate experiences. Over the years these outdated perceptions incubated in insular communities, creating a reality strikingly different than that in socialist Yugoslavia's Republic of Croatia.

The Croats who were scattered across the globe in the late 1980s were anything but a homogeneous lot. In neighboring Hungary, Austria, and Czechoslovakia, Croat minorities had made their homes for generations, and they were loyal to those countries, not Croatia. They were integrated and bilingual, with identities that had taken on the flavor of the contiguous cultures. The hundreds of thousands of Croat *gastarbeiter* (guest workers) who flocked to Germany, Austria, Switzerland, and Sweden during the 1960s and 1970s in search of temporary work were an entirely different phylum. They lived in workers' dormitories or shared cramped flats with fellow Yugoslavs: Serbs, Macedonians, Bosnians, and Kosovar Albanians. The migrant workers from Yugoslavia played on mixed soccer teams with names like *Bratstvo* (Brotherhood) and *Jugoslavija*. The Croat workers may have attended the diaspora churches, where clergymen spoke out against the communist regime, but they never formulated a political agenda. Most were apolitical, some even pro-Yugoslav, and after a few years on a construction site they returned to their homes in Yugoslavia.

The Croats, Catholic Slavs from the Balkans, first began to emigrate to the United States and Canada in the early nineteenth century, and by the 1880s the number of primarily economic refugees was growing. Most were unskilled peasants who joined the industrial work forces in blue-collar cities; the most welcoming were Pittsburgh, Chicago, Detroit, Milwaukee, and

Cleveland. Contrary to the contemporary image of Croat émigrés as diehard nationalists, the first generations of Croat émigrés were prominent in the labor movement and even in south-Slavic sections of the U.S. Communist Party. At the end of the century, rival socialist movements working out of Chicago began publishing the émigré newspapers *Hrvatski Radnički Pokret* (Croatian Workers' Movement) and *Radnička Borba* (Workers' Struggle). Such left-wing strains of diaspora Croats remained active in the United States into the 1950s, clashing ideologically with the postwar nationalists who they branded as "Hitler's fifth column in Yugoslavia" and in America.[8] Subsequent waves of ethnic Croats fled the Habsburg monarchy and then the post–World War I kingdom of Yugoslavia, settling in the Canadian cities of Toronto, Oakville, and Hamilton, among others. By 1914 there were twenty-two Croat Catholic parishes in the United States, as well as émigré publications, unions, and cultural organizations.

The aftermath of the ferocious bloodshed of World War II saw the first explicitly political exodus of Croats from their homeland, a migration that would form the first postwar generation of émigrés. The fleeing Croats were defeated loyalists of the Axis-allied regime of the 1941–45 Independent State of Croatia (Nezavisna Država Hrvatska), or NDH. Its ministers, officers, clergy, and henchmen were the sworn followers of the Ustashe movement, and they had ample reason to follow their *poglavnik*, or leader, Ante Pavelić, back into exile.

Pavelić and his fellow Ustashe assumed power in Croatia only when they returned to Croatia in April 1941 from exile in Mussolini's Italy, thus establishing a precedent for future political exiles. In Italy and Hungary in the early 1930s, as well as a few years later in locations as far afield as Pittsburgh and Buenos Aires, Ustashe training camps prepared young followers to infiltrate Yugoslavia to employ hit-and-run tactics and wreak havoc on the workings of the state. It was, however, in exile that the pre–World War II Ustashe did the greatest damage to royal Yugoslavia. In 1934 the Croat extremists, together with Macedonian separatists, assassinated Yugoslavia's King Alexander I while he was in Marseilles on a state visit to France. The experiences of Pavelić's Ustashe, a marginal movement of just several hundred before its abrupt assumption of power, was instructive for its successors decades later. If the original Ustashe could successfully carry out such an extraordinary coup from abroad, so could they. One lesson they absorbed was never to say never.

During its short rule, the fanaticism and brutality of the Ustashe were unrivaled. Only weeks after the NDH was established on April 10, 1941, racial laws went into effect and the first concentration camps were under construction for a daunting array of state enemies. Once in power, and initially with the blessing of much of the Roman Catholic clergy, the Ustashe needed no goading from the Germans to put its totalitarian vision of a "new Croatia" into practice. The litany of cruelty meted out by the Croat fascists—from communal slaughter to public dismemberment—was committed in the name of independent Croatia and properly gives the Ustashe a special place in the annals of human evil. Even the German Nazis at one point protested the Ustashe's barbaric methods of killing. The numbers alone are gut-wrenching: more than thirty thousand Jews, 70 percent of the Jewish population in NDH territory, which included Bosnia and Herzegovina, were put to death or deported to German death camps. Almost the entire gypsy population was liquidated, and more than three hundred thousand Serbs fell victim to the Pavelić regime. At the most heinous of the camps, Jasenovac on the River Sava, between eighty thousand and one hundred thousand people lost their lives, including anti-Ustashe Croats.

Diaspora Croats in North America, as well as elsewhere in the world, say that the legacy of the Ustashe created a stigma that they were forced to combat at every turn throughout the Cold War years. The émigrés complain that all Croats were unfairly branded as fascists or radical extremists because of the Ustashe's sins. They charged that Croatia's enemies intentionally exaggerated the Ustashe legacy in order to defame the entire nation. "It was next to impossible to find any article in the Canadian or U.S. press about Croats that didn't contain roughly the same three or four lines about the Ustashe crimes," complains former Otpor leader Sopta. "It used to drive us crazy. No matter what we did there'd still be the same three or four lines." Thus it became the common goal of almost all the émigré groups to polish the Croat image. In a counteroffensive, the Croats aspired to do "good deeds" in their communities, organizing soccer leagues and holding folk culture festivals. In 1986 they even considered donating funds for rebuilding the Zagreb synagogue. This idea, however, collapsed when the Zagreb Jewish community insisted that ethnic Serbs from Croatia also be included in the fund-raising campaign. This was entirely unacceptable to the Croat émigrés, who withdrew their offer of support.

Some among the Croat émigrés recognized and condemned the Ustashe atrocities, others soft-pedaled them, and still others denied them outright, but the Croats never undertook an open discussion within their own community about their past and its implications for the present. Croat wrongdoing during World War II certainly was not a topic in Sopta's arch rightwing magazine, *Otpor*, the mouthpiece of an organization itself disturbingly close to the original Ustashe in its convictions.

It is true that Yugoslav and Serb nationalist propagandists did blatantly inflate the numbers of the Ustashe's victims and often insinuated that the Ustashe crimes exposed some kind of "genocidal nature" intrinsic to the Croat people—an idea as historically inaccurate as it was politically divisive.

But the Ustashe ideology itself was textbook fascism with a xenophobic concept of the nation at its very center. The "independent" state owed its very existence to the Nazis' dismemberment and subsequent occupation of Yugoslavia.

Although the Ustashe promoted anti-Semitism to satisfy their Nazi allies, it was Croatia's ethnic Serbs, not the Jews, who were their paramount target. At the time, 1.9 million Orthodox Christian Serbs lived on NDH territory. Much of the anti-Serb hostility stemmed from the ill-fated post–World War I experiment called the Kingdom of Serbs, Croats, and Slovenes, which had deteriorated into a centralized Serb-dominated monarchy by the late 1920s. The Ustashe turned their resentment of Serb political domination into a radical creed. Hysterical Ustashe propaganda branded the Serbs as an alien, enemy people in Croatia, as traitors who betrayed Croatia to foreign interests. With so many Serbs in the NDH, complete liquidation was a practical impossibility. The compromise that was reached, to attempt to kill one-third of them, deport one-third, and convert one-third to Catholicism, would darken relations between Serbs and Croats for decades to come.

Another marker of the World War II era that was seared into the postwar émigré consciousness is Bleiburg, an Austrian village near the Slovenian frontier where thousands of escaping NDH sympathizers lost their lives. With the avenging victors closing in on them, NDH leaders, Ustashe cadres, soldiers, and many civilians fled the advancing Partisan forces. From Zagreb en route through Slovenia, columns of these panicked Croat refugees fled toward British-occupied Austria, joined along the way by German soldiers, Slovene collaborators, and the remnants of Serb monarchist units. But in the frontier region near Bleiburg, the unsuspecting refugees met a fate that would serve as a battle cry for future generations of émigrés, alleged evidence of the sinister anti-Croat nature of the Tito regime, and the inexplicable willingness of Western powers to meet it halfway.

Instead of providing asylum to the 100,000–150,000 refugees, the British command blocked their escape route and handed them over to the Partisans, a wartime ally of the West. Trapped, many of the refugees were executed on the spot. Tito knew that the Ustashe had originally formed and trained in exile; one way to prevent rightists from regrouping in anticommunist columns abroad was to physically eliminate them. This remained Yugoslav policy into the 1980s.

The total number of casualties at Bleiburg varies greatly depending on the source of the report. Western historians estimate that between thirty thousand and forty-five thousand died, a truly shocking death toll. But Croat émigré chroniclers such as Ante Beljo darkly hint at far greater carnage. Beljo, an electrician from Sudbury, Ontario, was one of the original core group to promote Tudjman in Canada and would become a key player later in the HDZ in Croatia and Bosnia. In his self-published book, *YU-Genocide*, he suggests that the number of Croat patriots to perish at the hands of the Yugoslav state stretches into the hundreds of thousands.[9] (The website of the Croat Academy of America, a U.S.–based émigré organization, claims that a total of 655,000 Croats "left or were driven out" of Yugoslavia during the war and communist rule.) Beljo had fled the grinding poverty of Čitluk, Herzegovina, in 1967, the same year his high school friend Šušak left nearby Široki Brijeg. He certainly considered himself among those "driven out" by the communists' anti-Croat campaign, a systematic extension of the Bleiburg massacre.

"Bleiburg" became a charged symbol for the alleged Serbo-Communist campaign to exterminate the Croat nation. Beljo was not taking poetic license when he titled his book *YU-Genocide* or its first chapter "Croatian Holocaust." He genuinely believed that he was documenting the premeditated mass murder of his people. "Throughout history there is no example of a nation that has suffered so much, has had as many victims, and has at the same time been paradoxically labeled as a villain," begins the foreword to this four-hundred-page book. The author of the foreword, Vinko Grubišić, a professor of Croatian studies at the University of Waterloo in Ontario, Canada, and another early Tudjman booster, continues: "I doubt that there would even be one ally who would be concerned whether the Croats could survive another tragedy like Bleiburg." Bleiburg functioned as one of the psychological keystones for the émigrés' self-understanding of their expatriation, their lives abroad, and their political work to rescue Croatia at all costs, and by all means necessary.

But some top NDH officials and Ustashe leaders, including Ante Pavelić, made it into exile—with a helping hand from the Croatian Catholic Church, the Vatican, and Anglo-American spy services. Among other sources, a book by Mark Aarons and John Loftus, *Unholy Trinity: The Vatican, the Nazis, and the Swiss Banks*, presents compelling evidence that a Vatican-sponsored network run by Croat priests provided escape routes to tens of thousands of German Nazis and other wanted war criminals from Hungary, Slovakia, Ukraine, and above all Croatia.[10] The destination of most of the fugitives was the fascist-friendly Perón regime in Argentina, but also Paraguay, Spain, Germany, the United States, Canada, and Australia, where small, organized Ustashe communities would base themselves and plot the resurrection of the NDH.

Pavelić slipped over the Austrian border in the summer of 1945. There, disguised as a monk, he hid in a monastery near Klagenfurt until the network could smuggle him to Rome. Just outside the Vatican's walls, the key figure in the operation was Father Krunoslav Draganović, an Ustashe colonel and secretary of the Croatian Institute of San Girolamo, the Ustashe's postwar hideout.

For outlaw Nazis, the ever-resourceful Draganović organized fake passports, plane tickets, and new identities abroad. It was through Draganović's anticommunist channels that the Nazi war criminal Klaus Barbie, among many others, escaped to South America. Draganović had been the unofficial liaison between Zagreb and the Vatican during the war, a cordial relationship marked by mutual respect. In Rome Pavelić met regularly with influential bishops, men who had backed his political movement from its inception. According to Aarons and Loftus, U.S. and British secret services knew all along about the underground activities and even coordinated them with the Vatican. The onset of the Cold War quickly eclipsed the debt the West owed to Yugoslavia's communists. Washington and London overlooked past allegiances in order to beef up their own clandestine networks of ex-Nazis, suddenly valuable resources in the fight against communism.

With U.S. and British support, Pavelić and Draganović launched the first armed exile-led assaults on socialist Yugoslavia from bases in Austria and Italy. The ill-fated Križari (Crusaders) operation was designed to spark an insurrection against the communists.[11] Like émigré incursions that would follow, the former Ustashe fighters were to infiltrate Yugoslavia and wage a campaign of terrorism, assassination, and sabotage: their plan was to connect with thousands of Ustashe loyalists supposedly still active in the country and overthrow the Tito regime. But in 1946–47, usually within days of crossing the border, the guerrilla units were ambushed by the Yugoslav security services, which deftly crushed the quixotic forces. After publicized trials, the regime executed or imprisoned for life all fifty-seven of the captured Križari guerrillas. But Pavelić, the strategist behind the incursions, again slipped away. With a wink and a nod from all involved, except the Yugoslav authorities, he and surviving cabinet ministers of the former NDH government relocated to Buenos Aires, the new base in exile of the émigré Ustashe movement. An estimated five thousand to fifteen thousand compatriots joined him in Argentina.

In trickles and spurts, thousands of Croats continued to emigrate abroad during the 1950s and 1960s, many a hybrid category of political and economic refugee. In the United States, Congress passed refugee acts opening the doors wide for anticommunist immigrants from Eastern Europe. The times in early postwar Yugoslavia were hard for everyone but especially for traditionally poor regions like western Herzegovina, northern Dalmatia, and Lika, areas that had also been Ustashe bastions. In Herzegovina, Yugoslav authorities had clamped down on organized smuggling after World War I, which, particularly when it came to tobacco, had been a mainstay of the region during the Ottoman and Habsburg empires. Over the centuries this reputation for smuggling and banditry fostered an image of the Herzegovinians as swashbucklers and highwaymen, or *hajduci*, a stigma that persists today. Remarkably it is not a badge most Herzegovinians strive to disown. It is their heritage, and they are proud of it.

These regions, because of their political past, were also squarely in the sights of the Yugoslav security services. Families that had members in the Ustashe or NDH army were routinely singled out for intimidation or worse. From one such family came Nikola Stedul, a man who would later figure prominently in the radical émigré scene. In Australia, and then in Europe, Stedul was the driving force behind the Otpor movement and would work next to Šušak in the Defense Ministry of independent Croatia in 1991.

Stedul grew up in postwar Yugoslavia in a village that was thirty miles south of Zagreb. His older brother, at age seventeen, had served as a volunteer in the NDH army. "When people talk about the Ustashe of that time, they automatically brand everybody involved as a war criminal," explains Stedul in the Zagreb office of his own small political party, the National Democratic Party. His deep-set amber eyes twinkle between a striking pair of oversized ears as he emphasizes the volunteer status of soldiers like his brother. "My brother probably hadn't ever even heard the words *fascism* or *Nazism*," he says.

Stedul maintains that his family supported the national-democratic movement of Stjepan Radić, the enigmatic leader of the Croatian Peasants Party. In 1941, when the NDH was established, Stedul's brother could either have joined the NDH army or gone underground to join the Partisans. But the goals and values of the communist Partisans were anathema to the Steduls. As Stedul says: "We didn't see the Partisans as the Croatian army at that time. They were against religion and an independent Croatia. The Croat people had a very bad experience with the first Yugoslavia and didn't want to go back into another Yugoslavia." In a freshly pressed blue suit and wearing a red and blue tie, Stedul gives the impression of being thoughtful and measured, hardly the reputation he earned while president of Otpor in Western Europe during the 1970s. He regrets that the NDH was forced into an alliance with Hitler, but at the time, he argues, a small country like Croatia had nowhere else to turn. Even the Soviet Union, he points out, made a pact of necessity with Hitler's Germany.

After the war, with the victorious Partisans in power, the Steduls, like many other such households, were labeled an Ustashe family. For young Nikola it was a curse that spelled a life of poverty and humiliation. "If you came from an Ustashe house there wasn't much chance of getting anywhere in the country," says Stedul, who, at sixty-three, is broad-chested and sports a closely trimmed graying beard, which only partially conceals a scar above his lip. The scar and a slight limp are what remain from the six bullets

Stedul took at close range in 1989—two in the face and four to his body—when a Yugoslav agent attempted to kill him in Kirkcaldy, Scotland, where he lived with his family. "You were completely excluded from a decent education, from a decent job, from anything. There was discrimination at every step," he says. An irreverent joke cracked about Comrade Tito would earn dissenters a prison sentence. On one occasion, communists ambushed and savagely beat Stedul's father, leaving him for dead on a village road.

In 1956, at age eighteen and expecting to be drafted into the Yugoslav army, the staunchly anticommunist Stedul opted instead to try his luck at the heavily guarded Austrian border. Somehow Stedul slipped between the Yugoslav border guards and their dogs and ducked the barbed wire, only to be picked up on the other side by Austrian guards and thrown briefly into an Austrian prison. Nevertheless it was the West where in different countries and on two continents he would agitate for an independent Croatia until the communist regime collapsed in 1990.

Like many thousands of Eastern European refugees, Stedul, following his imprisonment made his home in one of the many Austrian refugee camps which, at the crossroads of Europe, were brimming with people fleeing communism. The clock of history ticked fortuitously when Stedul was working as a farmhand near the camps. In October 1956 the popular uprising against the Stalinist regime in neighboring Hungary broke out. For Stedul and a handful of like-minded refugees at the camp, the revolt was exactly what they were waiting for: the first brick in the communist wall to jar loose. But marching to the Hungarian border to offer the insurrection their services, the small band of would-be revolutionaries were intercepted by Austrian border guards and sent back to the camp.

At one evening information session for the refugees, Stedul crossed paths with Father Draganović, the mastermind of the escape networks. Draganović counseled the refugees on the opportunities available in other countries. West Germany, desperately in need of manual labor for its undermanned work force, was the safest and easiest choice, he advised them. Stedul took a job fifteen hundred meters underground in the coal mines of the Ruhrgebiet. Almost at once he was recruited by the Croatian Liberation Movement (Hrvatski Oslobodilački Pokret), or HOP, Pavelić's pro-Ustashe movement based in Argentina. "At that time," laughs Stedul, reclining in his bucket-seated desk chair, overlooking a noisy Zagreb side street, "we really thought we'd be returning to Croatia as soldiers. We all thought communism was going to collapse a lot sooner than it did, in Yugoslavia and everywhere else." This is precisely what the HOP leaflets promised naive and embittered refugees like Stedul.

Pavelić and his fugitive government-in-exile called HOP to life on June 8, 1956, in Buenos Aires as the successor movement to the Ustashe. Its members were largely crusty Ustashe exiles, many of them former military personnel, but the movement actively strove to attract young followers, such as Stedul, in West Germany, Australia, the United States, and Canada. The remnants of the Ustashe vanguard plotted to liberate the millions of Croats suffering under communist tyranny when war broke out between the Soviet Union and the United States. Their vehicles to resurrect the NDH were trained armed units "prepared to die" for Croatia and to "drive out the Serbs." Secret training camps suddenly appeared in the Australian outback.

Rumors flourished including the notion that the movement financed its terrorist cells, printing presses, and the escape routes with the treasure the Ustashe had looted from Croat Jews and Serbs during the war, which they had either transported with them abroad or had laundered through Swiss banks. There are even charges that the last of this "Ustashe gold" went toward arming Croatia in the 1990s. There is no concrete evidence of the Ustashe treasury financing anything more than the early escape networks and the Križari commandos, and it seems highly unlikely that any of it was left to spend by the 1990s. While the HOP's fantasies of outfitting a guerrilla army fizzled and evaporated, followers of HOP—unreconstructed Ustashe loyal to the legacy of Pavelić—maintained a presence in worldwide émigré communities into the late 1980s. *Spremnost* (Prepared), the newspaper of the Australian branch of the HOP, was still being published in 2000.

By the late 1950s the heavy-handed persecution of NDH collaborators and suspected sympathizers in Croatia and Bosnia had eased considerably. Further, many Herzegovinians, including the hierarchy of the Catholic Church, had struck a kind of compromise with the communist regime. Those who cooperated with Tito's state (and many did, despite legend to the contrary) could indeed make their way up the ladder. Gojko Šušak's brother, for example, was in charge of the Široki Brijeg municipality office that oversaw the conscription process that filled the ranks of Yugoslavia's army, the JNA. But even the improved atmosphere did not stem emigration. Regions like western Herzegovina suffered from chronic poverty, a condition its inhabitants reflexively attributed to a concerted Yugoslav strategy of discrimination, a plot to keep them down and out. Whether real or imagined—often both—political persecution, combined with the dire economic situation, forced tens of thousands of young Bosnian Croats from Herzegovina to seek their fortunes elsewhere in the late 1960s and early 1970s. Men such as Gojko Šušak, Ante Beljo, Marin Sopta, and Mladen "Tuta" Naletilić, an émigré who would make a feared name for himself as a gangster boss in Mostar during the war, all hailed from the Široki Brijeg region in southwestern Herzegovina.

To natives of Široki Brijeg, their town is the very cradle of the Herzegovina. It lies at the far end of the snake-infested Mostarsko Blato Valley, just ten miles west of Mostar and another ten miles from the Croatian border. The Lištica River cuts through the low-lying central square, which exhibits a stout limestone cross, grossly out of proportion in the diminutive space. Chiseled into its ivory face is the *šahovnica*, the medieval Croat coat-of-arms with a red and white checkerboard. Another šahovnica, a giant mosaic pieced together with painted red and white stones, stares down over Široki Brijeg from the side of a pine-blanketed mountain. Above cash registers and on the walls of neon-lit coffee bars hang pictures of Široki Brijeg's favorite son, Gojko Šušak. Sometimes color glossies of the late president Tudjman or Pope John Paul II flank the Herzegovina native. "I love Tuta" bumper stickers in store windows, referring to the mafia boss Naletilić, signify that the right payoffs have been made to the right people.

Even before the recent wars that rid western Herzegovina of its Muslim and Serb inhabitants, Široki Brijeg's population of fifteen thousand was nearly 100 percent ethnic Croat. The town was a medieval outpost for the Franciscan Order, which built and still maintains the white limestone school and monastery on the town's high eastern ridge. The Franciscans first came to the region in the 1370s at the request of the Bosnian monarch to quash a popular heresy that dominated parts of Bosnia and the Herzegovina at the time. During four long centuries of Ottoman rule, the Franciscans enjoyed exclusive jurisdiction over the area's Catholics, a period during which Catholic rites became infused with local superstitions and pagan rituals. When the Austro-Hungarian Empire occupied Bosnia and Herzegovina in 1878, Rome tried to reassert its grip over the wayward Franciscan Order. But it met stubborn resistance. Friction between the Herzegovinian Franciscans and the Vatican persist today, as do striking differences of opinion between the Franciscans' Herzegovinian and Bosnian branches: during the 1992–95 wars the Sarajevo-based Franciscans demonstratively threw their support behind a multicultural Bosnian state, while the Herzegovina Franciscans stood firmly behind the Croat hard-liners and their separatist agenda.

During World War II Herzegovina was transformed into a battlefield where Ustashe forces clashed with both communist Partisans and Serb nationalist Chetniks, all sides suffering staggering casualties. Široki Brijeg itself was an Ustashe hotbed, with the Franciscan brothers in the movement's vanguard. The hilltop monastery was the hub of the Ustashe's regional operations and alma mater of several high-ranking Ustashe officials, including the infamous NDH minister of interior Andrija Artuković. Some of the war's vilest atrocities were committed in the vicinity of Široki Brijeg, often with the complicity of the Ustashe-loyal Franciscans. In 1941 and 1942, to the abhorrence of the Rome-appointed bishop of Mostar, thousands of Serbs were slaughtered in the district. A shocked Bishop Mišić wrote to his superior in Zagreb:

By the mercy of God, there was never such a good occasion as now for us
to help Croatia to save the countless souls, people of goodwill, well-
disposed peasants, who live side by side with Catholics. . . . While the
newly converted [Orthodox Serbs] are at mass they seize them, old and
young, men and women, and hunt them like slaves. From Mostar and
Čapljina the railway carried six wagons full of mothers, girls, and children under eight to the stations of Surmanci, where they were taken out
of the wagons, brought into the hills and thrown alive . . . into deep
ravines.[12]

When Allied planes attacked the armed monastery near the end of the war,
Franciscan friars and German SS fought side by side, machine guns in hand.

The details of Šušak's early life in western Herzegovina and of his emigration are veiled in secrecy, a family strategy to divulge little or nothing
about the Šušak past. His widow, Djurdja Šušak, a career social worker who
served in Croatia's military intelligence branch during the Tudjman administration, steadfastly refuses to speak to journalists. In Ottawa his one living
brother remains tight-lipped. During his tenure as defense minister Šušak
stayed at arm's length from the independent press, which, like other HDZ
leaders, he regarded with deep suspicion. The Ministry of Defense did what
it could to muddy the waters by building a personality cult around Šušak,
embellishing his curriculum vitae with fabricated accounts of his family heritage, reasons for fleeing Croatia, and his life abroad. Šušak did his best to
cover the tracks that led from the kitchens of Ottawa's fast-food industry
and the smoky back rooms of neo-Ustashe clubs to the Ministry of Defense
in the independent Croatia.

What we do know is that Gojko Šušak, the sixth son of Ante and Stana
Šušak, was born in Široki Brijeg on March 16, 1945, in the final weeks of the
NDH. One version of his family history claims that two months after his
birth his father and oldest brother, both Ustashe officers in the NDH army,
were reported missing in action, allegedly last spotted in Zagreb the day
Partisan troops entered the city. According to the Croatian Defense Ministry website, in a blunt act of retribution the Šušak house behind the Franciscan high school was burned to the ground—an event some Croat journalists question.[13]

The historical record does confirm, however, that the Partisans took
fierce revenge on little Široki Brijeg. In the stormy days in the aftermath of
the war, fourteen Franciscan friars were dragged from the monastery,
doused in gasoline, and burned to death. Others were shot and the monastery shut down. In 1953 the name of the town, deemed too reactionary even
to be spoken, was changed to Lištica. Across western Herzegovina the Par-

tisans ushered in a reign of terror, which included murder, torture, and incarcerations.

Carved into the steep ravine that forms one wall of a natural basin around Široki Brijeg, a pebbly road with hairpin turns leads busloads of Catholic pilgrims up to the Assumption of the Blessed Virgin Mary Church and the Franciscan monastery. Heavy-set, brown-robed friars with rope belts encompassing their midsections stroll across the walled grounds that loom over the town like a fortress. Inside the church, with its impressive white Romanesque columns, followers of various cults of the Virgin Mary—from Ireland, Spain, Italy, Canada, and the United States—kneel at the shrines that line the high walls. During peak pilgrim season the chapel benefits from the Mariolatry overspill from nearby Medjugorje, the location of alleged visions of the Virgin Mary in 1981. Hundreds of thousands of Catholics from around the world visit Medjugorje every year to communicate through the local seers with the Virgin Mary, known in the region as Our Lady, Queen of Peace. The Vatican has declined to confirm the veracity of the sightings, but among the local Franciscans they are an article of faith, as well as a critical source of legitimacy and income.

Behind the church is the Friar Dominic Mandić Gymnasia, an institution with a reputation as a first-class regional high school. Mandić was a high-ranking priest in the NDH who later established a center for Croat Franciscans in Chicago, an office that was part of the underground operation to smuggle Ustashe war criminals out of Europe and into the United States.[14] (The Franciscans' facility in Široki Brijeg lives up to its namesake. It reportedly remains a place of sanctuary for fugitive Croat generals who are wanted for war crimes and sought by the International Tribunal for Crimes in former Yugoslavia based in The Hague.)

It was here, under the tutelage of the Franciscan brothers, that the Ontario émigrés were educated and socialized. Šušak and his brothers grew up a stone's throw from the school, a little patch of neighborhood where a chic cluster of houses and tennis courts now stand, the exclusive homes of the recent wars' nouveau riche. Today well-dressed, healthy-looking children race up and down the school's polished steps into cavernous corridors that echo with their voices. In the principal's office yet another Šušak portrait, an unflattering charcoal sketch, adorns the wall.

Standing at the steps of the school, one wonders what it is exactly about Široki Brijeg and its hilltop enclave that produces graduates of such immoderate conviction. Indeed, what do the friars here teach their charges? How is it that two generations of militant nationalists refer to the direct vicinity of this obscure mountainside hamlet as their home? One explanation was offered in a 1941 report by British army captain Evelyn Waugh, the celebrated writer, who, during World War II, served on extended reconnaissance missions in Nazi-occupied Yugoslavia. He noted that many Franciscan priests had joined the Ustashe before the war. Waugh wrote:

> For some time the Croat Franciscans had caused misgivings in Rome for their independence and narrow patriotism. They were mainly recruited from the least cultured part of the population and there is abundant evidence that several wholly unworthy men were attracted to the Franciscan Order by the security and comparative ease which it offered. Many of these youths were sent to Italy for training. Their novitiate was in the neighborhood of Pavelić's headquarters at Sienna where Ustashe agents made contact with them and imbued them with Pavelić's ideas. They in turn, on returning to their country, passed on his ideas to the pupils in their schools.[15]

A visitor to Široki Brijeg cannot help but sense the rough, independent-minded spirit of the western Herzegovina. Even Croats from central Bosnia and Croatia proper are outsiders here, alien to the region's unique mentality which is distinguished by clan loyalty, recalcitrant pride, age-old superstitions, and an ethic of revenge. In *Medjugorje: Religion, Politics, and Violence in Rural Bosnia*, the Dutch anthropologist Mart Bax explores the volatile social relations and traditions in southwestern Herzegovina that over the centuries have created what he calls "volcanic territory" where "the eruptions of human violence were the rule rather than the exception. . . . Blood vengeance, vendettas and other forms of private justice were 'normal' phenomena that regularly reoccurred and barely seemed to be alleviated by the pacifying activities of either church or state."[16] The old tradition of warfare and revenge runs deep in the Herzegovina. "Here the knife does not blunt and the [rifle] barrel does not rust," runs one local saying. The law of the Herzegovina, though often cast in a modern mold, is essentially tribal. Clan feuds dating back decades, even centuries, are settled with weapons rather than through police or courts, which are considered recourses for shameless cowards. Violence between the clans can be as bloody and truculent as conflicts with ethnic motivations.

In 1967 the twenty-three-year-old Gojko Šušak moved from Široki Brijeg to the coastal city of Rjeka, where he began to study math and physics at a teachers' college. He married and fathered a daughter. In the late 1960s, Yugoslavia had opened its doors wide to its jobless men in search of work in Western Europe, as well to emigration to Australia and North America. Šušak was one of 15,000 Croats who emigrated to Canada between 1967 and 1973. At the time, literally hundreds of thousands of Yugoslavs were exiting the country. It is thus highly unlikely that the Franciscans disguised Šušak as a monk in order to help him "escape" across the Alps to the Free World, as he later boasted. It is more probable that he too entered Austria legally, on a train or bus, perhaps with the aim of working and evading military service. There he applied to follow his brothers to Canada. Whatever the conditions, Šušak left Yugoslavia (and his first family) in 1968 and then emigrated to Canada the next year, alone.

Šušak arrived in Canada in April 1969, perhaps even in time for the diaspora's April 10 festivities. The date recalls the anniversary of the proclamation of an independent Croatia in 1941, which was celebrated by Croat émigrés across Canada and the United States as Croatia Day, a day of dance and music, roast pork, and patriotic speeches. In Toronto, Ottawa, and Vancouver, the events, usually staged in upscale hotels, drew crowds of several thousand. If he had attended, the new arrival from Široki Brijeg would probably have thought he was dreaming.

The April 10 festivities in 1969 were probably not much different than the present-day gatherings that the Croat community sponsors regularly during the year. At Father Kamber Parish Park in Mississauga, a heavily Croat-populated suburb of Toronto, Croat picnics on clear summer Sundays still attract thousands of local Croat families. On one such sweltering mid-August afternoon, I made my way from congested downtown Toronto to the secluded picnic area, several miles outside Mississauga's vast urban sprawl. Canada is home to an estimated one hundred thousand ethnic Croats, the majority of whom live in Ontario. Many of these émigrés arrived in the 1960s and 1970s when Canada's immigration laws were far more accommodating to Yugoslavs than were U.S. laws. In the name of multiculturalism, Canada also provided generous funding for cultural activities, such as language schools and folk dancing societies, as a way to encourage migrant nationalities to retain their identities.

Just past the Church of the Croatian Martyrs on Mississauga Road, an inconspicuous fenced-off entranceway with a Croat checkerboard above it marks Father Kamber Park, an address known only to Mississauga's Canadian Croats. A shoulderless paved road winds downward through a sundappled birch forest, which eventually opens onto a flat expanse of freshly mowed fields. For this day it serves as a giant parking lot. At a wooden pavilion, a black-frocked priest delivers an open-air mass in Croatian. Behind him stand three nuns and a baby-faced younger priest, newly arrived from Croatia. Worshipers in white shorts, cradling baseball hats on their laps, sit under oak trees in fold-out lawn chairs. Later in the afternoon a Herzegovina folk group will perform there, the kind of cultural event that still receives official Canadian support.

Along the periphery of the car-lined fields there is a concrete swimming pool packed with screaming youngsters, an aproned vendor selling roast pork by the kilo, and a snack hut. Teenagers wearing Toronto Raptors basketball jerseys and earrings speak English to one another but effortlessly answer their grandparents in Croatian. A couple of muscular bare-chested boys casually throw a football.

In stark contrast to Toronto's ubiquitous multiethnicity, the one-dimensional ethnic harmony of the picnic is striking. On a brilliant day the atmosphere is serene, almost idyllic: a seamless *volksgemeinschaft* at peace with itself. This facsimile of the unspoiled Croat village, centered around religion, family, and nature, is almost kitsch in its imagery: living proof to the émigrés that, when good Croats are among their own kind, there is no dissension. Rupture comes from outside the organic community, from "the Other," the outsider. Here, far away from the complexity of multinational Yugoslavia, was the Croatia that the right-wing émigrés believed should exist—and would, were it not for communism, Serbs, and Western hypocrisy.

The political roots of this idealized vision of Croatia are not difficult to locate. The park's namesake, Father Charles (Dragutin) Kamber, was an officer in the NDH army. In the close air of the snack hut, a grainy black-and-white portrait of Ante Pavelić in military uniform is hung over the deep fryer. It is the only portrait of any kind on the premises. Along the gravel walkway, trinket stands sell gaudy Virgin Mary key chains, Croat pop music, and dozens of other items with the red-and-white Croat checkerboard emblazoned on them. An old woman presides over a table that also offers shot glasses and black T-shirts displaying the Ustashe "U." One T-shirt depicts a lit bomb inside the "U" with the inscription "Black Legion," a renowned Ustashe terrorist unit. At another stand is a video on cultural life in the NDH and a cassette of Ustashe march songs.

For most second- and third-generation diaspora Croats, the Ustashe symbolism is probably void of any meaning or experience. For the post–Cold War generation of picnickers, who have grown up with an independent Croatia, the NDH is completely irrelevant. Now May 30 is celebrated as Croatia Day, the date the democratically elected Sabor, Croatia's parliament, convened its first session in 1990. But for older émigrés, the Ustashe and the collapse of the NDH were the defining events of their lives, and, stuck in the time warp of emigration, they were unable to move beyond it.

According to businessman John Zdunić from nearby Oakville, Ontario, the annual Croatia Day festivities in April actually had little to do with the anniversary of the NDH. "This was just a day for Croats to get together. It had nothing to do with the Ustashe regime," Zdunić says, navigating his silver Audi smoothly through the beltways around Toronto. Zdunić, a big friendly fellow in his late fifties, is a first-generation émigré from Lika in central Croatia. Although an uncompromising Croat nationalist, Zdunić never joined organizations such as Otpor or HOP. Instead, he financed or co-financed Croatia-related projects ad hoc, most notably the drive to raise funds for a Chair of Croatian Studies at Waterloo University. A wealthy contractor, Zdunić exudes the confident air of a self-made man and proudly considers Canada as much his home as Croatia. In 1990 Zdunić became the first HDZ president for North America, a position he left several years later, disgusted with the party's political cronyism and its unwillingness to act on his recommendations. Zdunić learned the hard way that once diaspora money dries up, the homeland elite can quickly become distant. Tudjman listened—or feigned to listen—to the diaspora Croats when he needed them, and once they had outlived their usefulness, he dropped them without pause, as he did with Zdunić. But this bulky man in a dark blue windbreaker still supports the HDZ, even if it has left him deeply disappointed.

Zdunić admits that obviously some Croat émigrés identified with the Ustashe. "But not all of the people were completely blind," he says in his nearly perfect Canadian-tinged English. "Certainly I wasn't." Zdunić, repeating an oft-heard argument, claims that the salvageable part of Croatia's World War II experience was the legacy of an independent state, which Croats had for the first time since 1102 when the medieval Croatian state joined the crown of Hungary. The NDH, for all its faults and limitations, embodied independence from Serbs and other fellow south Slavs, which émigrés insisted Croats had dreamed of for nine hundred years. On April 10, says Zdunić, they were simply honoring the idea of an independent Croatia.

Father Josip Gjuran, pastor for the Croat Catholics in the greater Toronto area from 1969 to 1998, had more than his share of run-ins with his community's radical fringe. But April 10, he argues, was a legitimate date for celebration and commemoration. "Ninety-nine percent of the Croatian diaspora in Canada was expelled from Tito's Yugoslavia. They came here by force," says the elderly white-haired priest in his modest Zagreb apartment, echoing the general (fully unsubstantiated) perception of many émigré Croats. Notably Gjuran himself was never expelled from Yugoslavia but was ordered by the Catholic Church hierarchy to replace the late Father Kamber in Toronto. "They [Croat émigrés in the Toronto region] supported the NDH, as I did too, even though it was clear that Croatia was under occupation at the time," he says.

In the late 1960s the diaspora's April 10 commemorations provoked an embarrassing diplomatic tiff across the Atlantic. In Cleveland the home of thirty thousand or more Croatian Americans, émigré activists managed to talk the city's mayor, Carl Stokes, into publicly endorsing Croatian Independence Day and even raising the old NDH flag in downtown Cleveland! On April 10, 1968, Stokes proclaimed:

This date marks the anniversary of the beginning of the gallant struggle
of the Croatian people which, in 1941, was successful in bringing freedom after 850 years of foreign domination. . . . The people of Croatia are
held in respect and esteem by people of good will throughout the world
for their great contributions to the sciences, arts and literature.

Ohio Governor James Rhodes went even further a year later on the same
date, calling for a "determined fight for the reinstatement of an independent, free and democratic Croatian state which was declared on April 10,
1941."[17]

The Yugoslav embassy in Washington naturally caught wind of the
Cleveland celebrations and voiced its strong objections to the State Depart-
ment and directly to Ohio's politicians. In a letter to the mayor, the Yugoslav
Consul General even reminded Mayor Stokes that Pavelić's NDH, in its al-
liance with Nazi Germany, had declared war on the United States in 1941.
The mayor dismissed the letter, observing the occasion for two more years
before the State Department stepped in and leaned hard on the Cleveland
City Council to show better judgment.

Father Gjuran says he was not entirely comfortable with the Pavelić portraits, but he did nothing to protest their presence, even the one in Father
Kamber Park, a facility directly under his jurisdiction. "Ante Pavelić wasn't
any worse then Tito," he snaps, clearly sensitive about the issue. The difference, he claims, was that Tito was on good terms with the West because of
Yugoslavia's 1948 break with Stalin. Pavelić, he readily admits, was a dictator, even a war criminal, but nothing out of the ordinary in Nazi-occupied
Eastern Europe. "Our people [Gjuran's parishioners] were sympathetic to
Pavelić's state and I was serving those people as a church leader. I wasn't a
political activist. It would have been stupid to fight against my own people,"
he says.

Even diaspora leaders who personally condemned the Ustashe legacy
found it virtually impossible to raise the issue constructively in public. "I
was very embarrassed," says Martin (Mate) Meštrović, who for years taught
European history at Fairleigh Dickinson University in New Jersey. The son
of the world-famous Croat sculptor Ivan Meštrović, he served as president
of the Croatian National Congress in the 1980s, an umbrella organization,
founded in 1974, for the entire Croat diaspora. Meštrović took the position
in order to pry the organization from the grip of historically tainted ultra-
nationalists. "But the question of the Pavelić portraits is: What do you do?
Make an issue of it? I tried to ignore it because there were lots of people
who were just waiting to create incidents," he says, referring to Yugoslav secret service plants that infiltrated the diaspora leagues. "You never knew if it
was the UDBA that was ultimately behind it," he says, referring to commu-

nist Yugoslavia's secret services. It was the mission of Tito's agents, he explains, to provoke petty quarrels and sow seeds of discord in order to block meaningful work. The Pavelić portraits were a made-to-order pretext.

There may have been many like Meštrović with qualms about the Pavelić portraits and April 10 associations, but their voices were neither courageous nor loud. The Ustashe references did not indicate widespread support among the diaspora for the fallen dictatorship or its infamous deeds. Rather, they testified to a deep reluctance or inability on the part of these émigrés to face the burdens of Croatian history and articulate a new political vision. It seems mind-boggling that they failed to extract fresh impulses for their thinking from the democratic, multiethnic environment that Canada offered. They proved unable to imagine an independent, postcommunist Croatia without recycling the ideas and totems of the Ustashe and its discredited, volkish ideology. By failing to distance themselves from the past, these diaspora currents helped reintroduce a virulent strain of nationalism into Croatian society at a critical moment in its history.

CHAPTER TWO

Reconciling Croatia

When the future Croatian president, Franjo Tudjman, visited Canada early in the summer of 1987, he boasted a nationalist résumé second to few in Croatia. His historical work had made him an apologist for the Ustashe's World War II quisling state, and twice he had done time in communist prison cells for his beliefs. But it is unlikely that he anticipated the uncompromising visions and grandiose plans that North America's radical émigrés would whisper into his ear. In Tudjman's mind the program that would later be known as Croatian National Policy—the forging of an ethnic Greater Croatia—was still an amorphous hodgepodge of loose ideas and general ill-defined goals. Its essential outline, though, would become discernible over the course of his visits to North America in the late 1980s.

According to his Toronto host, John Čaldarević, on his first visit Tudjman did not mention the possibility of a Croatian bid for independence or any plan to form his own political party. At York University he lectured to audiences of several hundred people on the interwar Croat patriot Stjepan Radić, and at the University of Toronto Tudjman spoke on "The Question of Nationality in the Contemporary World." Not once in either talk did he explicitly call for Croatian statehood; but the contours of its rationale permeated both presentations.

On June 19, 1987, from behind a simple lectern at the Ontario Institute for Studies in Education at the University of Toronto, Tudjman outlined his world-historical views to an expectant audience of diaspora Croats. Couched in the convoluted phraseology of Yugoslav academia, Tudjman declared that the ethnic nation was mankind's most sophisticated form of social organization:

> From the earliest knowledge of mankind's history, nationalities or nations have been and remain, with all their manifestations of ethnicity and statehood, the highest social configuration of a human community. The whole of human history has concerned itself with the formation and self-determination of national societies and the creation of states. . . . The self-determination of nations, their freedom from external influences and foreign domination, their sovereignty of state, and at the same time

the desire for equality and ascendancy in the international arena have been and remain the main characteristics of contemporary historical fluctuation.[1]

World history, he went on, was one long geopolitical Hobbesian struggle of nation against nation. In a barely veiled swipe at Serbia, he admitted that nationalism, although the pinnacle of Western civilization, had occasionally sold out its lofty principles by enabling some nations to subject other worthy nations to tyranny.

No doubt more than a few in the diaspora audience squirmed when Tudjman heralded both Lenin and Tito as great thinkers. But their real genius, he argued, had nothing to do with Marx, wage labor, or class struggle. Their brilliance lay in the recognition of national self-determination as the unstoppable dynamic of "history's forward march." Tito's defiant stand against Stalin and Soviet hegemony should be chalked up as a noble defense of national sovereignty. There were not a few Croat communists, too, Tudjman hinted, who also grasped the "primary objective" of the socialist movement as the liberation of the Croat nation. But socialism ultimately leads the national cause into a blind alley, he admitted. The inherent contradictions of Titoism render the doctrine useless. In time, the God-given nationalistic forces of history will inevitably undermine the foundations of such multinational, one-party states.

"World unity," Tudjman told the Toronto émigrés, "prospers not through the negation but rather through the ever greater respect for national individuality." His example was the European Community. The suppression of the national principle could have dire consequences for Croatia. "In light of our historical experience," he warned, "wherein entire civilizations and many nations have disappeared, among them those of great intellectual and cultural wealth, even the most optimistic among us cannot be completely assured that our own civilization can escape the same destiny." Tudjman concluded that the aspiration common to the late Tito, the early Croat communists, and the 1971 Croatian Spring reformers was a "national democratic political platform," which is as close as Tudjman comes to hinting at the formation of his future party, the Croatian Democratic Community, the HDZ. The Ontario émigrés were so enthusiastic about the lectures, they published them in pamphlet form in English and Croatian, and mailed the booklets to diaspora communities as far distant as South Africa.

It was after the York University lecture several days later that Tudjman first met one of North America's most prominent nationalist radicals, the Croatian National Resistance (Otpor) president Marin Sopta. Sopta's reputation as a political extremist made it imprudent for the two men to meet in public, but in the evening at private residences they chatted late into the night. The impression Tudjman made on Sopta, as well as Ante Beljo, Gojko Šušak, and John Zdunić, was enormous. Sopta beams at the memory of it. "It's hard to say if it was some kind of instinct within us or just love at first sight," gushes Sopta, sitting outside at the Café Ban, the HDZ favored coffeehouse alongside Zagreb's bustling Jelačič Square. Every few minutes or so, Sopta interrupts our interview to greet friends or shake hands with former colleagues, most of them, in that spring of 2000, abruptly jobless after the fall of the Tudjman regime. After a decade in power the HDZ suffered a lopsided defeat at the polls in January 2000 to a reform-minded center-left coalition.

"Somehow we knew that he was the man, that he would be the leader to finally pull the Croats together," says Sopta, a loquacious, heavy-jowled man around fifty. The days he starred as a striker on Toronto's all-Croat soccer team seem a long way off. When he wasn't on the soccer pitch or in the Otpor headquarters, he worked part-time as a dental technician to pay the rent. He remembers his years in Canada fondly, a part of his life incalculably simpler than that in an independent Croatia, particularly one with the HDZ in opposition. In 1995, after a stint at the Defense Ministry, Sopta took over the directorship of the HDZ foreign policy think tank, the Ivo Pilar Institute for Strategic Research. "He had the charisma of a great leader," Sopta says, referring again to Tudjman, "like Churchill or De Gaulle." What impressed the exiles most about Tudjman was his potential to take charge and lead the nation toward its rightful destiny. Tudjman, the old Partisan general, was prepared to lead, and this group of émigrés was ready to follow.

Not surprisingly, the émigré nationalists and the former communist officer did not see eye-to-eye on everything. During the first Canada trip they locked horns on two issues. For one, Tudjman could not foresee the imminent collapse of socialist Yugoslavia, something the right-wing émigrés had assumed since 1946. He proposed a further gradual devolution of centralized power in Yugoslavia, which, either de facto or de jure, would turn Yugoslavia into a loose confederation of republics. A multiparty system might then emerge, followed by elections, and then independence, perhaps, down the road. "We kept saying that we didn't have time for this," explains Sopta, "that time was running out. We wanted full independence." But, in 1987, Tudjman could not be persuaded. Nevertheless, a fully independent Croatia sooner rather than later was a thought Tudjman would have time to mull over.

Second, there was Bosnia. Both Tudjman and the émigrés believed passionately that the Republic of Bosnia-Herzegovina was an artificial construction and that most of it properly belonged to Croatia. Ethnic Croats made up a total of only about 17 percent of the population of Bosnia and Herzegovina. But Tudjman and the diaspora activists agreed that the Bosnian Muslims were actually wayward Croats, one-time Catholic Slavs who converted to Islam during the Ottoman rule for reasons of convenience and who might one day be reconverted into good Catholics. Even unconverted, as Muslims, the Bosnians could still be loyal Croats—that is, if they *identified themselves and behaved* as Croats! Fantastic as it sounds today, the émigrés extolled the Bosnian Muslims as "the flower of the Croatian nation," as had nineteenth-century Croat nationalists, and the Ustashe's Pavelić, too. Given the bloody campaign directed only a few years later against Bosnian Muslims by these very same men in the Tudjman administration, it is nearly impossible to fathom, in hindsight, that they were sincere at the time. But it seems that they were. In the diaspora media there was no comparison between the vitriol lavished on Serbs and the benevolent indifference with which they ignored the Bosnian Muslims. In fact, attesting to the Croats' sincerity, a number of Croat-behaving Muslims ("Croats of Islamic faith") held high-ranking positions in some of the Croats' most radical émigré organizations, including Otpor.

An unquestioned tenet of the extremist émigrés was that Croatia extended to the River Drina, the eastern border of Bosnia and Herzegovina, just as it had in the NDH. "There was no Bosnia issue," says Zdunić bluntly, "only the Croatia issue." When Šušak first returned to Croatia in 1990 he automatically entered his birthplace as "Široki Brijeg, Croatia." (Technically he was right. When Šušak was born, Široki Brijeg was part of NDH, not Bosnia and Herzegovina or Yugoslavia.) Tudjman's early notions of Croatia's proper borders seem to have fluctuated. On some occasions he openly fantasized about the resurrection of the borders of the 1939 Croatian Banovina, which included parts of Bosnia and even Serbia, right up to the suburbs of Belgrade. At other times he talked about a division of Bosnia between Croatia and Serbia. At the very least he certainly saw Bosnia's northwestern Bihać pocket as critical for Croatia's strategic interests, while western Herzegovina and the northeastern Posavina were naturally part of Croatia in demographic terms.

Tudjman and the émigrés parted ways on the proper strategy to acquire those tracts of Bosnia and Herzegovina that they considered rightly Croatia's. They agreed that the majority of Bosnian Muslims would naturally gravitate toward Croatia. But, according to Sopta, Tudjman believed that the Bosnia issue could be solved peacefully, perhaps through some kind of deal with Serbia. The émigrés objected vigorously. "Šušak, Beljo, and I were from the region and we knew exactly," explains Sopta. "We said no way that the problem of Bosnia Herzegovina could be solved peacefully. It couldn't be solved without blood." Whereas Tudjman, who had lived for years in Belgrade, felt that some kind of deal with the Serbs to carve up the area was possible, the fiercely anti-Serb émigrés ruled this out as preposterous. The émigrés knew that a battle over Bosnia and Herzegovina was in store, and they were prepared to wage it. Quite amazingly, none of them guessed that the stiffest opposition would come from the Bosnian Muslims themselves.

Tudjman's first trip to Canada also presented an ideal opportunity to test the diaspora waters on his grand plan of "national reconciliation." Tudjman was by no means the first Croat nationalist to argue that Croats on both sides of the World War II barricades must shelve their historical animosities and unite as one, undivided nation. By the 1960s most émigré nationalists, with the exception of the oldest-school Pavelić Ustashes, endorsed some version of reconciliation between the left and right. Many Croat Partisans, the argument ran, were, at heart, also good Croat patriots. But at one time they had believed not only in the noble social ideals of communism but also, naively, in southern Slavic "brotherhood and unity." (Others at the time had even touted an independent "Soviet Croatia" that would be separate from Serbia.) But these lapses were excusable. How were well-intentioned Croat Partisans in 1941 supposed to know what a ruthless dictator Tito would become and how he would turn on Croatia? There was also nothing wrong with the essence of socialism, the émigrés insisted. An independent Croatian state should incorporate egalitarian ideals, just as the NDH did. After all, in the end, all Croats are equal. Anti-capitalist, illiberal ideas were not anathema to the cause of Croat nationalism. Various national and social philosophies had been wedded in the past, and could be again, in an independent Croatia.

Tudjman, the Partisan general turned nationalist dissident, not only espoused this plan, he embodied it. He was uniquely qualified to bridge the fractious divide in Croatia between the "sons and daughters of Ustashe," as he put it, and the "sons and daughters of Partisans." The Canadian diaspora was the perfect place to gauge how much distance had to be bridged. People such as Sopta and Šušak were ready to make the required leap of faith. Later that year in a letter to the moderate diaspora newspaper, *The Fraternalist*, based in Pittsburgh, Beljo spelled it out:

> Croatian solidarity—all for one and one for all—is our Croatian motto
> even more today than it was ever in the past. We are the sons of former
> Croatian Domobrans [the NDH home guard], Partisans, Ustashe, and
> who knows what other colors and camps. We respect them as our fathers
> but refuse to repeat their suicidal fights, no matter how angry some individuals will be with us.[2]

This version of national reconciliation had been a fundamental tenet of Otpor ideology since the group's founders broke with Pavelić in the late 1950s. But, in 1987, others needed convincing.

Older anticommunist Croats, particularly those who fled Croatia at the barrel of a gun, harbored deep reservations about the strategy. On the Sunday before Tudjman's first Canadian lecture, Sopta recalls, an old Ustashe supporter cornered him after mass at the Franciscan center in Norval. The man had heard about Tudjman's upcoming talk in Toronto and was not pleased. Sopta feigned ignorance. The man continued: "If I find the bastard who's organizing this, I'll kill the motherfucker," Sopta recalls him saying. The man broke out in a wide grin. "And Marin," he said, "I hear it's you."

In a 1996 interview for the Croatian publication *Hrvatsko Slovo*,[3] Šušak tells a similar story about Tudjman's first visit:

At first, in comparison with [other dissidents like] Savka [Dabčević-Kučar], [Vlado] Gotovac, [Dražen] Budiša, and many others, Tudjman had no chance, especially because of his past. . . . Imagine how hard it was for someone like me coming from Široki Brijeg, who had lost his family, to meet a former [communist] general. It was hard for me to say, "This is the right person for Croatia." During Dr. Tudjman's first visit, only 10 percent of Croat émigrés came to hear him speak, while the other 90 percent condemned me as the organizer for bringing him over. They said, "Who are you bringing here?" However, I talked with the president and asked him about the chances for the future. I realized that he had a vision, a plan, and a program. The question was whether he would find enough people and funds to implement his program. When other Croatian politicians came to Canada later, we were disappointed with them.

At the lectures, older Croats with World War II backgrounds peppered Tudjman with sharp-edged questions. One man stood up and defiantly announced that he had carried a rifle for the Ustashe. "If I had caught you in the forest forty years ago," he assailed Tudjman, "you'd be dead now. And if you had caught me, I'd be dead." The hall stood still. "But whatever the case," he continued with a nod, "I'm behind you now." "Everyone was tense because of who Tudjman was," says Zdunić. "Before, these people couldn't look one another in the eye. But Tudjman insisted that we had all been fighting for the same cause, the Croatian cause, just in different ways."

In addition to national reconciliation, Tudjman sampled the émigrés on another idea key to his emerging program: Iseljena Hrvatska. Roughly translated as "exiled Croatia" or "expelled Croatia," Iseljena Hrvatska implies that all, or at least most, of the Croats not in Croatia proper had been forced out of their rightful homeland—by war, repression, or poverty. This concept of diaspora emphasizes the element of *involuntary* resettlement. The 1945 Bleiburg tragedy, the diaspora's Alamo, was the model example.

When Tudjman looked out over the diaspora in Canada, for example, he did not see the Croat émigrés and their families as "Croatian Canadians,"

Canadian citizens who made up part of the country's rich ethnic composition. Rather, he saw generations of "Croats in Canada," displaced co-nationals who would, or should, eventually return home. For Tudjman and Šušak, this applied not only to the ethnic Croats on other continents but also to the ethnic Croat minorities of Romania, Kosovo, and Vojvodina, people who had lived as constituent peoples in those regions for hundreds of years. Iseljena Hrvatska suggests that all Croats should be living in one nation-state, Croatia. A bit ironically, since Tudjman relied so heavily on the diaspora, "exiled Croatia" implies that the very existence of diasporas is unnatural, an aberration of history that cried out to be corrected.

As unrepresentative as this paradigm was for most people with Croat ancestry living outside Croatia, the notion of Iseljena Hrvatska helps us understand the diaspora worlds of men such as Beljo and Šušak, people who never assimilated into Canadian society. This brand of émigré, not confined to Croats, lived in isolated diaspora communities, like those created by the Croats in Ontario. Ensconced in the suburbs and their ubiquitous shopping malls, they shared little sense of community with their Canadian neighbors or coworkers. Too often their existence was confined to their houses, their cars, and their jobs, on the one hand, and to the subcultural niches of the Croat community, on the other. The content of their stale discourses never strayed far from Croatia: Bleiburg, the NDH, historical Croat heroes, and Serb villains. In contrast to these Babylonian exiles, the majority of Croat émigrés were agreeably integrated into their new societies. They called themselves "Croatian Canadians" or simply "Canadians" and thrived in Canada's multiethnic surroundings. Iseljena Hrvatska represented a small minority that felt marooned on alien shores and vowed one day to return to the homeland. There, awaiting them, was the fortune, happiness, and respect withheld from them in exile.

This vision was taken so seriously by Tudjman that he expected large-scale "returns" of the "expelled Croats" and their families to the homeland. On assuming the republican presidency in 1990, one of his very first moves was to create a Ministry of Return and Immigration in order to expedite the process. The person selected to lead the ministry was Gojko Šušak. The Croat émigrés from Toronto and elsewhere say that Tudjman solicited them to return with promises of high-profile roles in the new Croatia. It was their duty to return, he stressed, arguing that Croatia would desperately need their international experience, investment potential, and business acumen to build a prosperous, independent Croatia.

But Croatia also needed their genes: red-blooded ethnic Croat families to restock a Greater Croatia. Beneath its innocuous surface, the concept of Iseljena Hrvatska suggests much more than the voluntary return of homesick patriots. It darkly implies an "exchange of populations" and the "reverse resettlement" of hundreds of thousands of people. As Tudjman and the HDZ later formulated more explicitly, Croatia would be "reconstituted" within its "proper ethnic borders" by biological Croats. The idea of Iseljena Hrvatska foreshadows the mass population movements that took place during the 1990s, though not voluntarily as Tudjman initially forecast. War and ethnic cleansing would uproot more than 500,000 ethnic Croats from Serbia, central Bosnia, and Kosovo who would relocate to Croatia proper and Croat-dominated parts of Bosnia. The 1995 Croat counteroffensives against rebel Serbs would send more than 150,000 non-Croats fleeing eastward out of Croatia. The number of émigrés who voluntarily repatriated from Western countries to independent Croatia was insignificant, no more than an estimated 3,500. During the same period, as Croatia's economy faltered, many times that number *left* Croatia.

In his inaugural speech in Croatia's parliament, the Sabor, on May 30, 1990, Tudjman articulated the plan more clearly, practically announcing sweeping exchanges of populations:

> Among the other successes of the HDZ that have contributed significantly to the hard-won democratic transformation, one must add the unquestioned creation of a spiritual unity between the homeland and exiled Croatia. The new Croatian government, at all levels, should undertake effective steps in order to facilitate the return of the largest possible number of Croat men from around the world to the homeland, as soon as possible. Serious consideration should be given to the possibility of relocating a certain number of Croat minorities to wasted homes in many Croatian areas.

Tudjman's passing reference to transferring ethnic Croats abroad to "wasted homes in Croatian areas" should have thrown up flaming red flags to the international community in 1990. What was a "wasted home," if not a reference to the homes of the 600,000-strong ethnic Serbian minority in Croatia?

"From the very beginning, this concept begged the question of where these thousands of repatriated people will go," says Milorad Pupovac, a professor of philology at Zagreb University and the leader of a moderate Croatian Serb political party. "It implies that these people outside of Croatia belong in places where other people, like non-Croat minorities, live inside Croatia." Pupovac argues that Iseljena Hrvatska was vital to Tudjman's concept of Croatia and integral to the processes that led to ethnic cleansing and war. He argues that while "national reconciliation" was designed to provide the political unity that had divided Croats, Iseljena Hrvatska was intended to bring about demographic unity. These were the pillars of what would become Croatian National Policy, the plan of Tudjman and Šušak to forge an ethnically cleansed Greater Croatia.

In 1988 and 1989 Tudjman returned to Toronto and also visited Vancouver, Ottawa, Norval, Sudbury, Montreal, and many points in the United States, such as Cleveland, Pittsburgh, and Chicago. By then he knew exactly what he wanted for Croatia—and for himself. The thoughts he had been pondering had coalesced into an ideological vision. "It was very different than the year before," says Čaldarević, who agreed in 1988 to have Tudjman stay in his home a second time. "He talked only politics. He talked about new states, about political developments in Yugoslavia, and about the future." It was evident that Tudjman, often seen in the company of Catholic priests, had made inroads into influential diaspora congregations, particularly among the Franciscans. The size of his diaspora audiences more than doubled, and his message grew more refined. After North America Tudjman toured Western Europe with the same agenda. The seed of the HDZ had been planted, and the diaspora would help it to flower.

But this second time around Čaldarević and Tudjman openly quarreled over the historian's contacts with the radical nationalists. Tudjman's interest in Sopta, Šušak, and a Franciscan priest by the name of Ljubo Krasić was deeper than Čaldarević had imagined. And to Čaldarević's chagrin, they controlled Tudjman's itinerary. "I told him straight out that I didn't want my house under RCMP [Royal Canadian Mounted Police] surveillance, which was bound to happen if he met with these guys," says Čaldarević. So Tudjman made his choice. It was the last time he stayed at the Čaldarević residence.

An element of flattery may have been involved when Tudjman, later in the 1990s, quipped that the HDZ was born in Canada, a remark the émigrés recall proudly. During those years, when not in the diaspora, Tudjman and his diverse allies in Croatia were networking furiously across the republic. But Beljo remembers discussing the name of a national democratic platform with Tudjman in 1988. The words *Croatian* and *democratic* had to be included. But they had difficulty choosing a third term. *Party* seemed too narrow for the world-historical quest at hand, and national reconciliation implicitly cut across all political borders. The name of their organization had to be suitable for a national movement that transcended the political divisions that had cursed Croatia throughout the century. Eventually Tudjman settled on *zajednica*, which can be translated as "community." The Croatian Democratic Community came to life on February 28, 1989, in the halls of Zagreb's Writers' Union, just off Republic Square.

Later in the year the first HDZ North America convention assembled in Cleveland, the U.S. bastion of HDZ support. John Zdunić from Toronto and Ante Beljo from Sudbury were named president and secretary, respectively. By November 1989, when Tudjman made his visit to North America as HDZ president, there were party branches in sixteen North American cities.

With socialist Yugoslavia entering its death throes, the moment was suddenly ripe for Croatia's right-wing émigrés to return in triumph to the homeland. The formal debut for the HDZ émigrés in Croatia came on February 24, 1990, in Zagreb's Lisinski Hall, with all the considerable pomp and pageantry that the young movement could muster for its first official congress. The jam-packed concert hall was draped in red, white, and blue Croatian flags, a donation of the émigré branches from the United States, Canada, Germany, Norway, Sweden, Switzerland, South Africa, and Australia, which accounted for about one-quarter of the twenty-five hundred participants. Only through diaspora associations could one obtain Croatian flags without the socialist insignia. "We brought as many flags as we could pack," smiles Zdunić.

The émigrés descended on Zagreb from all directions, many in Croatia for the first time in decades. Some had had visas arranged by Josip Boljkovac, HDZ vice president and former interior minister, who put his old connections to work to get the émigrés in. The Ohio-based loyalists secured visas from the Yugoslav consulate in Cleveland, run by a sympathetic Slovene. Others showed up without any visa at all.

Tudjman and Šušak met the émigrés at the airport. Tudjman's move to invite them en masse was an exceptionally bold challenge to the regime. If the dreaded "Ustashe émigrés" could return to the socialist republic of Croatia, anything was possible. "To invite the diaspora back to the homeland for a great meeting," recalled Tudjman years later, "was risky to the point that even those people who were later in my leadership waited to the last minute to see whether they would be arrested or not." Tudjman calls the decision "a turning point in [his] life in terms of decision-making."[4] He dared to test who would blink first. The regime did. Only one person was detained at the airport, an Otpor member from Toronto. The entire congress refused to convene officially until he was released, which happened several hours later.

The raucous, emotionally charged gathering set the tone for the HDZ election campaign. The republic's first multiparty elections since World War II were only two weeks away. Croat hymns and resounding standing ovations punctuated the long oratories of speaker after speaker. "We are Croatia, too," read one of the émigré banners. Tudjman's opening speech underlined the imperative of Croatia's "self-determination in its natural and historic borders," which he declined to define further. Buzzwords such as "self-determination" and calls for the émigrés' return triggered outbursts of wild applause. Similarly mention of Milošević or "Serb expansionism" elicited piercing whistles. One speaker, a notoriously conservative priest, for some inexplicable reason proposed sending a message of "peace and love" to the Serb minority in Croatia. He was roundly booed, loudest of all by the émigrés, and forced to discontinue his presentation.

Émigré representatives from four continents figured prominently in the congress lineup. First on the overcrowded stage was Zdenka Babić-Petričević from Frankfurt, Germany, who would enter the Sabor as one of the HDZ's "diaspora representatives." Over the next ten years she would define herself as one of Tudjman's most ardent and uncritical loyalists. The twenty-five HDZ branches in Germany, she announced, request that Croats abroad be allowed to vote, an oft-heard desire of many diaspora patriots. But if not, she promised theatrically, they will come to Croatia directly to vote for the HDZ—which, by the busload, is exactly what they did. Shouts of "Long live Croatia!" erupted in the hall.

The next to speak was the Sudbury electrician and amateur historian Ante Beljo, the new general secretary of the North American HDZ. (He, as did Šušak, listed his profession in Canada as "engineer.") After the elections, Beljo would take the top HDZ post in Croatia. Later he established the Croatian Information Center, a pro-government satellite news service, and in 1993 he was appointed director of the influential Croatian Heritage Foundation. For Beljo, his appearance at the congress, the first time he stepped foot in Croatia since 1967, was a vindication of all that he and the Canada émigrés had worked for. In fact, he argued immodestly, the new freedoms emerging in Croatia were the hard-won victory of the émigrés' "struggle for the respect of human and national rights." Political appointments had been as good as promised to the Canadian loyalists, and Beljo reminded Tudjman of his word: "The HDZ is the only organization in Croatia which showed that it cares for emigrants by asking our opinion. Others wanted only our reason, our fiscal potential, and our money, then they gave themselves the right to decide what to do with this." The Canadian émigrés were not prepared simply to be the vehicle for Tudjman's rise to power. They demanded a place in the driver's seat.

For the émigrés, the only conceivable political direction was independence, full speed ahead. While many non-émigré speakers, more attuned to the complex political and constitutional debates taking place within Yugoslavia, equivocated on the future status of Croatia, Beljo did not mince words on the émigrés' behalf:

> The historical right to statehood has to be put into reality. . . . By living abroad we have fully realized that every nation without its own state is a

nation without a name, a nation not respected by anyone, a nation about which little positive is said and a nation which is condemned to bear unsparingly each and everyone's sins and a nation at which everyone can spit, including its own sons.

This wounded tone persists throughout the speech. It reflects on Beljo as a person as well as a politician: a small, unaccomplished man with pseudo-intellectual pretensions. One could insert the word *person* where Beljo uses *nation* in his speech to begin to comprehend the inferiority complexes of diaspora figures such as Beljo and Šušak. The entire rambling speech is a generic template of the right-wing émigré mind-set. Communism was excoriated as "a Balkan abyss of evil and darkness" and "an unprecedented time of state terrorism." "Many heads fell and thousands of years in prison were arranged for innocent Croat sons and daughters in the homeland and abroad," he proclaimed. In a few gratuitous shots at the Serbs Beljo vents his indignation over the "violence and hatred" coming from Serb intellectuals in Belgrade, and promises "our full support to all the forces engaged in destroying these horrible and brutal methods of barbarians." At the time violence had yet to flare up between Serbs and Croats. That would change when the HDZ came to power.

Even before the Lisinski Hall congress, diaspora connections were employed to get the HDZ on its feet. In Croatia the fledgling HDZ needed cash and organizational competence. Zdunić, as one of the wealthiest Toronto émigrés, was just the man for the job. In the Canada contingent Beljo, Šušak, Sopta, and the Franciscan friar Krasić rounded out the core team. Their task was to initiate a "Western-style" campaign in Croatia and at the same time reach out to the diaspora. Office space was rented, telephones installed, and fax machines set in place, no small feat for a fledgling opposition party in socialist Yugoslavia. "The whole idea was that every village office [of the HDZ] would have a telephone and telefax," says Zdunić, who headed the HDZ coordinating committee in North America. About sixty fax machines arrived in the suitcases and backpacks of North American student volunteers, mostly via transatlantic flights from Canada. Croatian officers in the Yugoslav customs services turned a blind eye, either out of personal sympathy or, more likely, in response to direct orders from above.

The HDZ, less than a year old, mounted a global campaign for office in little Croatia, one republic of six in federal Yugoslavia, with a population of just 4.7 million. In addition to North America, South America, and Europe, the party dispatched representatives to as far afield as Australia to push for the HDZ and solicit funds. One scholar based at the time in western Australia, Dona Kolar-Panov, observed the stream of politicians and popular folk musicians, as well as Zagreb University's chancellor, who visited Perth's Croat clubs. The same campaign paraphernalia handed out in Croatia, such as posters, stickers, and badges, went like hotcakes in Australia, where in 1990 diaspora Croats were ineligible to vote. The touring HDZ troupes sold videocassettes, T-shirts and raised money through benefit auctions. One fruitcake adorned with Croatia's coat of arms went to the highest bidder for seven hundred Australian dollars, just a drop in the bucket that the Australia-based *Croatian Herald* estimated at three million Australian dollars (about $2 million) collected in the country by the HDZ for the race. Kolar-Panov notes that the unapologetic nationalism of candidate Tudjman and his HDZ provoked indignant cries from some Croatian Australians, who, like herself, identified with multinational Yugoslavia.[5]

By the time the HDZ arrived on the scene, other Croatian parties had sprung up as well—some of them openly courting the diaspora. Early opinion polls in Croatia showed Savka Dabčević-Kučar's Coalition of National Agreement (KNS) well ahead of the pack. Dabčević-Kučar, the popular leader of the 1971 Croatian Spring movement, was a name generally more familiar to most émigrés than Tudjman's at the time. But the KNS had nothing comparable to the HDZ network already in place in the diaspora.

Most observers agree that the émigré contributions to the HDZ far exceeded those to the KNS. Beljo claims that little money was required, given the politically charged atmosphere of the day. Šušak, in an interview with the German press, boasted that he alone orchestrated the flow of "a few million dollars" into the HDZ treasure chest. Sopta, on the other hand, claims that the sums were even higher. He tells of one HOP leader from Australia who contributed one million Australian dollars in cash. He says that unsolicited contributions streamed in from individuals, organizations, and church parishes across the world. Journalists from *Mladina* magazine in Slovenia calculate that the diaspora added as much as $8 million to the HDZ campaign coffers.[6] Whatever the exact figure, money arrived in quantities that in 1989 and 1990 no other party could rival, a testament to Tudjman's foresight. The fund-raising paid off: Tudjman and his HDZ surged to a narrow, first-past-the-post victory in May 1990. In line with Croatia's skewed electoral system, the HDZ's 40 percent of the popular vote entitled it to a commanding majority in the Sabor, and a mandate to push forward.

But émigré money was only one factor, and probably not the decisive one, in the HDZ's stunning triumph, after having trailed in the campaign. The HDZ beat the nationalist drum for all it was worth, not hesitating to play the volatile Serb card. "All people are equal in Croatia," pledged Tudjman, "but it must be clear who is the host and who is the guest." He proudly pointed out, in one grossly insensitive statement, that his wife was neither Serb nor Jewish. The remark made international headlines, and

Tudjman apologized profusely. Nevertheless, the comment contributed to the HDZ stance as the party most ready to disregard taboo in its drive toward independence.

The émigrés' boisterous return during communism's waning days was one of the lead news item in Croatia. The Zagreb airport was witness to joyous scenes of family reunions abounding in billowing red-and-white checkerboards and previously outlawed folk songs. The comparatively wealthy, ostensibly worldly émigrés basked in the limelight, relishing a status they could never have imagined during their days of "exile" in the West. In coffee bars and on television, the returnees shattered four decades of taboo, unabashedly championing the virtues of an independent Croatia. While praising Tudjman and the HDZ to the sky, they also struck out, in terms that had once been against the law, at Croatia's ethnic Serb minority.

Despite the name-calling, neither ordinary Croats nor most of Croatia's six hundred thousand Serbs were susceptible at first to the insidious baiting conducted by their respective nationalists. In Serbia Milošević had steadily cranked up the propaganda volume since 1987 and reached out to stir up passions in Croatia's Serb-populated pockets. But the initial response was remarkably tepid. The sparks did not catch automatically because Serbs and Croats had existed more or less amicably in Croatia for many generations, with the major exception of the violence of the World War II period. Almost every municipality in the republic had included a percentage of Serbs, which totaled 11 percent of the population. The Serbs, admittedly, were proportionately overrepresented in the local bureaucracy, police, and party. But the Croats suffered no tangible disadvantages. Croatian Serbs in the cities were well integrated into the urban fabric, many in mixed marriages. Even in more rural areas like central Croatia, in the so-called Krajina region where there were heavy Serb concentrations, Serbs and Croats spoke the same dialect, ate the same foods, and attended the same schools. Decades of living together had diluted, though not erased, the acrimonious memories of World War II. The daily exercise of balancing ethnic relations created a modus vivendi that most members of both nationalities could accept.

From the vantage point of their split-level duplexes in North American suburbia, the right-wing émigrés had no interest in the complexity of contemporary Croatian society. Some of them, such as Šušak, Sopta and Beljo, did not hail from Croatia and so never experienced living together with the Serbs of Croatia. Others, such as Zdunić, came from Lika, a poor, underdeveloped region where World War II resentments still poisoned relations between Croats and Serbs.

Quite simply, these émigrés had come to demonize all Serbs. It was "the Serbs" who had driven them into political exile, who had butchered their comrades at Bleiburg and continued to persecute their families in Croatia, to name only a few of the oft-recited crimes. Zdunić, who is otherwise a man of carefully weighed words, positively trembles when the topic comes up over a bacon-and-eggs breakfast in a Toronto diner. He refers to Serbs as "our arch enemies." "We were oppressed by Serbs, by the Yugoslav army, by Yugoslav diplomacy, Yugoslav trade, Yugoslav commerce, the Yugoslav banking system, Yugoslav organizations, Yugoslav domination," he fumes. Under the guise of communism, the émigrés charged, the Serbs in socialist Yugoslavia had already forged a Greater Serbia ruled from Belgrade. The émigrés believed that communism and the "terror machine" of the "bloody dictator" Marshal Tito were simply the means of enforcing Serb domination of Yugoslavia, or, as they called it, "Serboslavia."

For many of these émigrés, their passions and historical time were frozen in 1945 or 1952 or 1971, whichever year they emigrated. Yugoslavia's Serbs were the winners of the war, and they, the exile Croats, the great losers, chased from their homes across the world's oceans. Abroad in isolated communities, this resentment and anger fermented, growing ever more irrational and epic in proportion. If the Serbs of Serbia were the colonial lords of socialist Yugoslavia, those who comprised the Serb minority in Croatia were their agents. At their most polite, the Croat right-wingers referred to the minority Serbs in Croatia as "guests," a euphemism in nationalist jargon for second-class citizens. More often, though, they were castigated as the occupying forces who had invaded Croatia first with the Ottoman Turks, later with the Austro-Hungarians, and then with the Yugoslav armies. Whatever the case Serbs did not belong in Croatia, and the émigrés did. This is exactly the message Tudjman delivered to the émigrés when he visited North America in the 1980s.

When they returned to the homeland in 1990, the émigré radicals finally had a domestic forum for their ideas, and a vehicle, the HDZ, to peddle them. The resurgent Catholic Church was a powerful ideological ally in 1990 and 1991. Although the HDZ émigrés' brand of nationalism was initially foreign to most Croats, it found fertile soil in certain rural regions, particularly among peripheral social groups with mind-sets closest to the radical diaspora. These were rough regions, like the Dalmatian hinterland and adjacent western Herzegovina, where bad blood between Serbs and Croats had lingered throughout the postwar decades. Many émigrés hailed from exactly these parts. Moreover, migration from poor rural areas into Croatian towns and cities had created another strata of resentful, dislocated citizenry that was open to the call of firebrand nationalists.

"This peripheral part of the nation was the driving force for the ethnic tension and momentum toward war," argues Milorad Pupovac. A handsome academic with a thick shock of black hair, Pupovac was one of the many people working tirelessly in the early 1990s to keep Croatia from fracturing. Although a Croatian Serb, his scathing words for the radical extremists in both ethnic camps earned him a string of death threats in 1990 and 1991. "Without these peripheral elements, which were represented by the diaspora and aided by the Catholic Church, it would have been very, very hard to imagine a conflict between peoples who had lived together for so long," he says. Yet these people (and these ideas) penetrated from the margins of society into the mainstream and eventually took power. After moderates split from the HDZ in 1994, the hard-line factions, personified in the figure of Šušak, assumed undisputed control of the ruling party and, in effect, the country.

Their cause was substantially abetted by Belgrade, whose relentless anti-Croat vitriol enraged average Croats while it eventually radicalized the republic's minority Serbs. Milošević's spin doctors, intent on sowing fear and hostility, shrieked to the Croatian Serbs that "the Ustashe" was on the march again. Their definition of Ustashe was broad: it included the entire political spectrum of reform-minded Croats, not just the hard-liners in the HDZ who were employing terminology the Serbs associated with the old NDH. The Belgrade line was pure demagoguery designed to divide mixed communities and spur the ethnic Serbs in Croatia to take up arms. The reaction of rural Serbs to the Belgrade propaganda, on the one side, and to Zagreb's insensitive use of nationalistic slogans and imagery, on the other, was predictable. The Serb minority witnessed Croatia's new political class resurrecting the symbols linked to Ustashe rule, such as the šahovninca and the new currency, the kuna. (In fact, the šahovninca and the kuna had historical precedents that long predated the NDH.) But to the Croatian Serbs, it looked like the Ustashe, the rhetoric sounded like that of the Ustashe, and the Belgrade evening news swore to them that it was the Ustashe. Before long, no one could convince them otherwise: the Ustashe was back and the lives of the Serbs were in peril.

From month to month, through the latter half of 1990 and into 1991, Croatia lurched ominously toward war. HDZ hard-liners in the new Croatian government, men such as Gojko Šušak, the new minister of return and immigration, seemed at pains to alienate the Serb minority at every opportunity. Their intentions were thinly veiled: increase the ante, bring tensions to a boil, and eventually rid Croatia of its Serbs forever. Among the Croatian Serbs, Milošević proxies had drowned out all voices of reason. Weapons were distributed, militias formed, roadblocks set up, and, in December 1990, the self-appointed rebel Serb leaders proclaimed the Serb Autonomous District of the Krajina, a breakaway mini-state that would eventually subsume one-third of Croatian territory. Yet even at this advanced stage of madness, full-scale war was by no means inevitable. The Croat political elite still talked in terms of a reconstituted federation or confederation of the former republics of Yugoslavia. European diplomacy was belatedly waking up to the urgency of the situation. A window was there to negotiate a compromise solution.

When exactly—the day, the week, the month—that war broke out in Croatia is impossible to pinpoint. But the events in Borovo Selo, an industrial suburb of Vukovar in eastern Slavonia, marked a critical juncture in the descent into full-scale armed conflict. The old Habsburg city of Vukovar and its Danubian hinterland had long been the site of multiethnic coexistence. For hundreds of years Hungarians, Slovaks, Czechs, Italians, and, until 1945, Germans—as well as ethnic Serbs and Croats, of course—had farmed the fertile lands. By the late 1980s they enjoyed a relatively envious regional standard of living. But by the spring of 1991 the brewing tension had begun to destabilize the delicate patchwork of peoples that made their homes in the plains of eastern Slavonia.

Serb paramilitary units from Serbia proper, including the unscrupulous killer gangs led by the gangster nationalists Arkan (Željko Ražnjatović) and Vojislav Šešelj, had set up bases in and around Borovo Selo, a predominantly Serb settlement in Croatia's easternmost region of Slavonia. Barricades and control posts marked off Serb and Croat neighborhoods. Bloodshed had been averted, thanks in large part to the young police chief of Osijek, Josip Reihl-Kir, who came from a mixed marriage (German and Slovene) but considered himself a Croat. His selfless efforts to reach out to both communities had kept tempers from boiling over.

But in mid-April Reihl-Kir received an unexpected visit from a group of high-placed HDZ leaders, including Minister Šušak. In *The Death of Yugoslavia*, Laura Silber and Allan Little describe how Šušak leaned on Reihl-Kir to guide him through backroads and cornfield paths to the outskirts of Borovo Selo. Reihl-Kir thought that the idea was crazy and at first objected to the demand, since such a lark could undermine the tenuous peace he was fighting to preserve.

From the outskirts of the settlement Šušak and his men fired three shoulder-launched Ambrust rockets into Borovo Selo. One mortar round hit a house. Another landed unexploded in a field. No one was killed, but the escapade set off a chain reaction—as it was intended to do. The undetonated missile was brandished about on Serbian television, hard evidence of unprovoked Croat aggression against peaceful Serbs. A flurry of recriminations and countercharges followed between Zagreb and Belgrade.

In the poisoned atmosphere, Reihl-Kir continued to negotiate in good faith between the two communities. But, on the night of May 1, four Croat policemen attempted to enter Borovo Selo. Serb paramilitaries, lying in wait, opened fire. Two of the policemen escaped, but the other two were wounded and taken prisoner. The next morning disaster struck. When news of the hostage-taking made its way to the nearby city of Osijek, a busload of Croat policemen, mostly fresh recruits, set straightaway to rescue their colleagues. The rookie officers drove directly into a gory ambush. Serb paramilitaries rained gunfire on the bus as it entered the village, killing at least twelve Croats and wounding more than twenty.

The massacre sent shock waves through Croatia, pushing the political temperature higher and higher. Some of Tudjman's advisers hailed the attack as the perfect pretext for declaring independence at once. The media jumped on the incident announcing that dozens had been killed and that Croat soldiers had been mutilated and decapitated. The next day Tudjman virtually declared that Croatia was at war with Serbia and called Croats to arms "if that need arises" to "defend the freedom and sovereignty of the Republic of Croatia."

In the weeks that followed, Reihl-Kir fought a losing battle to restore mutual trust between the Serb and Croat communities of eastern Slavonia. He complained openly that HDZ extremists such as Šušak had highjacked the political process and were obstructing his efforts to broker between the two sides. On July 1 Reihl-Kir and two associates were gunned down by a Croat reserve police officer with links to the extremist wing of the HDZ. It was an assassination, insiders charge, ordered from above. The killer was promptly spirited out of the country and resettled in Australia. "It is a striking commentary," write Silber and Little, "on the direction in which Croatia was moving during those crucial weeks leading to the outbreak of full-scale war, that Reihl-Kir's moderation, his conciliatory approaches to the Serbs, had cost him his life, while Šušak's activities, stoking tension and provoking conflict, were to win him one of the most prominent places in Tudjman's government."[7]

Two months later, on September 18, 1991, Šušak was named minister of defense, the number two position in the Croatian government.

CHAPTER THREE

The Avengers of Bleiburg

ojko Šušak's 1991 foray into Borovo Selo was not the first time in recent memory that violence linked to Croat émigrés forced its way into international headlines. In the diaspora Šušak and his coterie circulated in a rough political milieu that had spanned five continents since the early 1950s. It was a hopelessly fragmented, sectarian scene, thoroughly infiltrated by various secret services and politically impotent. Dozens of radical nationalist groupings came and went, splintering along ideological lines and over personal animosities. Their revolutionary strategies and periodic attempts to convert ideology into action put them at odds not only with Yugoslavia and Tito's agents abroad but also with the law-enforcement services of their adopted countries, mainstream Croat diaspora groups, and even the Vatican.

In Australia, West Germany, Spain, Sweden, and Argentina, as well as North America, small militant pro-Ustashe groups such as Pavelić's HOP, Otpor, and the conspiratorial Croatian Revolutionary Brotherhood (Hrvatsko Revolucionarno Bratstvo) had operated since the mid-1950s. With their sights rigidly fixed on the armed overthrow of the Yugoslav regime, their strategies included backwoods camps to train Croat fighters who would one day infiltrate Yugoslavia and lead a popular anticommunist insurrection. "Today on the Murray River—Tomorrow on the Drina," boasted the Brotherhood's Australian publication, *Spremnost* (Prepared), in January 1963.[1] As utterly hopeless as their projects look in hindsight, taken together these fragmentary groups were probably no more marginal than Pavelić's Ustashe had been in the 1930s when it was banished to Italy. If Pavelić had managed to snatch power from exile once, they reasoned, why couldn't they do it again?

The Brotherhood had already made a name for itself as an effective terrorist organization in Australia when a contingent of sixteen commandos traveled from Melbourne to a base in the vicinity of Karlsruhe, West Germany, in early 1972, where they joined three more comrades. After a training stint there, the heavily armed unit crossed the Austrian-Yugoslav border and penetrated deep into the central Bosnian mountains around the town of Bugojno. The successors of the Križari operation twenty-five years earlier, the so-called Bugojnici believed that anticommunist resentment was so rife that their presence alone was enough to ignite rebellion. The guerrillas badly miscalculated, but they did not fail to spark the interest of the Yugoslav authorities, who dispatched several JNA units to nip the embryonic insurrection in the bud. Impressively the Bugojnici reportedly held out in the mountains for several weeks before succumbing to the overwhelming firepower of the JNA.[2]

It was not until the mid-1960s in West Germany that a campaign of assassinations and bombings propelled the Croatia issue into a broader international spotlight. In the immediate postwar period West Germany was one destination of choice for escaping NDH sympathizers and other Yugoslav political dissidents. German authorities estimated that roughly twelve thousand to fifteen thousand veterans associated with the Pavelić regime found political asylum in postwar Germany, where their status as political refugees even entitled them to state funds.[3] The Ustashe émigrés with political aspirations remained politically marginal until hundreds of thousands of young Yugoslav men, disproportionately Croats, unexpectedly began flooding West Germany to lend a hand in the country's "economic miracle" in the 1960s and 1970s. The number of Yugoslav gastarbeiter in Western Europe leaped dramatically from a mere 50,000 in 1965 to 280,000 in 1968.[4] By 1970, 390,000 Yugoslav citizens were registered as guest workers in the Federal Republic alone.[5] Three years later a staggering one million Yugoslav workers and their dependents lived in Austria, Belgium, Denmark, France, Great Britain, Luxembourg, Netherlands, Norway, Sweden, Switzerland, and West Germany.[6] Hundreds of thousands more would be employed across Europe during the decade.

The mix of the old Ustashe cadres already in Germany and the young, disenfranchised men fleeing the poverty of socialist Yugoslavia proved predictably combustible. The active memberships in groups such as Otpor, the Croatian National Committee, the Union of United Croats, the Struggle for a Free Croatia, the Drina Union, and others, received a fresh transfusion of angry, malleable energy. Cash-strapped publications such as *Hrvatska Država* (Croatian State) or the Spain-based *Drina* were revived with new membership dues, often coughed up by reluctant guest workers after threats and arm-twisting.

For the anticommunist émigrés (not just Croats), the Western powers' embrace of Marshal Tito after Yugoslavia's expulsion from the Soviet bloc in 1948 planted another painful milestone on their historical road map. When Stalin ordered Yugoslavia out of the Soviet ranks, Tito's regimen for the country had not deviated a millimeter from Moscow orthodoxy. But tensions between the two leaders had been simmering for years. Yugoslavia was not on a par with occupied eastern Germany, and Tito was not about to take direct orders from Stalin or anybody else. As a guerrilla leader of a victorious, homegrown communist movement, Tito ruled with a confident sense of purpose unique among the Eastern Europeans. But Stalin was not comfortable granting any one cadre special privileges. In June 1948 Yugoslavia was expelled from the Comiform, making it the only single-party socialist state in Europe between East and West, a status Tito would exploit to the fullest in the decades to come.

The West, thrilled over the first crack in the Soviet wall, soon jumped to Yugoslavia's aid. The United States above all lavished Yugoslavia with emergency aid followed by grants, soft loans, and trade concessions, and opened the door to billions of dollars of World Bank credits for future decades. Between 1949 and 1964 U.S. assistance to Belgrade, in return for bucking the Soviet line and minor economic reforms, totaled nearly $3 billion.[7] Tens of millions even went to arm the JNA. The West's coddling of the dictator Tito, the symbol responsible for their murdered compatriots and exile lives, was a stinging betrayal that the assorted Yugoslav émigrés could never forgive their host countries. For the Croats, coming just three years after the Bleiburg massacre, this odd East-West friendship rubbed salt in their open wounds. Just maybe, some thought, Moscow might advance their cause if the Atlantic allies would not.

At the time some of the Croat émigré groups began to show pro-Soviet leanings, based on the rationale that if the West had abandoned Croatia, at least the Soviet Union saw Tito for the fiend he was. The Berlin-based émigré club, the Croatian National Committee (Hrvatski Narodni Odbor), proposed that, in exchange for Soviet help in dismantling Yugoslavia, an independent and neutral Croatia—along the lines of Finland or Austria— would be prepared to declare the Adriatic a free-trade zone for East European countries; the port at Pula and the Mostar airport would also be open to Soviet use. In the spring of 1970 the organization's publication also recommended close relations between the representatives of independent Croatia and another anti-Yugoslav ally, Enver Hoxha's Albania.[8] Insiders say that the Soviet spy network reciprocated the Croats' interest, penetrating its ranks with informers and operatives.

Another shift in strategy among the would-be revolutionaries was the cautious retreat from the idea that an armed anticommunist uprising could be exported to Yugoslavia in the near future. The Tito regime, some acknowledged, had solidified its power, at least temporarily. The battles now fought against Yugoslavia would instead be fought abroad against its symbols and emissaries. The guerrilla handbook *Osvetnici Bleiburga* (The Avengers of Bleiburg) reflected one branch of the movement's direction and its thin intellectual underpinnings.[9] On its cover a crudely sketched caricature of a working-class man is emblazoned over a map of Croatia and Bosnia. He holds a Croatian flag in one hand, a machine gun in the other, and sports a belt of grenades around his waist. "The Croat revolution has been born and a strong flame burns in the heart of all Croat patriots," it reads, referring to the 1972 Bugojno Operation. "On the battlefield, the dark dungeon of the Tito regime will be destroyed." The manual, advertised for sale in émigré newspapers, calls for acts of sabotage in Yugoslavia as well as abroad and contains detailed instructions for making and using explosives.

By the 1960s sporadic outbursts of violence in West German cities caught the eye of German authorities and made the pages of *Der Spiegel* and *Frankfurter Allgemeine Zeitung*. In 1965–66 a string of assassination strikes against low-level Yugoslav diplomats claimed two lives, one outside Munich and another in a Stuttgart beer hall. In the Stuttgart case the chief witness for the defense was gunned down in his car two weeks later. Home-made bombs planted at Yugoslav consulate offices exploded in the night. Shootings, drug busts, and arson attacks were reported at restaurants with names such as Split, Dalmatia, and Adriatic Balkan Grill. In early 1976 the Yugoslav consul in Frankfurt was murdered, a fate the vice consul in Düsseldorf only narrowly escaped several months later.

Belgrade responded promptly to the challenge, dispatching new teams of undercover agents and hitmen to spy on émigré groups, agitate within their ranks, and liquidate its leaders. Between 1965 and 1976 at least nine exile Croats were murdered in West Germany. An atmosphere of fear and distrust permeated the émigré and gastarbeiter communities. West Germany and Yugoslavia went head-to-head in diplomatic standoffs over the extradition of Croat radicals, a demand by Belgrade that Bonn refused to meet. Tito retaliated in 1978 by providing temporary asylum to German militants from the radical left Red Army Faction. In the 1970s battles between militant Croat émigrés, Balkan mafia elements, Serb monarchist exiles, Yugoslav agents, and German antiterrorist units were being fought on German soil. The German authorities were often at a loss to distinguish who was shooting at whom, much less why. The bloodshed would only escalate over the next decade, bewildering the German public and media just as the outbreak of ethnic conflict in Yugoslavia would twenty years later.

The crushing of the Croatian Spring in 1971 by the Yugoslav authorities dealt a stinging blow to the freshly awakened hopes of Croat nationalists that change from within the communist structures was possible. The movement began in the late 1960s when nationally oriented reformers in Croatia had begun pressing for greater political and cultural autonomy for the republic within socialist Yugoslavia as well as substantial liberalization of the highly centralized economy. Students and intellectuals were also raising issues that had been off-limits since World War II. In the diaspora these events were followed with keen interest. But as the Croatian Spring gained momentum, Tito, who at first supported the reforms, became unnerved. He charged the top leaders with being open to the influence of the "reactionary diaspora." By the end of 1971 the peaceful "counterrevolution" had been quashed. Many leaders of the movement, Tudjman among them, were in jail. A new wave of political refugees fled the country.

But in the same period another development helped to fan the diaspora's smoldering ambitions. Tito, the man whose vision and immense personal authority had kept multinational Yugoslavia together, was in poor health, and many thought his death was imminent. The émigrés concluded that the time was right to push the decrepit regime as hard as they could.

In addition to the activities in Germany and Spain, a militant scene had coalesced in Sweden, which received spiritual leadership and practical guidance from a Catholic priest, Vjekoslav Lašić, who would later be excommunicated by the Vatican for his political involvement. On April 6, 1971, two Croat nationalists, both connected to Lašić and the Swedish Otpor faction, shot and critically injured Yugoslavia's ambassador to Sweden, who died a week later. The two killers, twenty-one-year-old Miro Barešić and twenty-five-year-old Andjelko Brajković, proclaimed, as they were arrested, "Free Croatia lives!" They were both given life sentences but did not remain behind bars for long.

After a failed 1972 jailbreak that ended with the capture of Barešić, three Croat nationals hijacked a Scandinavian Air DC-9 flight en route from Göteborg to Stockholm. Their demands were the release of Barešić and Brajković, and five hundred thousand Swedish crowns upon landing at the Madrid airport. At the time the Otpor organization and other pro-Ustashe groups worked in Spain with the tacit approval of the Franco regime. Although the hijackers' demands were initially met, the five men, including Barešić, who was apprehended in Paraguay, were later handed over to the Swedish authorities. In 1990, after Barešić's release from prison, he joined one of the first units of the newly formed Croatian militia and was killed shortly thereafter.

These events in the early 1970s in West Germany, Sweden, and Croatia were the topics of long, emotional conversations between Zvonko Bušić, a young Croat émigré from Gorica, Herzegovina, and his companion, an American flower child from Oregon named Julienne Schultz. The Swedish hijacking planted a seed in Bušić 's head that, five years later, would culminate in a bizarre thirty-hour hopscotch transatlantic hijacking that would end with the death of a New York City police officer—and, among Croat nationalists, turn Bušić and Schultz into folk heroes.

The couple first met in Vienna in 1969, where Schultz, an apple-cheeked American college student with long blonde braids, lived at the time. As Schultz, later Ms. Bušić, tells in her recently published memoir, *Lovers and Madmen: A True Story of Passion, Politics, and Air Piracy*, she fell head over heels for the tall, dark-bearded Zvonko Bušić who hailed from an exotic, faraway place called Croatia—in fact, Herzegovina. The two drifted from one Croat émigré scene to another in Austria, West Germany, France, and the United States, moving in the tiny underground circles that were connected by village and family names, carbon-copied manifestos, and phone numbers scribbled on scraps of paper. Zvonko told Julie about the plight of the Croat people, about the repression and poverty in his native Herzegovina, about the failure of the West to acknowledge the fascistic nature of the Tito dictatorship. Although Schultz does not mention it in her book, he also told her about Otpor, the NDH, and the Ustashe. Bušić was a prominent Otpor loyalist and leader of the North American branch in the early 1970s.

The idealistic Schultz, daughter of a West Coast classics professor, did not need much convincing to carry out her first mission for a cause and a nation she knew precious little about. Lugging a suitcase full of agit-prop fliers signed by the "Revolutionary Croat Youth," Schultz and a girlfriend arrived in Zagreb in late autumn 1970. On November 29, Yugoslavia's national day, they took the elevator to the top of the Neboder skyscraper in downtown Zagreb, had lunch, and let fly over the packed central square thousands of leaflets urging Croats to "rise up and revolt."

The revolution did not happen. But after one month in a dingy Yugoslav prison, Schultz was back with Bušić, broke and on the run between Berlin, Frankfurt, Vienna, Cleveland, Paris, and New York. *Lovers and Madmen* is a romantic tale in which Schultz explains her role in the hijacking, citing her love for the dashing Zvonko and her unquestioning acceptance of the noble cause of Croat independence. Zvonko, like Julie, makes an appealing character: he is an intense, fiercely cut revolutionary, both romantic and coldly calculating. In contrast to the HDZ nationalists who held power in Croatia for a decade, it is hard to imagine someone like Bušić stooping to enrich himself through the petty perks of power or the plunder of Croatian enterprises.

Yet his biography is familiar, with striking parallels to the Ontario émigrés. His poverty-stricken village, Gorica near Imotski (down the road from Široki Brijeg), seems straight out of an Ivo Andrić novel with its earthen-floor huts and stony hand-planted tobacco fields. Almost every family in Gorica had at least one member working abroad and had lost a relative in the war or its aftermath. Bušić's father had been in the NDH army and his uncle with the Ustashe, thus making Bušić, guilty by association, a "subversive element," "criminal," or "reactionary force," as the former Partisans labeled uncooperative Croats from Herzegovina. The Yugoslav government obviously had no plan to win the hearts and minds of these people.

A desperate and naïve attempt to draw the world's attention to Croatia's plight, the Bušić hijacking was a criminal act that ended in tragedy. The hijackers' first demand was that thousands of copies of a "Declaration of the Croatian Liberation Forces," written for this purpose by Croatia's foremost dissident intellectual, Bruno Bušić (no relation to Zvonko), be dropped from the air over New York, Chicago, Montreal, Paris, London, and the site of a popular festival in Croatia. The hijackers also demanded that the rambling sixteen hundred–word manifesto be published the next day in five major U.S. dailies. Notably the quixotic act was not directed against an object of the Yugoslav regime, such as a consulate or an ambassador, nor was it designed to ignite revolution. The hijacking was a ham-fisted effort to lobby Western opinion and policy makers, to inform them about the "real situation" in Croatia and force them to confront the dictatorial nature of the Yugoslav regime. In the future, professional Washington-based Croat lobby groups would take the more conventional route of buying advertising space in the same U.S. newspapers in which the 1976 manifesto appeared.

Schultz, Bušić, and three accomplices boarded Trans World Airlines flight 355 out of New York City on September 10, 1976. In airspace over upstate New York, they commandeered the jet en route to Chicago with its ninety-two passengers and crew members. In the cockpit Bušić demanded that the crew follow his orders or else he would detonate the explosives taped to his torso. In addition, should instructions concerning the written declaration not be carried out to the letter, a hidden bomb would go off in a "highly busy location" in the United States. Although the alleged sticks of dynamite strapped to the hijackers' bodies were fakes, a real bomb, with instructions on how to defuse it, was in a coin locker at Grand Central Station in Manhattan. This bomb, which Bušić alerted the police to, was meant as proof that yet another bomb existed at an undisclosed location. In fact, there was no second bomb. Whether the demands were met or not, no one was meant to be harmed.

Following a leaflet drop in Chicago, Bušić redirected the flight first to Montreal for another drop and refueling, and then across the Atlantic via Gander, Newfoundland, and Reykjavik, Iceland. A second TWA jet, a Boeing 707, joined the hijacked plane to guide the inexperienced pilot of the 727 to Europe and to drop the leaflets over London and Paris. The following day the manifesto was printed in all five dailies, including the *New York Times* and the *International Herald Tribune*.

Before the amateur team's perfectly executed skyjacking concluded with its surrender in Paris, twenty-seven-year-old Lieut. Brian Murray, a member of the New York Police Department's bomb squad, attempted to deactivate the homemade device that had been left in Grand Central Station. The bomb exploded in his face, killing him and injuring three others.

The Croat community around the world raised money for the group's defense but, in highly publicized trials, Julie and Zvonko Bušić received life sentences for air piracy that had resulted in death. Croat nationalists made the couple a cause célèbre. After thirteen years behind bars, Julie would attain positions in the Croatian Embassy in Washington, D.C., in the early

1990s, and from 1995 to 2000 she would serve as a senior adviser to President Tudjman, her post salaried by Šušak's Ministry of Defense. Zvonko Bušić's sister, Zdravka, who had lived in Cleveland, would become Tudjman's personal secretary and an HDZ parliamentarian. Twenty-five years after the hijacking, Zvonko Bušič is still incarcerated in a maximum security federal penitentiary in Leavenworth, Kansas, where he will probably remain until 2006.

Today Julie Bušić talks easily about the hijacking and with tempered nostalgia about her years on the move with Zvonko, although the death of Brian Murray continues to haunt her. At an outdoor cafe along the sparkling harbor of the Dalmatian port city of Zadar, she is immediately recognizable from the grainy photograph on the front page of the *New York Times* taken immediately after their arrest on September 12, 1976. In the photo a frightened, frowning, blonde-haired woman in a simple embroidered dress stands handcuffed to her four accomplices. One of them, the mustachioed Marko Vlašič, bares his teeth menacingly like a caged lion growling at his captors. At the other end of the shackled line is Zvonko wearing sunglasses and a cheap dark suit, looking every bit the defiant Eastern European revolutionary. He stands calm and erect with his head cocked back, staring off into the distance.

In a floral-patterned dress, denim jacket, and plastic sunglasses, Julie Bušić, at fifty-two, exudes a youthful openness and pure-hearted devotion to the cause she has never given up. With Tudjman's death in 1999 and the defeat of the HDZ at the polls in early 2000, Bušić lives in semi-retirement outside Zadar, devoting her time to de-mining projects and, of course, to her years-long campaign to win Zvonko's release. (In negotiations with the U.S. government, Croatia consistently pushed for Zvonko's transfer to a Croatian prison to serve out his sentence.)

With a self-deprecating half-smile, the former Oregonian rolls her eyes at the thought of the hijacking and her thirteen years behind bars. Yet, like the others who had been in and around the militant émigré scene, she defends the purpose of the movement. "It's gratifying to me," she says, now straight-faced and solemn. "The cause that we worked for and sat in jail for, that Zvonko is still sitting in jail for twenty-four years later, the objective of that cause has come to pass," she says, referring to Croatia's independence. "We were part of that process. We knew most of the players. I was part of the dissident faction before, and now I'm part of the official Croatian government after independence. That gives me a lot of satisfaction."

Julie Schultz Bušić and others such as the Ontario émigrés insist that they were legitimate liberation fighters, anti-imperialist revolutionaries forced to work underground and illegally, just as the African National Congress was forced to do in apartheid South Africa. For Bušić and the others,

Croatia's internationally recognized independence—and the wars for which Serbia shoulders the onus of blame—constitutes further post hoc justification of their actions. Julie compares her husband to Nelson Mandela. "There were a lot of parallels between South Africa and Croatia," she says. "But theirs was a black movement and the Croats' wasn't. In both cases, there was a minority government oppressing a majority, throwing dissidents in jail for wanting to have what they should have. Yet there are people who see Mandela as a hero and still call Zvonko a terrorist and outlaw."

By most any yardstick, the comparison of Tito's Yugoslavia with the apartheid regime in South Africa is strained, to say the least. Under Tito, ethnic groups in certain areas, such as Herzegovinian Croats and Kosovar Albanians, were branded "disloyal" and often singled out for abusive treatment. The single-party dictatorship did not hesitate to use its monopoly on power and its fearsome coercive apparatus to crush political opposition, particularly in the immediate postwar decades. Yet Tito's overriding concern throughout his thirty-five years of rule was to hold together the precarious, multiethnic federation, and his willingness to experiment with different forms of regional self-government in search of a workable ethnic balance was noteworthy. It is an entirely skewed view of history to suggest that the Croat nation as a whole was the victim of repression in socialist Yugoslavia.

In the 1960s and 1970s Croatia and Bosnia and Herzegovina underwent economic transformations unprecedented in their history, and many citizens by the late 1970s, particularly in urban areas, came to enjoy standards of living comparable to much of Western Europe at the time. The freedom to travel made Yugoslavia a more open society than its dour East European neighbors. During the socialist period ethnic differences never disappeared, but they were rarely an overt source of tension. Few Croats would have considered theirs to be a different language from Serbian, despite the regional variations. Nor would they have felt repressed by the prohibition of a handful of nationalist symbols. To a society preoccupied with development and modernization, the issues that galvanized the Bušićes were not compelling for the average Croat. Only among the diaspora rightists, obsessed with historical conflicts and isolated from the reality of contemporary Yugoslavia, could such symbolic matters serve to justify armed rebellion.

Whatever the radical Croat ex-émigrés may claim, theirs was never a popular movement enjoying even moderate support either in Croatia or among the diaspora. Although in hindsight the former émigrés contrive to give their struggle a democratic veneer, it was, in fact, deeply undemocratic, nationally exclusive, and profoundly authoritarian. "Democracy" meant a narrow vision of national self-determination, and not much more. The émigrés gave lip service to the Sabor, the traditional Croatian parliament, but advocated a strongly centralized state with power resting in the hands of a national leader. The late-night discussions over plum brandy and espresso coffee never encompassed the question of how to establish a free democracy in a complex, multiethnic state. Instead, their brand of nationalism contained a radical solution to the "national question," which decades later would help to shatter the intricate mosaic of multiethnic Yugoslavia.

One useful marker to trace the overlapping biographies and ideological continuity of the radical diaspora is the organization Hrvatski Narodni Otpor. Of all the militant splinter groups to come and go, Otpor, in one form or another, was one of the few that managed to survive three decades of splits and infighting, bans and infiltrations. This organization, which at its height probably never boasted more than a few thousand members worldwide, is the key to tracking the ideas, personnel, and strategy that link the distinct but interwoven strains of Croat nationalist activity over half a century. Men who never knew one another, such as Zvonko Bušić and Nikola Stedul or Ustashe General Maks Luburić and Gojko Šušak or Marin Sopta and Mostar gangster boss Mladen "Tuta" Naletilić, swam at different times in the same waters, in and around Otpor. Some of Otpor's guiding ideas, reworked and refined, as well as figures directly or indirectly associated with the movement, resurfaced decades later in connection with the Tudjman administration.

Otpor was born in early 1957 when former Ustashe general Vjekoslav ("Maks") Luburić broke with his former commander-in-chief, Ante Pavelić. The split ended a long working relationship between the two men, which began during the early days of the Ustashe movement in the 1930s. By mid-1941, just months after the Ustashe came to power, Luburić was entrusted to build and then direct the gruesome concentration camp Jasenovac. After the war Luburić established himself in Spain where he led the European division of Pavelić's Ustashe.

The falling out between the two was more than simply a petty power struggle. One version of the split is that Pavelić had broached some tenuous negotiations with exile Serb monarchists over the eventual division of Bosnia and Herzegovina between Croatia and Serbia, a move Luburić and his followers simply could not stomach. Luburić and others had also grown weary of HOP's crusty old-Ustashe rhetoric and pompous directives from distant Buenos Aires exile. It was Luburić's initiative to give the old movement an overhaul of sorts and put it into the hands of a younger generation, one closer to the real front lines. Luburić started with an ostensible dose of self-criticism. He conceded that the Ustashe movement had made mistakes during the NDH period and that he, too, was personally responsible for certain misdeeds, although he did not offer details about their nature or even mention the Jasenovac camp.

An early convert from HOP to Otpor was Nikola Stedul, who had migrated from the German Ruhrgebiet to Australia in 1958. "They [HOP] were promoting the idea that we were going to go back as victors to reestablish a regime more or less the way it had been. They didn't even know how out of touch they really were," he says. Stedul claims that by then he realized that this kind of 1930s revolutionary fascism could not possibly wrest Croatia from communist control. That Luburić, confined to Spain for fear of extradition, was on the international list of people wanted for war crimes did not faze Stedul. He, too, was inexplicably on the list even though he was born in 1937, just a child during the war years.

In terms of substance, Luburić's Otpor differed from HOP in several respects. First, unlike the unreconstructed and vehemently anticommunist Ustashes, Luburić's new force embraced an early version of the concept Tudjman would later call national reconciliation. Luburić accepted that there must be a rapprochement between Croat Partisans and Croat Ustashe under a supra-ideological national banner encompassing all patriotic Croats. The Croat checkerboard, as a symbol of national synthesis, must replace the antithetical Partisan red star and the Ustashe "U," he preached. Further, an independent Croatia would assume a neutral position between East and West, which to hard-line anticommunists amounted to a virtually heretical overture to the Soviet Union. And while Luburić professed to favor a peaceful transition in Croatia, should that prove impossible radical means had to be taken. Finally, there had to be active cooperation between the diaspora and the homeland, another idea that would crop up years later in the HDZ platform.[10] The diaspora could not liberate the homeland like a knight in shining armor, but neither could the homeland throw off the shackles of communism by itself.

Despite its departures from Ustashe–HOP orthodoxy, there was much that linked Otpor to its precursors. "General Drina," as his followers called Luburić, insisted that independent Croatia extend across all Bosnia to the River Drina, and even include parts of Serbia proper and the Sandjak. The future Croatian army should be infused with the Ustashe spirit, a critical factor for uniting all Croats. In his periodical, *Drina*, he signed articles "Ustashe Maks." According to Luburić, it was the responsibility of the Croat émigrés to finish what the Ustashe started, namely, the building of an independent Croatian state. The common enemy of this vision is the Serb nation. Shorn of the Ustashe's anticommunism, all that was left was a poisonous anti-Serbism.

In Spain Luburić set up the Drina printing press, a good-sized operation that printed the journal *Drina* and the newspaper *Obrana* (Defense) as well as other publications until 1969, the year of Luburić's assassination at the hands of one of Tito's agents. Luburić was found dead near his Valencia villa, stabbed and bludgeoned with an iron bar. The Otpor headquarters moved to Chicago and Toronto, where they received cover and funding from the émigré Franciscan network. The new organ, entitled *Otpor* and published out of Chicago, belies any pretensions of a new post-Luburić moderation that its leaders try to claim in hindsight. Every issue, for example, includes a quote on its cover from the deceased General Drina, alias Luburić. Front pages boastfully display pictures of the Bušićes and the mastermind of the Sweden hijacking, Barešić. Nearly every issue contains fundraising appeals for Croat "political prisoners" in jail outside Croatia as well as World War II war criminals such as the ex-Ustashe minister Artuković. One issue even includes instructions for making homemade bombs. This publication and other propaganda material were distributed in the diaspora and sent in stashed bundles to Croatia, often under the seats of Turkish or Albanian truckers passing through Yugoslavia.

Zvonko Bušić's connections to Otpor and the connections of other convicted Croat militants led West Germany, in late 1976, to ban Otpor, as well as the Croatian Brotherhood, from operating within its borders. In the United States a special antiterrorist unit was set up within the Federal Bureau of Investigation to look into the mysterious groups. In Canada, too, Otpor was placed under heavy police surveillance. Although these measures were a high price to pay, they did not stop Otpor from idealizing the Bušićes and their gang. "The Bušićes were our heroes. They did more to promote the Croatian cause than anyone else," the former North American Otpor leader Marin Sopta says today in his office in Zagreb's HDZ headquarters. Sopta visited Zvonko Bušić regularly when he was serving time in Pennsylvania. Šušak came with him once, on Thanksgiving Day, with a turkey under his arm for Zvonko. The hijacking was exactly the kind of pirate-style, hit-and-run operation that appealed to the Otpor tough guys, even though they contrived to distance the organization itself from the hijacking.

Stedul and Sopta deny any direct involvement in the violent acts committed in Otpor's name. They argue that "mainstream" factions in Otpor, which they say they represented, argued consistently against the use of violence abroad to carry out the struggle for Croatian independence. "We were for armed struggle in Croatia but not in Canada or Germany," says Sopta. "It was clear to me that these kinds of actions would only hurt the Croatian cause," says Stedul today, who took control of Otpor's European operations in the early 1970s when he moved to Scotland. "We tried to pull back the extremists in the Croatian movement somehow, to bring them under control. I think we had some success by the late 1970s."

Both men also point out that Otpor was often divided within itself, at one point with rival leaderships in Sweden, Australia, Argentina, and North America. The ultra-radical Argentine faction was at one point under the control of the fugitive World War II war criminal Dinko Sakić. (Sakić, a high-ranking officer at the Jasenovac camp, was finally extradited to Croatia in 1999, tried for war crimes, and sentenced to twenty years in prison.) Finally, Sopta and Stedul contend that a sizable chunk of the violence ostensibly linked to Otpor was, in fact, committed by, or at the behest of, Yugoslav-hired provocateurs, a charge that many neutral observers admit is possible. Indeed, some of those observers surmise that the entire phenomenon of Otpor was a creation of the Yugoslav secret services, and that Stedul and Sopta were their chief agents—something both men naturally deny. In the diaspora there is no simpler tactic to discredit one's rival than to charge him with secret service collaboration. It's a game the Balkan exiles never seem to tire of. Since no proof exists, or probably ever will, one wild accusation is usually as valid (or invalid) as the next.

So vicious is the name-calling and back-biting in diasporas—the Croats are not exceptional—that the phenomenon deserves some reflection. Paranoia and petty power struggles can consume exile communities, causing organizations with nearly identical goals and convictions to fracture like beads of mercury into ever tinier subsets. So much time and energy is spent on quarreling that diaspora groups often undermine their potential to engage constructively in their host countries' political processes. Since democracy within diasporas is usually underdeveloped or non-existent, particularly in groups promoting blatantly undemocratic ideologies, this in-fighting becomes the primary means for factions to shore up power, what little of it there is. In Ian Buruma's book on Chinese exiles, *Bad Elements*, he makes an observation equally valid for Balkan émigrés:

> Political exiles fight among themselves wherever they come from: Cut
> off from a common enemy, they tear into each other. In the course of
> talking to Chinese exiles and activists, I found almost no one who had
> anything good to say about anyone else. Mention a name and I would be
> told that person was a liar, a government agent, a spy, an opportunist, a
> gangster, an extremist, or corrupted by sex or power or both.[11]

For the Balkan diasporas one can add to that list of pejoratives: fascist, coward, Jew, cheapskate, embezzler, prostitute, bastard, homosexual, peasant, gypsy, member of and/or in the pay of a rival ethnicity, married to a person of a rival ethnicity. On the radical right, in groups such as Otpor, mud-slinging was a form of combat practiced unintermittently, and when the slurs failed to stick its activists often went a step further.

In the murky underworld in which Otpor operated, the line between the political and the criminal was never clear-cut. For these men, the ethic and the laws of the boulder-strewn Dinaric mountains held sway in New York and Munich. Extortion, blackmail, and racketeering were legitimate means to extract "contributions" from countrymen for the cause. In 1980 and 1981 FBI sting operations netted two Croat gangs both directly tied to Otpor. The first gang, five members of the New York chapter, were convicted of planning a murder and several bombings. The second, which included the de facto Otpor leader in the United States Mile Markić, received sentences ranging from twenty to forty years in prison for charges involving murder, arson, and extortion.[12]

Otpor's tactics were a constant irritant to the more mainstream émigrés such as those drawn to the opinions in the London bi-monthly *Nova Hrvatska*. For three decades Jakša Kušan was editor-in-chief of the prominent émigré newspaper, which also endorsed an independent Croatia but advocated its creation through a gradual democratic transformation in socialist Yugoslavia. A studious white-haired man in his seventies with a frail hunched frame, Kušan kept *Nova Hrvatska* afloat on a shoestring budget. The *Nova Hrvatska* circle, which included members of the interwar Croatian Peasants Party, maintained that the key to change in Croatia lay in reformist elements in the Croatian section of the League of Communists, the Yugoslav communist party. "In the early 1960s we began to bombard Croatian communists at home with appeals that they should do more for Croatian interests," says Kušan, who left Croatia in 1955 before settling in London and starting *Nova Hrvatska* in 1959. When he returned to Croatia in 1990, hoping to contribute to the rebirth of his country, he found himself excluded from the ruling circles around the HDZ and state-loyal media. Over the next ten years Kušan struggled to make ends meet as a freelance journalist in his homeland.

"It was impossible for us to be indifferent toward Luburić or Branko Jelić [Croatian National Committee president in Germany] but we didn't want to quarrel with them openly. This wasn't only against our principles but it was a waste of time," says Kušan, raising his thin voice over the din of Zagreb's Mittel-European Café Splendid. In contrast to the rough-hewn Herzegovina guys, Kušan's urbane demeanor bears something of the Austro-Hungarian empire. "But we slowly tried to take their subscribers. We really had to fight for every possible reader." The enmity between the émigré factions often got exceptionally nasty. "They couldn't suppress our influence in a more intelligent way than force," says Kušan, who tells of physical attacks on his paper's representatives. "They'd spread rumors that we were working for the UDBA or that we wanted a third Yugoslavia, that kind of thing."

Moderate émigré groups elsewhere, for example, in Ontario, had the same problem. A major thorn in their side was Gojko Šušak. In contrast to the misinformation spread during his tenure as defense minister, Šušak was never a significant player in émigré politics. Rather, insiders describe him as an Otpor fellow traveler who was often in the company of well-known Otpor representatives such as his good friend, Marin Sopta. In Sopta's wedding Šušak was his best man. His views and behavior, say Ontario sources, were indistinguishable from those of Otpor and other radical splinter groups. (Šušak denied ever having been a formal member of Otpor. Beljo never was. In fact, there were few "official members" but rather a body of more or less active loyalists—often undercover—around the leadership.) Like Sopta, Šušak took the "revolutionary" line on virtually every issue, more often than not throwing a wrench into the works of the projects at hand.

The Bušić hijacking captured the imagination of Šušak and the Canadian Otpor faction as no other event had. Šušak adamantly insisted that the incarcerated Zvonko Bušić be listed as a candidate for an office in the Croatian National Congress (CNC), the umbrella organization of the Croatian diaspora. The New York headquarters of the CNC had already voided Bušić's candidacy, which had been promoted in the first place by the radicals. But Šušak insisted that the votes for Bušić be counted anyhow. "It was a very, very hot issue at the time," remembers Ivan Zuger, an Ottawa-based émigré activist. "In the end, the whole Ottawa chapter just collapsed."

The Ottawa activists already knew the flavor of Šušak's tricks when he took over the CNC's Ottawa branch. Šušak's questionable judgment, for example, received considerable local press in 1979 with a publicity stunt that backfired badly. In dishonor of November 29, Yugoslav National Day, a state holiday complete with official celebrations in Yugoslavia and a day of spirited protest in the diaspora, Šušak and select friends had the inspired idea of painting the word "Tito" on a baby piglet and setting him in a black home-made coffin in front of the Yugoslav Embassy on Blackburn Avenue. On the closed coffin was scrawled, "Death to Tito." Presumably the piglet was to be slaughtered or perhaps just released to run through the embassy grounds.

But the farce never proceeded that far. The Canadian police learned of the event and informed the Ontario Humane Society. The pig was found frightened and squealing "trapped in an airless, coffin-shaped box." The Humane Society seized the eight-week-old animal and reported the incident to the local media, which then published embarrassing full-length articles on the stunt.[13]

In addition to instigating teenage pranks, Šušak was prone to exaggerating, if not lying, about his accomplishments. In fact, the claim that he held a high position in the Croatian Folklore Federation of Canada is readily disclaimed by Zuger, who has been president of the federation for ten years and is a leader in half a dozen other Canadian-Croatian émigré groups.[14] Zuger, today a court interpreter in the office of Ontario's attorney general, first met Šušak in 1969, two years after the latter arrived in Canada. He is one of the few Ontario-based émigrés who will speak on the record about Šušak. "He would attend many of the folklore events, which was typical of the revolutionaries since they couldn't bring together significant numbers of people on their own," says Zuger. "They would piggyback on other events in order to distribute their radical literature. It was a cover for them, but they didn't contribute to the organization itself." Zuger tells of one instance when Šušak and a gun-wielding Franciscan friar tried to intimidate him to hand over folklore funds, contributed by the Canadian government, for their own purposes. Zuger stood fast.

In the self-important macho fantasy world of Otpor, guns, tough talk, and daredevil stunts separated the real Croat patriots from the pack. In Šušak's pizzeria, at a 1977 meeting of the Ottawa chapter of the CNC, which Šušak and his allies had managed to commandeer, activists tell of Šušak brandishing an U.S. army rifle and suggesting that they take shots at a picture of Yugoslavia's late king, Peter I, hanging on the wall. Zuger says that even in the most inappropriate contexts Šušak and like-minded others pushed the idea of armed revolution. Other Croat émigrés tried to pin Šušak down on exactly what he meant by "armed revolution" or how he envisioned carrying it out in socialist Yugoslavia. "They tried to create a revolutionary spirit in which everything goes, not paying attention to Canadian law and order," says Zuger. Šušak would never debate or discuss these issues seriously or propose a concrete strategy to move this agenda forward. "If you didn't agree with him, then he'd say you're working for a foreign service or you're not a good Croat. It was impossible."

For mainstream voices such as Zuger, the behavior of Šušak and his group was so destructive to their ostensibly common cause that they were forced to conclude that he must be a paid agent provocateur of Yugoslavia or another country's secret service. "We saw these unrealistic radical demands as an attempt to compromise and incapacitate the entire Croatian movement. We were trying to integrate Croatian interests and the Croatian cause into the European and international political arena, while the extremists were always working to isolate it." Zuger and other Ottawa activists watched the events in Croatia during the 1990s in shocked disbelief: "They went from hijacking planes to hijacking the democratic process in Croatia," Zuger said.

In Ottawa Šušak's acquaintances and former fellow émigrés speak of him as an unsuccessful bit player in the work world. He went from his first job as a new emigrant in a Kentucky Fried Chicken outlet that his brother ran to the McDonalds academy in Chicago and eventually to a small space beside the highway next to KFC where he set up Tops Pizza with a partner. The hole-in-the-wall take-out shop was eventually sold at a loss, say Ottawa sources. From there Šušak went into construction, like many expatriated Croats.

Despite his two decades of life abroad, Gojko Šušak never strayed far from his roots. He had grown up under the wing of the Herzegovina Franciscans, had been schooled in their classrooms, and fled communist Yugoslavia with their help. In Canada Šušak remained close to the order, often serving as a driver and contact person. The Croatian Franciscans in Canada had several small parishes but no base comparable to their U.S. brothers' base at the Drexel Avenue house in South Chicago—that is, not until Norval.

In the late 1970s a Franciscan-run sect emerged in southern Ontario that would become the unofficial meeting place, think tank, and fund-raising source for the radical Croatian Canadian diaspora.

Tensions between the Herzegovinian Franciscans and the Vatican-backed Croatian Roman Catholic Church followed the Croats into the diaspora. In the Toronto region the ultra-nationalist Franciscans had long bristled at the compromises that the Zagreb-based seat of Croatia's Roman Catholics struck with the communist regime. When Father Kamber died in 1969, the Franciscans launched a tenacious bid to take control of the greater Toronto parish. But Zagreb held them off, replacing Kamber with their man, Father Josip Gjuran. The stakes were high. If successful, the Franciscans would have captured the linchpin to the regional diaspora.

Émigré organizations come and go, but the single institution that ties together mono-religious diasporas such as those of the Croats (and the Serbs) is the church, in this case the Roman Catholic Church. The political allegiances of diaspora Croats run a broad gamut. But they have one thing in common—they are all Catholics.[15]

The disgruntled Franciscans opted to go their own way. In 1977 a consortium of mostly Ontario-based Herzegovinians purchased a 180-acre tract of forestland twenty-five miles north of Toronto at a rock-bottom price. The acreage would become the Croatian Social and Cultural Center, the Franciscans' Ontario base, and, for a period, the cover for Otpor. The facility's founding father, Mladen Čuvalo, was not a newcomer to ultranationalist émigré circles. In 1977 the Vatican had excommunicated Čuvalo for his renegade stands and stripped him of his responsibilities in New York City. Čuvalo's proximity to Zvonko Bušić and the hijacking affair the year before was probably the last straw. No charges could be pinned on Čuvalo at the trial, but he was a known confidant of Bušić, if not the brains behind the skyjacking. When the commandeered jet landed in Paris, the first call the Bušićes made was to Čuvalo in New York.

In the middle of Ontario's rolling cornfields, the Norval center's red brick rectory is visible from Winston Churchill Boulevard, where the Croat checkerboard marks the driveway. On the edge of a sea of soccer fields and a sprawling picnic area lies a modest single-story building that doubles as a conference hall and chapel. Every year in June the Feast of St. Anthony celebration attracts about fifteen thousand Croatian Canadians, the largest gathering of Croats outside Croatia. The weekly masses bring Croat and Bosnian Croat followers from across Ontario, all members of the Norval parish, Our Lady Queen of Peace.

The parish name underlines Norval's close association with the Medjugorje shrine in Herzegovina and the cult of the Virgin Mary. Medjugorje's official newsletter, *Glas Mira* (Voice of Peace) as well as publications from the Franciscans' North American publishing house, the Croatian Franciscan Press in Chicago, are for sale in the hall's foyer. Other points of reference stare one in the eye. On one wall in the makeshift chapel a row of fifteen portraits of "great Croats" begins with King Tomislav and ends with Ante Pavelić. Behind the elevated altar hang the flags of Canada, Croatia, the Vatican, and Herzeg-Bosna, the 1992–94 breakaway Bosnian Croat mini-state in western Herzegovina.

According to Father Gjuran, who retired in 1998, the Franciscans in the diaspora strove to inject a radical nationalist element into the work of the Croatian Roman Catholic community. Under the authority of the Toronto archbishop, the Toronto Croats, like other Eastern European Catholic peoples, had their own church, Our Lady Queen of Croatia, and held daily masses in Croatian. Even though the Croatian Church had made an acceptable arrangement with the Yugoslav regime, it remained staunchly anticommunist, loyal to the Vatican and uncompromisingly Croat. The Yugoslav regime even forbade Gjuran to visit Yugoslavia once he had left. But the relationship was still too cozy for the radical Franciscans.

The creation of the Norval facility met with firm resistance from Gjuran and the Vatican. Rome refused to recognize the wayward Franciscan parish.[16] But the brothers' potent nationalism tapped a vein in part of the Croat diaspora. "They said that if you are Catholic and Croatian you must go to Norval because it represents the pure Croatian community," explains Gjuran. For the Norval priests, an independent Croatia was an article of faith. It was the task of the clergy and their faithful to bring about its resurrection.

Despite the Vatican's disapproval, Norval siphoned Catholic parishioners from the Toronto, Mississauga, Hamilton, and Oakville parishes. At stake in the internecine struggle was more than theological high ground. The concentrated southern Ontario parishes rank among the wealthiest in the worldwide Croat diaspora, and every head meant money.

Meanwhile, the aftermath of the Bušić hijacking was a rocky time for Otpor and other radical nationalist currents. The organization, banned in Germany, was under surveillance elsewhere and was effectively forced underground. It was at Norval that the radicals found a home. Norval served as Otpor's front, a place where Šušak, Sopta, Beljo, and their ilk could meet, brainstorm, give presentations, and raise money. The key figure behind Norval's political agenda was Čuvalo's successor, Friar Ljubo Krasić. Born in 1938, Krasić was a Franciscan priest from the southwestern Herzegovinian town of Čitluk. He left Yugoslavia in 1966 to do missionary work in Switzerland. Krasić then studied sociology in Rome at the University Pro Deo before emigrating to the United States in 1974. Today Krasić directs Croatian Franciscan émigré activities out of the Croatian Ethnic Institute in Chicago, the North American headquarters of the Croat Franciscans. He declines to speak to journalists of any nationality.

As president of the CNC in the 1980s Martin Meštrović traveled regularly to Canada and visited Norval many times. He confirms that the center sheltered the most radical wing of the Croat diaspora. Simply put, their ideology was to overthrow Yugoslavia, kick out the Serbs, and forge a greater Croatian state that included Herzegovina. Meštrović says that he always received a cordial reception at Norval, although the deep political differences between his more moderate convictions and those of the Norval group were clear. "They believed in revolutionary action," says Meštrović. "They didn't tell me they wanted to blow up anything, but they didn't believe you were going to get anywhere by lobbying the [U.S.] Congress." After his speeches donations were collected, but never for the CNC. Other causes, such as freeing Croat terrorists imprisoned in Germany, were deemed higher priority.

In 1987 and 1988 Tudjman had audiences at Norval. No one present then will discuss today the content of the meetings or the participants' identity. The topics of discussion, however, are not difficult to imagine. Just five months after taking the presidency of the Croatian republic in 1990 Tudjman visited Norval on another junket around the North American diaspora. Pictures show Tudjman in sunglasses surrounded by Canadian flags and red-white-and-blue carnation wreaths, flanked by Šušak, Beljo, and others from the émigré team, also wearing dark glasses. No transcript exists of his speech on that bright September day. Tudjman most probably promised the many thousand Ontario Croats that he would work to establish voting rights for the diaspora in future Croatian elections, which he did. (In 1995 and 2000, diaspora Croats, including those in Bosnia and Herzegovina, voted nearly unanimously for the HDZ, accounting for about 10 percent of the party's parliamentary seats. No other party won a single diaspora representative.)* Undoubtedly Tudjman also thanked the crowd for their generous support of his victorious campaign and alerted them that Croatia would need its diaspora's help again soon.

* The contentious HDZ-sponsored law for a special diaspora voting bloc stipulated that the diaspora would elect twelve representatives to the 127-member Sabor. The vast majority of diaspora Croats eligible to vote (398,841) lived in Bosnia and Herzegovina, where Tudjman had seen to it that all ethnic Croats qualified for dual citizenship. In 1995, the HDZ took 90 percent of the just 109,389 votes cast in twenty-seven countries around the world. Most of those voters came from neighboring Bosnia, primarily from the Herzegovina. Under sharp criticism from the international community and opposition, the fixed quota system was altered to make the number of diaspora seats proportional to the total votes cast by the diaspora. In 2000, there were polling stations in seventy-nine different countries. In North America, Croats could vote at the embassies in Washington, D.C., and Ottawa, as well as the consulates in Chicago, Cleveland, Los Angeles, New York, and Mississauga. There were also twenty-three polling stations in Germany, twenty-one in Australia and ten in Austria. Although the HDZ suffered a substantial set back at the ballot box in Croatia, dislodging it from power, it earned all six of the diaspora seats, winning nearly 86 percent of the 126,841 diaspora votes cast, 110,356 of which came from Bosnia and Herzegovina. In contrast, the Serb minority received three seats in 1995 and just one in 1999. (See Nenad Zakosek, *Politicki sustav Hrvatske* [Zagreb: Bibliotheka Politicka misao, 2000] 48, 59; "Croatia's Parliamentary Elections," prepared by the Commission on Security and Cooperation in Europe, Washington, D.C., 2000.)

CHAPTER FOUR

Making Baby MiGs

In Croatia's first HDZ-led administration, Gojko Šušak assumed the republic's newly created position of minister for return and immigration, an office Tudjman stipulated would be run by either Šušak or Ante Beljo. Other former émigrés moved into key positions in the 1990 republican government. The former Ontario resident Ivica Mudrinić became minister of transportation and communications, and then later director of state-run Croatian television, a strident mouthpiece of the regime. The economist Branko Salaj, who lived for years in Sweden and was counted among Tudjman's earliest European backers, became minister of information before moving on to different ambassadorial posts.

Other ambassadors and many top-ranking generals were drawn selectively from diaspora ranks. One assignment of particularly questionable judgment was that of the ambassador-designate to Argentina, Ivo Rojnića, an émigré with an Ustashe past who had eluded extradition to Yugoslavia since the 1940s.[1] In addition, Tudjman, exercising his constitutional right as president to fill five seats in the Sabor, appointed to one seat the eighty-five-year-old Argentine émigré Vinko Nikolić, a poet who had served in the wartime Ustashe Education Ministry and edited the cultural journal *Hrvatska Revija* for decades afterward in Buenos Aires. Nikolić, a prominent diaspora personality, was a key symbolic figure for Tudjman's "national reconciliation."

High-profile though they were, it would be unfair to contend that former exiles were running the first democratically elected Croatian administration. Tudjman's cabinet was a heterogeneous composition of Croat nationalists from assorted political traditions, only three of whom came from the diaspora. Of those, Mudrinić and Salaj were never connected to Otpor or other neo-Ustashe groups. But Šušak and the so-called Herzegovina lobby around him would prove infinitely more valuable to Tudjman in the long run. By 1994, after the party split, it was this clique that called the shots in the Croatian government.

Šušak's diaspora ministry was a curious creation. The Croatian Heritage Foundation (Hrvatska Matica Iseljenika) already existed and was being led by one of Croatia's most prominent exile literati recently returned from the United States, the poet Boris Maruna. The Croatian Heritage Foundation was responsible for relations with Croats abroad, and Maruna, in contrast to Šušak, was a known quantity in diaspora circles across several continents. But Šušak's ministry had a specific task: the implementation of Tudjman's Iseljena Hrvatska plan. Tudjman actually took seriously the chimerical idea of "repatriating" thousands, if not tens or even hundreds of thousands, of Croat émigrés to Croatia. Croatia even offered tax exemptions and monetary aid to lure back long-lost kinfolk.[2] One plan was to entice Croat–South American émigrés with offers of land in Croatia and cost-free transportation from Buenos Aires to Croatia by ship. Šušak even traveled to Argentina in 1990 to discuss the plan with Croat émigrés there. The plan was that the Croatian government would charter a freighter that would pick up the émigré families and their possessions and sail them (back) to Croatia.

These far-fetched plans would never materialize. Events in Croatia and Yugoslavia's five other republics were moving at breakneck speed and required the government's full attention. In the Yugoslav federation, to which the republic Croatia still belonged in 1990, Milošević's strong-arm tactics to manipulate and dominate the federal institutions, including the army, had provoked furor among the reformist republics. By mid-summer 1990, in southern Croatia along the former Austro-Hungarian military frontier called the Krajina, Croatian Serbs were calling to life their independent parastate, a direct challenge to Zagreb's authority. Even further to the south, in Serbia's ethnic Albanian-majority province of Kosovo, its dissident leaders were stepping up their nonviolent resistance to Belgrade's direct rule. And in Slovenia, on Croatia's northern border, the first of the region's wars would break out in less than a year. With a military showdown of some kind looming—either with Belgrade or the Croatian Serbs or both—Croatia needed more than the lightly armed republican police units it had at its disposal.

Martin Špegelj, a retired JNA general, was Tudjman's first minister of defense. Špegelj came to the position with the daunting task of turning a civilian police force into a battle-ready army. At the time the republic's armory was paltry. It included just fifteen thousand rifles (in the hands of the domestic police), one armored personnel carrier, and not a single piece of heavy artillery. This was inadequate even to respond to the local insurrections of the Croatian Serbs much less to the mighty JNA.

Špegelj went straight to work setting up an arms smuggling network with remarkable speed and results. At the time, between the spring of 1990 and early 1991, there was no international embargo on the export of weapons to Yugoslavia or to any of its constituent republics. Small quantities of arms began to pour in from the former Eastern bloc countries, the Middle and the Far East, and Germany. Later Špegelj managed to purchase vast shipments of anti-aircraft defense systems, rocket-propelled grenades, mines, and tens of thousands of machine guns from sympathetic neighboring countries such as Hungary. Salvageable parts of the former East German arsenal were unloaded to Croatia.

Špegelj's initial success apparently went to his head. By late 1990 the burly ex-general was advocating the retaking of rebel Serb positions by force, a risky move that would certainly have mobilized international opinion against Croatia. Even more audacious, he argued that Croatia's republican forces, locally organized paramilitary police units, could lay siege to JNA barracks and eventually confiscate enormous quantities of weaponry and ammunition. At the time the plan was too radical even for Tudjman and Šušak, who felt that the JNA, no matter how down-at-the-heels, could still crush the tiny Croatian force. For Tudjman, Špegelj's hubris went too far, too early. In February 1991 the portfolio for purchasing arms was transferred to the trio of Šušak; Franjo Gregurić, Tudjman's future prime minister and at the time director of a major trading concern; and businessman Hrvoje Sarinić, a former émigré recently returned after twenty years in France and Morocco.

The whirlwind events on the ground had whipped up emotions in the diaspora, which in many places was better organized and better placed to obtain military supplies than the new Croatian government, which had the Yugoslav army and secret services breathing down its neck. One former émigré ideally positioned to expedite the flow of arms to Croatia was the poet Maruna, the new director of the Croatian Heritage Foundation. Although Maruna was an ardent Croat nationalist and early HDZ supporter, he had a decidedly different profile than the Ontario group.

In the mid 1960s Maruna studied literature at Loyola University in Los Angeles. After that he drifted along the California coast, discussing poetry with the likes of Charles Bukowski and Allen Ginsberg, smoking dope with hippies and partaking in the summer of love, as he still remembers today with a nostalgic smirk. During the 1970s he lived in Madrid, Rome, and New York, where he penned numerous volumes of poetry and Croatian translations of America's beat poets. In 1977 Maruna covered the Bušić hijacking trial in New York, writing about the hijacking affair that he calls "a testament to Croatian political stupidity." From 1976 to 1977 he served as general secretary of the Croatian National Congress. In short, there was probably no one in the entire Croat diaspora with a name and contacts like Maruna. He knew virtually everyone.

While Špegelj and later Šušak operated in the name of the new Croatian government with large teams behind them, Maruna's gun-running operation out of the Croatian Heritage Foundation was a one-man show. The garrulous poet was suddenly the logical go-between for diaspora patriots looking to help the homeland in its hour of need, and police chiefs, paramilitaries, and commanders in the field desperate for supplies. Maruna's office behind the Zagreb train station became a conduit for military stock of every kind.

"The diaspora effort [to arm Croatia] began spontaneously," he says at his personal corner table at the Astoria Restaurant in central Zagreb, where he trades winks and little jokes with just about every waitress. "The exiles were very well organized, and at the time Tudjman had parts of the secret services against him. So the boys and girls of Croat origin in Toronto, for example, they knew exactly what to do without anyone telling them."

Dressed in faded jeans and a stone-washed denim shirt, the sixty-year-old Maruna grins mischievously from behind an oversized pair of 1970s-style plastic glasses with photo-gray lenses. His pear-shaped physique and perfectly round bald head bear little resemblance to the 1960s photos of him, which had recently appeared in a Croatian weekly, as a buff young man in swim trunks, standing akimbo in the surf off Mar de Ajo. But that does not in the least seem to blunt the waitresses' affection for "Boris."

The stories Maruna spins in rapid succession speak of the wild, panicked atmosphere in Croatia in late 1990 and 1991. "There were some days when so many people passed through my office I didn't know whether I saw my mother or the queen of England. I was the personal contact, a kind of middleman, between the officers in the field, whom I knew, and the exile groups, who had my trust. I never gave anything to the Ministry of Defense but to the individual commanders only."

Maruna's office and tiny bachelor flat were at times stocked to the ceiling with Kalishnikovs or old East German field fatigues. Maruna tells of twenty-year-old girls from Canada sending him U.S.–made M-16 machine guns in tennis bags via Air Canada. Friends in California, Vietnam veterans, arranged for small surveillance aircraft to be sent in pieces to Croatia. Trucks full of humanitarian aid from Germany would arrive at his office with a couple of rocket launchers hidden behind the boxes of secondhand clothing. Catholic Croat priests from Austria and southern Germany showed up at his door with garbage bags full of German marks. Stories abound, not just from Maruna, of diaspora kids who emptied their piggy banks for the cause or of ordinary working-class Croat émigrés who took out a second or third mortgage on their homes to make a contribution.

But Maruna was never tight with the clique around Tudjman, and he soon paid the price. "The first thing I said to Croat exiles is don't bring money into the country, bring supplies," explains Maruna. "The money placed at the hands of the Interior or Defense Ministries makes a 180-degree turn to banks in Austria or Switzerland. From there it can disappear very easily. Buy boots, I said, you can't miss."

Maruna refused to play by the new regime's rules, which included averting his gaze to the skimming of funds, issuing fake receipts, and taking cuts at every possible turn. But more damaging was Maruna's refusal to turn the Croatian Heritage Foundation into the primary channel for financing the Bosnian Croat security services in the Herzegovina. The Croatian Heritage Foundation, as the organization officially responsible for "Croats outside Croatia," had a natural cover that neither the Interior or Defense Ministries could claim. "It wasn't the diaspora money that they wanted to use," explains Maruna, "but my official budget, which was basically whatever I asked for." Before long, unmistakable signals were coming from the president's office that Maruna's time was up. "At a certain point they said, 'Boris, we think it's time for you to start writing again.' And I said, 'You're right.' I sat down and for five years I never stopped blasting the shit out of them."

In October 1992 Maruna resigned his post.[3] The foundation saw several interim directors come and go before Tudjman settled on an old acquaintance who would do the job without back talk: Ante Beljo from Sudbury, Ontario. Beljo, who had served as HDZ secretary for North America and then general secretary for Croatia (and thus worldwide), loyally turned the Croatian Heritage Foundation into an arm of the party and the regime. The former secretary of the foundation, Ćiro Grubišić, whom Maruna had removed from the position for his part in fraudulent financial dealings, became the government's designate for arming the Bosnian Croats and later the Croatian consul in Mostar. Like so many of the insider connections that underpinned political power in Tudjman's Croatia, Grubišić was the brother of Vinko Grubišić from Toronto, a good personal friend of Beljo and Šušak, and a Široki Brijeg native as well.

Šušak's building of a Croatian army began with the establishment of the Croatian National Fund (CNF), a Swiss bank account officially registered under the title "Aid for the Economic Renewal and Sovereignty of the Republic of Croatia." On February 9, 1991, the minister for return and immigration faxed an appeal to "all Croats and friends of the Croatian people across the world, all Croat clubs, societies, centers, and organizations outside the nation." Within hours a diaspora that spanned the globe learned how it could participate in its nation's struggle for independence. In this letter on behalf of the new government, Šušak entreated the diaspora to help the homeland in the form of financial contributions. Although nowhere in the letter did Šušak specifically state that the donations would go toward the purchase of weapons, the intention was transparent. The letter read, in part:

> You know that when democracy dawned in Croatia, the weapons that the republic had for its defense were confiscated. Now they [the Yugoslav authorities] again want to disarm Croatia, which has gone through great

pains and suffered many victims to succeed as a sovereign state and to obtain a portion of the arms it needs. It is understood that the Republic of Croatia will not permit this to happen again. It is obvious that with our young democracy in such a condition, we cannot ignore our own economic and national needs because of the needs of others. In spite of everything, Croatia must survive and will survive. For this, Croatia is depending on your help.[4]

The appeal informs the worldwide émigré community that contributions should be deposited in account 511–629 KH in the Central United Bank of Switzerland on Rue du Rhone 8 in Geneva. Every donor, the letter asks, should stipulate whether the deposit is a donation or a loan. It guarantees that the Republic of Croatia will return loans with accumulated interest. This never happened.

The first fund account was opened by Šarinić, who had considerable international connections, not least of all in Switzerland. The only people with access to the account were its three signatories: Šarinić, Tudjman, and Šušak. No sum could be withdrawn without at least two of the three men's signatures. Throughout the seven years of the fund's existence, the Finance and Defense Ministries were directly responsible for handling the money, with Šušak as the primary manager for those resources. An investigative report on the fund, conducted by the Zagreb weekly *Nacional*, found Šušak's signature on almost every documented transaction.

The urgent tone of Šušak's letter conveyed the sense that it was "do or die," now or never for Croatia. The response from the diaspora was overwhelming, dwarfing the sums collected for the 1990 HDZ election campaign. Within a few months, Šušak claimed in a 1992 interview, more than $15 million in different currencies had flowed into the account.[5] According to *Nacional*, Šušak's figure was a gross underestimate. (Or, as the feisty periodical put it, a blatant lie.) Bank receipts from the time revealed that the first wave of contributions probably totaled more than $50 million.[6]

In the diaspora the local CNF accounts that sprang up from community to community were periodically emptied into the central Swiss account. Fund-raising dinners, cultural events, and picnics collected millions upon millions of contributions. In the diaspora churches the hat was passed around one extra time for Croatia. At the Franciscan facility in Norval a blackboard posted the names and contributions of the biggest spenders for all to see. "Zagreb didn't demand anything," says John Zdunić, who helped set up the fund in North America. "We knew what was needed and we gave." Like Maruna, he, too, tells of seven-year old kids pooling their pocket money and of work-a-day émigré families digging deep into lifetime savings. Officially the contributions or loans were for relief supplies, such as medical equipment. "What the money really went toward, who knows?" smiles Zdunić. "We didn't do anything illegal." But from across his cluttered desk at the Agram Gardens warehouse for landscaping supplies, the big man's countenance darkens. "It's our business how we spent the money, no one else's. This was a family matter."

But the funds were decidedly more circumspect than Zdunić admits: Croatia's family affairs had far-reaching international implications. In early 1991 the international community had neither recognized Croatia as an independent state,* as Šušak implies in the first appeal, nor had it begun serious diplomacy to resolve the smoldering conflict in Croatia through peaceful means. By September 1991 the entire region was under a United Nations arms embargo. The funds, under the noses of authorities in the United States, Canada, and Australia, were part of an initiative that at the time ran counter to the foreign policy aims of Washington, Ottawa, and Canberra.

The bankers at Central United in Geneva soon got wise to the account's real purpose and ordered Sarinić to shut it down. The last complication they wanted was trouble with Western business partners or the UN, much less responsibility for stoking a Serb-Croat war. Just a few days later Sarinić opened a new account at the Bank für Kärnten und Steiermark in Villach, Austria, where the three signatories had to pledge that the funds would not be used for the purchase of arms or any other military-related purposes.

The new Austrian account prompted a second letter to the diaspora from Šušak on August 7, 1991, this time in his new function as deputy minister of defense, which he held simultaneously with the diaspora ministry post. The fund had to be relocated, he claimed, because a barrage of threatening letters from terrorist Serb "Chetnik" groups had unnerved the Swiss bank. In the letter Šušak protested the establishment of "rival accounts" for the purchase of arms and relief supplies over which the Zagreb government had no control. (Presumably he was referring to the other fund-raising initiatives, such as Maruna's, that did not go through government channels.) Only the official CNF, he promised, was transparent and legitimate. "The government of Croatia must be able to oversee and insure such an initiative so that all Croats who have invested in this fund have the possibility of seeing what happens with their money. . . . The Ministry of Return and Immigration takes full responsibility for each amount deposited into the fund. Do not be fooled by rumors spread around the world by our enemies who wish to divert us from investing with tales of misappropriation and embezzlement."[7]

The total sum of monies that flowed into and was paid out of the CNF

---

* Croatia declared its independence on June 25, 1991. Its statehood was recognized by the European Union states in January 1992.

will never be known—nor how they were spent. At no point, even after the war, did the government issue a public statement on the account as it had promised. Šušak and Tudjman are now dead, and Sarinić refuses to speak about the fund. Only fragmented records of deposit and withdrawal exist in the Finance Ministry, which have since fallen into the hands of the Croatian media. There were no receipts for donors. None of the loans were paid back. President Tudjman consistently resisted a regulatory mechanism for the account. The total figure could easily run in excess of $100 million.

"I once told President Tudjman that people were looking for some kind of certification of receipt for their money," says Stipe Mesić, the president of Croatia since 2000. Mesić was a founding member of the HDZ and close Tudjman confidant until the two men parted ways in 1994. "But the only response I received was 'Are you suspicious of me?' and matters were left at that," he says.

The CNF lacked any transparency whatsoever. In effect, it was the covert account of the Ministry of Defense and the president's office, a kind of all-purpose slush fund. Misappropriation and embezzlement were rife. That said, of the millions that passed through the Villach account, a significant chunk probably did go toward arms as most of the émigré donors had intended. Military and defense experts estimate that the creation and training of the Croatian army, which in the summer of 1995 would effortlessly rout the rebel Serbs from their UN-protected parastate, cost $5.5 billion.[8] Part of that, but only part, came from the diaspora.

How much of the total arms bill was paid for from the CNF is impossible to ascertain because the fund was tapped for other purposes as well. For example, the Villach bank account was also a functional channel for the Tudjman government to launder money, both during and after the arms embargo. The Croatian media reports that suitcases of cash went from Privedna Banka in Zagreb, the government's bank, to Austria before moving on to other locations.[9] Once the money's origins, namely, Croatia's currency reserves, were lost in the shuffle, it could be spent on arms or for other purposes.

Those "other purposes" were multifarious—and rarely above-board. The existing receipts and transaction records recovered from the Finance Ministry show that in 1991 two transfers of $3.7 million went toward the purchase of Tudjman's presidential airplane. Other transfers of similar magnitude wound up in the accounts of private individuals who would later emerge as part of Croatia's new tycoon class. Payments went to the Defense Ministry's pet soccer team, Hrvatski Dragovoljac (Croatian Volunteer). Still other transfers were made to private companies in Switzerland, the United States, Bangkok, France, and Cyprus that may or may not have been involved in trade in arms or military goods. The involvement of Jozo Martinović, the finance minister of the wartime Herzeg-Bosna parastate, dispels any doubts that at least some of the donations were going to the Herzegovina Croats: Martinović was given power of attorney by Tudjman to sign for withdrawals on his behalf. Martinović did this, generously approving deposits straight into his own private bank account.[10]

After Croatia's blitz military actions, Flash and Storm, in 1995, which retook most of the rebel Serb-held territory, contributions to the fund fell off sharply. Yet it was not until three full years after Croatia's battlefield conquests that the fund was finally dissolved. Immediately after Šušak's death in 1998, Sarinić approached Tudjman about the U.S.$1.4 million left in the account. Tudjman ordered that the balance be transferred to the accounts of the Foundation for the Croat Plight, an HDZ-sponsored cultural foundation close to the party's far-right faction. In other words, it was to be funneled into party coffers. Apparently Sarinić objected to the transaction so strenuously that he refused to co-sign the transfer order. But Tudjman pushed it through nonetheless. As one of the journalists following the scandal wrote, "The HDZ stole money from thousands upon thousands of honest Croat patriots who had given their hard-earned money from all over the world in order to help Croatia achieve independence. . . . At issue is theft and deceit ordered by the president."[11] In Tudjman's own mind, however, the complaints were unfounded, since there was no distinction between the nation, the state, and the ruling party.

In 1991 and 1992 the Croatian Ministry of Defense on Krešimir Square was a scene of wild activity and confusion. Šušak packed the department and new officer corps with people whose personal and political loyalties were beyond question: relatives, old allies from exile, and, above all, West Herzegovinians. Stories of shady deals gone awry, missing bags of money, and run-ins with unscrupulous arms dealers are a dime a dozen. Barely recovered from the six point-blank bullet wounds he endured in Scotland, former Otpor leader Nikola Stedul joined the ministry in the summer of 1991, where, ironically, and darkly so, he was working directly beside the very same people who, in their former capacity with the Yugoslav secret services, had ordered his botched assassination in 1988. In the spirit of national reconciliation, President Tudjman asked Stedul to put aside such petty squabbles of the past.

"I was just one of hundreds working to get whatever Croatia needed," says Stedul. But not everyone enjoyed the kind of connections he had from his Otpor days. It was rumored, for example, that Stedul was tight with various factions of the Irish Republican Army, not the first instance of Croat-Irish cooperation in such matters. "I had contacts with business people outside and from the diaspora who also had a lot of . . ." Stedul trails off ambiguously, "well, various contacts. We knew that some would fail and some would succeed." An example of one failure was Otpor member Andjelko Jurković, a U.S. citizen living in Chicago, who was apprehended off the Florida coast in 1991 attempting to ship more than $12 million in Stinger anti-aircraft missiles and other weapons to Croatia.[12]

Stedul crisscrossed Europe trying to pin down deals for weapons of every kind. Postcommunist Eastern Europe was an open arms bazaar for anyone with cash in hand. But as long as Washington remained skeptical about Croatian independence, even Stedul's old Otpor contacts would do him little good. "At the beginning, the deals would often fall through, blocked for this reason or another, accounts frozen," he says. "It was clear we were being obstructed by powerful secret services. But when the United States finally gave up the idea of saving Yugoslavia, well, then everything opened up for us." Ironically, by the time U.S. policy shifted in late 1991, the UN arms embargo was officially in place. But despite the new international ban, says Stedul, it suddenly became easier than ever for Croatia to smuggle arms.

The week the arms embargo went into effect in September 1991, Toronto resident Tony (Anton) Kikas found himself languishing in a ratty Belgrade jail cell, charged by the Yugoslav federal government with smuggling a shipment of weapons valued at $1 million into Croatia. On August 31, 1991, the fifty-five-year-old émigré, a Sarajevo native and wealthy contractor, was taken into custody after his chartered Ugandan Airlines Boeing 707, en route from South Africa to Slovenia, was forced down by Yugoslav jets at the Zagreb airport. Clearly Yugoslav military intelligence had a tip-off about Kikas. The airliner, with a crew of six, was carrying nineteen tons of Singapore-made SAR-80 assault rifles and ammunition. Upon landing, Croat police units and JNA soldiers exchanged fire to get to the cargo first, but the federal troops nabbed Kikas and the guns.

Kikas was no stranger to the new men in and around Croatia's Defense Ministry. He was a well-known émigré fund-raiser, close to the Norval Franciscans and the radical fringe of the Ontario émigré scene. Kikas had already proven that he could produce vast sums of money for the Croat cause at the drop of a hat. In the late 1980s Kikas, together with Šušak, headed a campaign to establish a chair for Croatian studies at York University. Kikas, president of the Canadian-Croatian Professional and Business Association, organized the gala fund-raising dinner at Toronto's Triumph Hotel. In one evening three hundred guests pledged the entire $500,000 required for the chair. Kikas chipped in $25,000 and his friend John Zdunić $100,000.[13] Two years later, Kikas came up with $300,000 for the Holy Trinity Croatian Church in Oakville, Ontario. These men knew how to raise money for the Croat cause.

Three months after his detainment, Kikas was released in a prisoner exchange for a federal army general captured by the Croats. As to where the $1 million came from or who organized the deal, Kikas was mum upon his release and remains so today. "I had no regrets for what I did," Kikas said at a press conference upon his arrival in Toronto. "I was not involved in smuggling guns. I am a patriot and, whatever I did, I fulfilled my moral obligation and expressed my patriotism to my old country."[14] Nor did the Toronto businessman speculate as to who had set him up, although the Yugoslav intelligence evidently had him in its sights every step of the way.

In four short years the Croatian armed forces underwent a breathtaking metamorphosis. By 1995, when Croatia launched blitzkrieg strikes on the rebel Serb enclaves, the minute man–style regional militias had been transformed into an effective, professional army. The Hrvatska Vojska was Šušak's creation, and he deserves full credit for it. Western observers were slow to take Šušak seriously, sizing him up as a Tudjman sycophant who, with his "chain of pizzerias," had bought his way into the president's inner circle. Šušak's thuggish looks and uncouth demeanor disconcerted many international interlocutors from the start. The 1989–92 U.S. ambassador to Yugoslavia, Warren Zimmermann, was clearly put off by Šušak. He described Šušak as "a Darth Vader doppelganger" with his long-lined face, hooded eyes, and permanent scowl.[15]

Croatia's defense minister simply was not the kind of statesman that the West's diplomatic elite could immediately relate to. Neither his regular-guy charisma nor his horse trader's intuition impressed them at first. After all, the president's right-hand man was Croatia's top arms smuggler, a job that required a certain resourcefulness and reckless disregard for the law that Šušak had practiced in his previous life as a professional exile. If exile politics resembled a macho fantasy world, Šušak, as defense minister, was acting out the real-life script. When it came to Croatia, his kind had always been convinced that everything was possible.

In 1994, when the *New York Times* Balkan correspondent Roger Cohen visited Šušak's spacious Zagreb office, he noted the minister's mocking deprecation of the international arms embargo. Šušak bragged that Croatia by then had access to anti-tank weapons, artillery, and multiple-rocket launchers, and could produce the T-72 tank as well as the ability to assemble MiG fighters. "It was easy to find Šušak risible," Cohen writes in his Balkan memoir, *Hearts Grown Brutal: Sagas of Sarajevo.*[16] "With his brazen manner, his broken English, his priggish contempt for Muslims, his glad-handing crudeness, and his almost childlike enthusiasm for all things American, he could come across as an unsavory buffoon—a pizza-peddler out of his depth, a hungry kid in a candy store with a bulging wallet. But he was smart, and America underestimated him."

When Šušak formally took the reins at the Defense Ministry in late September 1991, Croatia's plight was desperate. A third of its territory was in the hands of rebel Serbs. Vukovar's population crouched in cellars as Serb guns reduced their Habsburg city to rubble, and the Yugoslav armed forces promptly began pounding coastal Dubrovnik. By any objective account, the all-out defense of Vukovar should have been Croatia's number one military priority. Once Vukovar and neighboring Osijek fell into Serb hands, the Slavonian plains would be wide open to the JNA, which could then march straight across Croatia. But the first phase of Tudjman's Croatian National Policy was already under way: Zagreb's priorities at that moment lay elsewhere, to the south, in Bosnia and Herzegovina.

Tudjman was planning a division of Bosnia and Herzegovina and the new borders of a Greater Croatia at a time when Croatia was pinned to the wall: its sovereignty violated, statehood still unrecognized by the world and a UN arms embargo in place. Earlier that year in March, Tudjman and Milošević met secretly at one of Tito's old hunting lodges, Karadjordjevo, in northern Serbia. In discussions that have since come to light, the two men conspired to partition Bosnia and Herzegovina between Croatia and Serbia. The war in Bosnia would be a mutually agreed-on landgrab that would divide former Yugoslavia into a Greater Croatia and a Greater Serbia. What exactly would happen to the Bosnian Muslims was unclear, but not much, if any, of the country would be left to them.

The Zagreb hard-liners, with their base in the Defense Ministry, wasted no time in setting up the political, military, and secret service structures in western Herzegovina that would be critical to the enterprise of Bosnia's partition. Croatian president Mesić confirms that there was a direct line funneling "arms and money" from the Croatian Defense Ministry to the Herzegovina Croats by autumn 1991. "At the time when Vukovar needed arms desperately, when there were daily appeals for weapons, arms instead went to Herzegovina," Mesić says. "This appeared totally unreasonable to anyone who didn't understand that the partition of Bosnia Herzegovina was being planned. Tudjman thought that the problem of Vukovar would he solved today or tomorrow, sooner or later, but that he should see to it that he gets as great a part of Bosnia Herzegovina as soon as he could."

Seated in an ornate chair in the presidential palace, Tudjman's affable successor maintains that Šušak and the other émigrés were only carrying out Tudjman's orders: "Tudjman took advantage of their radical nationalism and turned them into the people to break up Bosnia Herzegovina." It was not, Mesić claims, the other way around, namely, that the right-wing émigrés goaded Tudjman to act against his better judgment. To the contrary, they were his accomplices, says Mesić.

By late 1991 the scent of war had already wafted into Bosnia and Herzegovina. An estimated twenty thousand Bosnian Croats,[17] mostly from

Herzegovina, had enlisted in the Croatian National Guard as volunteers. These fighters were thus prepared to mobilize in Bosnia well before the Bosnian government could begin to form its own units. A smattering of Croat émigrés from across the world also enlisted in the Croat militias at the time. There is no reliable figure, but they probably numbered no more than one thousand. In terms of soldiers, the diaspora volunteers added little to the Croat armies. More salient to the Croat forces were the ex-émigré officers with international fighting experience, including several with a background in the French Foreign Legion, who rounded out an anemic officers' corps.

The Bosnia and Herzegovina HDZ was born on August 18, 1990, every inch the offspring of its Croatian counterpart. Indeed, the Bosnian HDZ functioned as a regional branch funded and controlled from Zagreb. At its first congress a familiar cast of characters was on hand to push the agenda in the desired direction: Šušak, Beljo, and Babić-Petričević from Germany, among others. The émigrés' coercion was imperative since the Bosnian HDZ leadership was split from the beginning between a moderate faction, led by the bow tie–sporting Stjepan Kljuić, a Sarajevo sports journalist, and a nationalist faction faithful to its patrons in Zagreb. "It was clear that they [the émigrés] had Bosnia's division in their sights," explains Kljuić in his Sarajevo office. "Even at this time they wanted to unite Croatia and Bosnia." But at the first party congress this was not a decisive issue. The array of new opposition parties had an election campaign to wage against a communist party that had held power for 40 years.

The fault lines within the Bosnian HDZ reflected those that shot through the republic's 740,000–strong Croat community. In contrast to most of the 200,000 Herzegovina Croats, the more populous and geographically dispersed Croats from central and northern Bosnia had lived for centuries in ethnically mixed communities. Many even referred to themselves as "Catholics" or simply "Bosnians" rather than "Croats." They usually had more affinity to their neighbors, regardless of ethnicity, than with the mountain folk of Herzegovina.

Kljuić's tenure at the forefront of the Bosnian HDZ was short-lived. "They [the émigrés] brought money with them from Zagreb but it never went through the [Bosnian HDZ] Sarajevo office," Kljuić reports. Shortly thereafter, at a special party session, fittingly in Široki Brijeg, the Zagreb HDZ replaced Kljuić with Herzegovina supermarket manager and fanatic nationalist Mate Boban. "We were the same party divided into two factions and between two states. But the treasurer was common, namely Zagreb. This was Tudjman's advantage: Šušak was responsible for the money," says Kljuić.

The powers in Zagreb and the Bosnian HDZ ensured that the locally organized Bosnian Croat militias would coalesce into the Croat Defense Council (HVO), the official title of the Bosnian Croat army, by early spring 1992. When war first broke out in April, the Bosnian Croats and Bosnian Muslims fought side-by-side against the Bosnian Serb and Yugoslav forces. Many Bosnian Muslims enlisted in the HVO before the Bosnian army was capable of fielding a military force. But any real solidarity of the HDZ/ HVO leadership with the Bosnian Muslims was illusory. In July 1992, with fierce fighting under way across Bosnia, the HDZ hard-liners called to life the parastate they dubbed Herzeg-Bosna, a renegade Croat enclave in West Herzegovina that flew the Croatian checkerboard flag, did business with the Croatian kuna, and designated "Croatian" as its official language. Croat-Muslim relations soured quickly, and by March 1993 the bloody "war within the war" between the HVO and the Bosnian army was raging full tilt.

A grotesque experiment in social engineering, the phenomenon of Herzeg-Bosna illustrates just what becomes of a society when its most violent and unscrupulous elements assume total, unchecked power. During its short existence, the breakaway mini-state operated as a gangster-run island where untold millions were made on the black market, including the sale of arms to all sides. Non-Croats were systematically ethnically cleansed, women were raped, and men were thrown into camps such as the detention center at Dretelj. In Herzeg-Bosna's capital, West Mostar, or other strongholds such as Široki Brijeg, Grude, or Čapljina, there were no qualms about acknowledging the ideological forefathers of their movement: black-and-white portraits of Ante Pavelić, identical to those hanging in Toronto, hung in West Mostar's blaring techno cafes, along with giant Ustashe "U"s scrawled on the walls. HVO units and barracks proudly carried the names of prominent World War II Ustashe commanders such as Jure Frančetić and Rafael Boban.

In the fluid Herzeg-Bosna power structures, the competence and chains of command of the HDZ, the HVO, and the criminal underworld overlapped and merged. Warlords ruled over fiefdoms and controlled markets through the force of sheer terror. Units such as the infamous Convicts Brigade functioned as paramilitary mafias, directly answerable only to their local master, a branch of the security services or the Defense Ministry in Zagreb. At times the internecine warfare between the Herzeg-Bosna clans and gangs themselves was so fierce that it inhibited the war effort against the Bosnian Muslims.

One warlord with a special relationship to Šušak's ministry was Mladen "Tuta" Naletilić, the boss of the Mostar-based Convicts Brigade who for years held the city in a stranglehold. It was sometime in 1991 that Naletilić, a former secondary school acquaintance of Šušak's from Široki Brijeg, returned to Croatia from Germany. Naletilić was no typical Croat émigré.

Born in 1946, he left southwestern Herzegovina legally in the late 1960s, bummed around Europe for a while, and then settled in Germany, near the southern German resort of Bodensee, where he opened a casino restaurant and bordello. The Široki Brijeg native had worked closely with the neo-Ustashe Croat émigré groups, but his underworld history included a colorful ultra-leftist twist: Tuta was close with members of the Red Army Faction, Germany's radical left-wing terrorist group, as well as the IRA and the international terrorist known as Carlos the Jackal. Apparently he discerned in the German Marxist-Leninist splinter movement a "revolutionary" recipe for destroying Yugoslavia. Naletilić, however, avoided the fate of his two closest business associates from the Bodensee, who landed in jail for placing a bomb in one of Germany's Yugoslav consulates.

Tuta's political allegiances were not so resolute that they could not be negotiated, if the price was right. A 1989 memo obtained by the London-based *Guardian* newspaper[18] documents that the future Croat warlord worked briefly as an agent for the Yugoslav secret services. His task was to report to Belgrade on "the Ustashe émigré in Germany and all over." Several years later the "professional revolutionary" and political chameleon turned out to be just the right man to assist both Belgrade and Zagreb in their joint endeavor to carve up Bosnia and Herzegovina.

On his return to Croatia Naletilić fought on the Zadar front in Croatia before Šušak awarded him the plum job of heading up the Convicts Brigade, an HVO unit comprised of former prisoners who were released from Bosnia's jails to counter the Serb advances. Units such as the Convicts Brigade would do the dirty work necessary to implement Tudjman's Croatian National Policy. The Croatian president would remain in the distant background, and Šušak, while directly involved in events on the ground, would still be officially removed from the activities of his countrymen in an internationally recognized neighboring state. It was imperative for Zagreb that the trajectory of events in Bosnia and Herzegovina appeared to be guided by a dynamic of its own, and not from top officials in the Croatian capital.

On the western bank of the jade-green Neretva River, Tuta's thugs were a law unto themselves. Outside West Mostar's cafes, the young militia members with shaved heads and mirror sunglasses lounged about arrogantly with various displays of weaponry in their laps or at their sides. The brigade revered Tuta like an omnipotent, benevolent father. They called him "pal." He referred to each of them as "son." In contrast to his skinhead troops, Tuta cultivated the image of a laid-back child of the sixties, with beaded necklaces glinting from under his long stringy hair. In the evenings, Tuta, surrounded by a cavalcade of bodyguards, returned to his fortified mini-palace in Široki Brijeg, practically next door to the Šušak residence.

The Convicts Brigade was not entirely unique. It resembled dozens of other HVO units whose ratio ultimo was to rid their fiefdoms of Muslims and Serbs. They were the ethnic cleansing brigades that perpetrated some of the grisliest atrocities of the war. In the central Bosnian village of Ahmići more than one hundred people, including thirty-two women and eleven children, were massacred on Easter Sunday, April 1993. The hoodlums' reward was the usual spoils of war. They took over the apartments and looted the possessions of "cleansed" Muslims while hijacking humanitarian aid shipments, running stolen automobile rings, and controlling a myriad of black markets. At one point their attentions were so distracted by their criminal enterprises that volunteer reinforcements were sought in Croatia to help defend the Herzeg-Bosna lines. But despite the immense human suffering that the gangster units caused, the crime that would win them worldwide recognition was the demolition of Mostar's picturesque sixteenth-century stone bridge. After a ferocious artillery bombardment of the city's mostly Muslim-populated east bank, one HVO unit detonated the Ottoman-era *stari most*, or old bridge, sending its limestone ramparts to the bottom of the Neretva.

Gangster proxies such as Tuta were integral to Croatian National Policy. The implementation of the deal that Tudjman and Milošević struck at Karadjordjevo, the right-wing émigrés' years-long dream of an ethnically homogenous Greater Croatia, could never have been realized without the bloodshed, the atrocities, and the hatred employed for the purpose of altering Bosnia's demographic map forever. The war crimes committed in the name of this cause were simply a realization of Tudjman's plan for the ethnic demarcation of Bosnia. Although the émigrés knew of Tudjman's intentions, they were convinced that the Serbs, not the Muslims, would be their foes on the battlefield. As it turned out, they had woefully underestimated how tenaciously the Bosnian Muslims would defend their territory and identity. The Croats' historical quest would be foiled by the Muslim-led Bosnian army over the course of a few short months.

The arming of Herzeg-Bosna and the onset of the Muslim-Croat war marked a dramatic shift in the attitude of the Croat radicals to the Bosnian Muslims, a change that would fracture Tudjman's ruling party. In the diaspora it was an article of faith that the Bosnian Muslims were really Croats. And even if they did not acknowledge their genetic Croatianness, they were at least considered more positively inclined toward Croatia than toward Serbia. The émigré Croats joked about the indolent, slow-witted Muslims. They simply were not taken seriously. In the 1980s the émigrés naively assumed that the Bosnian Muslims would be their natural allies in carving out a Greater Croatia.

The Karadjordjevo talks, the 1992 international recognition of Bosnia's statehood, and the emergence of Sarajevo's mostly Muslim army changed things overnight. Zagreb's inflammatory broadcasts struck out viciously at the new enemy: the fanatic Middle Eastern–backed mujahedin terrorists bent on building a fundamentalist Islamic outpost in the center of Europe.[19] "There are already some 110,000 Bosnian Muslim students in Cairo," Šušak told the *Jerusalem Post* in November 1992, a flagrant fabrication supposedly intended to link the Sarajevo government with the Islamic world. Catholic Croatia was "in a very difficult situation with fundamentalist countries such as Iran and Libya. Can you imagine a fundamentalist state in the heart of Europe?" he asked. The new line was virtually identical to that propagated from Belgrade, intended to rally Western (above all U.S.) support for the Christian brothers against an Islamic threat. This, however, was one red herring that the West did not swallow.

During the summer of 1993 the Croat campaign in central Bosnia sent waves of Muslim refugees streaming into already overcrowded refugee centers on the little patches of territory held by the Bosnian government. The refugees from the now two-front assault swelled the ranks of the Bosnian army, which, by 1993, was receiving a steady flow of arms from sympathetic countries around the world, including some in the Middle East. The propaganda from Zagreb and Belgrade became, in part, a self-fulfilling prophecy. By fall the Bosnian army had delivered the HVO a string of serious military setbacks that had pushed the Bosnian Croat militia into retreat. This time it was thousands of displaced Bosnian Croats who took to the road. Even the Croatian army, whose commanders, foot soldiers, weaponry, and ammunition assisted the HVO, could not help their hapless compatriots.

The March 1994 Washington Agreement formally brokered an end to the Croat-Muslim war. But it did not extinguish Tudjman's intention to partition Bosnia; it only changed the strategy. The United States and Germany were blunt in their statement to the Croatian president: stop the aggression in Bosnia and Herzegovina or lose international support for integrating the rebel Serb-held enclaves back into Croatia. Tudjman had little choice but to accept the accord. Croatian public opinion was against the war. Tudjman's own party had split over his expansionist plans in Bosnia, and his popularity was at an all-time low. The HVO had retreated into sullen little pockets across central Bosnia. The very last thing Croatia needed was to become an international pariah state like Serbia, complete with economic sanctions against it. Tudjman signed the agreement that, however tenuously, reestablished a Muslim-Croat alliance within a federal partnership in Bosnia and Herzegovina. The Croatian president ordered Šušak to rein in his henchmen.

The Washington Agreement was a generous face-saving option for Zagreb and a nasty slap for the Herzeg-Bosna mafia structures. The accord put an abrupt end to their wartime goal of hitching West Herzegovina to Croatia proper by force and cut deeply into the profiteering that had turned common criminals into multimillionaires. One of Zagreb's first moves was to sideline such protégés as Boban and Tuta in favor of more reasonable voices such as Krešimir Zubak, a leading HVO official from central Bosnia with a reputation as a relative moderate. According to Zubak, Šušak had Tudjman's "full authority" in all questions dealing with Bosnia and Herzegovina. Once Tudjman signaled support for the Washington Agreement, Šušak fell in line. "Without Šušak it would have been very difficult to implement the Washington Agreement in the Herzegovina," explains Zubak. "I didn't have the necessary authority with these people. He did."

But Zubak says that even though Tudjman and Šušak consistently gave him the backup he needed, it soon became obvious to him that their agenda had not changed substantially. Tudjman and Šušak, loyal to the spirit of the Karadjordjevo agreement, envisioned the entire Muslim-Croat federation eventually linking up with Croatia in some kind of a confederative model while Bosnian Serb–held territory would join Serbia proper.

The Washington Agreement signaled another shift in U.S. policy toward Croatia. As dicey as the Croats could be, they were closer to Western objectives than Serbia was, and they appeared to be the only regional power that could pose a strategic counterweight to Belgrade. Even as the 1994 agreement was under negotiation and fighting ravaged central Bosnia, Washington picked Croatia as its favored player to end the wars in the Balkans. In exchange for its cooperation on Bosnia, Washington promised to help expedite Croatia's integration into Western political, economic, and security structures. More critically, it signaled Western acquiescence to a "military solution" to regain the rebel-occupied lands in Croatia, should a negotiated settlement fail. Not only would the United States turn a blind eye to arms procurements for the Croatian army, which had been policy for some time anyway, but there would be active assistance to the Croats. The Croatian army would get a helping hand in order to offset the military dominance of Belgrade and its proxies.

The West's contact man in the Croatian government was Šušak. Not only did he have Tudjman's ear, but he was the only person with the stature and clout in West Herzegovina to bring the Bosnian Croat extremists onboard—or push them overboard entirely. When talks stalled with the Bosnian Croats, says the then U.S. special negotiator Daniel Serwer, it meant a trip to Zagreb to see "Gojko." Serwer says that he and his colleagues had no illusions about the man they were dealing with, but they had no other choice—and they discovered that they could do business with Šušak:

> We could bend his arm and when we bent it hard enough he would yield.
> It was never a permanent solution but always bit by bit. While we were

always trying to extract from him what we wanted, he was extracting as much as he could from us.

Šušak, Serwer says, had a disconcerting style of conducting these negotiations. When asked a question, Susak would remain silent for an uncomfortably long period of time, staring his interlocutor straight in the eyes. The tactic unnerved some of the minister's counterparts but not Serwer. "I just stared right back and waited," he says.

Few Western diplomats saw as much of Šušak as the then U.S. defense minister William Perry, who befriended Šušak during their work together. Explaining his warm feelings for Šušak, Perry says that he respected his unswerving devotion to the national cause. Šušak also "shot straight" with him, he says, not a quality to be discounted in high-stakes diplomacy. But Perry goes further, describing Šušak, in a 2002 telephone interview with the author, as a "man of considerable integrity." That international diplomats such as Perry might have to curry favor with an array of dubious characters in order to realize U.S. goals is understandable. But to laud Šušak at his 1998 funeral, as Perry did (see chapter 1), or to extol his "integrity" posthumously seems gratuitous to the point of scandal.

The 1993–98 U.S. ambassador to Croatia, Peter Galbraith, describes Šušak as "easy to get along with" and his approach "businesslike" and "results-oriented." Over American coffee, Šušak was remarkably candid with Galbraith about his political past as well as Croatia's ongoing arms buildup. He would look Galbraith in the eye and say: "I don't know what happens. We put two MiGs in the hangar and then the next day we open it to find four there! They had baby MiGs!" Šušak would burst out laughing. But Galbraith says that he knew he was dealing with a shrewd operator in Croatia's defense minister:

> Šušak was up to his eyeballs in the smuggling of weapons, and he was not reticent to discuss it. But he understood that creating an army was not just about running arms, that it involves discipline, organization, logistics, the right kind of relationship between the officers and the enlisted men. All of those things Šušak understood in a way in which the former communist militaries in Eastern Europe, including the Serbian military, did not understand.

Šušak viewed Croatia's future in the Western alliance and looked to the United States, above all, for approval and assistance. He signaled that he was prepared to meet the U.S. diplomats halfway to get it. In March 1994 Šušak contacted the Pentagon with a letter urgently requesting its help.[20] "Our goal," the letter stated, is the peaceful transition of the Croatian military "to one which follows the model of the United States." The letter was referred to Military Professional Resources Inc. (MPRI), a company in Alexandria, Virginia.

MPRI boasts a prominent and controversial reputation in the debate over the privatization of military services. The company, founded in 1987, offers high-powered military expertise and training to U.S.–friendly foreign governments at not-so-friendly prices. Its payrolls are stocked with high-ranking retired U.S. armed forces brass, generals among them, and works in close collaboration with the U.S. military. MPRI is not the only quasi-official private contractor of its kind but it is the biggest player, with clients worldwide. Firms such as MPRI take on jobs deemed too sensitive or borderline inappropriate for the U.S. government to undertake, a kind of "out-sourcing" that goes on with the approval of the Pentagon and the State Department.

Šušak hired MPRI to "advise Croatia on the role of the army in a democratic society," according to MPRI, which had the indirect approval of the U.S. Department of Defense to offer the Croats a contract. The precise nature of MPRI's operations in Croatia in 1994 and 1995 remains the subject of investigative reports. U.S. officials say only that MPRI conducted training for noncommissioned officers and offered leadership courses—relatively innocuous assignments. Its license stipulated that MPRI could not provide the Croatian army with any direct military planning or advice on strategy. To do so would violate the UN arms embargo.

Its critics, however, claim that MPRI did just that: it aided Šušak in orchestrating the summer 1995 offensive against the hold-out Serbs, code-named Operation Storm. If this were the case, both MPRI and the U.S. government could be implicated in war crimes.[21] Croatia's top generals met many times with MPRI consultants. Among the firm's operatives in Croatia were its heaviest hitters, such as General Carl E. Vuono, U.S. Army chief of staff from 1987 to 1992, and General Crosbie E. Saint, commander of the U.S. Army in Europe from 1988 to 1992—a team, it seems, vastly over qualified to conduct "leadership courses." In the days before Storm, critics charge, MPRI provided the Croatian armed forces with "indirect" advice or "pointers" on how they might conduct an assault on territory occupied by rebel forces—all hypothetical, of course.[22]

In the summer of 1995 the military tide in the Balkans turned against the Serbs. But first the world would close its eyes while Bosnian Serb forces blitzed the Muslim-held enclaves of Žepa and Srebrenica in July, perpetrating the bloodiest massacre in Europe since World War II. Weeks later Croatia launched its long-awaited counteroffensive, Operation Storm, and wiped out most of the rebel Serb strongholds in their breakaway mini-state in Croatia. The strike, executed with textbook (Western) military precision, triggered the mass exodus of more than 160,000 of Croatia's Serbs eastward into Bosnia and Serbia, the largest single displacement of people in the war. The outnumbered Serb insurgents were no match for Šušak's modernized, well-equipped Croatian army.

While the Croatian government solemnly promised Western officials that civilians would not be harmed and that the Serbs would be welcome to return to Croatia, the reality on the battlefield proved otherwise. Entire Serb villages were torched, elderly men and women murdered. While the Croatian assault on the Krajina was not comparable to the brutal, systematic way that the Serbs ethnically cleansed eastern Bosnia in 1992–93, it had the same effect. As the Croatian Serbs left their homes on foot and by tractor, they were spat at and stoned by Croats. "They didn't even have time to collect their dirty currency and their dirty underwear," exclaimed Tudjman with glee, on a whistle-stop "freedom train" tour of the freshly liberated territories. "On this day we can say that Croatia stopped bearing its historical cross. This is not just the liberation of land but the creation of a foundation for a free and independent Croatia for centuries to come." The Serbs, the "historical cross" Tudjman refers to, would never return. Of that the regime made certain in the years to follow.[23] Croatia, for the first time in its history, had purged its borders of most of its Serb minority. "For Tudjman and Šušak, the result of the military action was one they had always intimately desired: the removal of Croatia's Serbs," writes Cohen of the *New York Times*.[24]

The West depended on Croatia to accept its gifts and to play by its rules, but it seems that Washington, indeed, underestimated the pizza baker from Ottawa. In making Šušak their go-between, Western negotiators thought they could exploit him to their advantage. But, in the end, it is unclear who was being used. Did the United States inadvertently give Šušak the green light (and perhaps the tools as well) to sweep out the Serbs from Croatia once and for all? Did they trust a man whose nationalist convictions and extremist background belied such trust? If Šušak had been a necessary evil as a negotiating partner, could they not have extracted more from him on the issue of human rights, on Bosnia or the return of the Serb refugees to Croatia?

Even with the trophy of Croatia's liberation in their cabinet, a prize that alone surely would have secured Tudjman's and Šušak's place in Croatian history books, the two men refused to relinquish the idea of partitioning Bosnia. When it came to Croatia, everything was possible. At least that had been the case so far. The Croatian president viewed the Muslim-Croat federation, the Dayton peace agreement signed in 1995, and the international peacekeeping mission in Bosnia as way stations to swallowing chunks of Bosnia and Herzegovina when those mechanisms fell apart, as he was confident they would. Tudjman, through Šušak and the other figures of the Herzegovina lobby, encouraged, advised, and funded the Herzegovina hard-liners throughout the 1990s, condoning their efforts to obstruct international implementation of the Dayton plan at every opportunity. The transcripts recovered from Tudjman's office after his death show that the Croatian president counted on Bosnia's disintegration and contemplated annexing Western Herzegovina, parts of central Bosnia, and even Banja Luka and Bihać as late as the spring of 1999.[25] The full goals of Croatian National Policy that Tudjman and the Canadian émigrés discussed into the wee hours in Ontario would end only with the deaths of Tudjman and Šušak.

One Ottawa-based émigré quipped that Šušak and company went from hijacking planes to hijacking democracy in Croatia. One might also ask whether Šušak and his allies "hijacked" the Croat diaspora as well. Diaspora Croats spent millions of dollars to aid Croatia in its hour of need—on arms, on humanitarian aid, and on political lobbying to push their host countries to recognize Croatia's statehood. But these people reached deep into their pockets for Croatia, not for Gojko Šušak, a minor diaspora player known to few outside the Ontario region. As a government minister, his appeals to the diaspora bore the stamp of the Croatian government, not that of Otpor or the Herzegovina lobby. Since there are no opinion polls in diasporas, it is impossible to tell where the worldwide diaspora stands on issues of the day. Certainly the greater Croat diaspora firmly backed Croatia's bid for independence and the liberation of the Serb-occupied territories. But neither Croats in Croatia nor diaspora Croats felt passionately about annexing Herzegovina and fighting the Bosnian Muslims. That hard-earned donations and "loans" ended up in the renegade mini-state of Herzeg-Bosna or the bank accounts of private individuals reflects on the nature of the Tudjman regime rather than the nature of the diaspora. Tudjman used the diaspora as a source to tap at his discretion, one that gave loyally and, to its discredit, asked few questions.

How was it, then, that these émigrés and not other, more moderate personalities managed to exert such a profound influence on Croatian politics during the 1990s? The answer, to a large degree, lies in the figure of Tudjman himself. The radical émigrés fit squarely into Tudjman's plans, a factor he astutely recognized in the 1980s. Tudjman not only relied on their money to finance his campaigns; he also relied on their extremism to help create the conditions for his rise to power. Šušak's foray into Borovo Selo, like the émigré hate speech and the gratuitous nationalist symbolism, taunted the Serb minority and radicalized both the Croat and Serb populations. The returned émigrés helped to shift popular discourse to the right, a prerequisite for Tudjman's success. Tudjman mobilized three key, like-minded constituencies in the early 1990s: the radical émigrés, the Catholic Church, and marginal, right-wing elements in Croatia and Herzegovina. This potent mix defined an agenda that would guide Croatia over the course of a decade concluding with the HDZ's fall from power in 2000 and the surviving executors of Croatian National Policy on trial in The Hague before the International Tribunal for Crimes in the former Yugoslavia.

PART II

Serbia: Little Helpers

The American identity is a strange concoction of cultures, but at its best it is a concoction prepared and cooked by each individual in his or her own kitchen.

CHARLES SIMIC, "Refugees"

CHAPTER FIVE

White Eagles over Chicago

"I was from a deeply patriarchal and patriotic family, and I was taught to love my homeland and America with equal measure," says Ohio-born Father Irinej Dobrijevich, a personable Serb Orthodox priest, director of the External Affairs Office of the Serbian Orthodox Church in the United States and Canada. Seated in his small, box-like Washington, D.C., office, where at first glance his traditional black priest's garb looks strikingly out of place, Father Irinej speaks passionately about the pain that Serbian Americans experienced during the spring 1999 NATO bombing campaign against Yugoslavia. The Clinton administration justified the military action on humanitarian grounds, saying it was the last remaining option to halt Serbia's brutal crackdown on the Kosovar Albanians. But this explanation rang hollow to Serbian Americans. "We, as Serbians living in the diaspora, especially the children of my generation, we could not understand America's turning on us," he says, sighing in resignation as he gazes out the window of his office toward Pennsylvania Avenue and the White House, only a couple of blocks away.

Father Irinej was born in 1955 in Cleveland, Ohio, the son of political exiles from a heavily Serb-populated region in eastern Croatia. Every Serbian American kid, he says, learns that the United States and Serbia were allies in two world wars. Nearly every one of them can rattle off the names of the seven Serbian Americans who were awarded Congressional Medals of Honor. And they learn—as Father Irinej emphasized in a private meeting with President Bill Clinton—about the "consistent underlying values" that bind Serbia and America.

"We couldn't understand how easily it happened that we, who were always allied with America, and proud of that fact, found ourselves on the other end of the deal. How was it that Croatians, Bosnian Muslims, and Albanians, the very ones who fought against America [in World War II], who were fascists, how was it they came to be allied with America? This is something that was beyond comprehension for us, and it was the first time we ever felt divided within ourselves. Being Serbian and being American were suddenly at odds with each other." Father Irinej pauses, thoughtfully strokes his gray-speckled auburn beard, and then shakes his head in disbelief, still genuinely perplexed by the past decade's course of events in the Balkans.

For seventy-eight days in the spring of 1999 U.S. war planes bombed Serbia until Yugoslavia's armed forces pulled out of the southern province of Kosovo. Throughout the campaign, diaspora Serbs such as Father Irinej, as well as thousands of others in Canada, Europe, and Australia, actively protested the foreign policy commitment of their adopted countries, a commitment just shy of a declaration of war. In the diaspora bastions of Chicago, Cleveland, London, and Sydney, émigré families picketed daily against the "NATO aggression," excoriating President Clinton and other NATO country leaders as war criminals and fascists. They perceived the "war against Serbia" as the apocalyptic finale of ten years of flawed U.S. policy in the Balkans. It was the last act in the gradual dismemberment of Yugoslavia by its historical enemies—abetted this time by Serbia's tried-and-true friend, the United States of America.

The diaspora Serbs in the United States insisted that they were not opposing America as a country, or their fellow U.S. citizens, but specifically the policies of the Clinton administration. Most of them, by the end of the 1990s, were equally adamant that they harbored no love for Yugoslav president Slobodan Milošević.[1] According to Father Irinej, or most any Serb you might ask worldwide, the U.S. administration had been badly duped by a coalition of adversarial forces ranging from the Vatican to Islamic-paid lobby groups. It was all a tragic mistake, they believed, which one day the United States would come to regret.

Father Irinej helped organize the day-long Lafayette Park rally in Washington on April 25, 1999, estimated to be the largest gathering of diaspora south Slavs since anticommunist Yugoslavs took to the streets in 1963 to upstage the U.S. visit of the then president of socialist Yugoslavia Marshal Tito. For this occasion the crowd of nearly five thousand had begun assembling in the capital the day before—arriving by chartered bus, plane, and automobile. The Serbs were joined by an assortment of antiwar groups, pacifists, Greek Americans, an isolationist right-wing fringe, and the far left, all of whom found common cause in protests against the interventionist policies of the United States. The day had special significance as it coincided with NATO's fiftieth anniversary summit, an upscale celebration taking place nearby in the Ronald Reagan Building.

The Serb émigré demonstrators, most of them presumably naturalized U.S. citizens, were there to let President Clinton, Secretary of State Madeleine Albright, and the NATO alliance leaders know how they felt about the attack on their "homeland." Whistles and sirens simulated the air raid alarms in Yugoslavia. Many protesters waved Yugoslav or Serbian flags and chanted pro-Serb slogans. "NATO is trying to demonize Serbia," complained Rev. Miroslav Lazarevich, pastor of St. Luke Serbian Orthodox Church in northwest Washington, venting his outrage to one reporter.[2]

"And they cannot do that without demonizing Serbian Americans. Those are our brothers, sisters, and children they are bombing over there!" Hymns were sung throughout the day for those killed in the strikes, while many in the crowd wore T-shirts printed with bull's-eyes, mockingly identifying themselves as "NATO targets."

Several times the crowd's anger against the Clinton administration turned nasty. "NATO Nazis!" jeered the crowd when it rushed the hotel residence of the Norwegian prime minister, mistaking the limousine of his visitor, the president of Azerbaijzan, for that of a high-ranking NATO official. "Hey! Hey! USA! How many kids did you kill today?" chanted demonstrators waving pictures of bombed buildings and hospitalized children. The next day the demonstrations were noted, if at all, in curt media reports.

"Our message wasn't being heard, not where it counted," rally organizer Father Irinej recalls, looking back over the weeks of demonstrations and a decade of lobby work. Father Irinej was right, ultimately. The protests had no impact on U.S. or western European policy. In fact, their tenor reflected the years of frustration with Western policy toward Serbia—and with their unsuccessful effort to reverse it. The bombing continued, and indeed was accelerated, in the weeks to follow. Finally, in mid-June 1999 the columns of Yugoslav army units lumbered out of Kosovo, possibly forever.

Serbia's withdrawal from Kosovo was a devastating final slap to the Serb diaspora, whose mythic conception of a "Greater Serbia" had never wavered. The state they envisioned, the one that Serbs deserved, encompassed all Serbia proper, including Kosovo, as well as Montenegro, most of Bosnia, and chunks of Croatia and Macedonia. Many diaspora Serbs watched in disbelief as their dream of a Serbia that stretched across most of the former Yugoslavia receded with every successive defeat of their armed forces—in Slovenia, Croatia, Bosnia, and then finally in Kosovo. At the dawn of the 1990s many diaspora Serbs welcomed the new nationalist spirit in Serbia, personified by Milošević, convinced the historical moment was right to forge a Serbian state from the remnants of Tito's Yugoslavia. They miscalculated badly and thus implicated themselves in the tragedy that befell their nation.

Unlike the Croat and Albanian diasporas, the Serb communities abroad never reached into their pockets to buy arms, nor did they send scores of volunteers to the fronts. They did not have to. In the wake of socialist Yugoslavia's disintegration, Serbia assumed de facto control over the JNA, which had one of Europe's most formidable arsenals. What was lacking was international sympathy for a greater state, the cause that inspired the bulk of the Serb diaspora.

Although the Western response to Serbia's wars in the Balkans was belated and timid, it was recognized early on that Milošević bore disproportionate responsibility for Yugoslavia's violent breakup. Even before armed conflict erupted in Slovenia in 1991, most of the major Western powers were wary of the Serbian president's belligerent tone and bullying tactics as he attempted to seize control of the six-republic federation. The allergic response of Yugoslavia's other republics to Milošević was predictable and triggered the disintegration of the country, a process that the Western embassies there saw unfold before their eyes. As Croatia and then Bosnia turned into killing fields, the weight of evidence against Serbia only accumulated. Most of the world's diplomatic players came to judge Serbia, embodied in Milošević, as the principal antagonist of the conflict, even if no one side deserved exclusive blame.

Despite million-dollar professional lobbying and public relations campaigns, the Serb diaspora failed to alter that underlying conviction, which ultimately determined the course, however inconsistent, of the West's approach to the Balkans. Nonetheless, the vociferous protests and energetic lobbying on the part of Serb communities worldwide did color the world's perception of the Balkan conflicts and, circuitously, the reactions of Western governments. By obscuring the debates of the day, the Serb diaspora deftly helped to confuse international public opinion and skew the foreign policy decision-making processes. In doing so it contributed to the half-hearted, indecisive response from the West that ultimately cost the entire region, Serbia included, so dearly.

Nor did the diaspora weigh in as a counterforce to Belgrade's excesses in the homeland, in postcommunist Serbia itself. The vocal support that the émigré communities initially gave Milošević was construed in Serbia as confirmation from their Westernized kinsmen of the righteousness and feasibility of the regime's expansionist project. "In the early 1990s the diaspora was perceived as, and indeed it was, Milošević's asset," charges Miloš Vasić, an editor at the irreverent opposition Belgrade weekly *Vreme*. "They bought the Greater Serbia idea hook, line, and sinker." Certainly the diaspora did not rush to bolster the upstart parties of the democratic opposition struggling to be heard in Serbia's first multiparty elections. To the contrary, the diaspora belonged to Milošević, as long as Milošević pursued a nationalist agenda—in the political arena and on the battlefield. The diaspora eventually backed away from Milošević in the mid-1990s when circumstances forced him to retreat from the Greater Serbia project.

Few diaspora Serbs today admit to indulging in the euphoria that greeted Milošević in the late 1980s and early 1990s. But at the time, in diaspora churches and Serb cultural clubs worldwide, Milošević was heralded as a bold nationalist reformer (a reincarnation of the nineteenth-century Serb hero Karadjordje!) who might restore Serbia to its proper place as first among nations in Yugoslavia. Even old-school monarchists who had fled

Yugoslavia in the sights of Partisan rifles excused the Serbian president's previous affiliations with the communist party in the hope of finally having their life-long dream materialize before their grandchildren's eyes. Should a Serb-run Yugoslavia not prove workable, as indeed it did not, the émigrés confidently believed that Milošević would stake out a Greater Serbia that linked all of those regions with Serb inhabitants.

There were notable exceptions to the rule of diaspora nationalism. One striking case is that of the California pharmaceuticals tycoon Milan Panić, who returned to Serbia in 1992 to take up the post of Yugoslav prime minister and spearhead one of the opposition's first serious challenges to Milošević.[3] But, as early as 1992, voices like Panić's were cries in the dark. For the most part the émigrés' chauvinistic instincts outdid, and outlasted, those of their cousins in the homeland. Serb peace activists in the United States and Europe tell of being shouted down as "traitors" and "Croat spies" when they launched events critical of the regime. There was no place for them in the diaspora organizations, they say.

By 1999, in the aftermath of the Kosovo catastrophe, most—but still not all—diaspora Serbs had given up on the authoritarian, corrupt, and internationally spurned Milošević regime. The diaspora abandoned Milošević because he betrayed the national cause in Croatia, Bosnia, and Kosovo, not because it finally grasped that this cause itself was responsible for Serbia's decimation. The enthusiasm for Milošević in the Serb diaspora ebbed over the decade with his every step back from the expansionist agenda. Eventually, after three wars and several hundreds of thousands dead, an important subsection of the diaspora, struggling for the soul of Serbia and fighting a worldwide network of Milošević loyalists, coalesced around Serbia's democracy-minded opposition. In October 2000 the mixed bag of anti-Milošević forces with support from the West finally ousted the Serb autocrat from power. But, in the end, the diaspora's part in the drawn-out overthrow of Milošević was stymied by the very dynamic it had encouraged a decade earlier.

Ten years before NATO's bombardment of Yugoslavia, an émigré by the name of Radmila Milentijević returned to Serbia in June 1989. Milentijević, a professor and university dean from New York City, was one of thousands of diaspora Serbs who, months in advance, booked commercial or chartered flights to attend the historic pilgrimage to Kosovo that would mark the six hundredth anniversary celebrations of the Battle of Kosovo. The patriarch of the Serbian Orthodox Church in Belgrade extended a personal invitation to all Serbs outside Yugoslavia to join the church on Kosovo's legendary Field of Blackbirds for the St. Vitus Day extravaganza on June 28, one of the Serbs' most revered holidays.

The diaspora churches, community groups, and newspapers bubbled over with talk of the anniversary all year. "Bon Voyage!" the front page of the Pittsburgh-based *American Srbobran*, the diaspora's biggest weekly newspaper, wished its traveling readers. The publication requested that they extend "love, respect, honor, blessings, and understanding to all Serbian Orthodox Christians at Kosovo and express to them—all—our best wishes on this glorious six hundredth anniversary." Orthodox parishes in North America and Australia had plans under way for long weekend "Kosovo programs" for those who could not travel. In addition to the other historical dimensions of the event, it was the first time that a diaspora community had been invited en masse to socialist Yugoslavia. It was a move that the church could not possibly have made without a nod from Serbia's new leader, Slobodan Milošević.

The date of June 28, 1389, is etched deep in the collective memory of the Serbs. According to legend, it was the day that the medieval Serb army fell to the Ottoman Turks, ushering in four hundred years of foreign rule over Serbia. The story of the valiant and hopelessly outnumbered Serb commander, Prince Lazar, who waged war against the infidel Turks and perished—rather than surrender—is an epic passed down in Serbia from generation to generation. The defeat at Kosovo Field launched four centuries of persecution and oppression at the hands of the Ottomans, which the Serbs broke only in the nineteenth century after years of tenacious rebellion. Entrenched in the Serb psyche is the conviction that Serbia was, and remains, a holy Christian bulwark against Islam, the frontline nation in a centuries-long battle between East and West. Kosovo is a potent symbol of that clash of values and civilizations.

Moreover, Kosovo, which lies due south of Serbia proper bordering Albania and Macedonia, is heralded by Serbs as the medieval cradle of their nation. The oldest monasteries of the Orthodox Church with their precious Byzantine frescoes are in Kosovo, and it is here where Lazar's bones lie in state. But Kosovo is also the historical home of a large, mostly Muslim Albanian community, which lays its own historical claim to Kosovo's rolling hills and fertile plateaus. The 1.7 million ethnic Albanians in "Kosova," as they say in Albanian, steadfastly maintain that they are the descendants of the ancient Illyrians who cultivated these lands for centuries before the Slavs arrived at the end of the sixth and beginning of the seventh centuries. It was a tremendous blunder, they believe, for the Great Power negotiators at the 1913 London Congress to place Kosovo under Serb rule rather than unite it with the newly created state of Albania.

By 1989 the Serbs' Orthodox monasteries had long been surrounded by the overwhelmingly non-Christian Kosovar Albanian population, and tensions between them and the politically dominant Serb minority had been steadily mounting since the 1970s. This reality fueled the perception of many Serbs that the Kosovar Serbs, and thus implicitly the Serb nation, were under siege again. Among Serbs in Serbia there were grumblings about the genocide in progress against their compatriots; incidents of rape and intimidation, grossly exaggerated by the Serbs, sparked calls for action by Belgrade to "protect the Serb minority." Estimates put the Kosovar Albanian population at 90 percent, while the police and administrative apparatuses were firmly in the hands of the minority Serbs. Earlier that year Serb security forces had cracked down hard on ethnic Albanian protests that had erupted in response to Belgrade's suspension of the province's political autonomy. The so-called pilgrimage to Kosovo in June 1989 was much more than a pious religious excursion. It was a flamboyant Serb display of patriotism, strength, and determination in the still undeclared war over Kosovo, and indeed over the whole of Yugoslavia.

Like many of the participants, Professor Milentijević drove to Kosovo through the length of Serbia. She held dual U.S. and Yugoslav citizenship and had visited Serbia regularly since she left as a young woman in 1953, but never had she set foot in the impoverished, faraway province of Kosovo, as indeed most ordinary Serbs had not. To an outsider, her decision to attend the St. Vitus Day celebration might have appeared strikingly out of character. A professor of history at City College of the City University of New York (CUNY) since the 1960s, she had specialized in southeastern European history until she entered the university's administration. During her years at CUNY, Milentijević declared herself to be a Titoist, a socialist loyal to the Yugoslav state. (Significantly she denies this today.) Faculty colleagues say that they never sensed a trace of nationalism in her academic work or in their conversations with her over several decades. Her abrupt switch from championing Yugoslavia's multinational socialism to endorsing Serb nationalism in 1989, they remember, caught them completely off guard.

Whatever her reasons for undertaking the journey to Kosovo, it would begin a tendentious final chapter in her not uneventful professional life. In 1992, at the age of sixty-two, U.S. citizen Milentijević would quit her job in New York to make the causes of Serbdom her own, leading her to hold two cabinet posts in Yugoslav governments, including the job of Milošević's minister of information. At the height of its international isolation, she would serve as the most prominent spokesperson in the world for the Serbian regime.

Milentijević and her companions from New York pushed on toward Kosovo as darkness fell. Their fears of being attacked by Albanians in Kosovo proved groundless. Rather, Kosovar Serbs in every Serb village they passed through welcomed them exuberantly with folk songs, country cooking, and plum brandy. At 3:00 in the morning a Serb peasant family put the group up for the night—an essential part of the full Kosovo experience.

In that rural dwelling Milentijević heard stories firsthand about the "terror" the Kosovar Serbs were suffering at the hands of their ethnic Albanian neighbors. "For the first time I realized the degree of persecution they were experiencing," she told me earnestly in her meticulously tidy Belgrade apartment, a choice piece of downtown real estate that she acquired at submarket price. The Belgrade City Council's special deal for Milentijević was the kind of perk the regime awarded its faithful, a token of gratitude for their services. "These people," she continued, referring to the minority Serbs in Kosovo, "were left and practically forgotten by the state. Nobody was protecting them."

The grievances that the Kosovar Serbs voiced to Milentijević do not rank as the most egregious of human rights violations, even if many of their concerns understandably produced anxiety. For example, their village, the Kosovar Serbs told her, was surrounded on all sides by Kosovar Albanian villages. They remembered that once, before a Serb holiday, an Albanian grocer reportedly refused to sell supplies, such as sugar and oil, to a Serb man from the village. And when Albanians offered Serb villagers tempting prices for their property, many of the villagers in the region jumped at the opportunity.[4] The exodus of Kosovar Serbs to Serbia proper and the explosion of the Kosovar Albanian birth rate combined to tip the ratio of Albanians to Serbs dramatically. Milentijević says that she herself saw the pockmarks on the outer walls of houses, allegedly potshots taken at the Serbs from nearby hills.

There is a vast discrepancy between the conditions the Kosovar Serbs and Kosovar Albanians describe in Kosovo in the late 1980s, one that speaks volumes about the gulf between the two peoples at the time. The Serbs Milentijević spoke with probably were not lying: tensions were high by then, and it is entirely conceivable that Albanian farmers used Serb villages for occasional target practice. But to claim that Serbs were defenseless victims in Kosovo, let alone the target of genocide—as she does—is absurd. The Serb police, paramilitary security units, and the Yugoslav army were thick in Kosovo, and the victims of their unchecked power were the Kosovar Albanians.

Independent international human rights groups, including Amnesty International, Human Rights Watch, and the Germany-based Gesellschaft für Bedrohte Völker, confirm that the Serb authorities were trampling over the rights of Kosovar Albanians with impunity. Following Milošević's unilateral decision to dissolve Kosovo's political autonomy, thus relegating it to the status of a virtual fief of Serbia, Kosovar Albanian demonstrations in 1989 were suppressed with brute force, leaving twenty-two dead and hundreds imprisoned. The indiscriminate violence of the state was a daily fact of life for the powerless Kosovar Albanians.

Thus the climate into which the Serb pilgrims stepped in June 1989 was already rife with animosity and fear, which the St. Vitus Day ceremony would only further inflame.

Even today Milentijević and other diaspora figures speak in hushed tones about the Kosovo rally at which many hundreds of thousands of Serbs met on the sacred old battlefield. The footage that would be broadcast for years to come on state television shows dense streams of people packed into the broad swaths that had been cut into the wild undergrowth of the hills. The diaspora communities, brandishing banners and flags that announced their city or club, were well represented. One snapshot shows Maryland Congresswoman Helen Delich Bentley, a Serbian American, and Robert (Rade) Stone, the president of the oldest émigré organization in the United States, the Serb National Federation, posing on the battlefield with a big American flag.

Milentijević's placid face becomes animated and her brown eyes light up as she recalls the event with undiminished pride: "It was a very exhilarating experience—spiritually, intellectually, emotionally." In her spoken English, a slight Slavic intonation fades in and out from underneath her acquired New Yorkisms. She strikes one at first as an eager-to-please great-aunt, one who might at any moment bring out a plate of freshly baked cookies. But at CUNY, as well as in Serbia during her tenure as a state official, both admirers and detractors agree that her innocuous air masked an ambitious, uncompromising personality. "I was one of a large number of people who shared something very important in Kosovo," she says, pausing, "a common sense of identity and history."

When not in Belgrade, Milentijević lives in her uptown Manhattan apartment overlooking the Hudson River. She never married or had children. Her colleagues in CUNY's history department barely got to know her before she joined the university's administration, climbing to associate dean and deputy to the chancellor for university relations. She retired early, earning $72,000 a year in 1992. Milentijević's academic publishing was scant, amounting to just a handful of book reviews. Instead, she chose to devote her energies to the administration and volunteer work in the university chapter of the faculty labor union. She holds season's tickets to the Metropolitan Opera and, in the old days, summered in her second home on the Croatian coast near Dubrovnik. Milentijević became a member of the Serb National Federation only in 1990, after the Kosovo rally.

On the Kosovo Field, Milentijević was among the multitude that waited patiently for hours in the glaring sun for the man of the hour to arrive. From a helicopter Milošević descended like a demigod onto the platform festooned in red, white, and blue Yugoslav flags. The famous words he spoke there would make Serbs king for the day in Kosovo. They would also set the stage for the country's disintegration:

> Serbs in their history have never conquered or exploited others.
> Through two world wars they have liberated themselves, and, when they could, they also helped others to liberate themselves. . . . The Kosovo heroism does not allow us to forget that, one time, we were brave and dignified and one of the few who went into battle undefeated. . . . Six centuries later, again we are in battles and quarrels; they are not armed battles, though such things cannot yet be ruled out.

But in 1989 the thought that armed battles would soon engulf Yugoslavia seemed alarmist. Diaspora Serbs were not pondering war; they were awakening from a long, restless slumber. In contrast to Croat émigrés' spectacular hijackings and bombing campaigns, the Serbs were relatively docile during the postwar years, expending more energy attacking one another than fighting the despised communist regime. During these dormant decades they nurtured a dangerous set of myths that they would mistake for reality when the Cold War came to an abrupt end.

One striking characteristic of Serbia's diaspora is that most of its members do not hail from Serbia proper at all. The first great influx of Serb émigrés into the United States in the 1880s came almost entirely from the Austro-Hungarian territories adjacent to Serbia, especially those along the Dalmatian coast of the Adriatic Sea. A large number of Serbian Americans, in particular, trace their origins to these old Serb communities in present-day Bosnia and Croatia, a fact that would influence their emotional reaction to the wars there in the 1990s.

Like many of America's other immigrants, the rural-born "old settlers" found jobs in the factories, mines, and steel mills of the American Midwest and Northeast. Humbly they worked their way up the socioeconomic ladder into the American middle class. Still today, in towns that once had a mine or factory—such as Lackawanna, New York; Steelton, Pennsylvania; or Windsor, Ontario—second- and third-generation Serbian Americans attend the local Orthodox church every Sunday for the holy liturgy. Afterward, in the parish social center or at home, families serve traditional feasts with plenty of plum brandy and strong coffee. An unread copy of the *American Srbobran*, printed half in English, half in Serbian, may be found scattered somewhere.

These working-class Serb immigrants had little in common with the next major migration from the Old Country. The so-called newcomers were the displaced officer corps and other royalist sympathizers escaping communist Yugoslavia after World War II, political exiles bitter about their lost property and status, resentful of their unwanted new neighbors, and convinced that a victorious return to the homeland was imminent. Despite their differences with the "old timers," they followed the early generations of emigrant Serbs to the regions where they had put down roots. The exiles' demeanor would recast the face of the Serb diaspora.

Almost to the last man the immediate post-1945 émigrés were Serb monarchists of one stripe or another, which most would remain into the 1990s. They escaped Yugoslavia with Tito's Partisans in deadly pursuit and pledged loyalty to the deposed and exiled king Peter II. In King Peter's veins ran Karadjordjević blood, that of one of two dynasties that had ruled Serbia (or Yugoslavia or both) since it threw off the Ottoman yoke. Rather than accept puppet status under the Nazis, the teenage king and his entourage fled into exile in 1941.

Many of the new émigrés had served under the royalist supreme commander General Draža Mihailović, leader of the nationalist resistance movement known as the Chetniks. It was in 1941, upon Yugoslavia's capitulation to Nazi German–led Axis troops, that Mihailović and his men took up arms as a nationalist guerrilla force. At first, with just a couple of dozen men, Mihailović holed up in the steep ravines of Ravna Gora in western Serbia. There he collected the shattered remnants of Yugoslavia's royal army to build a new fighting force. The royalists looked to London for orders, where King Peter presided over a reconstituted government-in-exile, which initially enjoyed the full confidence of Britain's wartime leaders. Mihailović's mission: to frustrate the German war effort until a popular uprising against Nazi occupation could muster itself.

The account of Mihailović's actions and associations during the war is complex and remains the subject of debate among scholars. Some say that Mihailović was more concerned with beating his communist rivals to power within Yugoslavia than with repelling the Nazis, a charge the Allies ultimately concurred with. But to émigrés loyal to the Mihailović movement, their larger-than-life "Draža" was a resolute anti-fascist and Western-minded Anglophile who fought the Germans tooth-and-nail.

In a North Chicago suburb, a bronze bust of the bearded, bespectacled Mihailović studiously surveys the hole-in-the-wall offices of the Serbian National Defense Council of America (SNDC). The organization, one of the largest and most active of the Serbs' diaspora groups in North America during the Cold War, was founded in 1914 and then taken over by the postwar exiles in the 1940s. Tacked into brittle wallpaper are fading maps and portraits of Mihailović. Loose stacks of the SNDC's monthly newspaper, *Sloboda* (Liberty) lie piled high against cluttered shelves. Early on a weekday morning, sixty years after the monarchy's demise, a handful of officious older gentlemen shuffle around the premises as if the struggle were as fresh as the day of Mihailović's capture. Taken by the Partisans in 1946, he was tried and executed several months later.

How could an 1893–born monarchist guerrilla leader straight out of a history textbook still be relevant today? Just ask SNDC president Slavko Panović: "General Mihailović is relevant as long as the Serbian people exist," he explains in his cramped office. The communists, he argues, as do most royalists, rewrote history to make Mihailović a Nazi collaborator. This, says Panović, is another communist lie. "He didn't know the word *surrender*! Mihailović stood up against the Nazis and for the Serb nation, but he was betrayed," he says, referring to the West's decision to support Tito's Partisans during World War II. Mihailović "stays in the souls and minds of Serbs today," a hero whose spirit will one day lead "Serbia to rise to its former glory." Young people in Serbia, says Panović, would do well to emulate a Serb hero like Mihailović.

During the Cold War years royalist émigrés in groups such as the SNDC labored to keep alive the supreme commander's fighting spirit in anticipation that one day it would burn brightly again in Yugoslavia. The obvious obstacle to a Chetnik revival was communism, personified in the Croat Tito, the murderer of Mihailović and tens of thousands more. Behind the guise of Yugoslav "brotherhood and unity," they charged, Tito's ambition was to tie Serbia's hands, keep it humble, truncated, and weak. Serbia was Yugoslavia's biggest nation with more than eight million citizens, nearly 40 percent of Yugoslavia's population. But a quarter of that number lived stranded outside the Serbian republic, above all in Croatia and Bosnia. Tito, of Slovene and Croat parentage, penalized Serbia for its size, sacrificing its greatness for the benefit of the smaller republics. What other republic, the royalists groused, had "autonomous provinces" within its borders such as Serbia had with Kosovo and Vojvodina? The West's support for Tito drove the fanatic anticommunists crazy with indignation. How is it, they asked, that Western leaders could back a devout communist rather than their movement, whose fighters in 1944 rescued five hundred U.S. Air Force personnel trapped behind enemy lines in Serbia?

Occasionally a radical fringe of the diaspora Chetniks would mimic the kamikaze stunts of their Croat counterparts. In 1975 one infamous SNDC denizen, Nikola Kavaja, acting without the group's approval, bombed the suburban home of the Yugoslav consul in Chicago, the first of a spate of attacks against Yugoslav state targets in the United States and Canada between 1975 and 1978. The Montenegro-born Kavaja and his co-conspirators were later apprehended in an FBI sting and convicted for the bombings as well as for plotting to blow up two Yugoslav receptions commemorating the country's national day. But on a November 1979 American Airlines flight to Chicago, where he was to receive his sentence, Kavaja managed to free himself and burst into the pilot's cabin where the convicted terrorist declared that he had fifteen sticks of dynamite strapped to his body. Taking crew members hostage, he redirected the plane to New York, where he transferred to a longer-range airplane and flew on to Ireland. His plan: to take over the cockpit controls and crash the jet into Tito's headquarters in Belgrade.

Fortunately, in the air, Kavaja's lawyer, on the flight and obviously acting in his own very immediate self-interest, talked his client out of the suicide mission. Kavaja, who received a sixty-seven-year sentence, now lives in Belgrade. His former lawyer, Deyan Brashich, represents Bosnian Serb officers on trial for war crimes before the international war crimes tribunal in The Hague.

The Yugoslav secret police responded to the bombing in Chicago and other sporadic attacks on Yugoslav targets abroad by gunning down one of *Sloboda*'s editors in broad daylight. The newspaper's dog-eared back issues show the tall, middle-aged man, Dragisa Kasakovich, fatally slumped in the doorframe of the Chicago office, his white shirt soaked with blood. The 1977 killing, if indeed it was the work of Tito's special agents, would support the charges of U.S. diaspora leaders that the Yugoslav spy services were present and active in the American émigré scene.[5] Tiny as these organizations might have been, and as ludicrous as their plans were, it seems that Belgrade was not taking any chances. Despite a long investigation, however, Kasakovich's murderer was never found, and U.S. authorities could uncover no concrete evidence that his slaying was the work of Yugoslav agents planted in the United States.

During these long decades of the Cold War, Serbian Americans cultivated a collection of historical illusions that became part of their thinking. Their account of the Mihailović legacy, a cornerstone of the postwar diaspora's worldview, is one such aberration in reason. It is true indeed that, when the Axis powers first occupied Yugoslavia, the Allies, in particular the British, put their support behind Mihailović to build an army and frustrate the German occupiers. And this the royalist forces tried to do. However, after some punishing initial strikes against the Nazis, the Mihailović forces were shaken by the Germans' brutal reprisals against Serb civilians. They eased up while Tito's Partisans proved decisively less squeamish. The Chetniks then had an unexpected rival on the battlefield, and civil war broke out soon after between Partisans and Chetniks. In addition, the Serb royalists boasted that they would "cleanse Bosnia of everything that is not Serb" and killed tens of thousands of non-Serbs in pursuit of that goal. At one point Mihailović entered talks with the occupying force, forging a short-lived pact with the Germans against the surging communist guerrilla army.

In the end, the British gave up on Mihailović and threw their resources behind Tito. The claim that Mihailović was the West's unquestioned ally-of-choice as well as an uncompromising foe of the Nazis simply fails to square with the historical record.

The émigré communities' heroic version of Mihailović's deeds is a choice example of how historical half-truths led to one diaspora's skewed perception of events in the 1990s. Take, for example, Father Irinej Dobrijevich's claim that an anti-fascist Serbia (behind Mihailović and the crown) and the United States were staunch allies in World War II. In fact, as noted, the British backed Mihailović only from 1941 to 1943, and the Serb general collaborated sporadically with the Germans. Further, the contention that "the Serbs" or even most Serbs were in a united royalist front against Nazi occupation is a myth, as is the insinuation that all Croats and Bosnian Muslims were committed Ustashe fascists. Serbs and Croats numbered prominently in the Partisan ranks, as did Bosnian Muslims. Moreover, the standard diaspora account fails to consider the collaborationist Nedić administration in Serbia, the caretaker regime installed by the Nazis. The Nedić government's anti-Semitic shock troops belong to another faction, headed, until his death in 1945, by the Serbian fascist Dimitrije Ljotić. In short, there was no consensus among "the Serbs."

Their selective, self-aggrandizing versions of World War II history led many diaspora Serbs to conclude that Serbia and Serbs are, by their very nature, anti-fascist and close to the West. This is the continuity in values that Father Irinej told President Clinton about, which makes Serbia and the United States "natural allies." The other side of the coin is that Croats, Germans, and others are somehow genetically disposed to fascism: they are "genocidal peoples," according to Serb propaganda. Through this kind of prism it is impossible for loyal émigrés to fathom the dark side of Serb nationalism with the sieges, massacres, and rapes carried out in its name in the 1990s. They firmly believe, instead, that the Serbs, the West's allies in two world wars, could not possibly murder and defile. These despicable acts are the purview of fascists like the Croats and the Muslims. No wonder Father Irinej shakes his head in disbelief when he reflects on the past ten years.

In late 1944 Axis-allied forces were in retreat across Yugoslavia. The Partisans and the Soviet Red Army marched into Belgrade and through Serbia arresting or killing the trapped Chetniks. Several of the monarchist units in Serbia directly under Mihailović's command were wiped out entirely, while the Chetnik forces from western Bosnia, eastern Croatia, and Dalmatia fled nearly intact through Austria and Italy. The first destination of some twenty thousand assorted Serb royalists was Eboli in southern Italy, where the British suited them up in Royal Air Force uniforms and set them to work in noncombatant positions, such as guard and patrol duty. The monarchists' pro-British leanings obviously still counted for something. In 1947 Serb prisoners of war were packed off to detention camps in Germany for screening. Even though more than one hundred men of the Serb "Surrendered Enemy Personnel" were listed as war crimes suspects, not a single one of them was delivered to Yugoslavia or stood trial elsewhere.

From the camps for displaced persons in war-ravaged Germany, the royalist exiles dispersed across the world, often following the path of their former field commanders. The Chetniks of western Bosnia and Croatia in "Duke" Momčilo Djujić's Dinaric division ended up in the United States and Canada. (In 1990, from his California headquarters, the elderly Djujić took it upon himself to bestow the highest Chetnik title, Vojvoda (duke), on Serbia's ultra-right leader Vojislav Šešelj, a man whose killer commando units operating in Croatia and Bosnia carried on the very worst of the Chetnik tradition.) Other Chetnik factions settled in the American Midwest, heavily in the Chicago region, and in Australia as well. There they promptly set up organizations such as the Movement of Serbian Chetniks Ravna Gora Society and Royal Combatants "Draža Mihailović." In Chicago the Yugoslav consul bomber Kavaja had his own militant-minded group.

Many of the fascist Ljotićevi, sympathizers of Nazi collaborator Dimitrije Ljotić, stayed on in Germany, particularly around Munich, where they operated their own publishing house and newspaper, *Iskra* (Spark). Several thousand other Ljotićevi made their way to northern England. In 1974 Ljotić's brother, the movement's leader for nearly thirty years, was shot to death by Yugoslav agents in Munich. The Yugoslav secret services obviously had more than just émigré Croats on their hit lists.

King Peter, in name at least, remained the leader of the now-exiled monarchist movement, but the deposed monarch and the royal family drifted between Europe and North America, financially ruined and without a proper home base, nurturing the fantasy that one day they would return to the throne. Karadjordjević struck a forlorn figure, a symbol to Serbia's political exiles but one without power or vision. Rival émigré groups drew the hapless king into their incessant schemings and quarrels. The royalist community resembled a bad caricature of a powerless, squabbling diaspora. Unlike its fictionalized account in Lawrence Durrell's captivating novel, *White Eagles over Serbia*, the plan that a hold-out Chetnik underground in central Serbia would link up with royalist émigrés in Europe to overthrow Tito proved hopelessly romantic. No white eagles, the royalist coat-of-arms, could fly over Serbia until communism was defrocked.

The year 1963 proved a bittersweet one for the Serb diaspora. Before a schism in the diaspora's Serb Orthodox Church split its flock from Los Angeles to Sydney, the Serbs savored an ephemeral moment of unity and, albeit briefly, the unusual taste of revenge. Shortly thereafter the church schism would render the Serbs politically powerless until the 1990s. But first the diaspora Serbs proved what they could do when working together.

President John F. Kennedy's invitation to Marshal Tito to visit the United States was a plum for the Yugoslav president. At age seventy-one the old Partisan commander craved recognition as a great world figure: as a victor in the war against Nazi Germany, as the unifier of Yugoslavia, and as an international statesman. He prided himself as the leader and symbol of the growing "non-aligned movement," an alliance of mostly Third World countries that spurned the rigid dichotomy of the Cold War blocs, lining up neither behind Washington nor Moscow. Tito the World Statesman and Visionary pronounced that a new era of peaceful coexistence between countries with different ideological views had already begun. The Cold War was winding down for good, he told the United Nations General Assembly in New York, obviously a bit prematurely. Kennedy was prepared to reach out cautiously to the maverick communist, not least to foil any chances of a Yugo-Soviet rapprochement.

The news of Tito's ten-day visit in mid-October 1963 galvanized the hodgepodge of Serbian American groups around the country for the first and last time during the Cold War. Independently of one another the south Slavic émigré communities in the United States prepared a rude welcome for the Yugoslav marshal. At the forefront of the Serbs' campaign was Bishop Dionisije Milivojevich, the diaspora church's top clergyman. Thousands of signatures were collected and sent to the U.S. Congress, where hard-line anticommunist Republicans were particularly receptive to the émigrés' ire. The House and the Senate passed resolutions against the visit. The Serb exiles organized press conferences and demonstrations, distributed pamphlets, and chastised Tito on the airwaves. Rumors circulated about a possible assassination attempt. With a nonstop barrage of phone calls, organized groups of older Serbian American women harangued San Francisco's Fairmont Hotel, where Tito was scheduled to stay. "We created a real mess in San Francisco," says Michael Djordjevich, who at that time was a young Serb émigré fresh from duty in the U.S. Army's Special Forces. A contented smile crosses his ruddy face at the memory of it. "It was a disaster for Tito," he says.

The protesters on the East Coast chased the Yugoslav president from event to event. "Ti-to, mur-der-er!" they heckled him. Young girls in peasant costumes carried placards outside the White House denouncing the $2.5 billion in U.S. aid extended to Yugoslavia since 1948. One unamused observer of the spirited demonstrations was the distinguished diplomat George Kennan, who had recently served as U.S. ambassador to Yugoslavia. "The hostile demonstrators," he later noted in his memoirs, "including some in full Nazi uniform, were assembled in droves across the street from the White House;

and their savage screams and chants were audible even over the strain of the two national anthems as the ceremony of welcome proceeded."[6]

In New York City one protester, dressed up as Marshal Tito, drove a fabricated chariot drawn by six compatriots in black-and-white skeleton costumes up and down Park Avenue. The long-bearded Bishop Dionisije seemed to be everywhere at once. On the picket lines near Tito's residence in New York, skirmishes broke out first with New York City police and then with the Yugoslav leader's burly security detail. When Tito succumbed to a bout of influenza and canceled the West Coast part of the tour, the San Francisco agitators naturally called the excuse bogus and proclaimed victory theirs.

On October 20 Tito's visit (and perhaps his life) nearly ended abruptly. Two twenty-year-old Yugoslav exiles from the Bronx sneaked through the security cordon to reach the thirty-fifth floor of the Waldorf Towers, where Tito was staying.[7] A mere few yards from his suite, patrolmen tackled and wrestled the two men to the floor. Tito was furious as was his American guide, the diplomat Kennan. The marshal complained directly to President Kennedy about the security lapse and acidly upbraided New York City's police commissioner in public. He then unceremoniously canceled a twelve hundred–guest reception that had been planned as his farewell party.

The trip ended in one final indignation when a bomb hoax delayed the departure of his ocean liner for nearly an hour. When Tito finally set sail from Pier 40 at Houston Street, the émigrés had every reason to cheer, at least for the moment. But their joy was short-lived, for storm clouds were gathering over the diaspora Serbs.

One émigré conspicuously absent from the picket lines in 1963 was the thirty-three-year-old graduate student, Radmila Milentijević. She had recently picked up stakes in Chicago, her point of entry to the United States, and moved to New York City where she was enrolled in a Ph.D. program in history at Columbia University. It was no secret that in Chicago she had been close to Orthodox church circles, especially to Bishop Dionisije himself, until a celebrated public falling out prompted her move to New York.

In fact, before Milentijević surfaced in Milošević's circle in the early 1990s, her name was known throughout the Serb diaspora. As the story goes Milentijević was a young, specially trained Yugoslav agent sent to seduce and discredit the vocal anticommunist bishop. The widely circulated charge within the diaspora was that she was in the United States to infiltrate and help split the diaspora church. The extent to which Milentijević directly facilitated the schism, if at all, remains the subject of speculation. But split the church did, with tremendous ill will and devastating consequences for the Serb diaspora.

By the early 1960s the Orthodox Church's stance toward the communist authorities had become a standing source of friction between Bishop Dionisije in Chicago and his superior, Patriarch German Djorić, in Belgrade. Like churches across Eastern Europe, the Serbian Orthodox Church was forced to strike a modus vivendi with the current regime in order to procure the minimal space it needed to operate. But the diaspora priests charged that Belgrade's "red bishops" had acquiesced too easily. When Belgrade finally excommunicated Dionisije, the renegade bishop announced the establishment of his breakaway "Free Church," which refused to recognize the legitimacy of Belgrade's patriarch. Across North America and Australia congregations were divided between those loyal to Dionisije and those loyal to Belgrade. The row even split the exiled royal family. In theUnited States the Dionisije-loyal *raskolnici* (schismatics) abandoned the church's seat at St. Sava Monastery in Libertyville, Illinois, for a new home in Grayslake, just eight miles down the road. Legal battles over property lasted into the late 1980s. Whether a plot of the Yugoslav leadership or not, the schism crippled the diaspora for the next two and a half decades.

No shortage of stories swirl around the enigmatic figure of Milentijević. What is known for certain is that she left Yugoslavia in 1953 (not illegally) to visit her exiled father in Paris, a former royalist officer. At that time, so soon after the war's end, she surely would have needed official approval to travel abroad, something not granted automatically to the children of right-wing political exiles, particularly not as early as 1953. Nevertheless, from Paris she traveled to Chicago where she met Bishop Dionisije, who had known her father. She lived in church residences and at some point, apparently, became his lover. Although Milentijević categorically denies the liaison, the rumors were powerful and persistent. The alleged affair and the extravagant gifts that Dionisije showered on the twenty-something Milentijević were gossiped about throughout the émigré community. The relationship assumed the dimensions of a public scandal, and in 1961 Milentijević left Chicago. In internal church deliberations one year later, Belgrade's Patriarch German presented the affair as evidence of Dionisije's flawed character.

Although Dionisije was expelled from the church, prompting the schism, the patriarch's ruling did not turn exclusively on Dionisije's ethical lapses. Nevertheless, in official records from the time, the Milentijević affair surfaces on a list of indiscretions that the Belgrade church authorities attributed to Dionisije.[8] He denied them all. Milentijević flatly denies that an intimate relationship with the bishop ever took place. "It's total and utter nonsense," she told the *Washington Post* in 1997. "What is very typical is our approach to throwing mud at people. If I were a man in this position, the [Serbian anti-Milošević] opposition would come up with all kinds of stories about how I robbed a bank. I mean it's absurd: a woman could not succeed without being a prostitute—that's the approach they're taking."[9] Today she responds calmly to the stale accusations and reiterates that there is simply not an ounce of truth in them.

What is true is that Tito and his agents worked strenuously to undermine the church abroad. In the diaspora the church was the potent focus of anti-communist opposition, the only institution and symbol that united North American Serbs of diverse political, class, and regional backgrounds. Émigré organizations come and go, but the churches of mono-ethnic diasporas are the glue that holds them together through thick and thin. The embarrassing fiasco of Tito's visit to the United States rubbed this in the marshal's face. In Yugoslavia itself the Orthodox Church was also a potential enemy, always better weaker than stronger. Ultimately the schism—never theological but solely political—would play directly into Tito's hands, fracturing the entire diaspora in North America and Australia, and depriving the Belgrade patriarch of large parts of his congregation (and its wealth) abroad.

As for Milentijević, there is no concrete evidence that she spied for socialist Yugoslavia and it is unlikely there ever will be. Even if the files of the Yugoslav state security services were opened, as were the secret police files in East Germany, their authenticity could never be verified. After fourteen years of Milošević rule, any files damning to a member of his administration could easily have been filched or doctored. The handful of former secret service officers publishing paperback memoirs in Belgrade today are notoriously unreliable.

Despite the absence of a smoking gun, perhaps Milentijević's explanation for skipping the 1963 anti-Tito protests reveals something significant about the continuity in her thoughts and actions over four decades. "I refused not because I was supporting Tito," she insists thirty-eight years later, adamant that she was never pro-communist. "But my position was, hey, we are citizens of this country [the United States] and we have a president who invited the president of Yugoslavia probably to do some important business. I'm going to respect that." She continues:

> I will not endorse communism as a way of life, as a system or ideology.
> But I will not try to interrupt the visit of the president of Yugoslavia, an
> elected [*sic*] president of Yugoslavia. He's a communist, he's a dictator,
> but it's up to the people of Yugoslavia to deal with that. So I took the
> same position that I did with President Milošević. He was elected, he was
> very popular. The best way I can help the Serb people is not going
> against the government but seeking the help of the government to ac-
> complish what I want to do.

Milentijević's seemingly jumbled explanation for staying home during the 1963 anti-Tito protests reads as a straightforward justification of her life's work. First, though, her claim to have abstained from the demonstrations out of respect for the U.S. presidency is deceptive. She had no such qualms in the 1990s about lashing out against the Balkan policies of Presidents Bush and Clinton. Moreover, she actually went to work for Yugoslavia, a foreign government under U.S. sanctions at the time. Further, it is blatantly contradictory for her to claim, on the one hand, that she was an anticommunist opposed to the Yugoslav dictatorship and, on the other, that she accepted Tito's life-presidency as legitimate. If one, then not the other. The contention that Tito was an elected leader is so preposterous—and out of place—that it must count as a gaffe, an unconscious slip back into the jargon she employed in the past, when she was a Titoist devotee and not a devout nationalist. Only hard-line communists would have the audacity to argue that the "elections" in the one-party state, a ritual with one name on the ballot, in fact amounted to a democratic expression of the peoples' will.

Why Milentijević stayed home in October 1963 is open for conjecture. Was it because she was loyal to Tito, and perhaps even in his employ? She, according to her own testimony, was willing to serve the government in power as long as she could "help the Serbian people" in that capacity. Coming from a dirt-poor village and a family with a monarchist past, her collaboration with the spy services could have been one way to escape the poverty and limited opportunities that faced her in Tito's Yugoslavia. But whether Milentijević worked undercover for the communist state, or even had an affair with Bishop Dionisije, is ultimately beside the point. In Milentijević, whatever her motivations, Yugoslavia could not possibly have wished for a more perfect agent. She was involved in a scandal that blackened Dionisije's name in 1961; she defended Tito against anticommunist protesters in 1963; she praised socialist Yugoslavia while a dean at City College for decades; and then, with equal adamancy, she stuck with Milošević to the bitter end in the 1990s. Her actions and statements served the purposes of the state for forty years.

In light of the diaspora's virulent antipathy to communism, it is curious indeed that it was the communist bureaucrat Slobodan Milošević who, in the late 1980s, effectively reunited their communities. (As of 1991 the two branches of the church are again under one roof.) The diaspora's willingness to forgive his leftist pedigree speaks to the power of Milošević's nationalistic bombast in the 1988–93 period. If the anticommunist diaspora could buy it, anybody could. The diaspora applauded the revamped constitution that dissolved Kosovo's autonomy and glowed with pride at Milošević's swagger. Scheduled reforms in the economy and a general glasnost in the arts and media raised hopes of further democratic changes, like those occurring in Poland and Hungary. They even hoped for free elections. But first on the agenda was the national question: the rightful borders of Serbia, be they inside or outside Yugoslavia.

One early beneficiary of the new openness of the state was the writer Vuk Drašković whose novel, *Nož* (The Knife), about the World War II Ustashe massacres of Serbs had shattered postwar taboos. In the mid-1980s Drašković, an avowed monarchist, toured abroad where he read to diaspora Serbs from *The Knife*. The royalist émigrés in North America, Australia, Sweden, and Germany swooned at Drašković's version of World War II, which, of course, glorified General Mihailović. "In 1985 they [diaspora Serbs] were very, very satisfied that I revealed the truth, all the truth about the genocide against the Serbs [in World War II]," Drašković explains today in his serviceable English. The tall, thick-bearded Drašković was an immensely popular figure in the diaspora, a fiery Chetnik and romantic bohemian poet rolled into one.

But on his return to North America a few years later, Drašković was stunned by the monarchist diaspora's embrace of Milošević. "I couldn't believe that so many of the Serbs outside Serbia would support Milošević. They promoted him as a national hero and a man who would create Greater Serbia, the man who will revenge them for the atrocities that the Ustashe committed against the Serbs in Bosnia and Croatia. I told them, 'You have no right to betray General Mihailović and to join the Partisans!'" he shouts at me, slapping the tabletop in front of him so hard that the coffee cups rattle on their saucers. He regains his composure, eyes still flashing. "Some understood, but the majority did not, unfortunately," he says.

It was not only monarchists who lionized Milošević at the time. He had entranced nearly the entire diaspora, political affiliations notwithstanding. One circle markedly less enthralled by the new man on the scene was that surrounding the monthly London-published newspaper *Naša Reč* (Our Word). Its editor and guiding light, Desimir Tošić, who founded the paper in 1948, had long agitated for a reworked social democratic version of Yugoslavia, a compromise model fashioned by reform-minded elements in the communist party and moderate currents of the anticommunist opposition. (Tošić became a founding member and vice president of Serbia's oppositional Democratic Party in 1990.)

A notable member of the *Naša Reč* group was Aleksa Djilas, a Serb historian of international repute, and the son of the famous Yugoslav dissident Milovan Djilas. The younger Djilas lived in England during the 1980s and participated, along with Tošić, in one of the few forward-looking émigré circles, Demokratska Alternativa, which sought to formulate a democratic multiethnic vision for a postcommunist Yugoslavia. "At the beginning," says Djilas, explaining the hysteria over the Serbian leader, "Milošević was everything to everyone." He continues:

For old-style communists he was as close as you could get to an old-style communist. To Chetniks he seemed like some kind of neo-Chetnik. To those who wanted to keep Yugoslavia at all costs he seemed like someone who might be able to keep Yugoslavia together with the help of the army and party. To those who were concerned about Serbian national interests, he could protect Serbian national interests. And to democrats, well, there was a certain liberalization that took place, for which he's not given sufficient credit today, but it did happen. He was also a banker who worked in New York, so some people were expecting economic reforms. They said here's a young guy who is primarily a manager and business-man rather than a party ideologue.

From the beginning the diaspora had a role in Milošević's script. The Serb leader's multipurpose popularity gave rise to a state-hatched scheme to put a money squeeze on the diaspora while the time was ripe. The Loan for the Reconstruction of Serbia, officially launched on June 20, 1989, eight days before the Kosovo celebration, was touted as Serbia's first step toward market reform. The idea was to petition the Serb diaspora, as well as Serbs at home, to raise more than $1 billion to fund development projects and eco-nomic modernization. Money would be borrowed from the diaspora and lent to promising applicants in industry, agriculture, tourism, and trade. The participants' investments in the bond scheme would be repaid with in-terest, eventually.

The campaign was kicked off with much fanfare. Packages of promo-tional material went out to the diaspora underscoring the patriotic message that it was the duty of Serbs everywhere to revive the Serbian economy. "The message was pretty crass," admits Brana Crnčević, one of the pro-gram's architects, also a key ideological advocate for the Milošević regime in the early 1990s. "It was: help us, we need money!" In Germany the gastar-beiter felt no small pressure to contribute to the public loan program—as much as two months of their annual salaries. If you were short on cash, bonds could also be bought with precious metals, valuables, or securities.

Although the scheme fell well short of its inflated goal, the diaspora chipped in selflessly. Radmila Milentijević, for one, lent the then unelected Serbian government $150,000 of her own savings, a hefty sum for a univer-sity professor. Chemical tycoon Milan Panić pitched in as well, as did mem-bers of Michael Djordjevich's family. In total, the loan program netted a lu-crative $151 million.[10]

But the fund's thinly veiled political objectives and practically nonexistent oversight mechanisms should have alerted any but a blinded nation to the rip-off in the making. After Milošević's fall from power in 2000, an official inquiry into "The Loan," as it is called in Serbia, revealed widespread fraud and misuse of the capital. The money loaned to economic projects went primarily to prop up Serbia's outmoded industrial sector, a bedrock of political support for Milošević. Nearly one-third of the funds disappeared without a trace. Ironically it was Milošević himself who enlightened an angry public about the project's missing accounts after his arrest in early 2001. When journalists accused him of having raided state coffers to pay for the wars in Croatia and Bosnia, he responded, no, the money came from the loan fund. In the end, few received back even a fraction of their investment.

In retrospect, the scam was typical of Milošević's manipulation of the diaspora. In contrast to his counterpart, Franjo Tudjman, Milošević unscrupulously milked the diaspora without ever reimbursing it in kind. Token gestures, such as appointing Milentijević to ministerial posts, won him nothing. There was never a diaspora figure in Milošević's circle with comparable stature to that of Gojko Šušak in Tudjman's administration.

One of the first crossroads where émigré Serbs might have nudged Serbia off its path of self-destruction was Serbia's first democratic elections in late 1990. In terms of resources and media, Milošević's Serbian Socialist Party had an overwhelming head start over all the opposition parties. The new radical nationalist parties received limited support from the Chetnik diaspora: both Drašković and his ultra-nationalist rival, Šešelj, managed to drum up campaign contributions from émigré royalists. (The U.S. diaspora response to Šešelj's coming out was as rapturous as its reaction to Drašković. The April 12, 1989, issue of the *American Srbobran* enthusiastically announced the U.S. lecture series of "Dr. Šešelj" describing him as a "real democrat and anticommunist." All his appearances were in the U.S. Midwest on the premises of Serbian Orthodox churches.)

These modest funds were sufficient to help Drašković and Šešelj mount decent campaigns, at least compared to those of the other nascent opposition parties. But a party like Tošić's Democratic Party, whose membership included many liberal intellectuals, went virtually unnoticed in the Serb communities abroad. Perhaps the votes would not have tallied up differently even if the diaspora had thrown its full weight behind the fledgling democrats. But it did not. And Milošević's party won Serbia's first free elections, hands down.

CHAPTER SIX

The New Lingua Franca

In July 1990 an eclectic group of high-profile Serbian Americans convened in Washington, D.C. The Serb diaspora's first lobby of the 1990s included the best and the brightest of the U.S. Serb community, men and women from strikingly diverse professions and political backgrounds.

Almost every one of the unlikely team would become a player—though on different sides of the shifting barricades—in the crises that would engulf Serbia over the decade. Congresswoman Helen Delich Bentley and bishops from both sides of the still divided diaspora church (not to be reunited until 1991) were joined by California insurance executive Michael Djordjevich, history professor Radmila Milentijević and the Serb National Federation president Robert Stone. Also in attendance was Milan Panić, the quirky founder and president of the multinational giant ICN Pharmaceuticals. Bentley assembled the informal committee to address what she charged was an ominous anti-Serb bias developing in the U.S. media and policy-making circles. On that score, at least, the personalities gathered in the U.S. capital were of one mind.

The group's participants all saw Serbia entering rough waters where it could benefit from their individual expertise and coordinated clout. (Less magnanimously, even then, more than one of the group harbored political ambitions in Serbia. Panić, for example, would serve as the Yugoslav prime minister.) The Bush administration, Bentley said, guided by the U.S. ambassador to Yugoslavia, Warren Zimmermann, had clearly positioned itself "against the Serbs." The U.S. media, too, had prematurely singled out Milošević as the top villain in Yugoslavia's unfolding tragedy. "We wanted to lobby for the Serbian cause," says Bentley, "to let people know that Serbians aren't all bad guys. People were only getting one side of the story."

Bentley's concern that Serbia was being short-changed in the U.S. corridors of power found a resonant echo in the diaspora. One of the explanations was the alleged pernicious influence of well-organized, well-funded Croat, Bosnian Muslim, and Albanian lobby efforts. The Serbs, on the other hand, had missed the PR boat. "The Serbs were totally oblivious to the importance of media in presenting a picture of you," explains Milentijević. "The Croats and the Catholic Church were experts in this. The Muslims were experts in this. So before we knew it, the Serbian people were being Satanized, labeled as oppressors."

In the United States the trickle of media reports out of Yugoslavia at the time had indeed begun to zero in on Milošević and his brand of nationalism as the main force fueling Yugoslavia's disintegration. U.S. policy makers also gradually came to this assessment, even if they could not agree on a fitting response.

In fairness to the diaspora Serbs' concern about media coverage, many Western journalists and policy makers relied reductively on the phenomenon of Milošević—a communist and an authoritarian nationalist—to make sense out of a complex and totally unfamiliar set of problems. Just as the Cold War expired, the Yugoslavia conflicts seemed to explode out of nowhere, sending journalists scurrying for a straightforward moral framework: good guys versus bad guys, oppressors versus victims. Yet, by the summer of 1990 the newly elected leaderships in Slovenia and Croatia were creeping toward independence, the latter heedlessly insensitive of its non-Croat citizens. Belgrade's nationalist posturing was met in kind by the new Croatian president, Tudjman, ratcheting up tensions across the region, particularly in those areas of Croatia with large Serb minority populations. Bosnia was nowhere on the map. Although Milošević was hit hard, the media failed to take the Croat leader to task with equal rigor. The German press was particularly guilty on this charge. The British and French media, in contrast, leaned toward the Serb position.

Although Tudjman may have gotten off the hook a bit easily, especially after 1991, the charges against the regime in Serbia and its minions in neighboring republics were not overblown. Milošević's manipulation of the federal constitution was making any compromise settlement between the six republics less likely by the week. In Kosovo the reports of human rights groups had begun to give a sharper picture of the daily repression and human rights violations that the ethnic Albanians faced. And in Croatia Milošević was busy setting the Serb minority on a collision course with the new Croatian leadership. At the time the lobby-forming diaspora Serbs refused to examine, with a critical eye, the policies being carried out in Serbia's name. To the contrary, they defended them as being right.

The question of the relative strengths and impacts of the Serb, Croat, and Albanian lobbies is nearly impossible to gauge. To be sure, Milentijević errs when she cites the PR campaign of the Bosnian Muslims, who had next to nothing in the way of spokespeople until well into the 1992–95 war. The Croat and Albanian diasporas, on the other hand, indeed had professional lobby firms active on their behalf throughout the 1990s. It is also true that they boasted substantially greater resources than the diaspora Serbs. (The figures the Serbs calculate for the operations of the Croat lobby, however, which stretch as high as $15 million, are certainly exaggerated.) The Albanian American Civic League wielded influence on Capitol Hill that the Serb groups could not hope to match (see Chapter 9). During the Bosnian war, the Croatian and Bosnian governments hired the New York– and Washington-based PR firm Ruder Finn Global Public Affairs to present a "positive Croat image" to members of Congress, administration officials, and the news media. The Croatian Americans enlisted top-name congressmen such as Kansas senator Bob Dole, the Senate majority leader, and others to back Croatia's bid for independence.

But the Serbs' contention that these PR and lobby campaigns stood offstage in the U.S. media's critical reports of Milošević simply does not hold water. The editorial offices of America's major newspapers and electronic media were not bought out by a few upstart ethnic lobbies. The actor responsible for those largely accurate reports was Milošević himself.

And as for U.S. policy, one could make a convincing argument that in the early 1990s (and beyond) Washington neglected the concerns of the Croats, the Bosnians, and the Albanians. Official U.S. policy in 1990–91 was to support the territorial integrity and sovereignty of federal Yugoslavia, despite Washington's grave reservations about Milošević. U.S. Secretary of State James Baker's famous quip, "We don't have a dog in this fight," accurately summed up America's hands-off approach to Yugoslavia at the time. Neither Ambassador Zimmermann nor the State Department expressed initial sympathy for the separatist yearnings of Croat or ethnic Albanian nationalists. The context for stability and peaceful coexistence in the region was a federal Yugoslavia, in one form or another. On the issue of Kosovo, Washington defended this position throughout the 1990s, despite the millions the Albanian lobby spent to shift the U.S. stand.

Nor did the diaspora Serbs acknowledge that Serbia had at its disposal all of the institutional structures formerly belonging to the six-republic Yugoslav state—embassies, consulates, press offices, and the like. It thus controlled an established propaganda machine with a worldwide staff.[1]

On several occasions in the early 1990s Bentley's high-powered contingent of Serbian Americans made rounds on Capitol Hill, at the State Department, and the editorial offices of major media, including the *Washington Post*. Separately they also visited Yugoslavia, where they called on Ambassador Zimmermann at the U.S. Embassy. According to Zimmermann, the diaspora Serbs he met with were incapable of distinguishing between Serbia's legitimate concerns and the person of Slobodan Milošević. They conflated the two. "Helen [Delich Bentley] can be considered a kind of litmus test for the Serbian diaspora," says the last U.S. ambassador to socialist Yugoslavia. "She started off as 100 percent pro-Milošević, even calling him a great democrat, and then slowly she became disillusioned." When it came to the Milošević hype, Zimmermann says frankly: "I wasn't buying it." Nor were his superiors at the State Department. In a discussion with President George Bush's top foreign policy makers, the coterie, according to Bentley, was told bluntly by Acting Secretary of State Lawrence Eagleburger: if you want to help your people, dump Milošević. It was a message the diaspora was not quite ready to hear.

The Bentley team's mission to Washington was not the first attempt by Balkan émigrés to influence the structures of power in their adopted countries—nor would it be the last. During the Cold War a host of émigré groups from the "captive nations" of communist-ruled Eastern Europe applied steady pressure on U.S. administrations and Congress. Their forceful message: stand up to the Soviet menace in its every manifestation, both internationally and at home. Any rapprochement with Moscow or its satellites, including the "Trojan Horse" Yugoslavia, was a sellout. The émigrés demanded that the Iron Curtain be torn down and Soviet Bolshevism rolled back. Their proponents in Congress were, first and foremost, right-wing Republicans who, in turn, welcomed their votes and campaign contributions. The propinquity of the émigré factions to McCarthyism in the 1950s attests to the depth of their obsession and its illiberal connotations.

The West's cautious friendship with Tito infuriated the Yugoslav émigré groups and fueled their strivings to sabotage it any way they could. Among its few accomplishments, the Cold War–era lobby ignominiously helped to finish off the decorated diplomatic career of George Kennan. Appointed by President Kennedy to the post of U.S. ambassador to Yugoslavia in 1961, Kennan immediately established an honest working rapport with Tito and promised the Yugoslav president that his country's Most-Favored Nation (MFN) status in matters of trade would continue without public debate or the usual tirades in Congress about taxpayers' money propping up a communist dictatorship. But in late 1962, despite Kennan's strenuous efforts, Congress ended a long-standing preferential commercial treaty with Yugoslavia and very nearly rescinded MFN treatment. The skirmish left Kennan looking ineffectual and foolish. He resigned his post shortly afterward, deeply disillusioned.

In his memoirs Kennan attributed the debacle, in part at least, to the campaign of "Croatian and Serbian immigrant elements." He noted that this was not the first time that ethnic émigré groups, often representing compact voting groups in large cities, were able to exert an inordinate influence on U.S. foreign policy. These groups, he claims:

> were not slow to wrap their demands, to suit Washington-congressional taste, in the relatively respectable mantle of a militant anti-communism,

denying the Yugoslav independence vis-à-vis Moscow, denying the
unique qualities of Yugoslavia as a Marxist-Socialist state, and doing all
in their power to establish the thesis that Yugoslavia was, to all intents
and purposes, no different from the Soviet Union. They were opposed to
the maintenance by the United States government of relations with
Yugoslavia; they would happily have seen us become involved in a war
against that country. This being so, they never failed to oppose any move
to better American-Yugoslav relations or to take advantage of any opportunity to make trouble between the two countries. And this they succeeded, with monotonous regularity, in doing.[2]

In Helen Delich Bentley Serbian Americans finally had one of their
own inside the U.S. Congress. She represented Maryland's Second Congressional District for five terms (1985–95), made an unsuccessful bid for
governor, and in 2002, at age seventy-eight, launched a campaign to re-
claim her former seat, which she lost only narrowly. A second-generation
American, she came from humble origins. Bentley's parents, both Serb
immigrants, settled in Nevada where her father worked in the copper
mines. She attended the University of Missouri (class of 1944) on a Serb
National Federation scholarship and then moved to Baltimore where she
eventually became maritime editor of the *Baltimore Sun*, the newspaper
that many years later would expose her links to the Serb lobby and dash
her political career. Later, she served as chairperson of the powerful Federal Maritime Commission and, in her spare time, ran the Serbian-
Americans for Nixon campaign committee in the early 1970s. In the
House of Representatives, Bentley's focus was on maritime issues and the
elderly, not Serbia. But American Serbs nevertheless contributed generously to her campaign accounts. Bentley was the star pupil from the
homeland who had made it good.

Bentley's first call to stand up for Serbia came in June 1988, when both
the House and the Senate drafted resolutions condemning the mistreatment
of ethnic Albanians in Kosovo. On the House floor, Bentley gave her fellow
congressmen a heartfelt sixty-minute lesson on the history of Serbia and
Yugoslavia. It was the same slanted version that Milošević and Serbia's nationalist intelligentsia were telling in the homeland, predisposing the population for the wars to come. "With [the 1389 Battle of] Kosovo, the Balkan
bulwark against the East was destroyed," she told America's lawmakers, referring to the defeat of the medieval Serbian kingdom at the hands of the
Ottoman army. "No longer would Balkan heroes protect the West from the
Hun and the Mongol, the Ottoman and the Russian," she said. "Coincidentally, even today, this field of battles, this widow maker, Kosovo, is in the
news and is the source of conflict among local peoples. Although Kosovo is

now part of Yugoslavia, Serbs and other Yugoslavs have become a minority people in their own country."

The Serbs, she contended, were good people: a proud group, fiercely independent, self-reliant, dependable as friends, loyal as citizens, family-oriented, and, of course, were U.S. allies in two world wars. Further into the monologue, Bentley branded the Albanians chauvinists who employ "murder, rape, pillage, humiliation, property damage, desecration—their age-old proven methods—to ensure their goal of an ethnically cleansed Kosovo" and ultimately a fascist Greater Albania.

In Congress, Bentley's long-winded speech probably fell on deaf ears. But diaspora newspapers such as the *American Srbobran* and *Sloboda* triumphantly reprinted her address on the front pages. It sent word to the diaspora that a new kind of battle was being waged, with a new lingua franca. The crusty rhetoric of "commies," "reds," and "Bolsheviks" no longer had currency. It also alerted chauvinists in Serbia to the fact that the diaspora, and maybe even the U.S. Congress, was behind them. Perhaps some of the U.S. congressmen in attendance that day should have paid more attention to Bentley's presentation. It was a chilling recitation of a kind of atavistic Balkan nationalism that most observers thought had perished in the 1940s. Coming from the mouths of Milošević and the extremist Bosnian Serb Radovan Karadžić, its consequences would occupy U.S. foreign policy makers for the next twelve years.

The Bentley-led initiative of prominent Serbian Americans concluded that the Serb community needed a professional, modern lobby and a full-time presence in Washington. The old Chetnik organizations such as the Chicago SNDC, its political coordinates embedded in the logic of the Cold War, looked sadly anachronistic in the new geo-political setting. But, as had been the case for decades, the effort to bring together the welter of diaspora groups and leading Serbian Americans fell flat, injecting fresh acrimony into their long-standing rivalries. Once again, diaspora unity proved elusive. Characteristically the loners Milentijević and Panić went their own very different ways. Bentley and Stone formed an organization called SerbNet (short for Serbian American National Information Network), and Michael Djordjevich founded the Serbian Unity Congress (SUC).[3] The SUC would emerge as the diaspora's most potent lobbying tool, and it brought Djordjevich back into politics after a long hiatus.

Upon leaving Yugoslavia in 1956, Djordjevich was thrown straight into the world of Serb émigré politics. He had come from an old Belgrade family with venerable monarchist roots, his father and an assortment of aunts and uncles having fled the country in the wake of the communist takeover.

Still today Djordjevich recalls his childhood impressions of the Wehrmacht's ferocious 1941 bombing of Belgrade, his family's flight to the countryside, and the reek of the corpses that littered the road to Belgrade upon his family's return. There was no possibility, he soon learned, for an ambitious young man with his blue blood to succeed in communist Yugoslavia. Moving first to Paris, then Milwaukee, then Chicago, Djordjevich finally settled in San Francisco, where he lives today with his family, one of the Serb diaspora's most influential figures.

"The goal was to overthrow communism, Tito," he says of the groups that he and his father, a former royalist officer, visited together. In diaspora circles, the Serb émigrés talked in terms of the restoration of a royal Serbia, not a kingdom of Yugoslavia. "They were anti-Tito, anticommunist, and anti-Yugoslav," explains Djordjevich, who was surprised at first by the rhetoric. A good monarchist, Djordjevich naturally believed that the Karadjordjević dynasty, with King Peter on the throne, should rule all Yugoslavia. But the groups that the Djordjeviches encountered saw it otherwise. They pleaded that Yugoslavia was a death trap for Serbia and the Serb people. It was something, says Djordjevich, that he began to think about.

The 1963 anti-Tito protests were the last campaign the diaspora Serbs would wage together before the church schism. The perpetual infighting and the knock-down, drag-out legal battles within the split church had disgusted Djordjevich. He opted instead to apply his considerable talents to U.S. politics.

"I thought I could be much more effective against communists in the [U.S.] Republican Party than those in Yugoslavia," explains Djordjevich with a wink over breakfast in Belgrade's Hotel Palace. A compact man with short-cropped gray hair and broad shoulders, he looks every bit as capable of serving up a volleyball as he did when he starred for the Red Star Belgrade team in the 1950s. His manner exudes the equanimity of the self-made California businessman that he is.

"American coffee," he tells the hotel waiter matter-of-factly in Serbian. The teenager, obviously confused, summons the head waiter who takes the order in duplicate, using carbon paper, and hands the pile of paper to a young waitress. Ten minutes later two traditional Serb coffees arrive at our table. "It's going to take a long, long time to get this country running again," he says with a grimace. Like other successful émigrés, Djordjevich is confident that he knows what his country needs. And though he does not express it, he knows he could make it happen, given the chance, and the ear of the right people.

During the 1990s Djordjevich's name had been bandied about in Belgrade as a possible future president or at least minister in a post–Milošević "government of experts." In addition to having "business smarts," politics was in his blood.

As a young émigré, Djordjevich cut his political teeth in the wild free-for-alls of California Republican Party politics. The year was 1964. The presidential candidate of the Republican right, Barry Goldwater. Djordjevich, his English still choppy, headed up the Young Republicans' campaign in the crucial California primary to defeat Goldwater's party rival, the "communist-liberal" Nelson Rockefeller. The red-baiting rose to fever pitch. One *Los Angeles Times* reporter, baffled by the hysterical mudslinging, called this new man on the scene, Djordjevich, a person with an "unpronounceable name and an incomprehensible political philosophy." But when the votes were tallied in California, Djordjevich's strategy proved to have been on the mark. Goldwater won, assuring him the top spot on the Republican Party presidential ticket.[4]

After Goldwater's landslide defeat to Lyndon B. Johnson in the 1964 presidential election, Djordjevich retreated from politics and immersed himself in family life and the insurance business. It was not until the Berlin Wall fell in 1989 that he reemerged with an essay in pamphlet form entitled "What the Serbs Want," which he distributed to his friends in Congress, to relevant policy makers, and throughout the diaspora community. It constituted a concise summary of much of the Serb diaspora's mind-set at the time, a vision of postcommunist Yugoslavia as seen through Serb-tinted glasses. The premise segued accurately with the monologue Bentley delivered to the House of Representatives a year earlier. Yugo-communism, as Djordjevich put it, was dead. It was now time for the Serb nation to extricate itself from Tito's yoke and its political, economic, and national subordination to other peoples. Only thus could a stable new order in the Balkans emerge from Yugoslavia's ruins. The Serbs had to assert their right to national self-determination, which had been denied them after World War II. The very first precondition for this was "ethnic and territorial unification of all Serbs residing in present-day Yugoslavia."

Djordjevich's short 1989 treatise is a straightforward manifesto for a Greater Serbia. Only once in the carefully worded essay is the existence of other nations or republics in Yugoslavia even acknowledged, and then not by name. At stake are Serbia's "vital interests," in particular the right to self-determination. There is no mention, however, of population exchanges, ethnic cleansing, or, as Milošević put it in Kosovo, "armed battles." The details of Greater Serbia (a phrase Djordjevich never employs), like its geographical borders or the fate of other peoples within those borders, are left unaddressed. But he warns: "The entire history of the Serbs has been but one superhuman effort and struggle to retain national identity and to secure national independence, freedom, unification, and a life of higher spiritual values. In this endeavor the Serbs are ready to pay any price and bear any burden."

Djordjevich chafes, as do most Serb nationalists, at the mention of "Greater Serbia." It is a term, he says, that Austro-Hungarian officials originally employed before World War I to discredit the idea of a unified Serb state. But essentially he concedes that, yes, the Serb people deserve to live together in the same country, just like other nations do. "Serbs have as much a right as any people to say where they want to live and how," he explains.

The borders of the six republics in socialist Yugoslavia were drawn up at Tito's caprice, he emphasizes, in a historical context that no longer exists. "Tito's philosophy was divide and rule. How can we today allow Serb aspirations to be put in a straitjacket created by Tito sixty years ago?" he asks. If the Croats opt to live in an independent Croatia, the Slovenes in an independent Slovenia, then the Serbs—including those in Bosnia and Croatia—can choose to live in an independent Serbia.

The Serbian Unity Congress, Djordjevich's brainchild, forthrightly advocated the cause of a Serb-dominated state fashioned out of former Yugoslavia. It included no explicit formula for its construction and underscored that the country would be democratic, constitutional, and free-market–oriented. Yet the process of creating an "ethnically and territorially unified" Serbia, as history would prove, could not possibly lay the foundations for such a state. In the ethnically mixed potpourri of Yugoslavia, the forging of mono-ethnic states could mean nothing other than ethnic cleansing and war.

The Serb lobby during the 1990s had a simple two-pronged public relations strategy of "promote and deny," which it executed with no small disregard for the truth. It advanced an uncritical picture of the Serbs and Serbia's aims, and denied absolutely anything that shed a negative light on Serbdom. By denying the brutal consequences of creating an ethnically and territorially unified Serbia, the Serb lobby made itself and Serbs abroad indirectly complicit in the disaster that befell Yugoslavia. Through their media, lobbying, and quasi-humanitarian campaigns, groups such as the SUC would champion the mind-set and processes that would rip Yugoslavia apart, leaving a truncated impoverished Serbia much smaller than anyone would have predicted.

Ironically the Serb lobby pursued its aims using the democratic platforms of its host countries. The SUC, as well as SerbNet, the London-based Serbian Information Center (SIC), and others, availed themselves of a wide spectrum of mostly legal options within the states they operated in. (Yugoslavia, under UN sanctions by 1991, was barred from directly hiring a PR firm in its own name.) The SUC was even registered as a tax-exempt, charitable organization in the United States, which meant that its lobbying work ("attempts to influence legislation") could not be a substantial part of its activities. In fact, though, it was.

Despite its campaigns, neither the SUC nor its sister organizations were able to win the allegiances of politicians, journalists, or respected experts in large numbers. But pro-Serb voices did manage to thrust their point of view into the heated public debate around the Balkan crises. In doing so they obfuscated the discourses and, arguably, indirectly influenced the response that Western policy makers would eventually take in the region. In the former Yugoslavia the symbolically important diaspora would be seen as a cheerleader for the warmakers, not, as it could have been, a cautionary voice on behalf of reason. Throughout the 1990s, its critics charge, the SUC acted as Serbia's de facto war lobby abroad, in contravention of U.S. law and Washington's foreign-policy objectives.

The SUC was never a big nor particularly well-endowed organization. Its activities coordinated out of one-man offices in Napa and San Francisco, California, and Washington, D.C. It relied extensively on the volunteer work of its network of only about six thousand members across the country, as well as individuals in much smaller operations in Great Britain, South Africa, Mexico, and Australia. (The SUC's London-based operation ranked second in size and scope to that in the United States. Among those on the SUC payroll was Sir Alfred Sherman, chairman of the Lord Byron Society for Balkan Studies, as well as a self-proclaimed adviser to Radovan Karadžić.) But the canny executive Djordjevich, a consummate professional, knew that professionals were required if the job was to be done right.

One of the SUC's first moves was to contract the services of the Washington lobby firm Manatos and Manatos,[5] the only reputable PR firm that would take its business—and also represent them at cut-rates. Manatos and Manatos is a familiar name in Washington political circles. Its president, Andrew E. Manatos, served as a U.S. assistant secretary of commerce under President Jimmy Carter. A Greek American, Manatos's PR and lobby firm holds the lucrative accounts of the United Hellenic American Congress and the Pan-Cyprian Association of America, among others. He is president of the National Coordinated Effort of the Hellenes.

In their faith the Greeks, like the Serbs, are Eastern Orthodox. The two nations also share a sharp antipathy toward Turkey, Albania, and Islam in general, common denominators that often caused their interests to dovetail in the Balkans. In the conflicts of the 1990s the Athens governments consistently lent a sympathetic ear to Serbia's grievances and periodically intervened in world forums on Belgrade's behalf.[6] In the diaspora the cooperation between the SUC and Manatos was just one instance of the friendly hand that the wealthy and large Greek community would extend to Serbian Americans.

Andrew Manatos, mustachioed and debonair with a deep baritone voice, claims he is not an expert on the Balkans, despite his years-long engagement with Greece and its neighbors, Macedonia and Turkey. It was, Manatos recalls, after meeting with Djordjevich in 1991 and listening to his arguments that he was persuaded that the Serbs were not getting a fair hearing in the United States. His firm's task was to help the Serbian Americans navigate the complex labyrinth of the U.S. political system. "We could show them how to get through the roadblocks, how to get the attention of a secretary of state, a senator, a congressman," he remembers telling SUC representatives in one of their first meetings. "And I explained this is an appropriate role, that as a U.S. citizen you are obliged to come forward if you have a particular expertise in a certain area."

Shortly thereafter, in the summer of 1992, the Serbs needed all the professional help they could muster to mount effective counterspin. The television images of emaciated prisoners in Serb prison camps and columns of Bosnian peasants fleeing Bosnian Serb and Yugoslav forces sparked an outcry around the world. The then-presidential candidate Bill Clinton vowed to stop—with force if necessary—the violent expulsion of non-Serbs from their homes. Among human rights groups, journalists on-the-spot, and most impartial diplomats, there was a consensus that Serb units and gangster-run paramilitaries were committing terrible atrocities in the territories falling under their control.

But lobbyist Manatos, based on briefings by the SUC, concluded that U.S. policy makers had prematurely singled out the Serbs as the sole perpetrators of the calamity unfolding in Bosnia and Herzegovina. In a line of argumentation that the Serbs would use throughout the course of the 1992–95 Bosnian war, Manatos attempted to convince both U.S. lawmakers and policy makers that the Bosnian Serbs were themselves the victims of persecution and ethnic cleansing *before* the full-scale fighting broke out. "When this was happening," he explains, referring to the alleged crimes against the Bosnian Serbs, "there was really silence from the world community, from the United States. Only then, when the [Serb] retaliation began was there extreme, extraordinary attention given to it."

According to most independent sources, Manatos's take on events is an inversion of the historical truth. The Serb lobby's evidence for concentration camps and massacres of Bosnian Serbs in 1991 and early 1992 is thin to nonexistent. Like the compendium of other claims the international Serb lobby would assemble, the contention that Serbs were the first victims of the war, and that their reaction was one of self-defense, exposed the diaspora campaign for what it really was: an apologia for the powers that be in Serbia and its proxy parastates. The Serbs posed their brief as "the other side of the story," the facts that had not come to light because of the ever-powerful Croat lobby, German diplomacy, and other anti-Serb conspiracies. Taken in total, though, the arguments of the diaspora Serbs amount to a straightforward endorsement of the Bosnian Serbs' war effort. They present a fairly accurate copy of the propaganda generated from Bosnian Serb leader Karadžić's mountain stronghold outside besieged Sarajevo and a rationalization for carving out a greater Serb state by force of arms.

The primary aim of the war for the Bosnian Serb leadership was to occupy all but small swaths of Bosnia, to rid that conquered territory of its Bosnian Croat and Bosnian Muslim citizens, and to join it to Serbia proper and Montenegro, along with the Serb-controlled parts of Croatia. This product would constitute (or, as the SUC put it, "reconstitute") Serbia in its natural and rightful borders. The first step for the national extremists was to convince both their own people and world opinion that this option was as inevitable as it was just. In Bosnia and Herzegovina, Serbs, Croats, and Muslims had lived alongside one another for hundreds of years. Turning neighbor against neighbor would not happen automatically. But the barrage of poisonous agitprop from Belgrade directed against Kosovar Albanians and Croats had already prepared the groundwork. With a flick of the wrist, it was redirected toward Bosnian Croats and Bosnian Muslims: the former assuming the cloak of genocidal Ustashe fascists, the latter (who were largely nonpracticing Muslims) transmogrifying into ruthless Islamic fundamentalists. The Bosnian Muslim leader Alija Izetbegović had the special honor of being branded both a raving Islamic fanatic and a Croat Ustashe war criminal.[7]

Now it was Bosnia, not Kosovo, that presented an urgent threat of becoming the bridgehead to an Islamic incursion into Western Europe. "This rise of Islamic fundamentalism has apparently resurrected the old zeal for Islamic expansion," wrote Djordjevich in the *San Francisco Chronicle* as early as April 1990. "There is an agenda for the extension of a Muslim "Green Belt," from Tehran to the Croatian capital of Zagreb, stretching westward across Turkey, Bulgaria, Greece and through Kosovo and Bosnia in Yugoslavia."[8]

Bentley's clash of civilizations, the West against the East, Christianity versus Islam, was suddenly being fought in Bosnia, with the Serbs, again, nobly on the side of the West. The casus belli, according to the Serbs, was not territorial greed but incompatible religious convictions. It was not a land grab orchestrated by Serbia and Croatia but a civil war, everybody against everybody. "The current civil and religious war in the former Yugoslavia," stated the first of "One Hundred Irrefutable Facts" on the SUC website, "is but the resumption of the 1941–45 civil war in which Croatian fascists . . . and Muslim extremists murdered between 600,000 and

1,200,000 Serbs. The issues are the same, the battlefields are the same, even the flags and army insignia are the same." To diaspora exiles, trapped in a historical time warp, this made perfect sense. This was the last Yugoslavia they knew or, as was often the case, that their parents knew. The propaganda of the Serb lobby would bombard diaspora Serbs with different versions of this story for years to come. The Serbs in Bosnia would buy it completely and act on it accordingly.

The SUC and its counterparts, for example, consistently reiterated the Karadžić line that the ethnic separation of peoples in Bosnia—whether directly into different national states or "autonomous units" such as cantons with the option of breaking away from Bosnia—was historically inevitable, natural, and, ultimately, the only way to stop the blood feuding and insure long-term regional stability. As Djordjevich argued in a 1992 addendum to "What the Serbs Want":

> Bosnia-Herzegovina must be cantonized, if it is ever to have peace again.
> The Serbs must realize that cantonization is the least favorable solution
> for Bosnian Muslims. . . . That, however, does not mean that the Christian majority of Bosnia-Herzegovina (Serbs and Croats) should, or could,
> be forced to sacrifice their national demands for the sake of the Muslim
> minority. The Serbs and Croats of Bosnia-Herzegovina wish to have
> their own separate cantons; neither of them wish to be under the Muslim
> rule, or even live with them in mixed communities or shared areas. This
> sounds horrible, but it is a fact amply certified by the ongoing bloody
> events in that unfortunate land.

"These people simply don't want to live together—why should we make them?" ran the standard brief. Karadžić reduced it still further: "Kittens and puppies just can't live together." Despite the fact that "these people" had lived together more or less amicably in postwar Yugoslavia, even intermarrying in the larger Bosnian cities, the nationalists hammered away at the supposedly irreconcilable differences between the cultures of Bosnia's constituent peoples, differences, they claimed, that had sowed hatred in the land. In an exemplary piece of circular logic, the best proof of this animosity was the war itself.

The Serb lobby portrayed the history of the Balkans as one series of massacres and countermassacres along ethnic and religious lines, destined to extend into the indefinite future. These voices tended to see deeply ingrained patterns of uncivilized behavior as the source of the wars of the 1990s rather than the aggressive policies of the Miloševićs and Tudjmans. The lobbyists repeated and amplified the myth of "ancient hatreds" that had supposedly plagued Bosnia and Herzegovina since time immemorial. Moreover, their thesis continued, the boundaries of the Yugoslav republics, like Bosnia,

Croatia, and Serbia, were artificial anyway, a product of Tito's Serbophobia. (In reality Bosnia and Herzegovina has had an uninterrupted existence as a political entity since the tenth century, except for the 1929–41 period of the Serb-dominated Kingdom of Yugoslavia and 1941–45 during the rule of the Independent State of Croatia.) The entirety of the Serb lobby's argumentation pointed toward one ominous conclusion: war in Bosnia was inevitable. There was no stitching it back together into what they said would be an artificial "multicultural" pseudo-state. Bosnia had to be destroyed, carved up, and parceled out. One way or another, the ethnic populations living on the wrong sides of the new borders would have to be moved.

In Western capitals, where policy makers were struggling to get their heads around the Bosnia problem, the argument about the Balkans' incorrigible animosities rang plausible. Why should these peoples live together if they don't want to? Why should the borders of these former republics in Yugoslavia be sacrosanct? The arguments of the Serb lobby also periodically served the purposes of Western policy makers. For much of the conflicts' durations, the Western governments sought every excuse not to intervene in the messy Balkan quarrels. The Serb lobby arguments were made to order, and they surfaced again and again in official briefs. The possibility of reestablishing a multiethnic Bosnia never had a chance. Every proposed peace plan for Bosnia from 1992 on envisioned some kind of ethnic partition of the country, usually less definitive and pro-Serb than what the Serbs wanted but rationalized with the same ethnic logic.

It would be difficult to prove that the campaigns of the Serb lobby directly influenced Bill Clinton or any of the hundreds of policy makers and journalists who espoused some version of its arguments. These ideas, however, were present in the public debate and arduously propagated by the Serb lobby, whose means of swaying the discourse were diverse and creative, low budget and effective. Both SerbNet and the SUC had their members bombard newspapers across the country with opinion pieces and letters to the editor. SerbNet placed paid full-page statements in the *Washington Post* and the *New York Times*. To present themselves as unbiased, radio call-in shows that addressed the issue usually had a "Serb voice." Influential members of Congress were targeted for letter and telephone campaigns. Extensive websites posted an array of materials, often bizarre and macabre, including doctored photographs of decapitated and maimed Serb victims. Newspaper and magazine articles that in any way served to substantiate the Serb view were reproduced in diaspora publications as well as e-mailed around the world. (The author was once pleasantly surprised to discover his own byline on the front page of *The Path of Orthodoxy*, the official publication of the Serbian Orthodox Church in the United States and Canada.[9] The article about Croatia's Catholic Church and human rights abuses in

Croatia had been written for a nationally known, nondenominational news agency based in Washington.) The Serb organizations produced videos, organized lectures, promoted journalists, and contributed funds to sympathetic politicians. In the United States, as well as Great Britain, representatives of the Serb lobby were regularly featured as "talking heads" on national news shows.

The message was pushed out and repeated ad nauseum, its effect insidious as the grasping public weighed the Serb propaganda against reports from frontline journalists, analyses from bone fide experts, and the testimonies of authentic war victims. Doubts about the legitimate reports seeped into the public's consciousness, and, in the end, the lobbyists succeeded in shaping the parameters of discussion.

One of the more durable falsehoods that Belgrade and its lobbyists put into circulation concerned a vibrant, well-connected "Croat lobby" in Germany. It was shocking how many journalists and even experts picked up and recycled the charge that organized Croat diaspora groups, bolstered by the Vatican, had pressured Bonn into its December 1991 recognition of Croatia's and Slovenia's statehood, an admittedly controversial move Germany made ahead of its Western European neighbors. The genealogy of the rumor can be traced back to socialist Yugoslavia's demonization of the "Ustashe emigration" and negative wartime stereotypes of Nazi Germany. The insinuation behind the charge was that Croat fascists and German proto-fascists had found common cause again, in league and plotting against their old anti-fascist foe Serbia. Those Western observers who fell for the ruse repeated the charge without making the slightest effort to track it down. In fact, Germany has no political Croat lobby (as it does in Washington), although several dozen Croat clubs, folk and church groups do serve the roughly two hundred thousand ethnic Croats living, above all, in southern Germany. These groups rallied to boost Tudjman and the HDZ in the early 1990s, but they had no access whatsoever to Germany's foreign ministry or the chancellor's office.

In the summer of 1993 representatives of the Serb lobby approached Brad Blitz, a Stanford University human rights activist and Ph.D. candidate, who later founded the campus-based group Students Against Genocide (SAGE). The area's diaspora Serbs tried to convince Blitz that he should take on the cause of the Serbs, the victims of genocide themselves in the former Yugoslavia. To Blitz, some of the Serb lobby's arguments sounded suspiciously similar to those that European rightists articulated to relativize and even deny the Holocaust. For the next eighteen months Blitz monitored the SUC and then posted a blistering report on its strategy and activities on the Internet.[10] In it he concludes that "the major achievement of the Serb lobby must be its infiltration of the media and the U.S. public through its disinformation campaign, bullying tactics, letter writing, etc."

The report argues that a chief tactic of the Serb lobby was to use flimsy counterevidence, Serbian state propaganda, and ostensibly credible "expert sources" to create an atmosphere of relativism around the actual events on the ground in Bosnia. The desired effect was to convince critically minded people that "truth" and "objectivity" lie "somewhere in the middle," between the reports from nonpartisan journalists and the version the Serbs presented. "The Serbian lobby has managed to camouflage the actual aggression and the commission of genocide behind supposed 'opinions' which can be neither 'verified' or 'denied,'" concluded the analysis. The SUC never responded to the SAGE report.

Despite their intense efforts, the Serbs failed to cast themselves convincingly as the real victims of the conflict. So they took another route: to equate disproportionate acts of wrongdoing, or alleged wrongdoing on both sides, in order to legitimize the Serbs' actions, which were then downplayed further or even denied. "We may have perpetrated atrocities, but so did they!" the line ran, and it was heard often from Milošević, both while he served as Serbian leader and when he was on trial in The Hague. The existence of Serb-run concentration camps were first denied and then somehow justified by claims that the Bosnian Muslims also had such camps, even though the hundreds of international journalists on location in the Balkans could not identify them. The secession of Slovenia and Croatia from the former Yugoslavia and their recognition by Germany, for example, was equated with the shelling of civilian centers such as Sarajevo, Dubrovnik, and Vukovar. Responding to the charges of the mass rape of Bosnian women by Serb troops, the North American News Analysis Group, an off-shoot of the Yorkville Station, N.Y.-based Belgrade Club, countered in a publication:

> This is preposterous and shameless propaganda. Rape in war is one of
> the most tragic but common forms of brutalization. Anyone who asserts
> that one side is guilty of it and other sides are not is either lacking all
> common sense or is an astute propagandist. The only way to stop rape in
> Bosnia-Herzegovina is to stop the war. The brutalization of Muslim and
> Croat women has been frequently reported. *The untold story about rape in
> Bosnia is about the rape of Serbian women by Muslim and Croat forces.*

The paper lists as its sources: Amnesty International, Reuters news agency, the United Nations, and Physicians for Human Rights. In the end, the Serbs claimed that all sides are equally guilty. Everyone is committing atrocities; there are no angels in the Balkan wars. These common motifs blurred the distinction between aggressor and victim, persecutor and persecuted.

The "pro-Serb" testimonies were meant to introduce an element of confusion into the public debate. The leading representatives of the Serb lobby comprised the front row of this lineup. Danielle Sremac, the official representative of Karadžić's Bosnian Serb mini-state, Republika Srpska, headed up the SUC's Serbian American Affairs Council, which was a front for the Karadžić regime. In 1994 Sremac filed with the U.S. Department of Justice Foreign Agents Registration Unit as the official spokesperson for the Bosnian Serb leadership. Later she broke with the SUC and worked directly for the Republika Srpska Ministry of Information. Further, the London SIC's Mike (Misha) Gavrilović and Marko Gasić, as well as Djordjevich, Milentijević, and others, made hundreds of appearances on national and international media in North America and Europe. These same lobbyists also appeared regularly on special Serbian state television and radio shows broadcast weekly across Serbia about the activities of the Serb diaspora worldwide. These programs had the desired effect of persuading ordinary Serbs that the Serb ethnic communities abroad were of one mind with the regime.

But the words of the unmistakably partisan diaspora Serbs packed less of a punch than persons who bore some claim to neutrality. *New York Times* journalists Abe Rosenthal and David Binder, for example, who openly sympathized with the Serb line, were quoted, reprinted, and referenced at length in the diaspora media and propaganda. The Serb lobby also found supportive voices in obscure niches—on the far left as well as the right. In the old Marxist left the Cold War conservatives of the Serb lobby found unlikely bedfellows. In the United States and Western Europe this left-wing remnant championed the perverse myth that the Serbs were the true antifascists of the Balkans, the last nation that believed in socialist Yugoslavia and was willing to fight for its preservation. Writers such as Alexander Cockburn from *The Nation*, Dianna Johnstone and Edward Herman from *In These Times*, and Joan Phillips from *Living Marxism* rallied, in their respective publications, against Western policy in the Balkans as a form of Cold War–era imperialism, a plot to snuff out Eastern Europe's last "mixed economy."

In Britain, as well as France, the foray of the Serb lobby into mainstream opinion, the media, peace groups, trade unions, academia, and the offices of policy makers in Parliament had an early foot in the door, thanks to a preexisting British belief in the myth of "gallant little Serbia." Britain's congenial historical relationships with Yugoslavia during the twentieth century further enhanced London's sympathy for the Serbs (and against the Germans) in the name of a unified Yugoslavia. This inclination expressed itself transparently in the Foreign Office's Balkan policies during the early 1990s. It has been well documented that ministers of parliament from across the political spectrum sprang to the Serbs' defense, repeating chunks of the Serb lobby's propaganda almost word for word.[11]

The North American diaspora groups also managed to enlist the services of a few big-name personalities, the former UN general Lewis MacKenzie being one of the most prominent. The big Canadian, who served as the top UN peacekeeper in Bosnia from March to August 1992, was also predisposed toward the Serb lobby's narrative when SerbNet hired him in 1993. Before going on SerbNet's payroll, Mackenzie already subscribed to the "all sides are guilty" version of the war in Bosnia. As commander of the UN blue helmets, he acted on this assumption of ostensible neutrality in Bosnia, refusing to distinguish between aggressors and perpetrators during the war's hottest period. Unlike the Serb lobbyists themselves, spokespeople such as MacKenzie carried an aura of clinical objectivity that lent credibility to their arguments.

On another front the Serb groups actively targeted select members of the U.S. Congress who they and their Washington lobby firms gauged as "Serb friendly." The goal was to create a nucleus of core supporters in Congress who would speak on their behalf. Blitz, the California human rights activist, attributes the opening of congressional doors for the diaspora Serbs to the Washington lobby firm Manatos and Manatos, which employed stratagems it had used successfully for its Hellenic American clients.[12] In fact, the Serb lobby's outreach to U.S. congressmen received generous financial assistance from many wealthy Greek Americans and the Greek lobby, another result of the work of Andrew Manatos.

According to Federal Election Commission records, in 1991–92 the SUC, which was registered as a Political Action Committee (PAC), made an array of smallish, piecemeal campaign contributions from between $500 and $3,000 to nearly a dozen members of Congress, including Maryland's Helen Delich Bentley. This early effort to win influence in the U.S. Congress was soon eclipsed by a more professional, coordinated strategy, one employed by almost all the organized ethnic lobbies. *Bundling* is a term that professional lobbyists use for the coordinated, simultaneous contributions of groups of individuals to a single politician on a given day of particular significance. This enables the interest group or groups in question to project an aura of magnitude and power, including the ability to raise large amounts of cash quickly, when necessary. Bundling also drives home the point that these multiple contributions are indeed directed toward a specific issue, one in which the donors expect to see results.

From 1993 to 1995 the largest single benefactor of the combined targeting practices of the Serbian and Greek American diaspora was the chairperson of the influential House Foreign Affairs Committee, Indiana Congressman Lee Hamilton.[13] The majority of these deposits, which exceeded those of any other special interest group made to Hamilton, landed in his bank account on a couple of specific, obviously targeted days. On September 29, 1993, for example, forty-five individuals, most with Greek or Serb surnames, paid a total of $24,000 into Hamilton's campaign fund.[14] Most of these donors, prominent diaspora figures among them, came from the Chicago area, not Hamilton's home state of Indiana.

During that period U.S. lawmakers and the Clinton administration were deeply divided over the proper course of action. In late September 1993 Bosnian president Izetbegović was doing everything in his power to have the UN arms embargo against his country lifted, which would significantly bolster its capacity to fight back, a measure clearly antithetical to the interests of Karadžić's Bosnian Serbs. There was also talk of sending U.S. troops to Bosnia to stop the Serb march, another move that would have spelled disaster for the breakaway mini-state.

Then, on April 25, 1994, another infusion of bundled donations flowed into Hamilton's campaign chest. Most of the twenty-five contributors were identifiable as clients or associates or both of Andrew Manatos (including Manatos himself), Michael Djordjevich, and Milan Panić. On the same day Manatos addressed the Appropriations and Foreign Operations Committee to appeal for nonrenewal of U.S. aid to Turkey. Manatos also took the opportunity to dissuade the United States from officially recognizing the former Yugoslav Republic of Macedonia as a state, which Athens and Greek Americans perceived as a threat to Greece's northern border.

Several weeks later Djordjevich testified before Hamilton's committee. His main points to the House committee repeated the Serb mantra: lift economic sanctions against Serbia; insist that the "warring parties" settle their "territorial claims" through arbitration (at the time the Bosnian Serbs occupied 70 percent of the country); and recognize the Bosnian Serbs' right to "self-determination." In other words, condone the war's redistribution of populations and accept the legitimacy of a Serb state on ethnically cleared lands.

Hamilton proved a reliable friend.[15] He spoke out against Greece's new neighbor, independent Macedonia, consistently opposed lifting the arms embargo against Bosnia and advocated suspending the economic sanctions against Yugoslavia. Hamilton used his position and vote to sway U.S. policy as he actively lobbied his colleagues on those issues and made numerous media appearances advocating the extension of the weapons embargo against the Sarajevo government.

The net impact of the Serb lobby on U.S. policy toward the Balkans remains a matter of speculation. In 1995 the House voted overwhelmingly (319–99) in favor of lifting the ban on arms sales to Izetbegović's Bosnia, a pointed setback for Hamilton and his Serb supporters. Yet "lift and strike" (the policy option of ending the embargo and intervening militarily on behalf of the Bosnian government) never became official U.S. policy. Washington's position toward the wars in the former Yugoslavia was woefully muddled, plagued by uncertainty and a proclivity to follow the path of least resistance. It often relied on arguments remarkably similar to those of the Serb lobby. In the international arena, the Clinton administration was perceived as pro-Bosnian. But, in the end, its verbal support for the Bosnian government came to little, and may even have hurt the Bosnian cause by fueling unrealistic expectations of a decisive U.S. intervention that, in the end, never materialized.

In November 1995 it was the United States that eventually invited Milošević to Wright Patterson Air Force Base in Dayton, Ohio, to conclude a peace agreement on Bosnia and Herzegovina. By then, the leaders of the international community had concluded that the division of Bosnia into ministates or greater states would only sow the seeds for a future of border skirmishes and repeat wars. But an interim consensus had emerged that any settlement would include some form of ethnic partition. The terms of the final agreement that emerged from Dayton met the Bosnian Serb nationalists "somewhere in the middle." It awarded the Serbs their own ethnic entity within Bosnia, Republika Srpska, on 49 percent of the state's territory. In part, at least, victory was theirs. (The other entity, known as the Federation, is populated with Bosnian Muslims and Bosnian Croats.)

Diaspora nationalists, however, treated the Dayton peace accord's insistence on a single Bosnian state as a crushing defeat. If the deal were to stick as signed, their dream of a Greater Serbia was history. They still held out hope that things could be finagled. In response to a June 1996 *New York Times* editorial, Djordjevich vented the diaspora's frustration, denigrating the Dayton accord as "fantasy":

> The Dayton agreement has at least one basic fault: blind insistence that people who started and carried out the bloodiest war in Europe since World War II in order to separate, now somehow want to be together because their leaders signed a piece of paper under duress from the big powers. Instead of forcing elections to create a complex and, in the end, untenable state structure, the United States should come out squarely and support a national referendum. Its purpose would be rather simple: let the respective people of all three groups decide whether they want to live together or not. But we can guess the outcome. While it would free us from the Bosnian burden, it would also shatter our myth of a multicultural, multiethnic, and multireligious Bosnian society and state.

Djordjevich and the diaspora had not given up quite yet.

The 1995 Dayton agreement spelled the definitive end of the diaspora's love affair with Milošević. The glowing admiration that accompanied his nationalist bravado in the late 1980s and early 1990s dimmed and then disappeared as he backtracked from the Greater Serbia plan. It was the Serbian leader himself, the diaspora activists cried, who at Dayton had "sold out" the Bosnian Serbs in order to strike his own deal with the West. Disillusionment with Milošević began growing within parts of the diaspora in 1993 when he sacked the popular nationalist writer Dobrica Ćosić, then president of Yugoslavia. In 1994 Milošević left many Serbs abroad spitting with disgust when he slapped his own sanctions on the Bosnian Serbs for their refusal to sign an international peace agreement. It gradually became clear to ethnic Serbs abroad that "the communist" Milošević was prepared to play the nationalist card when it suited his purposes—and to slough it off when it did not. The Greater Serbia rhetoric had been a ruse, and they had fallen for it.

Even before Dayton stark confirmation of his duplicity came in April 1995 when Croatian army forces overran the Serb-held pocket of western Slavonia, sending Serb refugees fleeing toward Bosnia and Serbia. Following Milošević's orders, Yugoslav armed forces remained in their barracks. A few months later, in July, the newly equipped Croatian army wiped out the entire Serb-controlled Krajina region in Croatia and prompted an exodus of more than 160,000 Serb refugees. Again, there was an eerie silence from Belgrade. The Yugoslav army was not going to intervene on behalf of its Bosnian Serb and Croatian Serb kinsmen, the very people Milošević had incited to rebellion.

Like the peeling of an onion, layer after layer of diaspora backing for Milošević fell away. (The Greek lobby backed away from the Serbs, wary that its association might soil its reputation and thus harm Greek causes.) Many discontents seamlessly shifted their allegiance to Karadžić—until his downfall. Karadžić was well aware of the diaspora's mood. In the salutory greetings he sent to the seventh SUC convention in Milwaukee in 1996, he wrote:

> I am addressing you after six years of struggle for political and military
> freedom, dignity, and statehood. I know that you were with us all the
> time. That was a tremendous encouragement for us because the Serbs
> living in the free world are in an excellent position to judge if our path
> leads to freedom and democracy or back to Communist tyranny. You wit-
> nessed the conclusion of the war and how we were forced to accept injus-
> tice. Nonetheless, we believe that peace has its redeeming values, and
> hence we intend to keep it in conjunction with our freedom and our in-
> terests. Republika Srpska is a reality that represents the culmination of

our six years of struggle. If it were not for the tragedy of the Serb Krajina, which we could not defend [*sic*] without the help from entire Serbdom, we could have been satisfied with the results accomplished in the
century. As it is, Republika Srpska represents a consolation for all our
suffering and losses caused by our disunity and lack of a national program and resources necessary to make it happen. Despite being surrounded by enemies and misunderstandings, Republika Srpska is developing as a modern democratic country. Throughout the war we neither
had a single political prisoner nor a political trial. The people are freer
than in the last six centuries. (SUC translation)

In the political arena of Serbia proper, the diaspora's discontents found a
new home in Serbia's nationally minded anti-Milošević opposition. To its
discredit, the "democratic opposition" opportunistically donned the mantle
of Serb nationalism and championed the Bosnian Serbs during the height of
the rift between Milošević and Karadžić. The diaspora nationalists gravi-
tated toward the opposition only once Milošević began to renege on their
plans for a Greater Serbia.

Despite these body blows, Milošević always retained a core of diaspora
loyalty. Until the very end, pro- and anti-Milošević forces waged gritty battles for control over and influence in the organizations of the international
Serb lobby. Some of the unyielding Milošević support can be attributed to
the work of Yugoslavia's secret services, which, according to well-placed
sources, remained active in the diaspora throughout the 1990s. Others were
prepared to pledge fealty to whichever leader wielded power at the time,
much like many ordinary Serbs in Serbia.

An additional factor, and perhaps the most critical, was that from 1991 on
Belgrade broadcast via satellite link its state-run news and cultural programming to North America, Europe, and Australia. The Milošević propaganda
machine had an enormous impact on Serbs abroad. Above all in Germany,
Austria, and Switzerland, as well as other Western European countries, migrant Serbs tuned in to the only news that mattered to them, in a language
they understood. Milošević never lost control over this route of access to the
diaspora.

By 1997, as the peace process in Bosnia began to take hold, the tainted
figure of Karadžić also began to lose its luster. Republika Srpska seemed
destined to remain part of the Bosnian state, however unwillingly, for the
foreseeable future. The image of Serbdom had been badly sullied by the
wars and by reports of atrocities that culminated with the July 1995 slaying
of more than seven thousand Bosnian Muslim civilians in Srebrenica. The
figures most immediately identifiable with the killing fields that Bosnia had

become—Milošević, Karadžić, and the Bosnian Serb's top general, Ratko Mladić—were suddenly liabilities. The Hague-based International Tribunal for Crimes in the former Yugoslavia (ITCY) had indicted the thuggish top rung of the Bosnian Serb leadership, printing their pictures on "wanted" handbills like common criminals.

Many diaspora Serbs recognized that the cause was lost. The chimera of a Greater Serbia was dead, but truncated Yugoslavia and Republika Srpska in Bosnia had to live on. A battered Serbdom needed a new image in Washington and elsewhere, and Yugoslavia had to have new leaders, economic investment, and repaired relations with the West. In 1997 the SUC turned away from Republika Srpska's hard-liners and Karadžić, and began openly backing his more moderate party rival, Biljana Plavšić. A position paper that year underlined the Serb lobby's commitment to expediting Serbia's democratic transition, formal support of the Dayton peace agreement, and stimulating economic recovery in Republika Srpska.[16]

The Serb lobby's efforts to put its spin on history had not ended; it just changed tack. The past had to be touched up post facto if Serbia's besmirched reputation was ever to recover. The rear-guard action focused on the ITCY in the Netherlands, where the first rounds of indictments concentrated exclusively on Bosnian Serb and Bosnian Croat commanders.

At the time, in 1996, the SUC's executive director, Mirjana Samardzija, had been busy for more than a year compiling a list of camps run by Bosnian Muslims and Bosnian Croats. On the SUC website, the pages "War Crimes Perpetrated Against Serbs" provide a list of two dozen alleged camps for the 1992–93 period, some of which, the author of the pages claims, operated into 1996. The SUC's own informal investigations into human rights violations concluded that "the ethnic cleansing of Serbs by Muslims and Croats started with the very beginning of the war on a massive and systematic scale throughout the territories under the control of the Croat-Muslim forces." Although the SUC could never furnish evidence for its charges of camps and atrocities before the first shots of the war were fired, reports of camps established after fighting began trickled back to Samardzija from refugees and the relatives of Serbs living in former Yugoslavia. She pressed the tribunal, asking why the court had not indicted a single Bosnian Muslim commander. The investigators responded that they lacked evidence as well as the resources to go after every alleged human rights violation in Bosnia and Herzegovina. Thus Samardzija, from her base in Napa, California, went after them herself.

"Through the SUC bulletin and through the Orthodox Churches in the United States and Canada we appealed to the diaspora, saying, look, we need to find people in your community who had been in these camps or otherwise victims of war crimes. Can you help us?" she explains in the

SUC's downtown Belgrade office. Former prisoners and detainees surfaced across the diaspora. The SUC appointed their own war crimes investigations coordinators and formulated a questionnaire for witnesses and victims. Samardzija faxed her findings to The Hague and several months later an ITCY team showed up in the United States to interview the witnesses one-on-one.

"When we finally met the investigators," Samardzija says, "we were so impressed. They were truly professional. There was none of that politicization that hung over the tribunal because of the kind of indictments they were issuing. We learned from them that they had a horrible battle internally, politically, to get any resources for investigations [of alleged crimes] against Serbs." Slowly, the investigating team zeroed in on the Ćelebići camp in central Bosnia where Serbs had been interned in 1992–93.

The investigation then moved to Bosnia and the refugee camps there, as well as in Serbia and Montenegro. Ten SUC scouts scoured the refugee centers for witnesses. Since Milošević forbade the ICTY from working in Serbia, the investigators met with nearly forty witnesses over the border in Timisoara, Romania. The outcome of the SUC-initiated investigations was the indictment of four Bosnian Muslims for grave breaches of the Geneva Conventions. "That was an extremely, extremely exciting thing," says Samardzija, "because it was the first time the mainstream media did anything about crimes against Serbs. It couldn't be ignored because, as politicized as the court was, it was the world's legitimate body for that subject. There was recognition, it was documented."

In November 1998 the court sentenced one of the camp guards and two of its commanders to sentences of seven to twenty years for war crimes, including murder.

With the Ćelebići sentence, the Serb lobby chalked up a small deserved victory. During the bloody war in Bosnia, Serbs suffered at the hands of non-Serbs in camps like Ćelebići. Yet the SUC's motive for pursuing the Ćelebići case was not a high-minded ideal of justice. Even after Dayton, the Serb lobby continued to press the point that "everybody" had had a hand in the war crimes. Injustices on one side balanced off or negated injustices on the other. The function of the Ćelebići case for the Serb lobby was to authenticate the historical view that Serbs were victims of equal magnitude in the war in Bosnia.

Ćelebići was small change for the ICTY. In comparison with the seven thousand Muslim men and boys murdered in Srebrenica or the hundreds of thousands driven from their homes in eastern Bosnia during the Serbs' 1992 offensive, the prison camps run by the Bosnian Muslims paled in significance. The court was going after the big fish: Milošević, Karadžić, and their generals.

That the SUC even took the ICTY seriously enough to pursue the case is encouraging. Most diaspora Serbs dismiss the tribunal as a tool of U.S. imperialism, a means to further degrade the Serb nation and justify the 1999 bombing campaign against Yugoslavia. They refuse to recognize its legitimacy. If more diaspora Serbs accepted the court's role, perhaps through its proceedings the diaspora could begin to puncture some of its myths and slowly come to grips with the nature of the wars they abetted in the former Yugoslavia. Mirjana Samardzija actually goes further than any other Serb lobbyist when she admits that, in terms of numbers, Serbs could be responsible for more war crimes than those committed by Bosnian Muslims or Bosnian Croats. The Serbs, she explains, had more land under their control at the beginning of the war and thus more territory on which war crimes might have occurred. But this, she shrugs, is the stuff of Balkan wars.

CHAPTER SEVEN

Turning on Slobo

On July 8, 1992, the California-based émigré millionaire Milan Panić sat down with Serbian president Milošević in the presidential office on King Milan Street to hammer out a deal that could have altered history.

For weeks prior to the meeting Milošević had urged Panić to accept the prime minister's post of what was left of the Federal Republic of Yugoslavia, by then only Serbia and Montenegro, an internationally isolated rump state, boycotted by most of the world. In hindsight, Milošević's choice seems pure folly. But the Serbian leader obviously thought he could handle the eccentric pharmaceuticals manufacturer. "Milošević," write his biographers, Dusko Doder and Louise Branson, "fancied himself a shrewd judge of character. Before offering Panić the prime ministership, Milošević had noted Panić's ostentation, his appreciation of press attention and flattery, and his restlessness. He expected Panić to become Belgrade's public relations general—a happy second banana with a very important title—who would deflect international criticism and present a smiling reasonable face to the world."[1]

Panić, brimming with confidence, was convinced that he could make a difference: stop the war raging next door in Bosnia, end the international quarantine of Yugoslavia and return his country of birth to the European fold. As Panić tells the story, he accepted the position with one essential condition: that Slobodan Milošević resign from office and leave the country. Only the president's removal, he had become convinced (with some nudging from the U.S. State Department) could pave the way for Yugoslavia's normalization.

Looking back, Panić's gambit sounds incredibly audacious, if not preposterous. There is not, in the turbulent history of the Balkans, a tradition of authoritarian leaders voluntarily handing over the reins of governance at the height of their power, in the prime of their natural lives. Milošević, who lived and breathed power, would seem as unlikely a candidate as any to set such a precedent. But the wide-ranging UN embargo had swiftly crippled the fragile Serbian economy. Long queues at gas stations and annoying shortages of other commodities were stoking a quality of discontent that the Serbian leader had never faced before. According to Panić, he had broached the topic of stepping down with Milošević previously, and the Serbian leader had never rejected it out of hand.[2] Yet the July meeting was the first time that Panić explicitly linked Milošević's early retirement to his taking the prime minister's job.

"I told him that it was my sincere view that he was the problem. Washington didn't like him or his system, that was clear," remembers Panić nine years later, his clear blue eyes twinkling. A small well-built man, the now seventy-two-year-old Panić plays the role of tycoon to the hilt, from his gold cuff links to a traveling multinational entourage of advisers. In a natty, dark-blue suit with a monogrammed shirt and red striped tie, he radiates a surplus of nervous energy, barking orders, reeling off jokes, and closing deals on his cell phone in one seamless tumble. As chief executive officer of ICN Pharmaceuticals, just as when he served as prime minister, his schedule is in constant flux, liable to change—even in mid-air over Albania—on a moment's notice.

"'You're going,' I told him. 'Get out of this mess. I'll offer you a job in America—$150,000 a year, a vacation on my yacht, visas for your entire family,'" Panić says, as he recalls the one-sided conversation. The job Panić had in mind for ex-banker Milošević was director of a planned Yugoslav-American investment bank. Milošević apparently stared at Panić first in stunned silence but then appeared to give it serious thought. "I said, 'Go to the television studio, say that you're sacrificing yourself for the good of the country, so that sanctions can be removed. People will cry for you. You'll come back in ten years the big winner,'" recollects Panić. "If he had listened to me," he flashes a mischievous smile, "he might be on that yacht today and not sitting in The Hague."

Throughout his life Milan Panić proved himself an astute, intuitive businessman. But in the world of high diplomacy and the very unique conditions of statecraft in the Balkans, Panić was an untested neophyte. Sitting across from Milošević in the sweltering heat of a Balkan summer, he gave the region's most cagey of manipulators ten seconds to make a final decision on his political future. Like a boxing referee, Panić, in English, counted backward.

Flustered, or feigning it, Milošević actually gave in and promised to step down! A tyrant who appeared addicted to power, whose instincts seemed trained on political survival, was calling it quits. Could it be too good to be true? Not for Panić. Remembering the moment, he grins ear to ear. The two men laughed, shook hands, and knocked back a whiskey. Panić proposed drawing up the resignation letter on the spot, but Milošević brushed it off. There'd be time for that later, he said.

In order to secure Milošević's withdrawal from politics, Panić first had to deliver some goods. He promised Milošević that the UN sanctions strangling Serbia's economy would be suspended if the Serbian president removed himself from the scene. The next day he jetted to Helsinki, Finland, to meet the U.S. secretary of state James Baker who was on state business there.

Panić's lofty pronouncements about a multiethnic future for Yugoslavia and cessation of violence in Bosnia favorably impressed many international observers. The laws of the free market—not of ethnic superiority—would turn Serbia into the "California of Europe." His tone was creatively impudent, optimistic, and forward-looking. In his memoirs the European special negotiator for the Balkans, David Owen, remembers Panić at their first meeting: "Always eager to please, he offered an opportunity of fresh Serb thinking and an effervescent mind in the midst of the many old Communists still in power in Belgrade."[3]

But the U.S. State Department had been lukewarm on Panić from the beginning, unconvinced that a health-care magnate playing statesman could outfox Milošević on his own turf. Panić's bossy style and rough edges rubbed seasoned diplomats the wrong way. And at times his grasp of political reality on the ground in Yugoslavia sounded as shaky as his out-of-practice Serbian grammar. Did this pill manufacturer from Orange County really understand the complex coalition of forces and interests fanning the flames of war in Bosnia and Croatia? Did he realize, in Milošević, who he was up against?

Panić's intentions were also understandably suspect to some, since he had been an early booster of Milošević. Many international observers wondered aloud whether this high-strung character was just a flashy front man for Milošević, a moderate face for a regime bent on territorial expansion. The State Department's Balkan people knew Panić from 1990, when he appeared in their offices next to Milentijević, Bentley, and Djordjevich, on the first expedition of the embryonic Serb lobby. If Panić had had a change of heart, Washington wanted proof.

In Helsinki, in July 1992, Panić strove to convince Baker to wield U.S. influence to get the UN sanctions against Yugoslavia lifted in exchange for Milošević's departure. Baker insisted that change at the top in Yugoslavia was only one precondition for the UN scrapping the embargo: the war in Bosnia had to stop, and the Yugoslav army had to withdraw from the country. Nevertheless, Secretary Baker said, he would confer with President Bush on the matter.

Panić returned to Belgrade confident, or bluffing the confidence, that he had enough in hand to secure Milošević's signature on a letter of resignation drawn up by his California team. For days the Serbian president vacillated. Panić persisted. Finally, at crunch time, Milošević balked. Baker's vague commitment wasn't enough, he charged. No deal. Steaming mad, Panić cried foul. Others, such as the diplomatic corps in Washington, shook their heads as if to say: told ya. Perhaps Milošević had been playing with the peppery little millionaire all along.

To this day Panić fiercely maintains that Milošević's voluntary exit from the political scene had been on the table. Whatever the case, the debacle soured relations between the two men, which would only deteriorate further over Panić's roller-coaster seven-month stint as a Yugoslav politician. It also proved emblematic of the Bush and Clinton administrations' consistently half-hearted interest in Panić. Washington had everything to gain and almost nothing to lose by backing Panić. Looking back a decade later the Panić chapter ranks as a fumbled chance to stem the bloody trajectory of the war in Bosnia.

As an émigré Serb, Panić is an intriguing character for the very reason that he is so profoundly uncharacteristic of the diaspora. Born in Belgrade in 1929 Panić, as a teenager, served as a courier for the communist Partisans in eastern Herzegovina. In the early 1950s he won a spot on the Yugoslav Olympic cycling team. En route to an international competition in the Netherlands in 1956, he jumped the train in Vienna, never to return until Milošević's invitation in the late 1980s.

Panić's rags-to-riches journey deserves a place in an anthology of American success stories. Arriving in Los Angeles in 1956 with two suitcases, a wife, two children, and twenty dollars, he propelled himself into the highest circle of the American corporate elite. Today ICN Pharmaceuticals Inc., based in Costa Mesa, California, has operations in six continents and is worth nearly a billion dollars. Panić hobnobs with the country's most powerful politicians, a token of appreciation, no doubt, for his consistently generous campaign contributions.

Unlike most of his émigré compatriots, Panić never identified himself as a member of the Serb diaspora. He had no time for the homeland or even for the Orthodox Church, the most common denominator among the Serb émigré community. On landing in America, he snipped the umbilical cord and never looked back. He forbade spoken Serbian in his house, paid little attention to political developments in Yugoslavia, and hung up the phone on Serbian American community groups. There was never any love lost between Panić and diaspora activists. A U.S. citizen since 1963, Panić even took the extraordinary step of discarding his Yugoslav passport.

His self-identity was neither that of a "Serb exile in America" nor a "Serbian American" but rather, as he says, "just an American." Panić went to extreme lengths to acculturate, even forgetting all but shockingly little of his Serbian, which today is broken and heavily accented. In marked contrast to the political persuasions of most Serb émigrés in the United States, Panić is a liberal Democrat. He was active in the U.S. civil rights movement in the

1960s, the street protests against the Vietnam War, and the presidential campaigns of just about every Democratic Party candidate since Bobby Kennedy.

Today Panić waxes philosophical about a vision of a world without atomic bombs, the death penalty, and narrow-minded nationalism. "These extremists, Serbs, Croats, Albanians, they're all the same. They all use exactly the same language, the same words, the same sentences," he gestures dismissively over a fish dinner in coastal Dubrovnik, in Croatia, where he had just delivered a keynote address to several hundred regional businessmen and policy makers. When Panić called for the immediate abolition of all borders in the Balkans and a single passport for all the countries of southeastern Europe, a murmur of discontent rippled through the pin-striped crowd. "That's what joining Europe means!" he tells me, his voice crackling with impatience, referring to membership in the European Union. "And that's exactly what they want! So go ahead and do it now. Why wait?"

Panić's life story and his scathing rejection of nationalism make his early engagement on behalf of the Serb lobby all the more mysterious. What drove him to throw in his lot with diaspora idealogues with whom he had little in common, a former Partisan who shunned his Serb roots? When asked, he testily waves off the question.

Inconsistency is one of Panić's hallmarks. Perhaps in 1990 Panić was overcome with a new-found and short-lived burst of Old World patriotism, an upswell of nostalgia that had been repressed for decades. Or, more plausibly, he was looking out for his new business interests as Serbia found its feet in the postcommunist order. Another possibility, which he denies, is that he had political ambitions early on, and saw the lobby as a way of establishing himself after decades of noninvolvement in Serbia-related affairs. He seems to recall his association with people such as Bentley and Djordjevich as a gaffe. But, as Brad Blitz's study on the Serb lobby noted, as late as 1995 Panić contributed to the lobby's bundled donations that were sent to U.S. Congressman Hamilton.[4]

Yugoslavia had pretty much disappeared from Panić's radar screen until the opportunity arose in the late 1980s to buy Serbia's sprawling state-run pharmaceutical plant, Galenika, at a rock bottom price. The plant was one of socialist Yugoslavia's biggest, providing the country with half its total pharmaceuticals. It wasn't the St. Vitus Day hoopla in Kosovo that caught Panić's eye, but Milošević's cautious first moves toward privatizing the economy and a bargain he couldn't pass up. After the drug-plant deal was signed in 1990, celebratory champagne flowed in Milošević's office until well into the night.

Milošević's idea to call in Panić as premier and simultaneously convince the esteemed nationalist writer Dobrica Ćosić to become Yugoslav president seemed like a stroke of genius. In Panić, he had a native son who had reached the pinnacle of success in the West and someone he hoped could patch up Serbia's tattered relations with Washington. Most critically, Milošević had to unshackle the country from the cumbersome international sanctions dragging down its feeble economy. The elderly Ćosić, on the other hand, was the grand old man of the nationalist intelligentsia, with moral credibility untainted by past political associations. It wasn't long, however, before Milošević realized how badly he had miscalculated.

Even though Milošević rebuffed Panić on the issue of his resignation, Panić kept the post. As Yugoslav prime minister he pieced together in 1992 a top-notch cabinet of predominantly independent experts, a government the likes of which would not be seen again until Milošević's fall eight years later. Strategically Panić appointed himself minister of defense, and thus the commander-in-chief of the Yugoslav army—at least on paper. Milošević insisted on filling several posts with his own people. One of them, as minister without portfolio, was Radmila Milentijević.

When Panić took the office, the frenzy of ethnic cleansing in Bosnia was at its peak, with the active participation of the Yugoslav army and Belgrade-backed Serb paramilitaries. In Serbia, state-sponsored hate speech filled the airwaves convincing ordinary Serbs that the war next door was defensive in nature. The Serb populace bought it completely. But Panić never did. The killing in Bosnia genuinely disturbed him, and he passionately rejected war as a means to settle political issues. Although exasperatingly inconsistent in his statements and positions, his crusade to derail the juggernaut of war was the first serious effort from within Serbia to stop the conflict.

Throughout the summer of 1992 Prime Minister Panić frenetically criss-crossed Europe in search of peace, opening the blocked channels of communication between capitals, including a daring trip to besieged Sarajevo where he met with an icy reception from Bosnian leader Alija Izetbegović. His irreverence and quirky antics raised eyebrows. The German weekly *Der Spiegel* dubbed him the "Clown of the Balkans." Undaunted, Panić's traveling circus pushed on.

At the August 1992 London conference, the first major summit designed to negotiate a peace for Bosnia, Panić elbowed Milošević aside to advance a maverick twelve-point peace plan that included Yugoslavia's recognition of all the former Yugoslav republics as states, including Bosnia and Herzegovina. It was a major breakthrough the international community had long sought. Panić called for UN monitoring of the border between Yugoslavia and Bosnia, as well as a complete disarmament of Bosnia and "if needs be . . . over a wider area," implying Serbia itself. In no uncertain terms, he pilloried the region's radicals as the source of the carnage.

Yet Panić operated under a handful of questionable assumptions that ultimately undermined his quixotic peace mission. For one, he failed to accept that it was the Serb forces that had instigated the war and were perpetrating the worst atrocities in the region. Although Panić rejected the nationalists' justification for the war, he steadfastly maintained that all sides were equally responsible for the conflict. Disarm all three [Croat, Bosnian, Serb] armies! cried Panić, apparently unaware that in 1992 the Bosnian government barely had an army. Its lightly armed, rag-tag forces were made up of neighborhood gangs, police officers, and volunteers. In fact, at times Panić appeared oblivious of the fact that Yugoslav forces were active on the front lines at all, pounding Bosnian cities to dust with heavy artillery. At the London conference, he swore that no military assistance from Yugoslavia was reaching the Bosnian Serbs. A piece of black irony: it was during Panić's seven-month tenure that the army under his nominal control inflicted the most damage on Bosnia during the course of the three-and-a-half-year war. The generals of the Vojska Jugoslavije would most probably have laughed in his face had Panić tried to order them out of Bosnia.

In addition, Panić shunned the political processes inside Yugoslavia, much to his own detriment. The chairman of the board ran the Yugoslav government like his own multinational corporation, as if he were unaccountable to the parliament or to Serbia's other power bases. "Panić was weak, actually the weakest in the parliament, where he should have shored up at least the minimum support for governing," quipped the daily *Borba* in late 1992. "This was the absurdity of his position: it was no use to him to win Russia for an ally, when he had [ultra-nationalist leader] Šešelj for an enemy, or China siding with him when [Milošević ally] Bora Jović is threatening him with a vote of no confidence."[5]

Panić vastly overestimated his own power, boasting, for example, that his position in Yugoslavia was tantamount to that of the president of the United States, whereas Milošević's position, as leader of Serbia, was equivalent to being governor of an American state. In fact, it was the other way around. The real power lay in the republic, in Serbia, not in the weak Yugoslav federal structures.

By autumn the bad blood between Panić and Milošević was an open secret, and the Serbian leader wanted nothing more than to banish his rival with his pack of foreign advisers back to southern California. Republican-wide elections for the presidency were scheduled for December. The logical opponent, and the man many believed could beat Milošević, was not Panić but Ćosić. But, at the last minute, Ćosić backed down. The only person left with a fighting chance was Panić. With only days before the registration deadline, Panić enlisted the leagues of Belgrade's university and high school students, a mainstay of the anti-Milošević opposition, to drum up the thousands of signatures he needed to qualify to run. By then, Panić had emerged as the bellwether of the democratic opposition, staking out radical positions that challenged even the nationalist positions of Serbia's democrats. Polls showed Panić neck-and-neck with Milošević or even ahead of him. The signatures required for his candidacy turned out to be the least of his worries.

Ćosić, with misgivings about the depth of Panić's patriotism, refused to back him publicly, a devastating blow from his former ally. State-run television kept the American showman off Yugoslavia's television sets, and his sassy campaign ads, produced by U.S. spin doctors, never ran. Milošević's allies and political frontmen screamed that Panić was a CIA spy and a traitor to Serbia. One of those who shrieked most shrilly was the former university dean Milentijević, who had already resigned from the wayward Panić government in protest. On the airwaves, Milentijević slammed Panić for his questionable allegiances and weak-willed commitment to the Serb cause. From across the oceans, other diaspora figures added their voices to the state-run smear campaign through call-in programs. The last place Panić could look for support was to his fellow Serbian Americans. "I understood that it was my responsibility to go in the campaign, not to campaign for Milošević, but to tell the Serbian people why Panić doesn't fit," explains Milentijević today, unapologetic and entirely certain her decision was right. "He knew so little about our history and our people. I was convinced that he had neither the moral nor professional qualifications to lead the Serbian nation."

The two émigrés first knocked heads when Panić proposed wide autonomy for Kosovo at the 1992 London conference. To Milentijević, this was tantamount to granting the province the right to self-determination, a giant step too drastic for any real Serb. "I said, 'Do you know what you're doing? That promises to alter the borders of the country. That's unacceptable. It's crazy!' At that point I decided this man is not good news."

But Panić did not need Milentijević or the diaspora behind him to win. He needed Washington, desperately. Again, Panić pleaded with the White House and State Department to offer him something tangible to promise the Serbian electorate, such as the partial lifting of sanctions or shipments of heating oil for the frigid Balkan winter—or anything at all. He got nothing. Adding injury to insult, the U.S. secretary of state Lawrence Eagleburger took this moment to brand Milošević a war criminal, a broadside from the United States that enabled Milošević to project himself as the victim of U.S. imperialism and Panić as one of its agents. Even the special international negotiators for the Balkans, Lord Owen and the former U.S. secretary of state Cyrus Vance, seemed to throw in their lot with Milošević, who they figured would win anyway and thus be the man they would have to deal with.

With only a week to campaign before the vote, the Panić team hurtled itself across the length of Serbia on a furious whirlwind campaign tour. In urban centers, the bastion of the opposition, Panić basked in emotional outpourings of support. In his campaign finale in Belgrade more than one hundred thousand people jammed Nikola Pašić Square and Pioneer Park as Panić excoriated Milošević for "building a Chinese wall around Serbia." In spite of everything, the outsider was making a real race of it after all.

In December the republic voted. The Panić people and international election monitors cited flagrant irregularities in the voting and counting processes. The Panić team charged that ballots were rigged, that students were blocked from voting, and that potential opposition voters were purged from the registers. Nevertheless, exit polls showed the two contenders even.

But the final count gave the incumbent Milošević 53 percent of the vote and the challenger Panić 32 percent. With a hair's breadth of a majority for Milošević, there would be no second-round runoff. All in all, it was an impressive finish for the hard-headed businessman who stormed forward against all odds opposing a vastly powerful state bureaucracy and without the help of the very countries who claimed that their foreign policy priority was to rid the Balkans of his political nemesis. On December 29, 1992, Panić's mandate as prime minister was revoked in a no-confidence vote. The exhausted crusader from Orange County packed his bags and headed for home.

From abroad, Panić continued to have a voice in the opposition through his Alliance for Change, one of the many unsuccessful efforts to unite the fractious opposition in Serbia. Panić's ICN operated the Galenika pharmaceutical plant until the government seized it in early 1999.

Virtually the same week that Panić plunged into the fray of Yugoslav politics, another émigré emerged on the scene. Crown Prince Alexander Karadjordjević, the forty-six-year-old heir to a throne vacant since 1941, returned to his ancestral homeland in the summer of 1992 for only the second time in his life. The London businessman, born in exile, paid visits neither to Milošević, Milentijević, nor Panić. He had his own agenda, which involved none of them.

"Serbia has seen enough of death," the son of Yugoslavia's last king, Peter II, told a cheering multitude of one hundred thousand in July 1992, gathered in central Belgrade for the largest peace march since Milošević came to power. "Victory will be ours," read the prince in halting Serbian from a prepared text. "Long live a democratic Serbia!" In the crowd royalist sympathizers waved flags and banners with the traditional symbol of the monarchy, the white doubled-headed eagle. Others looked on with polite curiosity. Around the perimeter of the demonstration, riot police in full battle gear made their imposing presence felt.

Opinion polls showed that popular support for a restoration of the monarchy was tepid, but Milošević obviously perceived Karadjordjević as a political enemy, perhaps a rallying point for the diaspora and the ever noisier opposition. The prince himself publicly promoted a constitutional monarchy for postcommunist Yugoslavia, pointing to the stabilizing influence that King Juan Carlos had on Spain. There were rumors that the British political establishment favored him as a possible successor to Milošević. He was, after all, the queen's first cousin.

To his credit, the prince was among the very few prominent Serb émigrés who never fell for Milošević. A chasm of history and interests separated the two forty-something men from the outset. Obviously a monarchy of any kind would have constituted a direct challenge to Milošević's power. Further, the Karadjordjević family would almost certainly demand the return of its once elegant properties that the communists had confiscated after the war. First on the list was the Royal Palace in Belgrade. The residence had been Tito's for decades and was then used by Milošević for receptions and entertaining dignitaries. The Serbian leader was in possession of a house stolen from Prince Alexander's father—grounds for ill will if ever there were any.

In Serbia, as in neighboring Bulgaria and Romania, the possibility of establishing a constitutional monarchy was an option being bandied about in the early 1990s. In the countryside as well as in the cities of central Serbia, the symbol of the crown still tugged at heartstrings, even if this Karadjordjević was an obscure and distant figure to most of them, known only by his prestigious grandfather's name. Serbia's largest opposition party at the time was monarchist, although it operated independently of the London-based monarch-in-waiting. In fact, for most of the 1990s the monarch and Serbia's leading monarchist party were not on speaking terms. That, however, did not deter Prince Alexander from agitating for nearly a decade against Milošević and eventually playing a small, symbolic role in his downfall.

The prince's hearty welcome in Serbia unsettled Milošević. The Serbian president countered with the simplest of strategies: he ignored the man completely. "He treated me as if I didn't exist," admits Karadjordjević dejectedly in his Piccadilly Circus office. In person, the portly, full-faced prince comes across as kind and good-natured. In the wings of the mahogany-and-leather suite, his second wife, the Greek-born Katherine, runs the show, watching his schedule like a hawk and marshaling the office staff with a commanding hand. When she says that an interview is over, it's over. The prince follows along.

Karadjordjević was born on a summer's day in 1945, in a suite in London's Claridge's Hotel, which the British government had declared Yugoslav territory for the day. King Peter II, the infant's father, requested that the Foreign Office grant his wish that his son be born on Yugoslav soil. In light of Britain's full backing for the communist Tito, who had banished the royal family to an indefinite future of exile, it seemed the least London could do.

His Royal Highness Prince Alexander of Yugoslavia is heir to the Karadjordjević dynasty, a house that has a checkered legacy in Serbia, as well as a long tradition of exile and return. It was the Serb clan chief with the nom de guerre Karadjordje (or Black George) who, in 1804, led an uprising that burst the shackles of four centuries of Ottoman rule. The revolt was quashed again several years later, and Karadjordje fled to Austria. His son returned from abroad to assume the crown in Serbia.

In 1941, when the Nazis occupied Yugoslavia, Prince Alexander's father, the teenage Peter II, fled the country together with royalist politicians who set up a London-based government-in-exile. Ultimately, though, King Peter lacked any real power, and the exile government disintegrated even before the communist forces liberated the country in 1945. That year Tito formally abolished the monarchy.

The decisive defeat of the monarchist armies cut the royal family and its newborn prince adrift in the world. Prince Alexander's childhood reflected the tragedy that fate had dealt his parents. Shunted from one boarding school to another, the young boy rarely saw his mother or father. In 1970 King Peter died in Denver, Colorado, from a disease related to alcoholism. He is buried in the Saint Sava Monastery in Libertyville, Illinois.

Unlike his father's generation, the triumphant return to a reconstituted royalist Yugoslavia seemed, for the young Karadjordjević, the stuff of fairy tales, not usually an impediment to exiles. "Then one day the fax machine started beeping and the phone ringing," says Karadjordjević, referring to the late 1980s. Behind him hangs a portrait of his father in full military attire, a jewel-encrusted crown beside him. "Things suddenly started happening in Yugoslavia, and I realized there was a role to play. I had not been tarnished by these incredible arguments that had been taking place [in the diaspora]. It's a good thing I wasn't involved in all this fratricidal mess."

Karadjordjević views the crown as "a uniting force," a symbol of national unity above political jousting. "I serve all people and not any political party or ideology," he says, trundling out his standard response, one of many. "We need this neutral person not as a member of any political party but that represents the people, the nation. If not we will have fratricidal politics, endless debates and arguments. That's the tragedy." The prince repeats the line "That's the tragedy" another four or five times in our hour-long interview. Silver-tongued, he is not.

As Yugoslavia began to unravel, Karadjordjević withdrew from the insurance business in order to devote full time to the business of being royalty. At first he envisioned a restored monarchy encompassing all Yugoslavia, including Croatia and Slovenia, just as it had under his grandfather. When that dream fizzled, he concentrated his efforts on Serbia and Montenegro. Despite being a founding member of Djordjevich's SUC, Karadjordjević shied away from the Greater Serbia option. He seemed willing to be prince or king in any kind of Yugoslavia that would take him. To his credit, his voice was moderate and consistently behind the democratic opposition.

Yet Prince Alexander's reception in Serbia was decidedly ambivalent. Serbs lined the streets for the occasion of his very first visit in 1990. Few on-lookers had ever gazed on Serbian royalty. But the trip turned Karadjordje-vić into the butt of jokes. As he kneeled over to kiss a section of turf, a symbol for Serbian soil, he looked to some observers like a swine rooting in a barnyard. The ungainly gesture earned him the nickname "Alex the Pig," and the label stuck into the next decade. With each visit the crowds that turned out for him diminished.

Frankly, even diaspora royalists admit that Prince Alexander fails to cut an impressive figure. During most of his adult life, he had little to do with Yugoslavia or the Serb diaspora, despite the fact that the crown, next to the church, was the diaspora's single strongest unifying symbol. Karadjordjević married, went into business, and divided his life between Europe and the United States. He never learned Serbian, thinking he would never need it. In the 1990s he fell out with Vuk Drašković's monarchist party, which left him no organizational vehicle for a royalist movement.

In July 2001, nine months after Milošević's fall, Prince Alexander and Princess Katherine returned to Belgrade to take up the responsibilities of full-time royalty—in a country that does not recognize the monarchy. They now live in the Royal Palace, where Milošević had offices for thirteen years. There they participate in a wide range of charitable activities.

Radmila Milentijević's exit from the Panić cabinet in 1992 in no way ter-minated her involvement on behalf of Serbia. Like hundreds of Serb émigré groups, church parishes, and individuals in North America and Europe, Mi-lentijević devoted her homeland-motivated energies to the delivery of "hu-manitarian aid" to Serbia and, in particular, to the war zones where Serbia contested territory. During and in the aftermath of the wars in Croatia, Bosnia, and Kosovo, thousands of tons of mostly nonmilitary supplies, pur-chased by diaspora organizations such as Milentijević's World Serbian Vol-untary Fund, made their way into the Serb-controlled Croatian enclaves, into Karadžić's breakaway Republika Srpska in Bosnia and, during the 1999 NATO bombing campaign, into Kosovo itself.

Most of the diaspora's charitable donations took the form of medical sup-plies and durable goods such as winter clothing, rubber boots, and blankets, usually shipped there through the diaspora's Orthodox churches. Berlin's

Vuk Karadžić–Brothers Grimm Society, founded in 1989, drove fourteen ambulances from the former East Germany (unloaded cheaply by the German Red Cross) down to Republika Srpska and Serb-controlled Croatian Krajina in 1994. Unlike the Croat diaspora's rampant arms smuggling carried out under the guise of humanitarian aid, the Serbs' shipments were overwhelmingly nonmilitary in nature. The well-equipped Yugoslav army and Serb paramilitary units did not need the cast-off weaponry of East Germany's defunct army.

The German authorities closely monitored the Serbs' consignments. "We couldn't have sent that kind of thing [arms or military-related technology] if we had wanted to," claims Miloje Meličević, a retired university lecturer and president of the Vuk Karadžić–Brothers Grimm Society. During the 1990s his home in an affluent Berlin suburb doubled as a warehouse for the collected supplies destined for the conflict zones. German police regularly searched his house and, claims Melićević, shadowed him periodically for years.

One of the few North American organizations with an official U.S. Treasury Department permit to conduct humanitarian activities in the former Yugoslavia was the International Orthodox Christian Charities (IOCC), a Baltimore-based group founded in 1992 and run by the Eastern Orthodox churches in America. "I realized we had to be engaged with the Serbs," explains the founding director and Greek citizen Alex Rondos. "People said you're crazy to start a new organization and begin with Serbia but I said, yes, precisely, that's where the needs are." Rondos knew philanthropic work, having held senior positions in Catholic Relief Services, and he knew that the project would be a thorny one. "My idea was to do good philanthropic work, which means you help everyone in need, not just one group," he explains. But he soon collided with the Serb diaspora. "Naively I didn't realize how a diaspora winds up being more royalist than the king," he says.

Contributors put Rondos under pressure to send aid to specific towns and villages, often ones near the front lines. "They wanted to do other things with the money. They said their people are under siege, they're isolated, and we must help them," Rondos trails off. "These people were engaged in ethnic politics, we were not. It was quite clear that food was being given to troops and that's why we [the IOCC] broke with the [Serbian Orthodox] Church."

Alongside the IOCC, individual church parishes and regional Orthodox communities in places with large Serb populations such as Chicago, Detroit, New York, San Francisco, and Los Angeles developed their own initiatives, though rarely in concert with one another. As the situation in Yugoslavia grew more desperate, a lifeline needed to be provided to an increasingly impoverished middle-class population in the homeland. "Lots of money was being raised and brought to Serbia. It became an informal but organized remittance system," says Rondos. He estimates that, during the 1990s, Serbian Americans sent "considerable millions" of dollars a year to their relatives in Serbia—though not tens of millions.

Rondos remembers the anguish and frustration he encountered when he toured the North American diaspora in 1993–94. "It was like a primal scream," says the Oxford-educated Rondos, today a senior adviser to the Greek foreign minister. "And I say it with a real sense of sympathy, because here are people in a land where their hopes lie and they're being demonized. Their kids are being talked to in a terrible way in the schools. 'You Serbs, we know what your people are doing.' This kind of thing. But I said that that screaming is exactly the way you reinforce other peoples' stereotypes about you."

In hindsight, Rondos believes that the diaspora missed a poignant opportunity to help its people. "They never turned around to say we're Americans, we have enriched ourselves thanks to the democratic system, and what we've got there is a communist bastard who's destroying the place. They never said we're Serbs, we're patriots, but we hate to see this being done to our country. The major characters must stand up to a double charge: of abusing the rights they were given in the United States that allowed them to grow and benefit, but also of reinforcing what was unethical and wrong in the homeland."

The message behind the aid shipments to frontline regions was unambiguous: they communicated the devotion of the diaspora to the cause. The local media in the Serb-controlled half of Bosnia, for example, trumpeted every delivery or the visits of émigré figures such as Milentijević, Djordjevich, and Meličević (the latter an honorary senator in the parliament of the wartime Republika Srpska) as proof of the diaspora's commitment to their ultimate objective—union with Serbia. A photo-op with Karadžić was standard. Milentijević personally escorted several truckloads of cigarettes into Republika Srpska and Croatia for Serb soldiers. And, once in the hands of the Republika Srpska authorities (for example, the Republika Srpska Red Cross run by Karadžić's wife), there was no mechanism to track the shipment's final destination: a school or a refugee center, the artillery positions around Sarajevo or an army hospital.

Tellingly the diaspora channeled substantial quantities of its material donations through the Belgrade-based Serbian Heritage Foundation (Matica Iseljenika Srbije, or MIS), headed by one of Greater Serbia's loudest proponents, the nationalist writer Brana Crnvević. Under Crnvević, MIS, the state agency responsible for the diaspora and a well-known front for the security services, became a critical conduit for funneling money, arms, and other supplies to Serbia's proxy armies in Bosnia and Croatia. The humanitarian aid shipments from abroad, whatever their content, usually took the same route. A key figure in this network was Father Filaret of Novi Pazar, the Orthodox Church's man in charge of humanitarian aid. According to Serbia's independent media, large quantities of this aid were sold on the black market, the proceeds going straight into the pockets of Crnvević, Filaret, and regional warlords.

Milentijević had no permit from the U.S. Treasury Department to send aid of any kind to embargoed Yugoslavia. In other words, Milentijević was personally breaking UN sanctions, if on a minor scale. Technically her charitable activities counted as smuggling, punishable by U.S. law. This she freely admits. Milentijević, now in her early seventies, theatrically drags two gigantic empty suitcases out of a back room. "This is how we did it," she beams, standing in the middle of her living room. As many as eight medicine-laden suitcases at a time went to the war zones from Milentijević on U.S. commercial flights. She personally made twenty-three trips to bring supplies to hospitals in the Serb-held Krajina, Republika Srpska, and Serbia. Other aid donated by her fund went through the Church Relief Committee of the Serbian Orthodox Church, which had U.S. and UN licenses to ship relief goods to Serbia. The medical supplies came cut-rate from Wayne General Hospital in New Jersey through Pavle Topolović, a doctor and the "vice president" of her charitable organization. The estimated value of the shipments over six years came to $5 million. In addition, Milentijević says she contributed over $350,000 of her own money to other kinds of philanthropic work in Serbia.

"I wasn't carrying guns to the Milošević government to enable him to shoot civilians," Milentijević says, attempting to justify her subterfuge. "But there were innocent people who were hurt, hit by whatever, who are bleeding and in the hospital and if they don't get some aid they will be dying. That is a crime against humanity. With sanctions they're killing people, while I'm trying to save them. I would have done the same if America were unfairly attacked."

The response, or lack of response, from the U.S. government to Milentijević's activities over a decade is curious. As a naturalized U.S. citizen, Milentijević took an oath not to serve a foreign government. She sought State Department approval neither for her post in the 1992 Panić government nor for the one in the 1997–98 Milošević cabinet. U.S. officials seemed to tacitly approve her dealings with officials in Yugoslavia, or at least she understood they did not disapprove. At one point, during the Bosnian war, U.S. Treasury officials investigated her humanitarian activities in Serbia and Republika Srpska but never followed up on the case. Observing the letter of the law, U.S. authorities at any point could have revoked her citizenship, or threatened to do so. But they did not. Perhaps the diaspora's humanitarian campaign to help Serbia struck U.S. officials as too meager and unimportant to pursue. So Milentijević went a step further.

Late in February 1997 Milošević called on Milentijević to head the Serbian Ministry of Information, the very department that had earned international condemnation for cracking down on opposition media and excluding dissident voices from state-run broadcasts. For one year Milentijević would serve as Serbia's chief propagandist, a spokesperson for a regime that Washington contended was criminal. Yet, inexplicably, even that questionable role did not rouse U.S. authorities to confront Milentijević.

At the time that Milentijević took her information post, the atmosphere in Serbia bristled with dissension. Three months earlier, in November 1996, Milošević had annulled a string of opposition victories in municipal elections, which sent furious democracy-minded protesters onto the streets. Tens of thousands of demonstrators marched daily through Belgrade, blowing whistles, clanking pots and pans, and screaming for Milošević's ouster.

The regime was under enormous pressure at home and abroad. The West's post-Dayton patience with Milošević had largely evaporated. The tall order facing Milentijević, the former public relations flak at New York's City University, was to present a reasonable face to the West, extend a hand to the enraged opposition, and perhaps also to reengage the diaspora, which had by then become disenchanted with the Serb leader. But, above all, Milošević chose Milentijević for her fidelity, which was unquestioned.

"I was honored," says Milentijević, describing her response to Milošević's offer. "It was an honor for an elected president of my people to invite me to come to help. Very few people had this happen to them." Indeed, she might well be unique among retired academics. During her tenure as the minister of information, Milentijević would become known for her uncritical devotion to Milošević and for her often garbled pronouncements. "I was perceived as having come to help Milošević," she says, "which I really didn't, although indirectly of course I was helping the president. But my purpose was to make a difference for the way the Serbian people are informed."

As Milentijević admits, in retrospect, she accomplished little in her twelve months in office. Her draft media law died in the republican parliament. The Western powers viewed her not as a moderate but as a hardliner, and the opposition media mocked her jumbled statements and fawning praise for Milošević. Nor did Milentijević have any impact in the diaspora. Older Serbian Americans associated her with the 1963 church schism and rumors of her collaboration with Tito's secret police. To her credit, though, Milentijević was never associated with the regime's bullying of the independent media. "She never had anyone beaten up, kidnapped, or killed, which is more than you can say about her successors," quips *Vreme* editor Miloš Vasić.

Belgrade's flagship opposition radio station, B92, regularly broadcast Milentijević's one-liners as sound bites to lampoon the regime. "When I talk to Mr. Milošević, I always learn something very interesting," was one of the station's all-time favorites. Another quote of the week: "When talking to foreign journalists one should always point out that Serbia is already a democratic state because the illegal behavior of the opposition parties is tolerated."

"Our point was to show the public the hypocrisy of these politicians and public servants who fell all over Milošević," explains the director of Radio B92, Veran Matić. He argues that Milentijević's public statements expressed something important about the nature of Milošević's system. "This kind of gibberish created a climate in which all social values and norms became relative. It announced that anything was possible, that there were no limits as long as you were a member of the regime. You could do or say whatever you wanted with impunity. It created an atmosphere in which everything goes."

By 1997 the diaspora's dreams of a Greater Serbia lay in ruin at Milošević's feet, their ancestral homes in enemy territory, their family members bunked in overcrowded refugee centers. Particularly in North America, among the postwar royalists and émigré Serbs with origins in Croatia and Bosnia, Milošević's "betrayal" of the Bosnian and Croatian Serbs turned their fading adoration into untempered scorn. In the name of the homeland, the diaspora had staked everything on a quest that Milošević had never taken seriously. To their nation's detriment, the diaspora played along, allowing itself to be used, until there was almost nothing left to lose—except Kosovo.

In addition, a new wave of emigration began to change the mix of the Serb diaspora, as well as its thinking. The "brain drain" émigrés of the 1990s looked as alien to the old-school monarchists as the latter must have appeared in the late 1940s to the immigrant steelworkers in America's Midwest. During the decade of Milošević, an estimated two hundred thousand to three hundred thousand Serbs, overwhelmingly educated and young, fled the dire conditions of Serbia's economic collapse and Milošević's authoritarian rule. They landed in Central and Western Europe, North America, South America, South Africa, and Australia, wherever they could get visas.

It was these urban-spirited, culturally Westernized college graduates, such as Desko Nikitović, who had first taken to the streets against Milošević in the early 1990s, who constituted the backbone of the democratic opposition. Their cultural points of reference were Sonic Youth, Quentin Tarantino, and Nike, not Draža Mihailović and folk dancing. Nikitović, a lawyer, left Belgrade in 1992, frustrated and angry at his pliant countrymen. "I left Yugoslavia because of Milošević, not because it was my dream to come to the United States," he explains from his eighth-floor office at the Chicago

real estate firm of Koenig and Strey. Nikitović had worked in different oppositional groups since 1989, until it became clear to him that real democratic change in Serbia was a long way off. "Milošević was a disaster not only
for the Serbs but for all peoples of Yugoslavia," he says. "It took the diaspora
longer to figure this out."

When he first arrived in the United States Nikitović could not find a
single diaspora organization that matched his own political coordinates. But
in 1995 he joined the SUC and soon became president of its Chicago chapter. "I knew we still had people in the SUC who liked Milošević and that was
unacceptable to me," he explains, "but you never have a perfect choice. I
tried to explain to people that not supporting Milošević didn't mean that
you weren't a good Serb."

On the other side of the Atlantic, twenty-three-year-old Jovan Ratković
had just completed a degree in environmental science at the University of
East Anglia when he entered the world of diaspora politics. In Serbia
Ratković was one of the youthful initiators of the colorful student troupe
Otpor (Resistance), an organization that would lead the charge that eventually dumped Milošević. He was a latecomer to the London-based Serbian
Information Center (SIC), which was founded in 1991 as a broad-based network that would, as its founders put it, fill the yawning information gap that
existed concerning Serbia. Its members included a diverse amalgam of émigré Serbs, most of whom, by the late 1990s, had long since written off Milošević. Yet protectively occupying the positions of spokesperson were two
media-skilled and staunchly pro-Milošević members, Marko Gasić and
Mike Gavrilović, who managed to gobble up enormous amounts of air time
on regional and international news shows. In literally many hundreds of interviews, their faces and uncompromising defense of the Milošević line became known to viewers around the world. But their positions had become
strikingly out of sync with those of the rest of SIC.

"These guys were highly patriotic," says Ratković, "but they had been
abroad so long they didn't know anything about the internal affairs of Serbia. They were thus very susceptible to government propaganda." According to the independent media in Serbia, Gasić and Gavrilović were also in
Milošević's pay. "They said that the new world order was crushing little Serbia, and so on," continues Ratković. "They really thought that opposition
leaders were paid by NATO and were traitors, foreign mercenaries and so
on. I tried to convince them that this was not the case, but it was impossible." Ratković concluded that somehow they had to be sidelined.

The backing of Serbia's fragmented democratic opposition from abroad
begged at least two critical questions: who to back, and how? More than two
dozen opposition parties crowded the Serbian political landscape. Internal

bickering and personal rivalries squandered the chances of the opposition to mount a unified challenge to Milošević. Knowing that the make-shift coalitions that the anti-Milošević forces had cobbled together in the past had disintegrated, the question was, could the diaspora help unite the opposition parties in a stable coalition? Or, in the absence of such a coalition, should the diaspora support individual parties? If so, which ones? And then there was the parallel question of whether the weary and disillusioned diaspora could come up with what the anti-Milošević forces needed most: the treasury necessary to compete with the state's intimidating propaganda machine.

Prior to the NATO military action against Yugoslavia in the spring of 1999, the sporadic efforts of diaspora groups and prominent individuals to rally the opposition largely fizzled. In the United States Djordjevich acted as an official representative for the opposition leaders Vuk Drašković, Zoran Djindjić and Vesna Pešić. The SUC facilitated the travel of opposition representatives to the United States to meet the diaspora and to testify before the U.S. Congress. They tried, without success, to convince U.S. policy makers to finally throw their full weight behind the opposition, which, they argued, was ready to lead the country to democracy.

The efforts of the democratic opposition in Serbia—and their allies overseas—to remove Milošević were abruptly interrupted when the brewing crisis in Kosovo came to a head. The harder the Serb police cracked down in the southern province, the more resolute became the Kosovar Albanians' determination to fight back. Blood flowed. Some eight hundred thousand Kosovar Albanian refugees streamed into neighboring Macedonia and Albania. When international talks to broker an internationally guaranteed settlement for Kosovo broke down, the West opted to bomb Milošević into submission.

On March 24, 1999, when the first NATO bombs fell on Yugoslavia, it was the first time Serbia had come under direct fire since the Nazi German bombardment in 1941. For a fleeting moment, Serbs everywhere in the world experienced the "unity" that had so painfully eluded them throughout their history. The Western-led bombing campaign against Kosovo united all Serbs—in Serbia, in neighboring countries, and across the diaspora. "There was no Serb anywhere in the world that wasn't devastated by this," says Nikitović, who led the daily demonstrations in Chicago. "It was an illegal, completely wrong-headed policy. For the time being we had to put the Milošević issue on hold."

When the last Yugoslav tanks rumbled out of Kosovo nearly three months later, the Serbs had suffered their worst military defeat of the decade. The old battlefield at Kosovo Polje, the site of Serbia's national resurgence only ten short years earlier, now lay in the hands of another people.

Kosovar Serb refugees were fleeing into Serbia, as Kosovar Albanians returned to their homes in triumph. Serbia's bridges and key industries lay in rubble, the nation's morale at rock bottom.

As grim as the situation was, the unity of the Serb nation dissipated with the sobering recognition of the extent of the tragedy of the past decade. "Milošević was exposed for what he was, a terrible blunder," says Djordjevich. "The time to push to topple him was now. It was also obvious to us that we finally had the U.S. administration behind us."

In London the SIC's Ratković and other board members expelled Milošević's media frontmen Gasić and Gavrilović from the organization. Through the SIC, now transformed into an informal embassy and vocal lobby group for Serbia's democratic opposition in Europe, dozens of the opposition's top leaders traveled to Western European capitals to make their case. At the time, the possibility of holding such meetings in Serbia was unthinkable. Ratković pounded on the doors of Europe's policy makers in London, Luxembourg, Brussels, and Berlin, using his considerable powers of persuasion to convince the West that the opposition was mature enough to run the country.

Yet one formidable obstacle stood in the way. Serbia's opposition remained fractured. Washington and London stipulated unequivocally that there would be no money or support until the members of the opposition set aside their differences. It was the brainstorm of Djordjevich and Prince Alexander to gather the diaspora and the opposition at a location outside Serbia proper. The task: to forge a common leadership and platform for the October 2000 elections. Their incentive was the promise of a $1 million donation from the diaspora should the array of opposition parties band together.

In Budapest, in November 1999, all the major diaspora groups worldwide met with the diverse components of the Serbian opposition: political parties, NGOs, women's and student groups. The meeting was the first of its kind, and it very nearly achieved its goal. More than twenty-five opposition parties came tantalizingly close to forging a unified bloc. But, at the last minute, monarchist Drašković's temperamental Serbian Renewal Movement pulled out. The million-dollar prize, which existed only on paper anyway, vanished. Nevertheless, the parties agreed on a common platform that formed the foundations of the future coalition, the Democratic Opposition of Serbia (DOS), which would officially come to life in January 2000. It was DOS that in October 2000 would narrowly defeat Milošević's Serbian Socialist Party at the polls and finally dislodge him from power.

In the final analysis, the diaspora contribution to the overthrow of Milošević was minimal. It was the U.S. government as well as other Western countries and aid agencies, not the diaspora, that bankrolled DOS and the student-led Otpor. In terms of money for the democrats, the diaspora came up with next to nothing. Diaspora figures counter that, without their lobbying efforts on behalf of the opposition, the Western funds from official sources would never have flowed.

The funding of the opposition by the West was understandably a touchy subject for DOS and Otpor. It played directly into Milošević's charge that they were the paid foreign agents of the West, of the same countries whose fighter planes had just bombed Serbia. As loudly as DOS and Otpor denied the charges, they had to explain the source of their considerable finances. The opposition leaders feared that an honest disclosure might turn popular sentiment against them. Their (dis)ingenuous response: the diaspora funded us! The story invented was that finally, at long last, the mythic Serb diaspora had come to bail out Serbia in its moment of desperation. The opposition pointed to Djordjevich as the mastermind behind the operation. He willingly accepted this mantle. Ironically the final contribution of the diaspora to the cause of democracy in Serbia was to take credit for something that it did not do.

PART III

Kosovo: Made in Yugoslavia

One son for the land, one son for the gun, one son for abroad.

Old Albanian saying

CHAPTER EIGHT

Skanderbeg's Way

"Well, welcome back to the Balkans!" Bent over awkwardly in the cramped plane, a grinning Chris Hill, the region's top U.S. diplomat, extended a hand to Dr. Bujar Bukoshi. Silver-haired and bespectacled, Kosovo's contested prime minister politely accepted Hill's gesture and passed into the Swiss Air flight's second-class seating. Bukoshi was just one of many returnees on the June 20, 1999, flight out of Zurich, packed to capacity with Kosovar Albanians. Outwardly composed, Bukoshi even dozed as the jet approached his intermediate destination, the Macedonian capital of Skopje.

At an al fresco restaurant on the city limits, Bukoshi convened the still-loyal fragments of his splintered government: cabinet members and political allies arriving from Switzerland, Macedonia, Albania, Slovenia, and Germany, where they had spent eight long years in exile. The prevailing mood at the table was anything but celebratory as one might have expected under the circumstances. Milošević's steel-blue army had that day completed its withdrawal from Kosovo after three months of NATO bombing. Thousands of Kosovar Albanian exiles, refugees, and migrant workers were pouring back into their liberated homeland. The war in Kosovo was over, and the Kosovar Albanians, to all intents and purposes, had won it. Yet few words passed between them as the somber entourage piled into private cars and set off toward Yugoslavia's southern-most border, the Blace crossing into Kosovo.*

In a suit and tie despite the oppressive heat, Bukoshi stared out the window at the border region's abandoned, litter-strewn refugee camps and the derelict fields in Kosovo, the crops choked by weed during a season of war. Along the highway, mud-splattered trucks roared past the convoy, horns blaring, giant black and red Albanian flags fluttering behind them. "We have a lot of work to do," says Bukoshi matter-of-factly, taking in the smells and sights of his native land for the first time since 1991. The top priority? "Of

---

* Ethnic Albanian populations are scattered across the southern Balkans. Their numbers in 2001 are estimated as follows: Albania, 3,227,000; Kosovo, 1,710,000; Macedonia, 475,000; Serbia proper, 100,000–150,000; Montenegro, 47,000; northern Greece, 50,000. (These estimates are from the United States Institute of Peace, with the exception of Serbia proper and Greece.)

course, we have to reestablish the institutions and structures of the legally elected government of the Republic of Kosovo."

Of course—well, not exactly. Whether or not Bukoshi accepted it, the years in exile had taken a heavy toll on his authority, to the extent that most Kosovar Albanians no longer recognized the legitimacy of his government. Darker voices warned that it might be better for him not to return at all.

Bukoshi, a urologist and surgeon by profession, had formally conducted the businesses of state—of an internationally unrecognized state—since the day he fled Serb-run Kosovo eight summers earlier. On that day, hours after he was named prime minister, the Serb police stormed his Pristina home and issued a warrant for his arrest. But Bukoshi had slipped away, hunkered down in the back seat of a car, speeding along the backroads of Macedonia en route to the Thessaloniki airport in Greece. His offices and ministries had never been in Kosovo but rather in empty research institutes in Slovenia, private houses in southern Germany, and other locations, places where host governments grudgingly tolerated a Kosovar government-in-exile.

There was no welcoming party to greet Bukoshi that hot June day in Pristina, Kosovo's muddy capital. No brass band or flags or little girls in folk dress to herald the man who had tirelessly pounded on the doors of the world's powerful to make Kosovo's case. The Fund for the Republic of Kosovo, which had been under his control, had collected more than $125 million in unofficial "taxes" to finance the parallel institutions of the Kosovar Albanians' shadow state. Yet, in front of the Hotel Grand, old acquaintances approached him tentatively before continuing on their way. Their timidity had its grounds: word on the street was that Bukoshi's name ranked high on a hit list. Unarmed and unguarded, he was a sitting target. This time, though, it was not the Serbs who had marked Bukoshi but fellow Kosovar Albanians.

"He's a traitor," snaps Dardan, lanky and twenty-something, his long legs extended brashly beneath a cafe table. After seven years in Canada, the young man left his job as a Vancouver rave DJ in the spring to take up arms with the Kosovar Liberation Army (KLA), the Albanians' underground guerrilla force, in the mountains of northern Albania. In Dardan's unit his fellow fighters grumbled about the millions Bukoshi had tucked away, which he stubbornly refused to hand over to fight the Serbs. Maybe, they surmised, he even worked for the Serbs. Why else would he stiff Kosovo in its hour of need?

"Even if he wasn't really a spy, and I believe he wasn't, then he acted like one. They couldn't have had a better one," says Dardan, launching into a loud harangue. "He thought by holding the money he held the power! Now look at him! No one cares about him," he gestures dismissively toward the plastic tables outside the hotel where Bukoshi and his ministers had modestly set up shop. "Sure, the KLA are a bunch of crooks but at least they did something. That was our money, my money. If Bukoshi had spent it the right way he'd be the most popular person in Kosovo now, no problem."

The assassin's bullet never came, but the decision to withhold the republic monies from leading KLA guerrilla commanders during the war would haunt Bukoshi. His fall from grace happened swiftly, undermining his claim to the prime ministership and, for years to come, rendering impotent the politician many Western diplomats thought should run Kosovo. Yet the genteel doctor, often underestimated by his enemies, refused to disappear from the stage in Kosovo. Bukoshi infuriated his political opponents and Kosovo's interim UN administration alike by turning the republic fund, basically the ethnic Albanians' treasury, into a humanitarian fund in Kosovo under his sole authority. By 2002, when eventually he muscled his way back onto the political scene, even Bukoshi's exasperated detractors acknowledged his mettle.

While the polyglot doctor was a favorite in the West, the heroes of the moment in postwar Kosovo were the rough-cut KLA commanders emerging from their frontline positions flush with victory. The KLA had part of its roots in the diaspora, too, above all in Switzerland, where militant activists had agitated among the gastarbeiter since the late 1970s. In contrast to Bukoshi and the intellectual leaders of the Democratic League of Kosovo (LDK), such as Kosovar president Ibrahim Rugova, the figures behind the KLA had operated for decades in clandestine networks, mixing in a brutish underworld that stretched from Stockholm to Tirana. For almost two decades these camorras had courted Kosovar workers abroad, attracting a nominal following with their bizarre ideological fusion of Greater Albanian nationalism and Marxism-Leninism. But that changed dramatically in the late 1990s when Kosovar Albanians, fed up with Rugova's pacifist policies and Bukoshi's dithering, turned to armed struggle to emancipate their homeland.

The turn of events in the late 1990s, ultimately so fortuitous for the Kosovar Albanians, would have been unthinkable without the mobilization of their communities in the diaspora. In contrast to the separatist Croats or Slovenes, the Kosovar Albanians lacked even a home base, such as a republic, from which to wage their campaign. In Yugoslavia, Kosovo had been designated a province, one notch lower than a republic in terms of the rights and powers it had in the country. And while the republics such as Croatia, Slovenia, and Macedonia were staking their claims to independence—and welcoming home their diaspora sons—in Kosovo the ethnic Albanians were fleeing Belgrade's repressive hand. The mass exodus from Kosovo would not simply bolster the existing Albanian diaspora, it would transform it completely. Ironically Milošević's own policies to subdue and "retake"

Kosovo for the Serbs created a diasporic force that would work with relentless energy to free its land from Serb domination.

The diaspora's engagement on behalf of their kinsmen was not considered unusually magnanimous by Albanian standards. It was expected of them. The Albanians date their rich tradition of diaspora activism back to the national hero Skanderbeg (1405–1468), a decorated general in the Ottoman army who defected from the sultan's ranks to lead his fellow countrymen in rebellion against the empire. The Albanians consider themselves a *wandervolk*, their migrations between the village and the wider world a normal condition. The exiles of the late twentieth century followed in the footsteps of Europe's nineteenth-century nationalists, including Albania's founding fathers, organizing abroad for the simple reason that their land was, in their view, under enemy occupation. As if second nature, they created an international solidarity and support network that kept the homeland afloat for a decade and funded not one but *two* guerrilla armies.

Bujar Bukoshi was not born to lead a struggle for national liberation. Like his father, a postal clerk, the young Bukoshi initially shied away from politics. In southern Kosovo, where he grew up, the post–World War II decades were unhappy ones for the province's Kosovar Albanians, then roughly four times as populous as Kosovo's Serbs. Few had carried arms for Tito's Partisans during the war. The experience of Serb-dominated interwar Yugoslavia had alienated the Albanian minorities to the extent that they welcomed the German and Italian occupation in the 1940s. In the aftermath of war, the communist victors sought to pacify Yugoslavia's "most hostile element," as they saw the Albanians, by shooting their nationalist leaders and many followers. More than forty thousand Albanians were rounded up and executed during the operation.

Most Kosovar Albanians thus perceived the Slav-run communist state as an alien authority. Tito's campaign to instill a "Yugoslav consciousness" in the country's multinational citizenry translated into heavy-handed policies of assimilation and de-nationalization in Kosovo. Bukoshi experienced the system's inequity, the Serb minority's domination of the local bureaucracy, and his Albanian teachers' nervous hesitation in the classroom. He sympathized with the informal and illegal anti-regime groups that surfaced in his high school. But he never joined them.

In fact, Bukoshi joined the Yugoslav League of Communists, the official state party, not out of conviction but as the only route for an aspiring professional. In 1964 Bukoshi embarked on his medical studies in Belgrade, one of a handful of Kosovar Albanians to earn the privilege. He exploited it, excelling in his science courses while branching out into literature, sociology, and history. At the time, in the late sixties, the campuses of Prague, Paris, and Berkeley were not the only ones with revolution brewing. With Sartre and Marcuse in hand, Yugoslavia's rebel students took to the streets to demand a new kind of socialism, a liberal, anti-authoritarian socialism permeated with the humanistic ideas of the early Marx.

Bukoshi marched along in the demonstrations, but with muted enthusiasm. Any overhaul that reshuffled the cards in Yugoslavia might bring changes to Kosovo, he calculated, perhaps a different status for the province within Yugoslavia, one less subservient to Serbia. But his Serb and Croat classmates refused to make Kosovo an issue. "There was a component of the student movement that tried to smuggle Serb nationalism in under the cloak of this new socialism," Bukoshi explains, recalling his first encounter with these ideas. He took note.

In 1968 demonstrations erupted in Kosovo as well, the first since the war's aftermath. While Bukoshi pondered French existentialism, Kosovar Albanian students demonstrated with banners that read "Down with colonialism in Kosovo" and "We want a Republic." Riots broke out, and arrests followed. Bukoshi listened to the reports by radio from the other end of the country. It would not be the last time that upheaval in Kosovo would find him far from the front lines.

By the time Bukoshi returned to Kosovo in the early 1970s, life for Kosovar Albanians had taken a turn for the better. The Yugoslav authorities granted the restless province far-reaching concessions, including its own university and, in 1974, special autonomous status, turning Kosovo into a full member of the federation with voting rights equal to the republics. Subventions flowed to the backwater region. But for Bukoshi, by then a newly licensed physician tackling his first job at a public health clinic in Glogovac, west of Pristina, the improvements only served to focus his eye on the enormous discrepancy between conditions in northern Yugoslavia and in Kosovo. His clinic had no running water. Sewage flowed in the streets. Primitive Glogovac's infant mortality ranked the highest in the country. "I realized that these conditions were the direct result of the policies of the Yugoslav state," he remembers, gesturing animatedly with his packet of Marlboro reds, never far from his reach. "Once the improvements began to take hold, people began to ask themselves, 'Why is Kosovo so underdeveloped? We need more rights, more development, new chances.' Kosovar Albanians began looking for their own place in Yugoslavia. In Belgrade it woke up nationalist voices who began to ask: what if we lose control of Kosovo?"

Resentment and frustration bubbled over. When the lid finally blew in the spring of 1981 Bukoshi was away again, on a year-long scholarship in Berlin, at a West German surgical clinic. The demonstrations in and around Pristina University—and the crackdown that followed—marked a critical turning point in Kosovo and effectively created the political diaspora of the 1980s. The protests began with student complaints over substandard food and long lines in the university cafeteria. In a few short weeks, discontent turned into riots across Kosovo. The calls for an ethnic Albanian republic within Yugoslavia were heard in even the smallest towns throughout the province. Placards read "Kosovo Republic" and "We want a United Albania!" and "Down with Revisionism, Long Live Marxism-Leninism." When the Belgrade authorities reacted, it was with full force, leaving several hundred dead and arresting hundreds more including scores of university activists, the suspected ring leaders.

Tito had been dead for less than a year, and buried with him was any pretense of "brotherhood and unity" between Serbs and Albanians. Serb nationalist elements began to reassert central authority over the province.

In 1987 Slobodan Milošević appeared on the scene, a party bureaucrat indistinguishable from his colleagues. It was in Kosovo at a small rally of Kosovar Serbs that Milošević first tasted the power of nationalism, and it was first in Kosovo that he won nationalist plaudits for bringing the Serbs' unruly southern province to heel. When, as president of Serbia, he orchestrated the dissolution of Kosovo's political autonomy in early 1989, he pushed the button that triggered a sustained, decade-long revolt of Kosovo's Albanians.

The gutting of Kosovo's autonomous status was a tremendous, shattering blow to the Kosovar Albanians. The provisions of Yugoslavia's 1974 constitution had made Kosovo virtually co-equal in most respects to the six republics. The province had its own (multiethnic) parliament, police force, judiciary, and educational system. The reimposition of direct colonial rule over Kosovo was a turn the Kosovar Albanians could not accept.

In the spring of 1989, 215 Kosovo Albanian intellectuals issued an appeal protesting the abolition of Kosovo's autonomy. One of them was Bujar Bukoshi, a popular professor of surgery in Pristina. The authorities did not take long to retaliate. Bukoshi was at the operating table when Serb police showed up at his university clinic. Scalpel in hand, he was escorted out of the building. When he tried to visit his patients the next day, he found the clinic under armed guard, his entry barred. That was the last surgery Bukoshi would perform in Kosovo.

More humiliation was to come. The abolition of self-rule constituted only the first phase of Milošević's program to "re-Serbianize" the province. For Serb nationalists, Kosovo was "sacred Serbian soil" that the ethnic Albanians had "usurped" over the centuries, through mass immigration from Albania, a sky-rocketing birth rate, and the intimidation of Kosovar Serbs, which had driven them from their ancestral homes. Milošević's strategy to reverse this balance amounted to a simple exercise in ethnic calculus: increase the number of Serbs and decrease the number of ethnic Albanians in Kosovo. Serb immigrants would be lured into Kosovo by financial enticements, loans, and offers of land and jobs, while the Albanians would be coerced to emigrate. "A policy of discrimination, economic and police pressure has been carefully planned with one goal in mind: the ethnic cleansing of Kosova," wrote the Kosovar Albanian sociologist Shkëlzen Maliqi at the time.[1] It is highly unlikely that Milošević or his co-conspirators pondered where the Albanians would go or what they would do when they got there. The diasporas of the ethnic "other" do not figure in the short-sighted calculations of demographic politics in the Balkans.

In 1990 and 1991 the Serbian parliament passed law after law aimed at reshaping the balance of peoples and power in Kosovo. Either directly or indirectly, the discriminatory provisions prompted the dismissals of many tens of thousands of employed ethnic Albanians. The Serbs purged all Albanians from the state sector, including the police force, public services, and industry. In addition to Bukoshi, 1,854 other doctors and health care workers lost their jobs when they refused to sign loyalty oaths. Serb authorities shut down the Albanian-language media, relieving 1,300 journalists of their jobs at the state-run TV and radio stations. When Albanian teachers rejected the modified Serbian instruction plan, more than 25,000 teachers were fired.[2] By 1992 an estimated 70 percent of Kosovar Albanians had been removed from their places of employment.

Only a year after the dismissals began, sociologist Maliqi described the situation:

> Serbs and Albanians live separated from each other, the former as a privileged minority who, with the assistance of the police and the army, administers and controls Kosova, while the others, although in an overwhelming majority (in the ratio of nearly 9:1), are subjected to powerful repression and complete marginalization in political, social and economic life. The system that is being built in Kosova has almost all the characteristics of national apartheid and segregation: the Serbs were not content with the abolishing of the previous autonomy and takeover of absolute control in administration, economy and in cultural institutions, but went on to usurp almost all public goods and civil institutions. . . . Hotels, restaurants, sports centers and stadiums have become "Serbian," as well as all institutions of secondary education, university buildings, school and college dormitories, libraries with reading rooms, cultural centers, all public halls, workers' resorts, swimming pools, etc.[3]

Not every fired or persecuted Kosovar Albanian left Kosovo. But thousands and then tens of thousands and then hundreds of thousands of Kosovars would pack their bags.

Bukoshi, devastated by his own expulsion from the hospital, channeled his workaholic energy into his new career—politics. Strikes, protests, and the brutal reprisals of the Serb police shook the province. The new vehicle that gave voice to the Albanians' grievances was the Democratic League of Kosovo, in name a political party but with such broad appeal and wide-ranging functions that it has been better described as a mass movement. Born on December 23, 1989, the driving forces behind the LDK's creation were intellectuals such as Ibrahim Rugova, chairman of the Kosovo Writers' Association, and Bukoshi; the two became, respectively, president and general secretary of the LDK. Within weeks, the LDK mushroomed into a movement with half a million members and branches across the province. Bukoshi, for the first time in his life, was on the front line. He would not remain there for long, however.

The LDK would dominate the Albanian side of politics in Kosovo throughout the 1990s and beyond. Although Western analysts dubbed it "moderate," the LDK pursued a nationalist agenda no less straightforward then its militant-minded rivals, whom foreign journalists referred to as "nationalists." The LDK, often criticized for its authoritarian structures and mentality, started off with thin democratic underpinnings. Bukoshi elaborates:

> The LDK was a spontaneous reaction to events in Kosovo. We settled upon "league" in the name because we didn't want a selective, narrow political party. A "party" would've been more risky, too. And "democratic" [he laughs] was an "in word" at the time. We included it to gain some kind of immunity, since Albanians were frequently branded as extremists and terrorists. It's not a particularly proud story but we knew we had to use this word for strategic reasons. In the back of our heads, of course, we knew that first we had to get out from under these Serbs. Democracy wasn't a priority at the time.

The LDK also struck a nerve in the Albanian diaspora communities that had burgeoned with ethnic Albanians from across Yugoslavia since the early 1980s. The formation of the LDK ignited an exuberant outpouring of solidarity in a previously unorganized diaspora. Ethnic Albanians from Macedonia, Montenegro, and Albania proper signed up, too. Hundreds of branches sprouted from Slovenia to Scandinavia and laid the foundations for an international network that would serve the Kosovar diaspora for years to come. "At the very beginning there was no organizational impetus from the Pristina leadership," explains Dardan Gashi, a Vienna-based activist and writer in the early 1990s. "The LDK was finally saying what everybody wanted to hear, and Kosovar Albanians [in the diaspora] flocked to it. Sections popped up everywhere not only in Vienna but in every village in Austria with more than three Kosovar Albanians," he laughs. "The diaspora was even more outwardly enthusiastic than people in Kosovo because, for them, there was no direct danger involved."

In Germany sixteen LDK branches had been set up by May 1990. Three years later Germany boasted as many as three hundred branches and sub-branches. During that period the number of Kosovars in Germany more than doubled. Joining the pre-1989 Kosovar Albanian population, mostly gastarbeiter families that had put down roots, the newcomers were refugees, the by-product of Milošević's demographic machinations. The LDK's Stuttgart-based diaspora director, Hafiz Gagica, estimates that the ethnic Albanian population in Germany jumped from around 100,000 in 1990 to nearly 250,000 in 1994.[4] LDK offices with full-time staffs sprung up in Stuttgart, Vienna, Melbourne, Tirana, Toronto, Zagreb, Stockholm, Istanbul, Brussels, Oslo, and New York City.

Only at rare historical junctures, usually in times of crisis, do diasporas experience anything approaching the moment of unity, the oneness of purpose, conviction, and organizational cohesion that so obsesses nationally minded diaspora leaders everywhere in the world, and yet usually eludes them. The LDK captured this moment during the first half of the 1990s. The diaspora Croats rallied with a focused sense of purpose when their homeland came under attack in 1991, just as nonresident Serbs rose in solidarity when their nation went to war. But in neither case did a single organization, save their respective churches, garner the diaspora's allegiance the way that the LDK gained the loyalty of the Kosovar Albanians. These moments, however, pass quickly; the cohesion of the Kosovar diaspora would withstand the test of time better than most. But it, too, would eventually dissolve.

Bukoshi soon appreciated the risks of his new profession. Returning to his Pristina apartment late one evening in September 1990, four masked men jumped the slight doctor, threw a sack over his head, and bound his hands and feet. The methods of the Yugoslav security services were not unfamiliar to Kosovar Albanians, and Bukoshi had every reason to believe that the hour was his last. At a country hide-out the team interrogated him through the night and into the morning, a pistol at his head. Eventually they dumped him in a field—exhausted and terrified, but alive.

Bukoshi's ordeal was not an isolated case. Police intimidation, beatings, and arrests ratcheted up the pressure on the Albanians. Known activists faced expulsion. It was becoming impossible for Kosovar Albanians to engage publicly in political activity in Kosovo.

Since the formation of the LDK, events in Kosovo had lurched forward. In the summer of 1990 the Kosovar Albanian deputies in the demoted provincial parliament, a shell of its former self under autonomy, tried to obstruct passage of the new Serbian constitution. Tit for tat the Kosovar Serbs locked the ethnic Albanian deputies out of the assembly building. On its steps the Kosovar Albanian parliamentarians defiantly voted to proclaim Kosovo a republic—separate from Serbia but within Yugoslavia—equal in status and powers to Yugoslavia's other republics.

The move pulled up short of full independence but, legally, republican status included the right to secede from Yugoslavia. Bukoshi claims that by then he harbored no illusions about Kosovo remaining part of Yugoslavia, in any constellation. His people's differences with Belgrade had become irreconcilable. The Serb authorities seemed also to understand it this way, but from their point of view that spelled separatism, treasonous activity that imperiled the state. The Kosovar parliament was dissolved, Albanian radio and television shut down, and direct rule imposed from Belgrade. Like outlaws, the fired parliamentarians carried on with their political activity, working at night by stealth and sleeping during the day in different locations.

The situation was clearly untenable. The first step toward exile came in September 1990 in the small southern town of Kaçanik, where the expelled Albanian deputies gathered to promulgate a constitution for their self-proclaimed republic. The delegates concluded that their (illegal) parliament and an appointed interim government, not originally including Bukoshi, would fan out from Kosovo to seek support from the other republics in Yugoslavia. The political parties would stay in Kosovo to work on the ground.

The first stop of the fugitive Kosovar assembly was Zagreb, Croatia. The circumstances of exile require exile politicians and governments to rely on the good graces of foreign governments, hosts who rarely profit directly themselves from the outcasts' subversive activities. Perhaps the Kosovar Albanians considered their cause so self-evidently righteous that they, as fresh exiles, would be welcomed by their ideological allies with open arms. If so, they were mistaken. It seems that none of the Kosovar deputies thought to call ahead to Zagreb for an invitation. On their arrival, the Tudjman government unceremoniously informed the one hundred politicians that Croatia had enough of its own headaches. They were unwanted guests.

The next destination was the independence-minded Alpine republic of Slovenia, which in the past had shown some sympathy toward the Kosovar cause, especially when it dovetailed with its own. "Slovenia guaranteed our safety, which was very considerate at the time since Slovenia was still part of Yugoslavia," explains Halit Muharemi, the former general secretary of the Kosovar parliament and then the justice minister in Bukoshi's 1991–99 exile government. The Yugoslav security services were still active then [in Slovenia] so there was a real danger of us being shot or kidnapped. The Slovenes gave us licenses to arm ourselves, and their security people guarded us, too.

Remember, our presence was an act of defiance for Slovenia. We had the same goals—independence—so it was like a pact between us." Typical of the exile's desperate hope, Muharemi thought that his return to Kosovo was around the corner. The status quo, he figured, simply could not last. Asked how long he remained outside Kosovo, he answers in a flash: eight years, three months, and four days.

The Slovenia experience proved instructive for the Kosovar Albanian politicians. On June 25, 1991, Slovenia declared its independence from Yugoslavia, as did Croatia. The Kosovars watched from the picturesque northern Slovenian town of Bled as Yugoslav tanks tried to squelch Slovenia's bid for sovereignty. Slovenia's week-long war against Yugoslavia concluded when the JNA sheepishly withdrew. Little Slovenia had humbled the Yugoslav Goliath. "It was exciting for us," remembers Muharemi, "because we knew the secession of Slovenia would further our own goals."

Muharemi, a constitutional lawyer, studiously began drawing up Kosovo's own plans for independence. In Slovenia, in September 1991, the remnants of the defunct, communist-era Kosovar assembly approved the Resolution on the Independence and Government of Kosovo. It went a giant step further than the Kaçanik declaration that proclaimed Kosovo a republic inside Yugoslavia. It was Kosovo's own declaration of independence. Several weeks later, in Kosovo, a hastily organized popular referendum conducted by the Kosovar Albanians brought to life the Republic of Kosovo, which, according to its founders, was the newest independent and sovereign state in southeastern Europe.

This independent Kosovo, called into being from exile, from the other end of war-racked Yugoslavia, existed primarily in the minds of Kosovar Albanians. Unlike Croatia and Slovenia, whose republican police and territorial defense forces formed the nucleus of future armies, the Kosovar Albanians were defenseless, their homeland occupied by one of the largest armies in Europe. Kosovo's independence, explains British journalist Tim Judah,

> was, of course, a state of virtual reality. In other words it existed in some form, but definitely not in the sense of Kosovo Albanians running Kosovo. The Serbian and Yugoslav institutions remained, Albanians carried Yugoslav passports and the Yugoslav army and Serbian police remained very much in control. But, this is where the experiment began, guided by the LDK. Instead of trying to mount a violent insurrection to realize this independence the party began to simulate it in the hope that, by force of demographic and other pressures, Kosovo would, one day, simply drop into Albanian hands like a ripe fruit.[5]

To the extent that this wishful proposition constituted a plan, exile and the diaspora were central to making it happen. First, in order to breathe life into this phantom state they had to believe in it, which meant treating its constitution, even if only a blueprint, with due respect and formality. With the creation of institutions such as an elected parliament, a government, a presidency, and a parallel social system, they could put flesh on its skeletal frame. But it would all mean nothing from the confines of a Serb jail cell. "Exile was the only alternative. It was the lesser of evils," recalls Bukoshi ten years later in his Pristina office. "The other option was to stay here and be arrested by the Serb police. We knew how difficult it would be to operate from exile, to be effective, but we wanted to send the clear signal that we have a democratic, legitimate, and legal government." The Serb authorities may have tolerated opposition Kosovar Albanian parties in Kosovo, Bukoshi notes, but they could not accept an alternate government that claimed sovereignty over the same land and citizens as Belgrade did.

On the ground in Kosovo, Albanians opted for the strategy of mass noncompliance, a boycott of all the Serb-run institutions as a means to deny their legitimacy and thus that of Serb rule. An extraordinary experiment in nonviolent resistance, they set about constructing an entire self-organized society parallel to, but not obstructing, the one the state sanctioned. The teachers who had been fired gathered their classless pupils together in underground schools, instructing them in living rooms, garages, cellars, mosques, and shops. University classes also met on private grounds. Medical professionals erected makeshift clinics to offer Albanians at least minimal health care. Jobless workers, civil servants, and others had no option but to branch out into the private sector, one they first had to create.

In Kosovo at the time some people harbored grave reservations about the strategy of parallel and exile institutions. A small group of influential intellectuals argued that the government and parliament should remain in Kosovo—and face arrest, should that be the consequence. Could the regime really lock up 130 parliamentarians and a government? they asked. If it did, then the Kosovo Albanians could elect another 130 to replace them, they argued. Exile would hopelessly marginalize the leadership and make it ineffective. It would lose touch with the struggle. Resistance, they contended, had to be waged on location. If the nation's leaders ran away, who would lead the nation? And would the government's example spur ordinary Kosovars to flee, too? The province was already being drained of its best minds.

It was in the leased rooms of the Slovenian Academy of Sciences in Bled that the exile government had its first seat. Bukoshi's cabinet was a mixed bag, including independent-minded intellectuals, ex-radicals, and former communist party members. Bukoshi was prime minister and foreign minister; Halit Muharemi, justice minister; the accountant Isa Mustafa, finance minister; university dean Muhamet Bicaj, education minister; the Swiss-based journalist Xhafer Shatri, minister of information; and Nikë Gjelosi and journalist Ramush Tahiri, the deputy prime ministers. The health minister, Adem Limani, operated inside Kosovo. And, critically, each ministry also had an undercover counterpart, in effect a co-minister on-the-ground in Kosovo. The co-ministers for each portfolio were to work with one another in close coordination, a demand often complicated by distance and poor communications.

"Our options were so limited that at the time it felt hopeless," says Bukoshi, who was living out of a suitcase like the others. The shadow state desperately needed a budget to finance the Albanian schools and health care system. Internationally, Kosovo needed allies. And the leadership knew it also had to plan for the future, for the day, perhaps, when Kosovo, like Bosnia and Croatia, had no choice but to shoot back.

Bukoshi's first foray into the arena of international politics hit a brick wall: "Nobody was willing to accept us as a negotiating partner," he says. "All the doors were closed. We had to pry them open." Bukoshi started his entreatments and worked around the former Yugoslav republics sounding out their officials on Kosovo's independence, among other issues. In Western Europe Bukoshi scheduled appointments with junior desk officers at the foreign ministries, human rights groups, and political party functionaries—anyone who would give him the time of day. It was not a lack of sympathy or interest in the plight of the Kosovar Albanians that Bukoshi encountered. But he found extreme caution about even appearing to condone Kosovo's drive for independence. The international community insisted that the province remain in some form of revamped state together with a democratized Serbia and Montenegro. Even Albania proper never officially recognized Kosovo's statehood, although it treated the exile government, which had an "embassy" in Tirana, with all of the courtesies afforded legitimate state officials.[6] All other foreign officials met with Bukoshi as a representative of the Kosovar Albanians, never as prime minister.

The diaspora Kosovars, on the other hand, turned out in droves to cheer on their new leaders. Organized largely through the extensive LDK network (virtually identical with the Bukoshi government in this early phase) the prime minister and other activists stumped through Europe's Kosovar Albanian communities: LDK branch offices, Albanian cultural societies, gastarbeiter clubs and provincial beer halls. This network, particularly in western Germany, Austria, Switzerland, and Scandinavia, proved indispensable to the Kosovar cause throughout the 1990s. Before the creation of the republic fund in 1992, the Kosovar Albanians passed the hat to pitch in for schools and health clinics. A few wealthy Kosovar businessmen in Switzerland chipped in to cover the government's operating expenses. The vast financial potential of the Albanians' European diaspora was no secret to

Bukoshi or anyone else. The trick was how to prime the pump, as no one else ever had.

Kosovo's bid for independence galvanized the diaspora in a historically unprecedented way. Followers of other smaller preexisting parties peeled off to join the exciting new movement that was the LDK. It was part of Bukoshi's job to keep them onboard. Despite its expedient use of the word *democracy*, the LDK and the exile government were Western-oriented, outspokenly committed to nonviolence, and ultimately interested in a Kosovar state that could one day join the European Union. As we shall see, this vague set of goals constituted a qualitatively new direction for Kosovar Albanians, one requiring vigilant reinforcement.

Nonviolent resistance, for example, was not an idea that came naturally to the Albanians, a people proud of their martial culture. As Bukoshi slogged from town to town he painstakingly explained the government's policy of passive struggle, whose revered symbol was President Rugova, a Sorbonne-educated literary scholar with a benign professional air. The Kosovar Albanians had no alternative at the moment, Bukoshi reiterated. Neither was Kosovo in any way ready for an armed uprising against the Serbs, nor would the West tolerate it. Statehood, he insisted, could be achieved through peaceful means. But after his stump speeches, over a glass of wine, he assured his countrymen that their republic was silently preparing for darker days, should passive resistance fail. Behind the scenes, the Kosovar Albanians had set secret plans in motion to build their own army.

Bukoshi's reluctance to move boldly on the military question would ultimately split the Kosovar leadership, precipitate his downfall, and drive a wedge into Kosovar political culture into the twenty-first century. But in the early 1990s the prime minister's first steps toward consolidating embryonic defense structures commanded the full support and participation of an unlikely coalition of actors, including Rugova, the diaspora LDK, and Kosovo's radical fringe, whose skepticism of the LDK intellectuals ran deep. The government started virtually from scratch, under conditions of the utmost secrecy. The covert defense and interior departments, both in Kosovo and abroad, initiated rudimentary intelligence-gathering operations that charted police and troop movements, and mapped the sites of Serbia's military installations. Regional intelligence networks were pieced together from the fired police force and Kosovar Albanians who had been Yugoslav army officers.

In order to counter the inevitable repercussions of Serb infiltration, the Kosovars organized the net on a horizontal "chain-link" principle. Each member of the network knew the proper name of only two other members: the persons one link above and one link below on the chain. Should someone be exposed and arrested, the contacts on either side would immediately flee abroad out of reach of the Serb police. The chain broken, damage to the network would be confined.

"Of course it would have been better if we could solve our problems non-violently, better for Serbia, for us, for everybody," concedes Anton Kolaj, the former LDK vice president and Bukoshi's 1991–94 defense co-minister in Kosovo. For the professional schoolteacher Kolaj, his was arguably the most dangerous job in Kosovo. Parallel schools and hospitals did not threaten Serbia, but a secessionist rebel army did. Moreover, the preparations for armed insurgency were just the pretext Belgrade needed to clamp down on the Kosovar Albanians with its full might, settling the question of Kosovo once and for all. Should Kolaj's cover be blown, he could count on being tortured, at the very least. Kolaj estimates that the Kosovar Albanians had 450 professional former officers inside and outside Kosovo. He knew that the will to fight Serbia existed, but he asked his officers a simple question: as professional soldiers, can you tell me whether we are militarily prepared to wage and win a war with Serbia today? "They couldn't say yes," he recalls.

Patience and meticulous groundwork were the order of the day. In this early phase the militant splinter groups in Switzerland and the clannish extended families in rural Kosovo operated in close coordination with the Bukoshi structures. Together they set up covert training camps in "several countries," in Albania and presumably Croatia. According to Kolaj, Bukoshi's republic fund was conceived as a war chest. "This is how the diaspora understood it. And I'd say clearly to them what Bukoshi and Rugova couldn't," explains Kolaj, who toured the diaspora as an LDK representative to raise funds. He emphasizes today that he had both Rugova's and Bukoshi's full and explicit support to do so. "I'd tell them [diaspora Kosovars] that we were willing to consider different ways to liberate Kosovo. They understood. They weren't donating money for Albanian schools in somebody's cellar but to get their kids out of the cellars and back into the school buildings." The diaspora's knowledge of this strategy was never leaked to the Western press. In effect, the Kosovar leadership was lying to its Western interlocutors, swearing that their struggle was and would remain nonviolent. International diplomats dismissed the Serbs' accusations that ethnic Albanians were involved in armed separatist activities as more Milošević propaganda.

As for military allies, the Kosovars could count few. Albania proper signaled it would not help them, even if it could. The political costs—like disfavor with the West or war with Yugoslavia—were too high for the dysfunctional, impoverished motherland still gasping in the wake of communism's collapse. Most promising appeared Croatia, desperate itself for friends with a third of its territory under rebel Serb control and no sign in sight of reversing battlefield losses. The possibility of a two-front war against Serbia naturally intrigued the Croatian president. Tudjman wheedled the Kosovar Albanians to launch a popular uprising in Kosovo's cities and a guerrilla war from the mountains. But the Kosovars demurred: they just weren't ready. Not only were they short of firepower, they instinctively distrusted Tudjman who, as they correctly surmised, was in cahoots with Milošević to divvy up Yugoslavia's corpse between them.

Nevertheless a battle-ready Kosovar unit, the Guard of the Republic of Kosovo, manned front lines alongside the Croatian army in 1991. The Guard fought with the Albanian coat-of-arms, Skanderbeg's black eagle, emblazoned on their uniforms. But the tenuous alliance with the Croats petered out in acrimony over its command. The Croats wanted the unit fully integrated into the Croatian army, subject to its chain of command, whereas the Kosovars demanded their own officers. After the unit's disbandment, the Kosovar ministers living in Croatia, such as the de jure defense minister Ramush Tahiri, were requested to leave. Radio Kosovo in Zagreb was shut down. Shortly thereafter the Slovenian authorities informed Bukoshi that their hospitality, too, had run out, no reason given. Bukoshi and his finance minister left Slovenia for Germany in April 1992, and the other ministers moved to Macedonia, Switzerland, and Albania. Slovene exile had come to an end.

On matters military, the Bukoshi government's contact from the militant diaspora circles was Xhavit Haliti. A thick-set man with heavy-hooded eyes, known then only by his code name, Zeka, Haliti was a key figure in the Swiss underground. Gruff and tight-lipped, he does not usually meet with foreign journalists. And when he does, he gives away little. When I first met Haliti in March 2002 in Pristina's Hotel Ilyria, his terse condemnation of Bukoshi was so unkind that it took some leap of imagination to envision the two of them ever meeting on compatible terms. As far as Haliti is concerned, Bukoshi should be locked up for robbing the Kosovar people. Bukoshi hoarded the Kosovars' money and divided the nation at the height of its liberation struggle, he charges. If Bukoshi had really been on a hit list in June 1999, then it was men such as Haliti who were behind it. At the time of our interview, however, it was Haliti who was under investigation for a range of criminal activities. The UN and German finance authorities had scoured Bukoshi's accounts and found nothing improper or unaccounted for in the books, somewhat to their dismay. But Bukoshi sat sidelined from politics while Haliti boasted a top position in Kosovo's second largest political party and was one of the parliament's vice presidents.

Haliti and his co-conspirators in the Swiss-based Popular Movement for Kosovo (Lëvizja Popullore e Kosovës, or LPK) had staked out diaspora turf for more than a decade before the LDK and Bukoshi appeared in the early 1990s. Their revolutionary slogans and adoring praise of Albania's ultra-orthodox communist leader, Enver Hoxha, attracted a modest following in the late 1980s, when the Popular Movement was the only game in town. But the LDK's enormous appeal lured diaspora members and activists away from the radical camp. The LDK's diaspora chief, Gagica, and the Bukoshi government's minister of information, Shatri, both had histories in the militant movement during the early 1980s. The Popular Movement shut down its own Swiss-based bank fund (Help for Kosovo), paying instead into the Bukoshi treasury for a time. But the likes of Xhavit Haliti never trusted Bukoshi or the LDK. They were just too different. Seldom had the course of their lives or the coordinates of their political visions intersected, even on Kosovo's miniature grid. During most of his service to the Popular Movement, Haliti was a paid agent of the Albanian secret services, the Sigurimi. Later, during the war, he put those contacts to good use as the KLA's Tirana-based operative responsible for smuggling arms.

Haliti and Bukoshi grew up on opposite sides of the tracks. Born in 1956, in the city of Peć in western Kosovo, Haliti came from a family with close ties to the interwar Albanian nationalist movement Balli Kombëtar, or National Front. The anticommunist "Ballists" had long championed an "ethnic Albania" that included Albania proper, Kosovo, part of southern Serbia, western Macedonia, and a piece of Montenegro—the classic Greater Albania scenario. The World War II Kosovar Ballists collaborated with the German and Italian occupation, explains Haliti, for the simple reason that the Kosovar Albanians wanted out from under Yugoslavia. Their enemies were the Serbs—Chetniks or Partisans—it didn't matter. The stripe of their allies' flag was less germane than advancing the cause: freeing Kosovo from Slav rule.

In the aftermath of the war Haliti's uncles and older cousins fled the wrath of Yugoslavia's communist authorities and took up new positions abroad, in the United States, Italy, England, Belgium, and Turkey. Many Kosovo Albanian exiles initially melted into the anemic organizations of Albanian émigrés from Albania proper. Unlike the Serbs, the Croats, or the Slovenes, the multidenominational Albanians (mostly Muslim but also Catholic and Eastern Orthodox) never had a single religious institution that underpinned the diaspora. Seething with anger, the defeated flotsam of Balli Kombëtar, the Second League of Prizren and the royalist Legaliteti (followers of Albania's Egypt-based King Zog) reestablished themselves in back-alley headquarters with small printing presses where they plotted the overthrow of communist Albania and the unification of all Albanian lands. Their master plan: first liberate communist-controlled Albania, then free Kosovo, and finally western Macedonia and Montenegro, in that order. Major currents in the Albanian diaspora would remain wedded to versions of this strategy into the 1990s.

As a teenager, Haliti visited his relatives in the diaspora, including his father in West Germany, a migrant worker who left Kosovo in 1971. In Western Europe the émigré activists sewed literature into the boy's luggage for him to distribute back home and assured him that one day the Albanians would prevail. Albanians had endured exile in the past, they told him, and had returned home in triumph. It was Albanian communities in Romania, Bulgaria, Anatolia, and Italy in the 1800s that had nurtured the nation's intellectual traditions during direct Ottoman rule in the Albanian-inhabited lands. The first political program for an independent Albanian state stemmed from these circles. Even into the early years of the twentieth century (Albania and Kosovo were still under Ottoman control) Bucharest remained the epicenter of the Albanian world community. Through channels in Egypt and Bulgaria, funds, propaganda, and weaponry were funneled into Albanian revolutionaries. In 1913, at the fateful London conference following the Balkan wars, the European powers intervened to settle the Albanian question. An independent Albania was allotted a fleck on the map but Kosovo was placed under Serb tutelage, where it would remain, with one brief intermission, until 1999.

Another story recounted by Haliti's uncles, one told to him in hushed tones, was of an embarrassing little episode in the Cold War which came to public light only decades later.[7] Official sources in Washington and London originally mocked the reports that in the late 1940s and early 1950s Western-trained Albanian exiles had infiltrated communist Albania with the top-secret mission to subvert Enver Hoxha's regime. But the reports were true. One of Haliti's uncles, a surviving member of the émigré sabotage units—one of the few survivors—attested to the existence of the operation, and its inauspicious failure.

In the aftermath of the Berlin airlift and the Soviet Union's consolidation of Central and Eastern Europe, the West perceived Stalin to be on the offensive and perhaps even gaining a competitive edge. Little Albania, wedged between rebel Yugoslavia (Tito had just broken with Stalin) and civil war–torn Greece, appeared the prime candidate to be prised from the Soviet orbit. Perhaps the West could chalk up an easy victory over Moscow and, more important, deny the Soviet Union the Mediterranean port it craved.

Britain's Secret Intelligence Service (SIS) first approached the Albanian émigré community in early 1949 at their provisional headquarters in Turkey, Greece, Italy, and Egypt. Thousands of wartime Albanian refugees languished in Italian displaced persons camps waiting for permission to return home or to emigrate elsewhere. The British officers floated the idea of spiriting small armed units into the Albanian mountains to test the climate and lay the grounds for an anti-Hoxha insurrection. To no one's surprise, the exile resistance leaders jumped at the idea and plans were hastily set in motion. Several groups of émigrés, picked from the rival factions around King Zog and Balli Kombëtar, convened on the Mediterranean island of Malta. There Western intelligence experts, led by the British, had prepared a training camp to instruct the volunteers on the basics of counterrevolution. Often the SIS and CIA officers had their hands full just sorting out quarrels between the royalists behind King Zog and the republican supporters of Balli Kombëtar. Perhaps the tensions in the camp helped divert attention from Kim Philby, one of the top British agents on the project. No one in the operation suspected that Philby was a double agent, in Moscow's pay, relaying details of the doomed mission to the Soviets every step of the way.

The military side of the operation commenced in October 1949 when SIS officers deposited the Albanian commandos off the coast of southern Albania. The Albanians' mission entailed making contact with anticommunist elements in the country, convincing them of Western support for their cause and then slipping back over the border into Greece. The units would leave behind gold, communications equipment, and propaganda material, including photos of King Zog. They promised to return with more if the requisite enthusiasm was present. The first foray into the Albanian hinterland fared no better than those that would follow. Whether a result of Philby's tip-off, other leaks, or simply the diligence of Albanian intelligence, Hoxha's military police and army units were lying in wait for the so-called pixies. In a bloody ambush, three guerrilla soldiers were shot and killed almost at once. The five who made contact with their families and former comrades-in-arms had a hard time convincing them that the Western powers were serious about overthrowing Hoxha. What proof could they offer? Why were they only a handful, and no Westerners among them? And where were the arms?

Over the next five years at least a dozen such units infiltrated Albania to spread propaganda and foment insurgency. Most of the agents were shot down in the field or captured, put on trial, and then executed. Tirana reaped huge propaganda windfalls: to catch agents of U.S. imperialism red-handed was a coup indeed. The West laughed off the "show trials" as the delirious concoctions of a warped dictatorship.

The Western agencies obviously never took the inexpensive, low-risk operation as seriously as the men who lost their lives for it, or their families and contact people in Albania who suffered the repercussions of abetting counterrevolutionaries. Exiles often prove willing pawns, and these men were sterling examples. Desperate and determined, people with nothing to lose, the exiles made perfect accomplices. When the operation flopped, the Western powers washed their hands of it. A decade later, the United States would mount another exile-led invasion, if on a much bigger scale, with more than one thousand anticommunist Cuban émigrés at Cuba's Bay of Pigs. The 1962 operation would have no more success than had its Balkan predecessor.

In the latter half of the 1970s Pristina's newly founded university emerged as a hotbed of radical anti-regime thought and activity. The Albanian Studies Department, in particular, attracted nationally minded young ethnic Albanians from across southern Yugoslavia. One of them was Haliti, who spent less time in the overcrowded classrooms than he did circulating *samizdat* manifestos and scribbling anti-Tito graffiti on Pristina's buildings. Inexplicably Haliti and his mates had not latched onto the royalist or interwar nationalist traditions embraced by his exiled family members, at least not directly. Rather, and to the horror of the aging Albanian émigrés looking on from Europe and North America, the Kosovar resistance had seized on other traditions to achieve the same goal. Its young activists had come to see Enver Hoxha, the hard-line leader of communist Albania, as Kosovo's savior and mentor! The illegal groups around the university sported such names as the Revolutionary Movement for the Unification of Albanians, the Marxist-Leninist Revolutionary Youth Group, the Albanian Leninist Party, or the Youth Movement for the National Liberation of Kosovo, Haliti's organization.

By that time neighboring Albania had perked up its ears to the calls of ethnic Albanians in Yugoslavia, even if it never—explicitly or implicitly—backed their demands for a unified Greater Albania. In the 1970s and 1980s travel between the two countries was still strictly forbidden. Few Kosovar Albanians had ever stepped foot in Albania proper, their southeastern neighbor with a forty-five-mile contiguous border. But textbooks and newspapers flowed over the closed frontier as did the broadcast messages of Radio Tirana, the official mouthpiece of the communist regime. It seemed to Kosovar Albanians that their rightful motherland was finally taking note of them. They tuned in gladly to hear Albanian folk music or programs on Albanian culture and history, all off-limits in Yugoslavia. With outlandish propaganda mixed into the daily reports, how were Kosovars to know that Albania was a suffocating nightmare of a dictatorship and not the egalitarian paradise Radio Tirana depicted?

"It was basically a reflection of our love for Albania, the motherland," says Haliti, a bit shamefacedly, speaking today about the Albania-Hoxha cult. "They were bombarding us with strong propaganda twenty-four hours a day. We thought Albania was very powerful, that it even had an atomic bomb," he laughs. "It was an Albanian state but it was hermetically sealed. When I first went there in 1990 I had planned to kiss the ground, but I couldn't even speak. I immediately lost my illusions." This disillusionment, however, did nothing to sour Haliti's superb connections with the communist party's "socialist" successors in Albania. In contrast to Bukoshi, Haliti maintained special contacts with the socialist's intelligence services throughout the 1990s and particularly, when it counted, in 1997–98 when war broke out. As the KLA's top gunrunner, Haliti had an office in a building provided by the Albanian government.

Also, since their struggle was revolutionary in nature, they picked out some useful tricks from the early Bolshevik movement. The university-related groups organized conspiratorially, relying on the organizational principle of "cells." The stakes were high: detection spelled prison or heavy fines. During the 1970s hundreds of ethnic Albanians were arrested and convicted of plotting the secession of Kosovo from Yugoslavia. In the period between 1974 and 1981 Yugoslav security forces claimed to have rooted out seven underground Albanian separatist organizations operating in Kosovo and two in Macedonia. Their crimes against the state fell under headings such as "counterrevolutionary behavior," "hostile propaganda," or "inciting national hatreds." The student groups' cloak-and-dagger methods would remain the organizational principle of the underground groups in Kosovo after 1981 and would follow them into exile.

Haliti, one of the "Class of '81," was arrested after the violent demonstrations, released on grounds of insufficient evidence, arrested again, and released again. In 1983, away without leave from military duty, authorities apprehended him on the Austrian border attempting to flee. He spent a year and a half in jail before emigrating to Switzerland in 1986.

Others, such as Bardhyl Mahmuti, a core member of the Popular Movement/KLA leadership in the 1990s, served jail sentences of up to eight years for sedition. The jails, he remembers, were packed with ethnic Albanians. "There were so many that it was impossible to isolate us. Even in prison we organized ourselves so that as soon as we were out we'd be active as soon as possible," says the Macedonia-born Mahmuti. At the time, he emphasizes, no distinctions were made between ethnic Albanians from Macedonia, Montenegro, Kosovo, and southern Serbia. "Back then," he laughs, "the border between Kosovo and Macedonia was marked with a painted stone. From 1981 to 1991 we were all working for the same cause, that of a single Albanian republic in Yugoslavia," he says.

Old Popular Movement propaganda from the time shows the proposed Albanian republic extending over all of Kosovo, half of Macedonia (including Skopje), about a fifth of southern Serbia, and corners of Montenegro. "We knew that unification with Albania at that time was impossible," explains Mahmuti. "Unification with Albania implied a military strategy that we didn't have. That's why we wanted a republic in Yugoslavia first." And that is why he and his counterparts set about developing a military strategy.

Republican status was a tactical stepping-stone to outright secession, just as the Serb authorities had charged.

Gradually, after their release from prison and short stints working underground in Kosovo, Mahmuti and Haliti and others from the Class of '81 trickled abroad to hook up with comrades in Western Europe who had been plotting Kosovo's liberation since the 1970s. The natural first port of call, Albania proper, was closed. Tirana authorities took an active interest in the Kosovar activists but not openly, not to the point of making public waves with Belgrade. Ironically the U.S., West German, and Swiss authorities exhibited more generosity toward post-1981 asylum seekers than Mother Albania did. But the early radicals forgave Albania the cold shoulder. Backstage, they told themselves, the picture was different.

The Popular Movement for Kosovo was born first as the Popular Movement for a Kosovar Republic, in Istanbul, Turkey, in February 1982 and united several fragmented strands of the Albanian underground in Germany and Switzerland. The helping hand of the Albanian secret services guided its creation. "Albania as a state was never interested in the dissolution of Yugoslavia," explains the editor of *Zëri* (Time) magazine Blerim Shala, who interviewed former Albanian intelligence operatives for a book on the subject. "They wanted somehow to damage Yugoslavia but not to destroy it. After 1981 they thought that somehow they could influence events in Yugoslavia through these groups."

In the late 1970s tiny groups had surfaced abroad with names that paralleled those in the Pristina University circles. The Popular Red Front, the Marxist-Leninist Organization of Kosovo, and the National Liberation Movement of Kosovo and Other Albanian Regions of Yugoslavia (the latter with the ponderous acronym LNCKVSHJ) struggled to find the money and readers for their irregular, mimeographed publications. The front page of the "organ" of the Marxist-Leninists, *Liria* (Freedom), sported a blood-red Albanian flag with the black double-headed eagle and the communist star attached to the barrel of a rifle. "Proletariat of the world unite," it proclaims. The more sophisticated *Lajmëtari i Lirisë* (The Messenger of Freedom) includes, among its poetry and essays lavishing praise on Albania, a full-page photograph of the teenage, cherubic-cheeked Enver Hoxha in a Partisan uniform.

The Kosovar exiles' strategy was twofold: to produce propaganda material for distribution in Kosovo (and the other Albanian-inhabited parts of Yugoslavia) and to court the ranks of the Albanian guest workers who had flooded Western Europe since the 1960s. Ultimately they envisioned a guerrilla insurgency from the mountains or an intifada-type uprising in the cities or both. The propaganda targeted the gastarbeiter both as ethnic Albanians and as members of the proletariat. A 1983 flyer distributed across

Germany on May 1, International Labor Day, provides a taste of the revolutionary rhetoric:

> Workers of the world unite! Bread, work, and a republic for the Albanians in Yugoslavia! Kosovo, inhabited primarily by Albanians (over 80 percent), is a province inside the Serbian republic. The poverty and unemployment is always greater than the Yugoslav average. At the moment joblessness is 22 percent above the Yugoslav average. The national income is six times lower than in Slovenia. This poverty and unemployment has forced more than 120,000 workers to go abroad in order to sell their labor power to the monopolies (especially in Western Europe). . . . In order to triumph against reactionary governments and powers, against U.S. imperialism and the social imperialism of the Soviet Union, against both the military blocs of NATO and the Warsaw Pact, we must trust our might, as our own nation does. Regardless of how strong the Yugoslav government appears—our nation has risen up in order to demand its elementary rights and to fight. It wages now heroic opposition against the terror; it fights willfully until victory. The reactionary regime, the opportunists, the troublemakers—organized in different movements and with their terrible propaganda—try to divert us, the nations, and the workers of the whole world not to trust our inexhaustible powers.

It was a hard sell not only because the message rang so stale. "It was extremely difficult to get through to the gastarbeiter," explains Ibrahim Kelmendi, one of the Kosovar movement's first pioneers, who lives today in Cologne, Germany. "First there was fear. The UDBA was everywhere, and the guest workers knew that if they were discovered in our groups or with our literature they might not be allowed to return. Also, they were uneducated, often illiterate." The first generation of Albanian gastarbeiter were road workers, the lowliest of the migrant jobs. "Sometimes at meetings I had to read our literature aloud to them," says Kelmendi. Interestingly, despite the left-wing slant, the Kosovar Marxists received little sympathy from Western leftists. Socialist Yugoslavia's experiment with workers' self-management, whatever its shortcomings, understandably intrigued German radicals more than the struggle for a Stalinist Greater Albania.

The guest workers' angst about secret service infiltration and its repercussions was not fantasy. By 1982 Germany's federal police counted seventy fatalities connected with Yugoslav exile groups on West German territory over two decades.[8] In the city of Heilbronn in southwestern Germany, on the evening of January 17, 1982, Yugoslav agents gunned down three top Kosovar leaders: Kadri Zeka and the Gërvalla brothers, Jusuf and Bradhosh. The twelve bullets fired at close range from a 7.65-mm Beretta were the calling card of Yugoslavia's professional hitmen. Coming on the tail of the bloody back-and-forth between the Yugoslav spy services and the exile Croats in Germany, the Heilbronn executions infuriated the already displeased West German government, which took up the prickly issue directly with Belgrade. "We simply cannot accept," fumed the *Stuttgarter Nachrichten*, "that foreign security services send their killers here. That goes for the hitmen of the Shah, Qaddafi's men in black, and naturally also for Belgrade's executioners."[9] German police never cleared up the murders despite a nationwide manhunt. Fearing for their lives, Jusuf Gërvalla's family—his widow and three young children—left for Albania, where they lived until 1990. Gërvalla's eldest daughter, Donika, would return to Germany in 1992 and serve as the LDK's diaspora vice president throughout the 1990s.

With the assassination of thirty-six-year-old Jusuf Gërvalla, Tito's agents eliminated a formidable opponent, perhaps the one man who could have forged a credible movement out of the 1980s Kosovar diaspora. No less loyal to the idea of a Greater Albania, Gërvalla, a newspaper editor, poet, and pop singer, cut a more sophisticated figure than the other early Kosovar activists. People such as Kelmendi and Haliti proved too limited to transcend the sad caricature that became the Popular Movement.

Like other political exiles, the mind-set of these men remained stuck in the stifling confines of the events that produced and defined their expulsion from the homeland. Inevitably their curricula vitae included persecution, prison sentences, and often torture. Even well into the 1990s many of them clung to some form of crass ultra-nationalism rather than explore the democratic political culture in which they had lived for ten or twenty years. Their covert ways and underground mentality remained ingrained in their modus operandi for years to come. Why, one wonders, did they so stubbornly resist the influences of the West? Haliti, for example, despite his more than ten years in Switzerland, never learned to speak German, Italian, or French. The Popular Movement leaders lived between the milieus of the proletariat gastarbeiter, a criminal underground, and the world of the Balkan secret services. Most eked out livings from unskilled labor. The West was a platform for their struggle, nothing more.

Kosovo would later pay for its diaspora leaders' uninspired political imaginations. One deficiency shared by all the Kosovar exiles, including Bukoshi and the diaspora LDK, was an unwillingness to think much beyond the short-term goal of independence. The LDK's liberal shortcomings would leave it nearly as ill-prepared as its rivals in the post–Popular Movement parties to lead Kosovo toward a democratic future, when the time came. A symptom of the thinness of exile discourses, neither faction had formulated a thoughtful vision of what Kosovo would look like after its liberation. For example, no mention was made of the future status of ethnic minorities, such as Serbs or gypsies, in an independent Kosovo. Serbs were only spoken of in connection with Serbia proper and the instruments of repression, never as neighbors, potential political allies, or future equal citizens in an Albanian-led Kosovo. Diasporas rarely become constructive forums for dialogue and forward thinking, and certainly not on issues addressing the homeland's ethnic others. The Kosovar Albanian diaspora proved to be no exception.

CHAPTER NINE

Birth of a Lobby

"This is Sami Jonuzi! He and his brothers own the best pizzerias in Atlantic City!" barks Joe DioGuardi, dwarfed in the
throng of Albanian American businessmen around the eve-
ning's guest of honor, Delaware senator Joseph Biden, chair of the influential
Senate Foreign Relations Committee. On his toes, DioGuardi waves Jonuzi
through the pack. Biden smiles a fixed ear-to-ear smile. Cameras click and
flash. "Shake the senator's hand, Mr. Jonuzi! Mr. Jonuzi is another 'max'
donor! Yeah, it's OK to say that, this is a fund-raiser!" bellows DioGuardi
playfully, as he scans the group for another $2,000 "maximum" donor.

On this special evening in Manhattan's Sheraton Hotel, the former U.S.
congressman Joseph J. DioGuardi, the founding father of the powerful Albanian American lobby, appears as fully in his element as a man could be. A
five-foot-five, one-person show pulsating with adrenaline, the master of
ceremonies is everywhere at once: making introductions, double-checking
the guest list, tending to a dozen VIPs, and distributing the promotional literature that he and his wife, Shirley Cloyes DioGuardi, produced for the
event. As he passes one table he hurriedly adjusts a plastic stand holding
miniature Albanian and American flags. The $100-a-plate function qualifies
as much more than a one-off fund-raiser for DioGuardi's organization, the
Albanian American Civic League. The star-studded array of U.S. and Albanian politicians in the Sheraton's Imperial Ballroom, packed to the rafters
with more than six hundred Albanian Americans, translates into stock of another kind for DioGuardi. It confirms that in the spring of 2002 he is still a
major player, if not *the* major player, in the U.S. Albanian lobby.

In fact, sixty-one-year-old DioGuardi's pretensions are even grander: he
touts himself first among diaspora Albanians in the world. Just who exactly
does Joe DioGuardi represent? It is a knotty question, the kind that could
be posed to any diaspora leadership figure. Certainly, if you ask him, he represents the half million Albanian Americans in the United States.[1] Sometimes he appears to speak on behalf of the entire Albanian diaspora worldwide; at other times no fewer than the world's fourteen million (his figure)
ethnic Albanians. When he acts, he does so in the name of the Albanian national cause—as he interprets it. This, in diaspora politics, is par for the
course. Though unelected and unappointed, he serves as a point man in

Washington for the Albanian people of Albania, Kosovo, Macedonia, Montenegro, Greece, and Serbia. At the same time, he promotes individual politicians and patron parties on the ground in the Balkans. He is an adviser, fund-raiser, and powerbroker. It is turf DioGuardi guards like a terrier.

In the mid-1980s the junior congressman DioGuardi and a handful of New York–based Albanian American businessmen founded the Albanian lobby and forced the issue of Yugoslavia's Albanian minority into the sights of U.S. policy makers. The lobby raised millions of dollars to promote its agenda and, under DioGuardi's tutelage, deftly worked the corridors of power in Washington to line up big-name congressmen and to apply hard-nosed pressure on consecutive administrations. The 2002 Manhattan event marked the twelfth anniversary of a dinner in 1990, the first visit of Kosovo's Albanian leadership, including Ibrahim Rugova, to the United States. The Kosovars later testified at a DioGuardi-organized hearing before the Congressional Human Rights Caucus in Washington. According to DioGuardi, the visit was a historic step in internationalizing the Kosovo issue and thus was a milestone on the road toward Kosovo's liberation. "We wouldn't be where we are today without the work of the Civic League!" he lectures the Sheraton crowd. Minus the pomp, there is a grain of truth to his boast. But fifteen years down the road, long since ousted from Congress, his original supporters gone, DioGuardi is no longer the only game in town. The Civic League—run by DioGuardi and his wife, who doubles as his "Balkan Affairs Adviser"—is just one of several U.S. diaspora groups that compete for the wealth of North America's Albanian communities, a foot in the doors on Capitol Hill and political clout on the ground in the Balkans.

Despite misgivings about DioGuardi's rabble-rouser style and the imperial nature of the mantle he claims for himself, he still commands enormous respect from across the community. Even his detractors admit that, without his savvy, Albanian Americans would not have the voice they do today. "His energy is incredible. It's just not always constructive energy," quips one guest at the Sheraton dinner, a member of the National Albanian American Council (NAAC), a Washington-based group that includes many of DioGuardi's former allies. The New York City dinner shows that DioGuardi and the Albanian lobby as a whole still pack a formidable punch, even after the dust of the wars has settled. Its sustained activity is something the other diaspora lobbies, those associated with the former Yugoslavia, no longer muster. In contrast, they are spent forces.

On the elevated rostrum facing the dining room floor sit Biden, Congressman Benjamin Gilman from New York, New York Senator Charles Schumer, and leading Albanian politicians from Albania, Kosovo, Macedonia, and Montenegro. Kosovo's muscle-bound war hero, Ramush Haradinaj, rarely leaves DioGuardi's side. "Now let's everybody turn off our cell phones, we don't want to embarrass ourselves tonight," DioGuardi reminds the guests in his broad Bronx drawl. But no one seems to mind the patronizing slight. When Biden enters the room or, after him, New York City's mayor, Michael Bloomberg, DioGuardi pumps his fists in the air and leads the cheer "Biden! Biden!" "Bloomberg! Bloomberg!" The hall erupts on cue. Only Joe DioGuardi could pull off such a show.

After the New York fete DioGuardi accompanied seven of the Albanian politicians to Washington where he had arranged audiences with House and Senate committee leaders, State Department officials, and a hearing before the Congressional Human Rights Caucus. The message the troupe carried to Washington may have sounded less imperative than those of similar expeditions in the past, such as when Kosovo writhed under Serb rule during the 1990s or when civil war threatened Macedonia a year ago. But it was delivered with no less vigor and conviction. It is, with minor variations, the agenda that most of the Albanian diaspora has come to endorse over the last few years: full independence for postwar Kosovo, full equality and human rights for Albanian minorities in Macedonia, Montenegro, Serbia, and Greece, and democracy and economic development for Albania. While DioGuardi describes the Balkans' Albanians as "divided by borders imposed by others" and speaks of a new era of Albanian "empowerment" and "self-determination," the Civic League and its friends and rivals in the Albanian diaspora insist they neither demand nor wish for a Greater Albania. This shift away from "ethnic Albania" illustrates that the communication flow between diasporas and their host states can be a two-way street. The diaspora organizations such as the Civic League, NAAC, and others received and transmitted the message that Washington had sent them loud and clear: to push for a greater Albania is futile and ultimately counterproductive. The diaspora Albanians wisely took the advice and moved on.

DioGuardi's involvement with the Albanian diaspora began the moment he realized he was an Albanian American. It happened rather late in his life, at the age of forty-five, by sheer coincidence during his first term as a U.S. Representative. DioGuardi grew up in the Little Italy section of the South Bronx, the elder son of Italian immigrants. His father, who ran a neighborhood green grocery, never spoke much about the Old World, and DioGuardi assumed that the language his father spoke with his own siblings was a rare Italian dialect. After graduating from Fordham University in 1962, DioGuardi went straight to the international accounting firm of Arthur Andersen and Co., where he climbed the ladder for the next twenty-two years, including twelve years as a partner.

"At age forty-three I had enough accounting," he explains in the Civic League's drafty offices above a garage in Ossining, New York, a sleepy upstate hamlet on the Hudson River where the DioGuardis make their home.

From the window DioGuardi admires his pride and joy, a 1965 metallic-blue Cadillac convertible in vintage condition, the first car he ever owned. On this particular afternoon DioGuardi's voice is raspy and his demeanor uncharacteristically subdued: the price he paid for the week-long New York–Washington junket. But after some small talk and a coffee he springs out of his chair. Pacing the room's creaky wooden floorboards he animatedly recounts the life story of Joe DioGuardi.

In 1984 the Republicans were desperately seeking a candidate to run in the traditionally liberal 20th District of Westchester County, where the DioGuardi family had moved in the late 1950s. Normally no Republican, much less a conservative like DioGuardi, would have had a chance in the district, which spanned poor minority neighborhoods in Yonkers to upscale suburban towns such as Scarsdale, Larchmont, and Rye. But the Democratic candidate was weak, an aide to the retiring incumbent, and DioGuardi opted to give it a go. A bit ironically, in the campaign he played up his ethnic roots—the son of Italian immigrants. House Republicans were ecstatic when this political neophyte, an unknown certified public accountant with the loudest New York City accent they had ever heard, squeezed out the thinnest of victories and entered the 99th Congress in 1984.

In his first race DioGuardi didn't receive a dime from the Albanian community. He still didn't know he was an Albanian American. The next year, at a birthday party for DioGuardi, some of his Irish American supporters brought along a group of ethnic Albanian contractors to flesh out the crowd. The Albanians, from Kosovo and southern Serbia, included Ramadan and Jim Xhema, the latter the owner of a local construction business in Rye, New York. They overheard DioGuardi's father speak with his younger sister in Albanian and soon ascertained that the DioGuardi family were Arberesh, an ethnic Albanian minority in southern Italy that had fled Ottoman-ruled Albania in the fifteenth century. "We're Albanians from Kosovo," they told me," explains DioGuardi. "And your father's people left Kosovo more than five hundred years ago. Congressman, we need to talk to you about what's happening to your Albanian brothers and sisters in Kosovo today." With this news, Joe DioGuardi became part of the Albanian diaspora.

The Kosovars sat down with DioGuardi and unfolded a map of the Balkans. They explained the worsening human rights situation in this faraway province in socialist Yugoslavia. Few U.S. politicians had detected that since the 1970s Albanian political refugees and immigrants from Kosovo, Montenegro, and western Macedonia had begun to change the face of the Albanian American communities in the United States. A particularly high concentration of ethnic Albanians were settling in the tri-state region of New York, New Jersey, and Connecticut—men such as the Xhema brothers. (Xhema, who would go on to make a fortune in construction and real estate, became a major contributor to the campaigns of the Albanians' friends in Congress for years to come.) A national constituency was taking shape with the human rights issue close to its heart, and with potential votes and money to give. DioGuardi went to work pronto. Together with the heavy hitters whom he recruited for the issue, including Holocaust survivor Tom Lantos, a California Congressman, and Kansas senator Bob Dole, DioGuardi, in 1987, hastily cobbled together the first of many congressional resolutions addressing Albanian issues. The concurrent House and Senate resolutions "condemning the repression of ethnic Albanians by the government of the Socialist Federal Republican of Yugoslavia" immediately encountered stiff opposition from the State Department and congressional allies of the Greek lobby.[2] No need to ruffle feathers on this issue, was the consensus in the State Department. The resolution was snuffed out before it came to a vote.

DioGuardi and Lantos began talking about the Albanian American community as a possible constituency, something no one had yet done. Lantos, of Hungarian Jewish origin, knew the issue, and DioGuardi was learning fast. The ethnic Albanians, so many fresh to the country, had to learn the ropes in the arena of U.S. politics. "They [the Albanian Americans] had to understand that they not only had to become better citizens by voting, but that even if they weren't citizens yet they could legally contribute to congressmen like Lantos as well as make charitable contributions to the Congressional Human Rights Caucus, run by Lantos. I got one of these guys to make a $25,000 contribution. That got Lantos's attention!" DioGuardi cries. "We quickly got them [the Albanians] to understand that you've got to support people who you want to support you."

An underdog even as the incumbent, DioGuardi in 1986 secured a second two-year term in one of the priciest, most fiercely contested congressional races in the United States that year. New York's 20th Congressional District was considered up for grabs, and the anti-abortion candidate DioGuardi was an easy target. But DioGuardi's $1.2 million tooth-and-nail campaign pummeled his opponent, the nationally known liberal Bella Abzug. DioGuardi's fund-raising prowess and constituency building had paid off. Having won by only three thousand votes in his first race, DioGuardi's winning margin this time was fourteen thousand votes. Only a small fraction of his monies in this race came from the Albanian Americans, such as the contractor Xhema, but that would soon change. Back in Congress, DioGuardi redoubled his efforts to pass a resolution that would put the Albanian issue on the map.

The product DioGuardi offered the Albanian Americans was a nonbinding congressional resolution, basically a kind of message from Congress to the executive branch. "I told these Albanian guys that they needed a vehicle for their issue," explains DioGuardi. "In Congress the language is a bill. It educates the staff, educates the congressmen, it allows you to cite it, you put it on the Congressional Record. And you start building a constituency on the inside. They had never done that before."

"The second time around I understood the issue. It was Kosova," he says, using the province's Albanian name. The expanded resolution zeroed in on the plight of the Kosovar Albanians whose numbers, not coincidentally, were growing by the year in the United States. DioGuardi personally knocked on the doors of his congressional colleagues and cornered them on the House floor explaining the seemingly distant, complicated issue: Kosovo, Yugoslavia, Albanians, human rights. Slobodan Milošević had not even come to power when DioGuardi, Lantos, and Dole reintroduced the resolution, this time with dozens of co-sponsors. The bill did not pass, but this time the State Department, which had weighed in against it, was forced to respond. "They said this issue shouldn't be raised at this time because of our good relationship with Yugoslavia, *our friend Yugoslavia*," says Dio-Guardi in a mimicking tone. Little did he know then, he says, the strength of the "pro-Serb lobby" inside and around both the State Department and the National Security Council (NSC). Its chief personalities, according to DioGuardi, included the assistant secretary of state Lawrence Eagleburger, the NSC director Brent Scowcroft, the U.S. ambassador to Yugoslavia Jack Scanlan, and Henry Kissinger. DioGuardi would come to blows with these men again down the road.

By 1988, in his next race for reelection, DioGuardi finally connected with the Albanian American constituency, which would make generous contributions to the campaign and loyally finance his (chronically unsuccessful) attempts to win back his House seat over the next decade and beyond. More important, they would form the nucleus of the first modern Albanian American lobby, the Albanian American Civic League. DioGuardi stumped through the Albanian churches and mosques in New Jersey, Brooklyn, Staten Island, and the Bronx, establishing a national database and mailing list with two thousand ethnic Albanian donors. Two-thirds of the donations he received from Albanian Americans came from contributors outside his congressional district. But despite the new money source, DioGuardi lost by two thousand votes (a margin of 2 percent) to the Democratic challenger Nita Lowey, in her first run for office. It spelled the end of his short congressional career: he would never again tread on Capitol Hill as an elected representative.

Even today, fourteen years later, DioGuardi pines for his old seat. It is this aspiration, insiders say, that drives his involvement in the affairs of Albanian Americans, his "natural constituency," as he calls them. A registered PAC related to the Civic League, the Albanian American Public Affairs Committee regularly makes direct donations to People for DioGuardi, a campaign-related account that was never shut down. Few observers give DioGuardi, tainted by scandal and spurned even by his own party, an outside chance of making a comeback. Running against the Republican Party–endorsed candidate Sue Kelly in 1996 and again in 1998, DioGuardi's tally dropped from 13 to 4 percent of the total votes. But in the direct aftermath of the 1988 squeaker, his chances for another successful run looked decent enough—and his ambitions dovetailed conveniently with those of the Albanian Americans. The situation in Kosovo was deteriorating, and the ethnic Albanians needed a tenacious voice in Washington more than ever.

DioGuardi, Xhema, and a handful of Albanian American businessmen launched the Albanian American Civic League in January 1989. Xhema and eleven others kicked in $12,000 a head for the salaries of DioGuardi and three of his former key staff. The Civic League kept up the pressure on the "pro-Serb" State Department and helped stage ever larger demonstrations in Washington. In July 1989 the Civic League scored the biggest success for Albanian Americans to date. House Congressional Resolution 2655 and Senate Congressional Resolution 20, which condemned Serbia for human rights abuses in Kosovo, passed both houses of Congress. The resolution "expressed grave concern" over the "rapidly deteriorating condition of ethnic Albanians" living in Yugoslavia and requested that President Bush convey to Belgrade his support for Kosovo's continued autonomy within Yugoslavia. The issue was now on the map.

The resolution set off alarm bells from Chicago to Athens. Serbian American congresswoman Helen Delich Bentley and Greek American legislators blasted the resolution with all the artillery at their disposal. The State Department rushed to emphasize its engagement on the issue. Infuriated, Belgrade withdrew the Yugoslav ambassador to the United States. And the Greek lobby suddenly realized it had a formidable competitor on its hands. Nearly two years before war broke out in Yugoslavia, a war of a different kind was being waged in the U.S. capital.

In a small two-story house, directly across from the leafy southern periphery of the Bronx Zoo, are the offices of Vatra—the Pan-Albanian Federation of America, the oldest of the Albanian American community's many organizations. The group's congenial president, Agim Karagjozi, has plenty of time for me. After we chat for several hours he leads me back into a musty one-room library where a pastel portrait of the Rev. Fan Noli, Vatra's founder, is propped up amid the chaotic collection of books and newspapers.

Diaspora-produced literature must qualify as a genre unto itself. The usually self-published histories or biographies are unabashedly one-sided tracts with no pretense to academic rigor or balance. They trumpet the praises of long-forgotten national heroes or purport to "document" something previously undocumented, such as a glorious national struggle or the heinous crimes inflicted on them by another people. Inevitably, as I leave the Vatra office, Karagjozi fills my arms with books, as well as diaspora journals, literary reprints, and a stack of Vatra's quarterly, *Dielli* (Sun).

Months later, as I weeded through a box of such materials, one of Karagjozi's gifts caught my eye. A remarkable exception to the rule, this 1939 study of Albanian immigrants in the Massachusetts region, *The Albanian Struggle: In the Old World and New*, was an extraordinary product of President Franklin Roosevelt's Federal Writers' Project (FWP), part of the New Deal–era Works Progress Administration. Researched and written by a team of Harvard social scientists, clearly in close cooperation with knowledgeable Albanian Americans, the succinct study tells a flesh-and-blood story of the first Albanian arrivals to the United States, their early years in the country, and the evolution of their transatlantic discourse with the homeland. By a stroke of luck, perhaps, the Albanian Americans possess in this study an obscure gem that offers a fascinating account of the U.S. diaspora's engagement in promoting Albania's national independence, a story brimming with parallels to the experiences of the Albanian migrant communities nearly one hundred years later.

When the first Albanians set sail to the New World in the 1880s and 1890s to escape the destitute conditions of their remote Ottoman-ruled province, their steamers deposited them not only on another shore but virtually in another epoch. The economic refugees, predominantly unlettered peasant men from southern Albania, settled in New York and New England, landing jobs in mill towns, in the shoe factories, or as menial day laborers. Lonely and secluded, they worked themselves ragged to save up a pocket full of dollars and return home to their families and farms. In tenements or slums on the city outskirts, the Massachusetts Albanians huddled together in single shared flats called *konaks*, sometimes a dozen or more male workers to a room. Often listed as Turks or Greeks, to the ordinary American they did not exist at all.

These early immigrants had probably never given much thought to politics back in their rocky mountainside villages where they scratched out existences in vineyards and olive groves. They did, however, know that their people was an ancient one and that their ethnic identity was different from their Greek neighbors to the south and the Slavs to the north. The Albanians had long since struck an acceptable modus vivendi with the Ottoman authorities, even though Albanian schools and publications were forbidden in the province as late as the end of the nineteenth century. But an exiled nationalist movement with centers in Istanbul, Romania, Greece, and Egypt harbored intellectuals and agitators who longed to partake in the national awakenings sweeping Europe. They kept a watchful eye on the migrations to America.

In the American factory towns the grind of the workers' daily lives spawned a potent nostalgia for the homeland. In addition to the fertile soil of expatriation, these first-generation gastarbeiter enjoyed liberties that their compatriots under Turkish rule, or even in the European diaspora, could not dream of, such as freedom of speech and assembly. And, relatively speaking, they also had money. The diaspora headquarters in Europe sent over emissaries to enlighten the mill-town migrants about their nation's patriotic struggle. In the konaks, teachers with primers printed in Bucharest began to tutor the illiterate workers in the subject of their own language.

In Boston, in 1906, the first issue of the Albanian weekly, *Kombi* (Nation), rolled off a backstreet press. The paper espoused the wishes of Albania's upsurgent nationalists: an autonomous Albania within the framework of the Ottoman Empire; Albanian schools; native Albanian judges, administrators, police, and prison wardens; and the adoption of the Albanian language for all public transactions. *Kombi*'s editor was Fan Noli, a Harvard-educated, Eastern Orthodox bishop.

From the pulpit of Albania's first independent Orthodox Church (1908), in publications such as *Kombi* and *Dielli*, and through his 1912–founded organization, Vatra (Albanian for "hearth"), Noli rallied his countrymen around an outspoken nationalist agenda. Yet in 1912, when the first Balkan war broke out, the Albanian Americans unexpectedly balked at full independence for Albania. The time was clearly ripe to throw off Ottoman rule, with Bulgaria, Greece, Serbia, and Montenegro set to dismember the "sick man of Europe." In a gaffe explained by distance rather than weakness of will, Noli and his Boston followers horribly misread the situation. They stuck with their demands for autonomy and even pledged military aid to Turkey! Better to do business with the devil you know, they reasoned, than risk partition between the Slavs and the Greeks. Although the Albanian American community hastily backtracked when the Ottoman regime collapsed like a house of cards, it was the first of many stunning lapses in judgment that the Albanian diaspora would commit over the years. The Albanian American leaders were pro-German in World War I, flip-flopped on the issue of interwar monarchy, and then sedulously backed the communist dictator Enver Hoxha for years.

Never again, though, would Vatra waver on the principle of Albanian sovereignty. Presumably the pioneering Albanian American lobby effort, Vatra weighed in with all its might to petition the victorious Great Powers to recognize an independent Albania. The Massachusetts Albanians sent Noli himself to the negotiations at the London conference to make the Albanians' case. Greece, Serbia, Montenegro, and Bulgaria all had their sights set on a piece of Albanian territory, and they would certainly have consumed it all had the 1913 conference not condoned the creation of the modern Albanian state.

From the first days of independence, the native Albanians in the United States felt a vested interest in the affairs of the infant state. In 1920, at the Vatra convention in Boston, the delegates, perhaps a bit presumptuously, elected Noli to the Albanian parliament, thus setting an early precedent for diaspora voting rights. The penniless government pleaded with the Albanian Americans not to stop sending remittances. When Albania needed backing for a major loan, it was floated through Vatra.

Independence spurred an idealistic wave of emigration back to the homeland, which gathered momentum after World War I. Most of the work-a-day migrants had never planned to settle in Massachusetts or anywhere else in America, and the euphoric moment seemed like the right time to withdraw savings and return to help reconstruct the war-ravaged homeland. Between 1920 and 1925 an estimated twenty-five thousand Albanians left America for Albania proper, roughly half those in the country. As an expression of gratitude for the U.S. contribution to independence, active Vatra members received officer posts in the new national guard and choice political appointments. The thinking was that their worldly experience and knowledge would help to pull Albania out of its archaic rut. Fan Noli emerged as the paragon of the political forces in Albania that advocated transforming the country into a modern European republic.

The high hopes of the *Vatrani* and the *Amerikani*, as they were called, were soon dashed. The Muslim ruling elite in Albania, opposed, above all, to land reform, dug in its heels. "As this group came into the ascendancy," reads the FWP study, "the welcome that had at first been extended to the Amerikani rapidly chilled." Returned natives found themselves ridiculed for their "visionary notions" and discriminated against in government circles. Pains were taken to remind them that they were only peasants, despite their American ways and their pretensions to worldly wisdom. They were warned that they had better "look to which side their bread was buttered on." They became the butt of jokes, vicious but often not so far off the mark: "So you dishwashers from America want to get the better of us, eh? Tell me, my American, why do you carry those pens in your coat pocket when you do not know how to write your name?"

Disillusioned with the intransigence of the landed aristocracy, many of the Albanians sailed back to the United States, this time to make it their home. Whole villages packed up and left. More Christians chose to return than Muslims, which explains the disproportionate concentration of Albanian Christians in today's North American diaspora. The returnees brought their families with them or, once back in the United States, sent home for prospective brides. They gave up the konaks for apartments and the life of day labor for one of shopkeeper. They set about becoming Americans.

Noli also called it quits after a brief stint heading up a curiously illiberal reform-minded administration in 1923. Ironically he came to power in a feeble military coup and declined to hold an election during his six months as prime minister. In response, the royalists overthrew Noli's government with the help of foreign mercenaries, thus nipping in the bud the odd experiment in democracy. Noli fled the country, eventually returning to the United States. His failure, writes historian Anton Logoreci, was that he "had spent most of his life in the United States, where he was educated, and had little or no real knowledge of the grave political, economic, and social problems facing his countrymen. . . . He was no match for consummate politicians such as [the royalist Ahmed] Zogu or some of the former bureaucrats of the Ottoman Empire."[3] Much the same words could be written about a long line of ex-émigré politicians.

The FWP study makes some astute observations about the nature of the early Albanian diaspora, insights that remain pertinent today both for the Albanian diaspora and for others. The study notes the remarkable effect of the Albanian immigrants' geographic "transplantation" on their national consciousness, the way that it stimulated "their interest in Albanian culture and traditions, and in paving the way for their active participation in the struggle for Albanian independence. Instead of becoming Americans and taking part in American political and social movements, they became conscious Albanians." The writers expressed astonishment at the sacrifices these simple men were ready to make for their distant nation: "The Balkan struggles for national unity and independence came over with them to the United States, and the Albanian worker lived in a self-imposed poverty even greater than that which his meager earnings imposed upon him, either sending his wages home, hoarding them against the day of his return, or using them to further the national cause." So typical of the classic Babylonian exile, the Albanians sought "vicariously abroad the restoration of that dignity and fruition of life which seemed denied him in the mechanized and alien circle of his life in Massachusetts." "It is a fascinating commentary on the civilization of the United States," the 1939 study concludes, "that we should have here, almost utterly unknown to the people among whom they live and work, groups of devoted adherents to causes even the names of which often carry no meaning to the rest of us."

Twenty-five years after Fan Noli's death in 1965, the Vatra headquarters moved from Boston to the Bronx. His present successor, Agim Karagjozi, reflects proudly on the organization's ninety-year history. "If it weren't for

Vatra, would we even have an independent Albania today?" asks the seventy-five-year-old retired engineer rhetorically. Vatra may no longer be the biggest Albanian diaspora organization, but, says Karagjozi, its reputation commands respect in the community and a voice in its affairs.

In the United States, Karagjozi worked for half a century to spur communism's overthrow in Albania. But when he finally returned to the land of his birth in 1990, his feelings of disillusionment echoed those of the interwar Albanian émigrés. "When communism fell I thought very seriously about buying an apartment in Albania, or a summer house, to spend two or three months a year, maybe even half the year there," he explains. "I had a great love for Albania, the memories of my childhood and summers in the country." Proof of his faithful devotion to Albania, Karagjozi declined to become a U.S. citizen until 1994. The elderly, gravel-voiced man looks down at his desk. "But I am very disappointed about Albania today and about the kind of human beings that communism has produced. Right now I don't even have a desire to go to Albania, much less live there. I cannot stand it. It's too painful for me." Karagjozi swallows hard, lost in thought.

Karagjozi credits the Kosovar Albanians with reinvigorating the Albanian diaspora in the United States. "In the 1990s the Albanian community [in the United States] repeated in Kosovo the role that Noli and Vatra played so long ago," he says. "The whole Albanian community was mobilized when we started to get the news from Kosovo."

The Kosovo issue briefly curbed the decades of infighting and division that had kept the Albanian diaspora occupied during the long years of the Cold War. Karagjozi, born in southern Albania, wore a Balli Kombëtar uniform in World War II and fought as a volunteer against Serb nationalist units in Kosovo. When the communists took over, he fled Albania with thousands of others to the squalid displaced persons camps of Italy. He regrouped there with other survivors of the smashed nationalist forces before moving on to Turkey and then the United States. Karagjozi vividly recalls the painful experience of arriving in the United States as a young man in 1956, an unbending anticommunist, to find Vatra and many Albanian Americans praising the communist government in Albania.

The postwar political exiles, numbering between thirty thousand and thirty-five thousand, gasped at Vatra's coddling of communist Albania. Vatra and most Albanian Americans had stood staunchly with the Allies against Nazi Germany. The German and Italian occupation of Albania undermined everything Noli believed in. He thus saw Hoxha's Partisans as liberators—and, more important, the guarantors of Albanian sovereignty against the unrenounced territorial claims of its neighbors. Better a communist Albania than no Albania at all, they reasoned, until the very late date of 1959, when Vatra again changed its thinking.

It seems that the U.S. government was quicker than Vatra to tap this hostile, activist strain of anticommunism that had entered the bloodstream of the Albanian diaspora. In 1949 the Committee for Free Albania came into being, a branch of the CIA-financed Committee for Free Europe. This U.S.-based anticommunist front was basically a propaganda tool to do battle with Stalin over Eastern Europe. It was founded, notably, the same year that the first U.S.- and British-trained commandos landed on Albania's shores. "The rationale was that the West should have some kind of mechanism to react should the communist regimes fall," explains Idriz Lamaj, a former staffer, today an apartment house superintendent in uptown Manhattan. "The committee was a means to fight the Cold War. If a hot front really opened up with the Soviet Union, then Albanians like us, and not Americans, would rise up and go fight in Albania."

The committee's newspaper, *Free Albania*, sent the unambiguous message that "we had to continue to raise our voices against communism and challenge communism in every way," says Lamaj. The committee, in cooperation with the State Department, orchestrated the immigration of an estimated fifteen thousand to twenty thousand wartime refugees, sworn enemies of communism, to counterbalance the "red influence" of Vatra. In 1954 the Assembly of Captive Nations brought together the Free Europe committees of Albania, Bulgaria, Czechoslovakia, Estonia, Hungary, Latvia, Lithuania, Poland, and Romania, which diligently issued volume upon volume of proclamations, warnings, and open letters against world communism. But in the 1970s Washington cut back the budgets of the assembly and the Free Europe committees. In the end, Lamaj admits, the efforts of the Committee for Free Albania did not add up to much. Washington reneged on plans for a military penetration of the Iron Curtain, favoring, instead, a policy of detente and coexistence with the Soviet Union. "We were affected by the too peaceful U.S. policy against the communists," says Lamaj, still chagrined about the missed opportunities. "It wasn't pacifism as such, but it resolved problems in the most peaceful way. That cost us a lot."

Kosovar Albanians, and ethnic Albanians from elsewhere in southern Yugoslavia, began to trickle into the United States in the late 1960s and 1970s. Many exited Yugoslavia through Slovenia and then moved on to New York and New Jersey by way of Italian refugee camps. In the aftermath of the 1981 riots, others received political asylum first in Germany or Switzerland, and then emigrated to North America. And unlike the other communist countries, Yugoslav citizens had passports and were freer to travel or move where they wanted. Whole families—large Kosovar families—transplanted themselves to the U.S. East Coast, a heavy concentration settling in the Bronx borough of New York. Diaspora activists estimate that nearly 70,000 Kosovar Albanians came in the 1980s. By the end of the 1990s, as many as 200,000 to 250,000 Albanians from the former Yugoslavia had entered the United States over two decades. Before long, Kosovars dominated the Albanian diaspora.

In addition to numbers, the Kosovar immigrants brought with them a mentality worlds apart from that of the thoroughly Americanized grandchildren of the early immigrants or the World War II political exiles. For one thing, the Kosovars had the fresh taste of persecution on their lips. They were bristling with resentment and convinced that the situation in Kosovo was untenable. Moreover, their relatives still languished in the country, some in Serb prisons. They shared the trauma of their kinsmen across the ocean, perhaps with a tinge of a guilty conscience. Even those who had never lifted a finger for the political opposition movements inside Kosovo were moved to action.

One prickly issue, a source of contention between the Kosovars and Albanians from Albania proper, was the former's reverence for Hohxa's Albania. Like the 1980s Kosovar migrants arriving in Western Europe, many Kosovars fresh off the boat idealized Albania as a proud, independent motherland. To the great embarrassment of the Albanian Americans, at demonstrations the Kosovars waved Albanian flags *with the communist red star* on its face. At one point Joe DioGuardi had to step in to mediate between the two factions. Organizations such as the Jusuf Gërvalla Association, named after the 1982 assassinated poet-dissident, defended outlandish hard-line positions that were nearly identical to those of Europe's militant Popular Movement.

But as the Kosovars acclimated to life in the United States, they soon found themselves in search of a political home. Florin Krasniqi, born in Peč, Kosovo, emigrated to the United States in 1986. In the late 1990s he would run guns between the United States and the front in Kosovo. Even as a student at Pristina University in the early 1980s he did not fall for the Hohxa line. His first foray into the world of diaspora politics made him laugh out loud. "I went to the Jusuf Gërvalla [Association] and saw these Enver books and said, 'Shit! They even have that here! What's going on, this is America!' Then I went to the other organizations like Vatra and Balli Kombëtar, but they were so outdated I couldn't take them seriously."

Deep in Brooklyn's Flatbush section, Krasniqi's first job was with his cousin's roofing firm, Tirana Roofing. Before long he had his own contracting business and was making decent money. Like Krasniqi, the hardworking Kosovars seemed to take naturally to the U.S. market economy. Construction, gastronomy, real estate—so the Kosovars built their wealth.

Flipping through the Albanian Yellow Pages, a Bronx-produced business directory of the Albanian diaspora, one derives a sense of the steely business acumen of the U.S. Albanians—and an insight into the sources that funded

DioGuardi, dozens of top-name U.S. political campaigns, the Kosovar government-in-exile, countless humanitarian drives, as well as a guerrilla movement. The 238-page booklet is a testament to the entrepreneurial spirit. Should you need an Albanian-speaking veterinarian or *tax advokati*, or a printing press that offers bilingual wedding invitations, or a catering service that bakes a tasty spinach *byrek*—not a problem. And if you are short on time, you can buy it on the web at www.albanianshopping.com, "where Albanians shop on-line." The Yellow Pages, distributed for free in the United States, Germany, and Switzerland, as well as in the Balkans, reads like a "Who's Who" of the Albanian diaspora's business community. It radiates a sense of self-esteem and accomplishment, symbolically crying out: "Look at us, look how far we've come!"

The Albanian Yellow Pages reflects the Albanian diaspora: young, financially astute, resourceful, and tightly knit, precisely the ingredients that make it a potent political force. It is this cohesion, not size, that determines a diaspora's potential for mobilization. "Exactly!" beams the proud creator of the Yellow Pages, Ismer Mjeku, a handsome young executive type in a chocolate-brown suit. The Pristina-born Mjeku first set foot in the United States only ten years ago. Today, he brags, every second ethnic Albanian family in the United States and Canada has a copy of the Yellow Pages. He admits that he lifted the idea from the Chinese and Jewish communities and that it still receives financial subsidies from interested businessmen. But it is big and is getting bigger. In its fifth year, the circulation has climbed to eighty thousand. The Yellow Pages is the kind of institution that creates diasporas: it provides links, it communicates, and it preserves bonds and a communal identity. And unlike the majority of diaspora by-products, it serves a useful purpose.

Mjeku concedes that the Yellow Pages works best with a strong first-generation diaspora. Only the recent immigrants, for example, order the special Albanian sausage, *suxhuk*, or prefer conducting business in Albanian with other Albanians. For these people, unlike the integrated generations, their bonds to the Old World still exert a strong pull.

The wealth on display in the Yellow Pages typifies young immigrant populations. Many New Yorkers might be dismayed to learn, for example, that their favorite Italian restaurant or pizzeria is, in fact, Albanian-owned. There is a simple explanation: most Albanian immigrants passed through Italy on their way westward—as refugees in the camps or as temporary workers—naturally picking up some of the tongue as well as the recipes. (In Albania proper, Italian is practically a second language.) On arriving in the United States their first stop when looking for employment was Italian restaurants. After working their way up, they eventually bought into the business.

In real estate, too, the Albanians started off at square one, often as janitors or handymen. In the depressed Bronx of the 1970s, property prices were at rock bottom. New tenants-rights laws made it increasingly difficult for landlords to collect rent. The buildings were not profitable until the Albanians bought them—four or five investors pooling their resources to buy a single building. A little sweat equity, nothing the Albanians shrank from, helped to insure the steady payment of rent.

The Yellow Pages office looks out onto Arthur Avenue, a quaint tree-lined thoroughfare of the Bronx's Little Italy. Tie dangling, Ismer Mjeku leans out the window pointing to the red brick buildings next to and across from his. "That one's Albanian, and that one," he gestures. "That one over there and those three." The newspaper offices of *Illyria* and *Bota Sot*, the LDK office, and other Albanian American institutions dot the neighborhood. The All Star Café, with its "members only" sign in the door, is a favorite meeting place for coffee and byrek. Today the Bronx's Little Italy is the hub of the Kosovar community in New York—and more than half of it is owned by Albanians.

The period from 1989 to 1992 was the high-water mark for DioGuardi's Civic League. In 1990 alone the league's books recorded $450,000 for operational and lobbying expenditures. Added to its lineup were such names as Senator Claiborne Pell of Rhode Island, Senator Alfonso D'Amato of New York, Senator Carl Levin of Michigan, Congressman William Broomfield of Michigan, Senator Larry Pressler of South Dakota, and, most important, Representative Eliot Engel of New York. From 1990 to 1992, according to DioGuardi, the league raised more than $260,000 for presidential candidate Bob Dole. In total it solicited more than half a million dollars for its political candidates. In 1990 DioGuardi raised the profile of Kosovo by traveling to Belgrade and Kosovo, billing it as a showdown with the brutal dictator Milošević. On subsequent trips he managed to get Lantos and Dole to come along. DioGuardi was raising hell, and Kosovo was getting press.

The birth of the Democratic League of Kosovo (LDK) shattered Dio-Guardi's short-lived monopoly over the Albanian American lobby. The LDK set up branches in the New York–New Jersey–Connecticut region and in Chicago, Detroit, and Canada, siphoning off members and resources from DioGuardi's operation. Some of DioGuardi's staunchest backers, including the Xhema brothers, defected to the LDK. A simmering discontent with DioGuardi and his bossy, hard-edged style exploded into full-blown enmity. "DioGuardi was a hired gun, that's all he was, and that's all he is," says Harry Bajraktari, one of the Civic League's early supporters and founder of the diaspora newspaper *Illyria*. "We paid him to work for us, not tell us what to do." Bajraktari and others believe DioGuardi hangs onto the Civic League in order to promote his own thinly veiled political ambitions.

Marijan Cubi, a Manhattan building superintendent, was a founding member of the North American LDK and its president from 1998 to 2002. He remembers the ugly friction between DioGuardi and the American Kosovars when the LDK arrived on the scene:

> DioGuardi responded very negatively to the LDK, even declaring openly at one demonstration his opposition to Rugova. He saw that everything wasn't going to center around him anymore. We thought it was more important to support people [U.S. politicians] who were in Congress such as Sue Kelly, Eliot Engel, etc., not DioGuardi who was no longer there. He demanded that everything go through him, even the demonstrations. He'd say that he was a representative of all Albanians in the world. He declared himself the great ruler of every Albanian. But we wanted to represent the people of Kosovo. We wanted to represent our case directly. DioGuardi thought he knew better than Rugova, Kosovo's own president. We didn't agree.

The story of the Albanian diaspora groups in the 1990s speaks profoundly about the nature of diaspora politics. Observers tend to attribute the intense factionalism in émigré communities to the egocentric personalities involved and to the underdeveloped political traditions of their homelands. But these explanations are inadequate. The world of diaspora politics itself is a no-man's-land with few written rules, one in which basic democratic concepts such as accountability, checks and balances, term limits, representation, and pluralism are meaningless. Neither DioGuardi nor his wife, for example, are mandated to speak on behalf of anyone other than the members of their organizations, generously counted at several thousand. Ultimately these are the people they represent and are accountable to. Ironically, more than a decade down the road, DioGuardi still is not on speaking terms with the now legally elected Kosovar president Rugova, and he refuses to recognize the current elected government in Albania proper. Yet, incredibly, he conducts the business of Albanian politics in Washington, although no longer alone.

The diaspora LDK had its own built-in flaws. Technically the LDK was a Kosovar Albanian political party, one of many in Kosovo. It received a certain number of votes in the Kosovar elections in 1992, making it the biggest Albanian party in Kosovo. (Of the 105,300 people who voted in the diaspora, presumably, as in Kosovo, over 75 percent voted for the LDK.)[4] The party nominated a president who then appointed a government. But what is the legitimate function of LDK diaspora branches? One arguably legitimate answer is to raise money to support the LDK in Kosovo, a kind of solidarity network. But the LDK leaders in the United States did much more: they represented the Republic of Kosovo, all of its Albanian citizens and the diaspora Kosovars, too. Admittedly the LDK was more of a mass movement than a traditional party and indeed possessed some legitimacy in the early 1990s to "speak for the Kosovars." But what, then, was the purpose of Bukoshi's exile government? Moreover, by the mid-1990s both Bukoshi and the LDK had lost a good part of their legitimacy. How, from exile, do transitions of power take place?

The legitimacy of the self-appointed diaspora "leaderships" often boils down to competing claims. He who shouts the loudest or raises the most money or both carries the mantle until someone louder and wealthier appears on the scene. Upon its arrival DioGuardi's Civic League dislodged the old groups such as Vatra from their positions as first among émigré associations. The LDK shoved DioGuardi aside. When the authority of the LDK and Bukoshi waned, another louder, more aggressive contestant for power barged onto the scene. The emergence of Homeland Calling and the Kosovar Liberation Army again turned everything upside down.

CHAPTER TEN

Exile on Königstrasse

When Bujar Bukoshi, Kosovo's appointed prime minister, took the self-declared Kosovar government abroad in 1991, he brought with him scant political experience and zero knowledge of running a government-in-exile. He knew that Albanians before him had sought haven abroad in order to promote the national cause, but these historical episodes provided meager instruction for the hands-on task in front of the forty-three-year-old surgeon. It was on the job that he learned the ropes of exile politics—and the lessons came fast. Though Bukoshi caught on intuitively, he discovered the hard way that exile governments have notoriously short operational life spans. By the onset of 1996 his government's legitimacy had worn paper-thin.

During the twentieth century, exile governments have largely left behind poor track records. By definition, they are the losers from domestic battles who, usually by necessity, flee their homelands to seek sanctuary abroad. One scholar has noted that the term *government-in-exile* is indeed an oxymoron since exile administrations neither control their own home territory nor wield authority over its inhabitants.[1] They are thus incapable of rendering services to their countrymen or fulfilling international obligations as normal governments would. The government-in-exile, writes political scientist Michael Riesman, is "not a government at all but a political and legal technique. The purpose of the technique is to influence, undermine, or replace a particular government in situ by trying to challenge and deprive it of its authority."[2] It is according to these demanding criteria that the success or failure of exile governments is ultimately measured.

Most often the precarious status of exile executives facilitates their demise. Even when lawfully elected, time erodes their core support in the homeland. Stranded abroad for years or decades, distance and poor communication leave exile politicians removed from their people and the problems of their country. The absence of democratic mechanisms such as elections or parliamentary oversight opens the door wide for infighting and factionalism. Usually penniless, exile governments look to the diaspora for money and thus place themselves in direct competition with existing diaspora groups. Internecine quarrels break out over who most accurately represents the national interest. Moreover, the objective at hand, to overthrow the home government, is tremendously difficult to accomplish so far from the front lines. The regime in power presides over the institutions of the state—an army, intelligence services, a proper treasury, and a propaganda apparatus—which the exile governments usually cannot hope to match. Uncertainty, political sterility, and frustration tend to eat away at its corpus until only an empty title is left.

Perhaps the first of the unvarnished lessons handed Bukoshi was that exile governments are at all times beholden guests, their tenuous existences dependent on the good graces of a sympathetic patron. Moreover, the state offering asylum often harbors its own selfish motives for playing host. The Kosovars' first base, the northern republic of Slovenia, was still part of Yugoslavia when Bukoshi and his ministers arrived in 1991. For the independence-minded Slovenes, the Kosovar exile government constituted another scrap of evidence to lay before the international community, further documentation of the undemocratic nature of multinational Yugoslavia. But once Slovenia had secured its sovereignty in early 1992, the Kosovars had outlived their usefulness, and the exile government had become baggage for the new state. A last slap, Slovenia, fresh from its own battle for official international recognition, declined to recognize the validity of an independent Kosovo or the Bukoshi administration as Kosovo's rightful executive.

The decision to make Stuttgart, Germany, their next port of call came almost automatically to the exiles. Bukoshi and his ministers had used the office of the Democratic League of Kosovo on Königstrasse as their entry point into Western Europe and their de facto second home since the first days of exile. At the time the government and the LDK worked hand in glove, with little discernible difference between the two. For the exile administration, the instantly accessible resources of the LDK, for example, the network of branch offices and their personnel, could not have been more ideal, a luxury enjoyed by few governments-in-exile. And nowhere outside Kosovo was the LDK stronger than in Germany.

Diaspora activists estimate that by 1992 there were approximately four hundred thousand ethnic Albanians in Western Europe, about a third of them in Germany and a quarter in Switzerland—with more on the way. During the early 1990s Kosovar Albanians (and other refugees claiming to be such) automatically received political asylum status in most Western European countries. Even when the requirements for asylum were tightened, any young Kosovar man brandishing a call-up letter from the Yugoslav army had an entry ticket to the West. The trickle of politically persecuted Kosovars from the late 1980s exploded into a mass exodus. In 1992 sociologist Hivzi Islami counted the number of ethnic Albanians (not exclusively Kosovars) from the former Yugoslavia living in the following countries: Germany, 120,000; Switzerland, 95,000; Croatia, 40,000; Sweden, 35,000;

Albania, 25,000; Austria, 23,000; Slovenia, 15,000; Belgium, 8,000; France, 5,000; Denmark, 5,000; Italy, 4,000; Norway, 3,500; Britain, 3,000; the Netherlands, 2,000; Finland, 600; and Luxembourg, 200.[3] By the late 1990s, according to a World Bank report, the Kosovar Albanian community had swollen to 350,000–400,000 in Germany alone and 160,000 in Switzerland.[4] This was the potent constituency of Bukoshi and the LDK.

The period of mid-1992 to late 1995 marked the apex of the Kosovar government-in-exile, starting with its transfer to Stuttgart and terminating with the internationally brokered peace agreement for Bosnia and Herzegovina, which failed to include Kosovo in the settlement. During these years the exile government logged an impressive run, even if it ultimately fell short of its declared goals: to prevent an all-out Serb onslaught against the Albanian Kosovars and to win international recognition for the Republic of Kosovo as an independent state. But when it did return to Kosovo in June 1999, to its partial credit, Serb rule was no more. Most exile governments never savor that moment.

The Fund for the Republic of Kosovo counted as the Bukoshi government's defining achievement and the backbone of its authority. The fund, which netted a total of more than $125 million in contributions from diaspora Kosovars, functioned as the official treasury of the shadow state. (A second government-run fund, Everything for an Independent Kosovo, collected an additional $30 million.) The republic fund was identified with the government-in-exile to the extent that many simply referred to it as "The Bukoshi Fund." From its central accounts in Ulm, Germany, and Geneva, Switzerland, the exile government financed Kosovo's parallel schools, health care and social welfare systems, a Tirana-based bank, satellite television programs, President Rugova's diplomatic activity, information offices (de facto embassies) in seven European cities and the Bronx, the services of an American public relations firm, as well as its own operational expenses. Even as his authority slipped away, Bukoshi clung tenaciously to the fund. It proved an asset that sustained his political power long after the downfall of his government.

Bukoshi, his cabinet ministers, and the LDK's Hafiz Gagica launched the republic fund in March 1992. Until then, an LDK-run solidarity fund in Aachen, Germany, had collected diaspora contributions to support striking workers in Kosovo, and to help finance the underground school system and makeshift health clinics. But the republic fund was much more than another charity. It constituted the treasury of the self-styled Republic of Kosovo. If independent Kosovo existed at first as a phantom state called into being by the Kosovar Albanians, the fund added another limb to its skeletal body politic—and its multimillion dollar budget would finance other institutional appendages.

Unlike most states, which collect taxes to finance their expenditures, the

Bukoshi government had neither the power nor the mandate to levy tithes on anyone, much less on Kosovars living outside the homeland. Contributions were voluntary, but the government decreed that all Kosovar Albanians in the diaspora and in Kosovo were duty-bound to pay 3 percent of their monthly wages into the republic's accounts. The republic fund was thus also nicknamed the "Three Percent Fund." (Businesses were requested to contribute up to 10 percent of their profits.)

Diaspora Kosovars, or anyone else so inclined, could pay into one of the eighteen fund bank accounts registered in Europe, the United States, and Australia. The LDK branch offices spread the word, and regional "Three Percent Committees" oversaw the individual accounts, which were emptied monthly into the two central accounts at the Bayrische HypoVereinsbank in Ulm and Credit Suisse in Geneva. The government could only withdraw monies from the central accounts, and every withdrawal required three signatures: that of Bukoshi, the finance minister Isa Mustafa, and either Gagica or the information minister Xhafer Shatri.

In contrast to other examples of diaspora funds, during the life of the republic fund there were no reports of strong-arming to induce payment. People closely connected to the operation say that Bukoshi resisted calls for indirect coercion such as the use of veiled threats to procure higher rates of remittance. One idea was to threaten to deny visas (presuming Kosovo achieved independence) to those who had refused to pay their dues. In other words, a black list would be drawn up, perhaps even just as a bluff. But Bukoshi stood firm. "At first we thought everyone would pay which turned out not to be the case," says Peter Coli, director of the Germany-based funds. "There was some disappointment about that and we were constantly talking about how to get a higher rate of payment." Coli and the sixteen German local fund managers presided over twelve hundred part-time activists in Germany who worked for the fund, traveling across the country to drum up contributions. The fund, registered in Germany as an NGO, had its own office in Weissenhorn, near Ulm, where the books were kept.

Bukoshi contends that the remittance rate was just about as high as could be expected. The Kosovars flooding Europe were mostly destitute refugees, many forbidden to hold jobs under the political asylum guidelines of the host states (Switzerland was an exception). They lived in temporary housing or refugee centers, subsisting on small state entitlements. Others worked menial jobs as day laborers. Bukoshi estimates that in Europe about forty thousand people contributed monthly to the fund, roughly 60–70 percent of employed Kosovars. In the United States, he says, the numbers were much lower. Rather than concentrate on the fund, the U.S. Kosovars were encouraged to focus on their lobbying campaigns and fund-raising activities for U.S. politicians.

In the Balkans, and their diasporas, money is the touchiest of subjects. When sums the size of those that flowed in and out of the republic accounts are involved, charges of personal misuse, corruption and embezzlement inevitably swirl around those near the till. The custodians of the exile fund were not immune to such innuendos and accusations. Yet the charges against them were usually leveled from the corners of Bukoshi's political opponents and were rarely accompanied by material evidence. Although questions remain about the wisdom of the way the republic fund's monies were allocated, no one ever furnished proof of criminal wrongdoing. Bavarian finance department authorities combed through the Three Percent Fund's books every year. Their findings: *alles in Ordnung*. (In January 2001 Bukoshi opened the records of the fund before the Kosovar parliament.)[5] It seems that Bukoshi and his finance minister, Isa Mustafa, took every precaution to keep the transactions of the fund aboveboard. Given the structure of the Three Percent Committees, fraud would have been next to impossible. Cash deposits, for example, were not accepted, and donors received receipts for every contribution and a final statement at the year's end. In Germany the contributions were even tax-deductible!

The personal integrity of Bukoshi and the honor of the fund as an institution were inextricably linked, and this was key to the success and longevity of the fund. Given the hurly-burly of diaspora politics, and the ease in which the wildest accusations can become magnified, it is remarkable indeed that Bukoshi managed to preserve the republic fund's reputation both on the ground in Kosovo and abroad in the diaspora. "If it [the exile government] really accomplished one incredible thing, it was to keep the fund clean," explains Donika Gërvalla, who lives in Hamburg, Germany, and was the LDK diaspora vice president from 1993 to 1998. "If the fund had been misused, it would have been a catastrophe for the Kosovars. This was the first time in history that Kosovar Albanians could freely invest money in their own country. It was a great thing for them," she says. In the past, it was different, maintains Gërvalla: "Those little radical [diaspora-based] groups would go around from [gastarbeiter] club to club and put a hat on the table and say, 'Listen up all you patriots, throw some money in here.' That's how it was. Then who knows what happened to it."

But, according to Gërvalla, Bukoshi and Mustafa went overboard to shield the fund from criticism. Mustafa guarded the coffers like a dragon, she says, but to the extent that the government, in effect, hoarded monies that should have been spent. They were too fearful that rumors of misappropriation or frivolous expenditures would stain the scheme's reputation, says Gërvalla. Throughout most of the fund's existence, large untouched sums lay in the main accounts. These were monies, say critics of the fund, that could have been designated for economic initiatives, for youth programs—or for equipping a guerrilla army.

Transferring the diaspora money from Germany and Switzerland to Kosovo entailed risks that called for creative improvisation. At first, bundled stacks of German marks were transported across the borders packed in plastic garbage bags. But too often the Serb authorities caught wind of the operation and confiscated the money. The exile government countered with a credit-based transfer scheme that had served other transnational networks in the past, including the Irish Republican Army and the Palestinian Liberation Organization, and would serve Al Qaeda in the future. The simple but effective scheme, commonly known as "hawala banking," used Kosovo-based businesses with offices or branch outlets abroad to circumvent sending cash over international borders. In short, Kosovar businesses in Kosovo would pay into the republic coffers, and the exile government would reimburse them in bank accounts abroad. The government, for example, would arrange for a Kosovo business, say a publishing house, to transfer a given sum, say $25,000, from its main account to the Kosovar administration's central finance office in Pristina. The republic fund's overseers would then issue the publishing house a foreign credit for that amount. At any time, the firm could request that this credit be paid into a foreign bank account of its choice or directly to a foreign creditor. Dukagjini Publishing House, for example, could pay international bills for paper supplies, printing presses, and ink through the exile fund, while Dukagjini paid into the Kosovar budget at home in Kosovo. To expedite the process, the government set up its own bank in Albania in 1993, Dardania Bank, which became one of the country's leading banks.

In this way the exile government financed the parallel state without sending a penny across borders. About $1.3 million monthly went through this circuitous route from the Three Percent Fund to the Kosovo budget. Roughly half that monthly figure was earmarked for teachers' salaries, the fund's biggest expenditure.

The ultimate objective of every government-in-exile is to return to the homeland and take political power. One critical step toward that goal, central to the strategies of all exile contenders, is winning diplomatic recognition from other independent states. "Recognition of one contender," writes political scientist Yossi Shain in his book on exile governments, "as the sole representative of the state automatically implies non-recognition of competing claims to govern the same state's territory."[6] When the Kosovar Albanians unilaterally declared their independence in 1991, announcing that Kosovo no longer belonged to the Socialist Federal Republic of Yugoslavia, it proclaimed itself a new sovereign state. The ethnic Albanians offered historical, demographic, geographical, and moral rationale for Kosovo's statehood. Over the course of the 1990s they built up their own quasi-state institutions. This all mattered for naught, however, if only the Kosovo Albanians were to acknowledge the validity of their break from Yugoslavia.

It wasn't for lack of trying that Bukoshi never secured international recognition for a sovereign Kosovo or for his own government as the official executive of the Republic of Kosovo. Bukoshi, President Rugova, and their teams relentlessly beat paths to the offices of the UN and the European Union as well as a gamut of political parties, NGOs, think tanks, parliamentary commissions, human rights groups, and national governments in Europe and North America. The Kosovars' arguments did not change substantially over eight years, and, in retrospect, they ring prophetic. If their international interlocutors suspected the ethnic Albanians of exaggerating Kosovo's plight or crying wolf about Serb war plans, history would prove them wrong.

In vain, Bukoshi tried to convince the Western agencies that only swift and resolute international action in Kosovo would prevent it from becoming the next battlefield in the Balkans. Serbia, he argued, had already begun ethnically cleansing Kosovo and his people would soon face the same fate as the Muslims of Bosnia. Serbia was bent on forging a greater, ethnic state, which entailed ridding Kosovo of 90 percent of its population. "Our country is next on the ethnic genocide list of Serbia," he wrote in a November 1992 *Washington Post* editorial, a line he repeated ad nauseam throughout the 1990s. But the urgency of his message failed to impress the diplomatic corps. "Peace is fragile," he told the European Parliament several months later. "There is still time for a political solution but the conflict holds very powerful and destructive potential. It will explode if nothing is done soon."

"We are deeply concerned, Dr. Bukoshi." The surgeon-turned-politician switches into English from his precise German, mocking the tone of a bored diplomat. "We are deeply concerned," Bukoshi repeats. "I heard this so many times!" he sighs, again speaking German, picking at his fish dinner in Pristina's Rio Restaurant. He wears a jet black button-down sweater and black trousers, which contrast sharply with his silver-gray hair and gold-rimmed glasses. "I knew it was just lip service and I told them that, too. They kept talking about diplomatic pressure and economic sanctions, this kind of thing. I said this was ridiculous because Serbia would deal with the situation in Kosovo first, then worry about the economy. That's the way things are in the Balkans."

On the issue of Kosovo's independence, the international diplomatic community never budged: Kosovo would remain part of Yugoslavia, reiterated the foreign ministries in different languages. The redrawing of international state borders in southeastern Europe would only spark further instability, they said. An accommodation with Serbia, within Serbia, had to be found. The Kosovars shot back that the majority Albanians had been treated as second-class citizens ever since the territory was put under Serbian rule in 1913. Today the majority ethnic Albanians deserved the same right to self-determination that the Croats and Slovenes had exercised. But, says Bukoshi: "Their response was always: 'No, that's just not going to happen. How about autonomy in a democratic Yugoslavia where rights are respected? We'll put more pressure on Yugoslav authorities and maybe things will get better sometime.' They always saw Kosovo as just another human rights issue. In reality, it was about territory."

These standard responses in diplomat-speak exasperated the normally even-keeled doctor. But he persevered, hammering away that the Serb campaign against ethnic Albanians was part of a larger demographic strategy. The killings, the imprisonments, the firings, and the daily harassment were calculated provocations. The Serbian government was doing everything in its power to instigate an uprising, just the alibi it needed to crack down on the defenseless Albanians and sweep them out of Kosovo once and for all. The Kosovars' struggle was still nonviolent, Bukoshi emphasized, but his peoples' patience wasn't limitless. One way or another, the world had to move boldly to stave off the worst. The diplomats nodded politely and reminded Bukoshi that were the Kosovars to resort to armed insurrection, they would forfeit the moral high ground and lose whatever sympathy they had.

Despite the snail's pace, the diplomatic initiatives of the diaspora Kosovars slowly began to chip away at the impenetrable embassy walls. As Rugova and Bukoshi became known faces in the foreign ministries, the basics about the situation in Kosovo were no longer terra incognita to the international community. Unexpectedly it was the Americans, rather than the Europeans, who first started to take Bukoshi seriously. The U.S.–LDK sections and Joe DioGuardi's Civic League had certainly helped pave the way with their campaigns in Washington. The Three Percent Fund paid the New York PR firm Ruder Finn, Inc. generously to line up Washington meetings and do basic publicity work. Arguably an indirect result of the early lobbying, outgoing president George Bush warned in late December 1992 that the United States was ready to use military force if the Balkan wars widened to include Kosovo. The Clinton administration repeated the famous "Christmas warning" early the next year.

"Ironically our contacts with the West European embassies ultimately went through the United States," says Bukoshi. The German foreign ministry maintained a cautious distance from Bukoshi, despite the fact that, from 1995 on, the office of the exile government was just down the street in Bonn. The ministry passively tolerated the Kosovar exiles, who had registered their itinerant administration not as an exile government (had there been such a category in Germany) but as the Kosovo Information Zentrum in Bonn. "The [German] foreign service couldn't put him in a box because he didn't belong to a proper diplomatic mission or have a business card with a recognized title," explains Stefan Schwarz, a German parliamentarian who worked on Balkan issues. "When we'd come back from speaking to an assistant secretary of state," explains Bukoshi, "only then would the Western Europeans say, 'Ah ha, in the United States they met so-and-so.' Only then would they open the doors. This is the way it was right up until we met President Clinton in 1998. The Europeans were always one step behind. Classic."

On the ground in Kosovo, the prestige of the exile government peaked during the first half of the 1990s. The republic fund financed ever higher portions of the parallel institutions (about 30 percent in 1994 and 50 percent in the years to follow),[7] and the international diplomatic activity of the Kosovar leadership had Kosovars convinced that international recognition, or intervention, was imminent. It looked to them as if Rugova and Bukoshi commanded the attention of the world's powerful and mighty.

The work of the Bukoshi government at the time was one with that of Kosovo's president Rugova and the LDK. All three were symbols of the shadow state and the Kosovars' campaign of passive resistance. Rugova had, in fact, earned the reputation of an "Albanian Gandhi." During these pinnacle years of the movement, ordinary Kosovars rallied almost unanimously around the triumvirate and pitched in collectively to incarnate their phantom republic.

Though the idea of nonviolent resistance was not one that came naturally to ethnic Albanians, they threw themselves wholeheartedly behind the campaign. Eyewitnesses and participants attest to the Kosovars' stirring ethos of social solidarity and sense of popular empowerment as they shaped their own parallel society, using the barest of resources. In the improvised schools teachers worked for minimal salaries, if they were paid at all. The charitable organization, the Mother Theresa Association, which had offices in Munich and other Western cities, set up Albanian-run health clinics across the province that offered free treatment to all.

In his fine book, *Civil Resistance in Kosovo*, the British pacifist Howard Clark describes the impassioned spirit among Kosovar Albanians at the time. In every aspect of life—culture, sports, commerce, and media—Kosovars fended admirably for themselves, demonstrating a talent for improvisation. Clark points out that the movement also took aim at some of the most conservative attitudes embedded in Kosovar society. Campaigns to eliminate the tradition of the blood feud and to address the issue of women's rights reflected a rejection of centuries-old customs and the embrace of a more modern, democratic society. "People's eyes would light up when they talked about how their generation had ended the blood feuding that had blighted their society for centuries," writes Clark. "Parallel schooling might mean that students were sometimes sitting on people's floors, but it was also a sign of the strength of the people's will."[8] But, Clark concludes grimly, instead of building on this spirit, the movement stood still. When it did, the Kosovars' rock-solid faith in its leadership began to show cracks.

Already by 1994 Kosovo's experiment in civil resistance had begun to lose steam. The parallel institutions kept Kosovar society afloat, but the creative energy present during their initiation had dissipated. A malaise settled in over the Kosovar Albanians, while some factions voiced growing impatience with the strategy of nonviolence. The Kosovars' underground parallel society was never meant to drag on forever, they charged. The majority of ethnic Albanians survived day by day, waiting, hoping, and expecting the world's centers of power to impose a settlement that would eventually, if not immediately, deliver independence.

This status quo suited Belgrade just fine. There was no rebellion in Kosovo while the Serbs were tied up with wars in Croatia and Bosnia. And the Kosovar Albanians' withdrawal from official society relieved the Serbian state of responsibility for providing services to 90 percent of the population. As for the international community, it seemed content enough with the deadlock as well; the peace in Kosovo may have been fragile, but at least there wasn't another war in the Balkans.

The source of the movement's degeneration could be traced straight back to Rugova and the LDK. Even among the raft of eccentric, idiosyncratic, and unsuited men who find their way into Balkan politics, Rugova defined his own category. The 1944-born professor of literature never abandoned the chain-smoking, bohemian-poet image he adopted while studying in Paris for a year under the celebrated philosopher and linguist Roland Barthes in the mid-1970s. He penned ten books and edited several scholarly periodicals in the two decades he taught at Pristina's Institute for Albanian Studies. With his long stringy hair, plastic glasses, and rumpled suit, he looked like anything but a president, of any country. His trademark garment was a silk scarf he wore wrapped around his neck at all times.

As a politician, he was shy, often distracted, and known for his vague pronouncements. His stubborn indecision would infuriate those who worked with him. "Rugova has no talent at all for what he's doing, or what he thinks he's doing," the Kosovar newspaper editor Veton Surroi once quipped. "He should go back to teaching French." "Rugova is a 'passivist,' not a pacifist," fumed Bukoshi. Rugova personified the Kosovars' nonviolent struggle as no one else did, and he repeated the mantra of peaceful resistance to his people and to the international diplomatic community for ten years. "Rugova was like a Buddhist guru," says the Vienna-based writer Dardan Gashi. "He wanted you to believe, not question." He himself believed that time and patience would deliver Kosovo its statehood, and no amount of argument or cajoling would budge him from that stand. Notwithstanding the criticism that became increasingly vocal after 1995, ordinary Kosovar Albanians revered him as their leader, as the internationally known symbol of their struggle, and even reelected him in Kosovo's first free vote in 2000. But in the mid-1990s he was unable to rejuvenate the movement he defended with such conviction.

The LDK, for its part, had from its birth demonstrated stark authoritarian tendencies. Even though other parties existed, the LDK held nearly hegemonic sway over political life in Kosovo. The Kosovar media, such as the exiled daily *Rilindja* (Awakening) in Switzerland and Albania, regurgitated the LDK line. Dissenting and even questioning voices were pushed to the side. When the civil resistance movement began to falter, the wooden bureaucracy that had become the LDK clung to Rugova and business as usual. By late 1994, writes historian Miranda Vickers, "it was becoming increasingly obvious that the LDK had no clear strategy beyond boycotting official institutions and any electoral process and hoping that eventually the international community would grant it recognition."[9]

The movement's stagnation and the unwillingness of Rugova and the LDK to activate Kosovo's principal democratic institution, the 1992-elected parliament, or to hold new elections implicitly undermined the authority of Bukoshi's exile government. Bukoshi was in an awkward position to begin with: the head of an unrecognized government of a country that officially did not exist. To compound the Kafkaesque scenario, he, the prime minister, could not even step foot in this fictional state. Thus some semblance of the democratic-legal legitimacy of his mandate was imperative to make the exile government more than an absurd, hollow title. Its claims to formal and popular legitimacy endowed the government with the authority to act as the official representative of a people rather than as an ordinary NGO; it made the Kosovo republic fund a state treasury rather than a charity; and it turned the issue of Kosovo into a question of state sovereignty rather than yet another minority rights issue. Critically it also kept rival exile groups at bay, factions that doubted Bukoshi's competence from the beginning. In other words, everything hinged on the perceived vitality of the government's legitimacy. When it expired, the only component left to fortify its authority were the monies in the fund itself.

The exile leadership, like any other democratic government, maintained that it received its executive authority indirectly from its people, through a constitutionally prescribed democratic process. Before the May 1992 elections, an interim government (with Bukoshi as prime minister) had been appointed by the Coordinating Council of Albanian Political Parties, an assembly of Kosovar Albanian parties that operated in the vacuum created by the disbanding of the provincial assembly. After the 1992 elections the newly elected president of the republic, Rugova, and the party council extended the government's mandate without the approval of the new parliament, which could not meet openly at the time in Kosovo. In light of the extenuating circumstances, and if one accepts the premise of the Kosovar's secessionist drive, the Bukoshi government fulfilled many of the generally accepted requirements for formal (legal) legitimacy. And the popular legitimacy of the leadership was undisputed in the first half of the 1990s. The government, Rugova, and the LDK accurately reflected the aspirations and interests of the Kosovar Albanians.

Although this tentative legitimacy deserved the benefit of doubt in 1992, it did not contain the stuff of a durable, long-lasting mandate. With the conditions for democracy anything but ideal, the authority of the Bukoshi government had to be considered interim in nature. "In contrast with periodically elected bodies in a democratic parliamentary system," writes political scientist Shain, "exile organizations are faced with the problem of how to renew their legal status without elections, plebiscites, or other popular mandates."[10] Without viable democratic processes on the ground in Kosovo, even its mandated four-year term would prove very tricky to sustain. In fact, the parliament would never convene and the next elections of any kind would be 1998. Time works against exile governments, and the mandate Bukoshi derived indirectly from Kosovar Albanian voters in 1992 would wither quickly.

Friction between Bukoshi and Rugova was another development that exacerbated problems for the exile government. Though at the time, around 1993, still opaque to ordinary Kosovars, Bukoshi was not the only Kosovar politician whose frustration with the quirky Rugova boiled over into animosity. Within the LDK's intellectual-led leadership, impatience with Rugova's aloof air, his dictatorial manner, and slow-motion pace had been growing by the year. More radical currents in the LDK (and outside the party, too) were already fed up with the experiment in nonviolence. But Rugova conceded nothing. Even protests or public demonstrations, he maintained, could provoke a vicious backlash. Bukoshi says he never agreed with this:

> I argued that we can't use these Gandhiesque methods forever. What does civil resistance mean if police go into a village, beat up people, and nothing happens? I was never a pacifist. Pacifism was an appeal to the Serbs to do whatever it is they wanted to do. And I was right, the repres-

sion increased and increased. I thought that maybe when people organized themselves in villages and demonstrated in the cities en masse, like daily demonstrations—half a million in Pristina every day!—then the world's journalists would come and say, "Ah, it's really cooking here."

Rugova and his LDK backers responded indignantly that Bukoshi should stop shooting off his mouth from Germany. He didn't have the Serb police breathing down his neck. It wasn't his decisions that spelled war or peace for the people in Kosovo. Bukoshi neither could nor should lead the movement in Kosovo from distant exile. Bukoshi admits as much: "It would have been very difficult for me to call a demonstration from Germany—or to order someone to kill [Serb] policemen while I wasn't there. I knew that I couldn't lead effectively from abroad." Learning about the day-to-day situation on the ground through secondhand reports, the exile prime minister no longer had his finger on the pulse of ordinary Kosovars. And though he had his supporters in the LDK, Bukoshi feared that commands issued from along the Rhine would not necessarily be heeded in Kosovo. His powerbase was the diaspora, and his control over its purse strings was the potent source of whatever muscle he had. The parameters of exile politics, narrow to begin with, were closing in on the surgeon-politician by the month.

A further blow dealt to the Kosovar leadership in 1993 would have devastating, long-term consequences for the government, and for Kosovo into the next century. In a summer sting operation, the Serb security services exposed the ethnic Albanians' clandestine preparations for a rebel army. The existence of embryonic military organs inside Kosovo and abroad had been top-secret; even most high-ranking members of the LDK and the exile government were not directly informed about the ongoing plans to create a guerrilla force. Few knew the real identities of the covert ministers for defense and interior, or if they existed at all. But exist they did, with one co-minister in exile and the other undercover in Kosovo.

The Serb raid captured only a handful of arms, but it decimated the Albanians' operation. First a dozen, and then more than one hundred ethnic Albanian activists, including former JNA officers and ex-political prisoners, were arrested and charged with plotting an armed uprising.[11] The sting punctured the horizontal chain-link network, forcing thirty activists to escape to neighboring Albania proper. The on-the-ground defense minister, Anton Kolaj, fled Kosovo on Rugova's orders. At the time the Kosovar Albanians insisted that the charges were bogus and that the criminal proceedings were "political show trials." Western journalists joined the chorus. But the charges were accurate. Military training, arms smuggling, and intelligence gathering had been going on since 1990, part of the Kosovars' "two-track" strategy to create a fallback should passive resistance fail.

The Kosovar leadership knew that any kind of military preparation, even at the lowest levels, entailed supreme risk. The disclosure of defense-related structures would cast doubt on the sincerity of the Kosovars' nonviolent campaign, the main source of the concerned sympathy they enjoyed in the West. For the Serb authorities, evidence of an armed rebellion was just the ticket to justify the reimposition of martial law or to order new waves of arrests. The Kosovar Albanians rightly expected the Serb security services to be on high alert for signs of nascent military formations. Indeed, the Kosovars anticipated that sweeps like the one in 1993 (and then again a year later) would sporadically cast a wrench in their operations. But personnel could be replaced, structures rebuilt. The conspiratorial network in Kosovo was organized to withstand such body blows. And the corresponding exile structures could not be hit so easily, the rationale for their being in exile in the first place.

But the 1993–94 stings stopped the Kosovars' military preparations cold—just when they should have taken off. To the disappointment of those on the inside, the military preparations in exile had never really amounted to much. Bukoshi's defense and interior ministers, Ramush Tahiri and Nikë Gjeloshi, had resigned their posts in frustration by late 1992, even before the crackdown in Kosovo. No successor was named to either ministerial position until 1997, when it was too late. The vacuum left the field open for the militant Swiss-based groups and other freelancers to step in, factions that had long since given up on Rugova and Bukoshi. Thus the Kosovo Liberation Army was born.

Today, nearly a decade after the fact, explanations for the lapsed defense preparations remain a source of vigorous contention. To accept responsibility for the debacle would surely spell political suicide in today's Kosovo. Bukoshi lays the blame squarely at Rugova's feet. He charges that he himself pushed hard to bolster the government's military component, to fill the posts of defense and interior, and to start reorganizing in Kosovo. Rugova, he says, refused to give him the green light, and without that he couldn't possibly move forward. It was Rugova, he contends, who repeated again and again that it was too dangerous, too risky, that passive resistance was the only option.

That's one side of the story. The Swiss-based militants, such as Xhavit Haliti and his friends, charge that Bukoshi wasn't one shade bolder than Rugova. Both were true-blue LDK pacifists, under the thumb of the international community. They were doing the Serbs' work for them, they say.

Another version is told by the ex–de facto defense minister Kolaj, who contends that it was Bukoshi's mandate from the beginning to oversee the buildup of paramilitary organs and networks from exile. Rugova's hands were tied, but not Bukoshi's. "What was he [Bukoshi] waiting for? Some piece of paper from Rugova?" asks Kolaj indignantly, who today lives in Geilenkirchen, Germany, employed as a social worker. "Bukoshi was being disingenuous, always asking for something that Rugova couldn't give him. The fact is that this [the military planning] was his job from the beginning. That's why he was sent into exile. He had the money, but he vacillated and the structures crumbled." Kolaj and other expelled activists ended up applying for political asylum in Western Europe. With just the clothes on their backs, Kolaj and his family checked into a refugee center in Germany, not far from the exile government's Bonn office.

Whatever the explanation, Bukoshi let the military question sleep for three critical years. One of Bukoshi's defining qualities is his caution. He moves methodically and purposefully once he has chosen his path, but he is not quick to decide and is rarely spontaneous or sharp under pressure. To the contrary, when pressured he appears to freeze like a rabbit caught in headlights. Perhaps his hesitation, to some degree, can be attributed to inexperience. He had never called the shots while under fire. Others had been on the front lines during the 1968 and 1981 demonstrations in Kosovo; Bukoshi himself was out of the country, pursuing his surgical training. In exile, he formed the rear guard for those in the trenches in Kosovo. When he had the opportunity to move decisively, to step up and lead forcefully as Rugova would not do, he deliberated about protocol. Where a bold leader was needed, a thoughtful stickler held the job.

The peace activist and author Clark argues that another route existed, a course that steered between submission and armed struggle. In contrast to the narratives popular today, he maintains, the descent into war was not a fait accompli, and military preparations were not where Kosovars needed to direct their energy. He suggests that a path of "*active* nonviolence," combined with negotiations with Belgrade, could have saved many lives and advanced the cause of democracy in Kosovo as it entered the twenty-first century. The Kosovars, so Clark argues, could have focused on transforming civil society much more aggressively and thus gradually reclaimed Kosovo for themselves. The faltering movement had to recapture the momentum and spirit of innovation that it had in the early 1990s, challenging the status quo with a confrontational strategy that took risks but stopped short of provoking the ethnic Albanians' expulsion from the province.

Greater activism on the ground and less bluster over Kosovo's statehood would have opened doors that most probably would have led to national self-determination at some point down the road. Clark describes Kosovo as a "battle of wills." The Kosovar Albanians had the means to break down the will of the Serbs to hold on to Kosovo at all costs. By 1996 the emotional fervor in Serbia over Kosovo had died down considerably since the Kosovo Field extravaganza in 1989. In spite of Serbia's campaign to "re-Serbianize"

Kosovo, Kosovar Serbs were still exiting the province. Moderate Serb groups and even currents in the Orthodox Church realized that Kosovo was lost for Serbia. In other words, a window for compromise existed but the LDK refused to exploit it. Negotiations and inter-ethnic dialogue had to be reopened with the Kosovar Serbs and Serbia proper, argues Clark:

> A *process* was essential. The point was to focus on transition, identifying and responding to the interests and concerns of the communities in Kosovo—Albanian, Serb, Turkish, Roma, Slav Muslim, and Croat—and rebuilding inter-ethnic relationships and confidence in a way they could make this "intractable" problem finally "tractable." Without such a process, no option for the future status of Kosovo would be viable unless it was imposed by force of arms.

In Kosovo it was Rugova and the LDK bureaucracy that blocked a reinvigorated campaign of civil resistance and negotiated transition. But what about the diaspora? Could not Bukoshi, for example, or someone else from abroad have picked up the reins? The exile prime minister sat marginalized in the Bonn office, a one-man institution with deep pockets. The rift between Bukoshi and Rugova was, by 1996, an open secret, and Bukoshi had begun taking potshots at Rugova in the media, alerting ordinary Kosovars to the friction in their leadership. But Bukoshi confined his challenge to Rugova's authority to jibes from the sidelines. He made noises about a more active brand of resistance but declined to mount a frontal challenge to the president. In the LDK diaspora circles, even those who harbored reservations about Rugova believed that their job was to support their people's movement and its leadership in the homeland, not to undermine it from abroad. For better or for worse, they had placed their trust in Rugova. Diasporas do not lead or challenge, they said, they generate solidarity.

As for the issue of dialogue with Serbia or the Kosovar Serbs or both, the diaspora was in even less of a position to break ranks on this most delicate issue. In general, diaspora leaders and organizations are poorly placed and negatively inclined to reach out to their nation's adversary. By definition, the exile "politician" has been excluded from the political process in the homeland precisely because of his unacceptability to the ruling consensus. Also, from the shores of exile, the "other" in the homeland looms as a disembodied, intangible enemy, both the source of the exile's condition and his people's victimization. Milošević was demonized, and the eight million other Serbs were imagined as a nation of little Milošević clones. From the diaspora, complex, nuanced issues become black and white, often reduced to a handful of one-liners aimed at a foreign audience. And on matters of principle, diasporas tend to be holier-than-thou, quick to denigrate compromise of any kind and to charge their rivals in the movement of betrayal and "going soft." This is exactly what happened to Bukoshi who was, at one point, accused of favoring transitional autonomy for Kosovo. He immediately rushed to the diaspora information services to deny the rumor. And finally, a pragmatic point, in exile there is no negotiating partner or interlocutor from the other side with whom to strike a compromise. The Kosovo Serbs lived in Kosovo. Belgrade naturally looked to Rugova. Diasporas are isolated, mono-ethnic worlds.

In Germany, as elsewhere in Europe, the Kosovars organized regular demonstrations, attracting tens of thousands. If Bukoshi, disgusted with Rugova's obstinacy, had sincerely wanted to heighten the political pressure, theoretically he could have done so through his real constituency—the diaspora. He had more than one hundred thousand diaspora activists who looked to him! But the protests were remarkably muted. Year after year they became perfunctory. "The Kosovars were so very well behaved, too well behaved," notes one German journalist. "They'd come with their signs and banners, demonstrate for a couple hours, and then back in their cars to go home. They didn't make enough noise, raise enough hell. Maybe if they had, somebody would have listened to them." Bukoshi says he urged Rugova to push the envelope in Kosovo, but he wasn't ready to do so himself in exile.

By late 1994 the Kosovars' internal divisions and the dwindling energy of the movement had begun to marginalize the Bukoshi administration. The government itself rarely met with all present as it had in Slovenia and Stuttgart. Important decisions were made on the ground in Kosovo by the de facto ministers and parliamentary commissions. Word of the tensions between Bukoshi and Rugova had seeped out, confusing ordinary Kosovars and splitting the ranks of the leadership. Remarkably, though, the diaspora LDK and the Bukoshi structures continued their formal cooperation on the Three Percent Funds. But Bukoshi withdrew into the Bonn office, no longer appearing at LDK functions.

The close communication between the exile structures and the LDK in Kosovo—key to making an exile strategy succeed—had broken down, and pettiness filled the void. One slight that infuriated the LDK was Bukoshi's decision to stop financing the president's diplomatic trips. Contending that Rugova's extravagant choices in hotels and gastronomy was out of line, he ordered that they not be funded by Kosovar taxpayers. (Bukoshi prides himself on his asceticism. When he was not with his wife and two daughters on weekends in Ulm, Bukoshi slept on a mattress in the Bonn office.) Rugova would surely have replaced Bukoshi by 1994, had he been able to, but the president of the republic had no control over its exile prime minister. After less than four years of exile politics, the Kosovar constitution was a dead letter.

The last gust of tailwind slipped from Bukoshi's sails in November 1995 outside the barbed-wire gates at Wright Patterson Air Force Base in Dayton, Ohio. For nearly five years the Kosovar leadership had encouraged its people to believe that the international community would intervene benignly on their behalf. Both the media in Kosovo and the diaspora press trumpeted every meeting of Rugova or Bukoshi with foreign leaders as another irreversible step toward independence. The Kosovars were convinced that their status would be on the table at the next major international conference on the Balkans. But, at Dayton, the world's top diplomats excluded Kosovo from negotiations over a peace settlement for Bosnia and Herzegovina. First Bosnia, they promised, then Kosovo. On the periphery of the air force base, Bukoshi and a rain-soaked pack of Kosovar Albanian protesters were literally left out in the cold.

Irate Albanian Americans, however, refused to take no for an answer. They picketed the negotiations, insisting that Kosovo be included in the peace talks. Several hundred protesters, mainly from U.S. diaspora centers such as New York, Chicago, and Detroit, chanted "USA Free Kosovo." Photographs in *Illyria* show a trench-coated Bukoshi in the crowd with a megaphone in hand. Protesters carried signs that read "Include Kosovo," "Jail Milošević," and "Albanians will fight for freedom." At one point the diaspora activists broke through the heavy security line and stormed the gate of the base, reportedly ripping it off its hinges. The militancy was a sign that the Kosovars' patience was finally at the end of its tether.

The agreement on Bosnia reached at Dayton stipulated that one tier of the UN sanctions against Yugoslavia would be lifted in exchange for Belgrade's compliance with the peace plan. This rubbed salt in the Kosovars' wounds. It was an unscrupulous sellout of their years-long campaign: the international community was sacrificing them for peace in Bosnia and Herzegovina. Without full sanctions, what leverage would anyone now have against Milošević, who had showed no sign of easing the repression in Kosovo? Milošević was now being heralded as a "man of peace." Disappointment and fury stretched from the corners of the diaspora to the streets of the homeland. Without the pressure of sanctions, Bukoshi candidly told the *Cleveland Plain Dealer* on November 11, 1995: "The situation will deteriorate. Our population will lose their hope that any sort of peaceful solution will be found. The people are desperate and they can be radicalized suddenly, which would be a catastrophe not only for the Albanians but for the region."

The writing on the wall was that clear.

CHAPTER ELEVEN

Frankie Goes to Kosovo

Just before dawn on May 26, 1999, Operation Arrow commenced from a ten-mile stretch along Albania's remote northern border. The three brigades of Kosovo Liberation Army (KLA) fighters, about three thousand–strong, could barely discern the upper reaches of the Paštrik mountain range when their gunners began shelling its Serb positions. For the ethnic Albanian soldiers, these strategic peaks, just over the border inside Kosovo, were occupied territory. It was the objective of Operation Arrow to liberate them.

About eighty of these frontline troops were U.S. citizens of Albanian ancestry, members of the Atlantic Brigade. Another twenty Albanian Americans stationed in Košare, north of the Paštrik lines and already inside Kosovo, had joined the KLA units pushing southward toward the new front. The Americans in the jet-black uniforms with the red-and-yellow patch on their arms that read Ushtria Clirimtare e Kosovës (KLA, in Albanian) were not the only diaspora contribution to Operation Arrow. The lion's share of the KLA soldiers along the base of the Paštrik range had come to Albania from Western Europe. Non-Albanian volunteers, professional soldiers from as far away as Denmark and Israel, were also sprinkled through the lines.

A junior at New York's John Jay College of Criminal Justice, nineteen-year-old Florim Lajqi, had been assigned sniper duty. Gangly and wide-eyed, this was Florim's first taste of war. Four weeks in the KLA training camps of northern Albania had taught him how to handle the Russian Draganov sniper rifle he carried, and the Chinese submachine gun in his pack, a vintage piece that recalled the long-forgotten days of Albanian-Chinese friendship in the 1970s.

The commander of his company, Fadil Idrizi, hailed from Djakovica, a city that lay just beyond the Paštrik chain. Fadil, a brooding, well-built man in his mid-thirties, had not been so close to his hometown since he and his wife and daughter had fled Kosovo in 1993. They lived in Brooklyn, now with two more children. In the 1980s, in socialist Yugoslavia, he had worn the gray-blue uniform of Yugoslavia's national army. He had been in special operations, a sharpshooter, stationed in Macedonia next to fellow soldiers from Serbia proper, Croatia, Slovenia, and Bosnia.

By the time the push up Mount Paštrik began, the one hundred–odd members of the Atlantic Brigade had dispersed between the 121st Brigade "Paštrik" and the 128th Brigade "Agim Ramadani" in Košare. But, in spirit, the Atlantic Brigade still existed, as real as the day the U.S. volunteers took off together from JFK International Airport a month earlier. Next to their KLA insignia, every one of them had a patch with the American flag sewn onto his uniform. The group's composition reflected the mixture of first- and second-generation immigrants that had signed up to fight for Kosovo. It included students and bartenders, pizza bakers and building superintendents, roofers and maintenance men. For some of them, Albanian was their first language; for others, English. By the time the guns fell silent well after nightfall on the first day of the offensive, the fighters of the Atlantic Brigade had forged bonds that would endure long after they returned to their adopted homes in America.

The Paštrik offensive was key to the overall game plan of the KLA high command. The units along the border had to take the prize range from the Serbs—and hold it. From the heights of these barren mountains that form the southwestern border of Kosovo, its master surveys the vast basin that holds key Kosovar cities and much of its farmlands. The southern flank of the Yugoslav army stretched along the mountain chain and down into the fertile plateau below it where the towns of Djakovica and Prizren lie. The KLA strategy was to fight into the Dukagjin Valley from the west and the south, take Djakovica and Prizren, and split the Serb lines. If they could break open a corridor, nothing could stop the KLA units in northern Albania from linking up with their guerrilla comrades in central Kosovo. Should the coordinated offensives prove successful, nearly one-third of Kosovo would fall into KLA hands.

The Kosovar rebels were hopelessly outmanned and outgunned by Milošević 's professional army. But they boasted a mighty ally, one that would cut short their campaign and hand the Kosovar Albanians one of the quickest victories in the history of guerrilla warfare. In the skies over Kosovo and Serbia proper, NATO fighter planes had been pounding Serb targets since late March. With a disaster all too reminiscent of Bosnia staring it in the eye, the West had finally opted to confront Milošević on the battlefield. In contrast to the Albanian émigrés who tried to overthrow Albania's communist dictatorship in the 1950s, the patriots in the Atlantic Brigade had U.S. Stealth bombers overhead conducting a fierce air war against their foes. In less than three weeks after Operation Arrow started the war was over, and the Albanian Americans on Mount Paštrik, which they captured, would go back to New York as veterans and war heroes.

But the men in the Atlantic Brigade did not know this when they signed up to defend their relatives and countrymen in the homeland. The chance of a Western military intervention looked impossibly slim just a year ago.

Neither the United States nor the Europeans were eager to risk involvement in a protracted war in the Balkans. Had Milošević signed the agreement presented at the Rambouillet negotiations in February–March 1999, Kosovo would have remained part of Serbia, just as the West had always insisted it must. Most likely, rather than become NATO's de facto ground troops, the rag-tag KLA would have become the West's adversary on the ground in a hopeless, drawn-out guerrilla war.

In the United States Fadil and Florim had "enlisted" for the KLA several times before their phones finally rang. It was in the spring of 1998, at the crowded New York and Washington demonstrations, that a previously unknown group, Homeland Calling, had circulated sign-up sheets for Albanian men to fight for the Kosovars' new guerrilla army. Hundreds of men at the angry rallies grabbed for the pens and clipboards: name, address, phone number, military experience. "We'll call you," the unknown organizers said. Florim and Fadil weren't sure if the lists were genuine. For months no one contacted either of them.

"I understood it as a message from the homeland that they needed recruits," says Florim, who had lived in the United States since he was three. As a child, Florim had visited Kosovo every summer with his parents, his grandparents still residing there. Like Florim, nearly two thousand men signed up to fight; there was nothing to lose by scrawling one's name and number on a piece of paper. But Florim was dead serious, even though he had never done a day of military service or training in his life. He had read lots of military history, he says, and his father had brought him deer hunting upstate. For him, though, the lack of experience didn't matter. He simply couldn't stand by and watch his people slaughtered the way the Serbs had slaughtered the Bosnian Muslims. "I thought this was the only way to stop Milošević. I'm only one person, but there's more," he explains earnestly. "Bosnia showed that the world doesn't care what happens there, in the Balkans. We have to defend ourselves." This sentiment, virtually word for word, echoed across the Kosovar Albanian diaspora.

Florim's commanding officer, Fadil, had learned English in the United States, adding incrementally to the phrases he needed as a waiter in a Manhattan restaurant. He introduced himself to his colleagues as "Frank" rather than Fadil, hoping to blend in and avoid nosy questions. He didn't talk much to Florim or anyone else about the regular phone calls to his parents in Djakovica, when he learned the latest grim news from southern Kosovo. "I had military experience," he says curtly. "I thought that I could use what I know to make a difference."

Their cell phones finally did ring in early April. They were told to be at the Il Galleto Restaurant on April 8 in Hoboken, New Jersey, just past the Lincoln Tunnel. About 450 fighting-age men turned up, with as many supporters and onlookers in tow. They were told that the KLA command, based in Tirana, had announced a general mobilization of all Kosovar men, including those in the diaspora. "This is no joke, you're really going to go," the organizers said. Some of those who had showed up full of bravado melted back into the crowd. Those ready to fight, it was said, should be at the Royal Regency Hotel in Yonkers in three days: with uniform, pack, and paperwork, ready to go. "That's it," says Florim. "We only had three days to drop everything in our lives."

Over the next few days the new recruits scrambled to quit their jobs, terminate their studies, and say good-bye to family and loved ones. The Army-Navy surplus stores in New York and New Jersey did a record business. "You couldn't *not* knock into another Kosovar Albanian," laughs Fadil. They walked out with armfuls of black fatigues, helmets, flack jackets, military backpacks, and hunting knives.

On April 11 between four hundred and five hundred volunteers appeared at the Royal Regency, in uniform and looking prepared for immediate deployment. In reality, the event was partly a public relations ploy. Several hundred of the would-be soldiers had no intention of leaving the United States. They were there for the media, which had appeared in full force. The Atlantic Brigade was not slipping out of the country under the cover of night. CNN's cameras rolled as the recruits performed a mock swearing-in ceremony and then pretended to split up into squads. As media stunts go, this one hit the bull's-eye. Diaspora Albanians across the world watched the Americans as they declared their loyalty to the cause. As its organizers admit, the performance was aimed at the hundreds of thousands of Albanians in the European diaspora. It was they who would pay the bills and fill the ranks of the KLA.

The Atlantic Brigade was the brainchild of the men behind Homeland Calling, the KLA's front organization in the diaspora. "I knew it would make a big difference in propaganda terms," says Florin Krasniqi, a Brooklyn contractor and key figure in both Homeland Calling and the Atlantic Brigade. "I remember when they swore in, in Yonkers, it was on every radio and TV station in the world!" Krasniqi admits that he never imagined that the U.S. volunteers would see frontline action. "I did everything in my power not to have them sent to the front," he says. "It didn't matter whether they went or not, the important thing was that they showed up in uniform [in Yonkers]. With that alone they would have done their part."

Despite all the acting, more than one hundred Albanian Americans were, in fact, off to Albania. But at JFK the men's adventure of a lifetime was nearly stillborn. The first two charter plane companies that Krasniqi had contracted somehow learned the true nature of the operation and backed out quickly. The would-be soldiers waited for several days. A third charter company, Miami Air, ostensibly accepted the explanation that the men were humanitarian aid workers and took off with the volunteers from New York. It was not until the contingent landed at the Mother Theresa Airport in Tirana that it informed the pilot that his passengers were not charity workers at all, but soldiers! The pilot apparently feigned the proper shock.

Yet the real shock was still to come. Most of the recruits had never before been in Albania proper, and the reality of the country's postcommunist misery hit them like a cold slap. The poverty and grinding living conditions were worse than they had even imagined. Many found the Albanian dialect, different from that spoken in Kosovo, incomprehensible. At the Burrell Camp in northern Albania, the flood of diaspora volunteers and refugee recruits overwhelmed the camps' organizers. There were only enough toilets, beds, and kitchen equipment for about one thousand soldiers, not four times that number. At first there was barely enough to eat: just bread and raw onions. "Onions!" laughs one of the Atlantic's soldiers, Frank Mehmeti from the Bronx. "That's all we had, onions! I said, you've got to be kidding me. I'm not eating raw onions!"

There were plenty of jokes in the brigade about onions. But little did the *Amerikani* know that they, too, were the butt of jokes. Word of their bitching had spread. "A spoiled pack of mommy's boys," their compatriots chided behind their backs. "Did they think they were going to a party?" "We need soldiers, not pizza bakers," they said. The barbs were remarkably similar to the snide comments that Albanians flung at their returning Americanized cousins in the 1920s. But the Americans had shown up, prepared for combat, and for that they earned their fellow soldiers' grudging respect.

Until the Dayton conference the men who would join the Atlantic Brigade, like most Kosovar Albanians, abided by the LDK gospel that patience and nonviolence would eventually be rewarded by the powers-that-be. Florim's father and older brothers were active LDK members and had paid regularly into the Three Percent Fund. Fellow soldier Uk Lushi, before he emigrated to the United States, had worked in the LDK's Stuttgart office next to Bukoshi in the early 1990s. But the Kosovars' exclusion from the historic peace talks only proved to them further that, in the Balkans, the force of arms produced results, not good behavior. For their brutal war in Bosnia, Serbia and the Bosnian Serbs reaped rewards. And adding insult to injury, in 1996 the European Union countries officially recognized rump Yugoslavia, made up of Serbia and Montenegro (and thus Kosovo, too), as one of the legitimate successor states to socialist Yugoslavia.

The glimmer of hope that Dayton might be followed up by a conference on Kosovo, as the Albanian Americans were informally promised at Wright-Patterson, faded quickly. In fact, as the peace process in Bosnia got under way, the Kosovo issue slid even further down on the international agenda. Germany, Sweden, and Switzerland judged the situation to be so stable that they started repatriating Kosovar refugees!

So what then, as of 1996, had eight years of sustained diaspora engagement done for Kosovo? In the United States the combined efforts of Dio-Guardi's Civic League, the U.S.–LDK branches, the Bukoshi government, and the array of wealthy and well-placed émigré Kosovars, dwarfed the campaigns of the other diasporas from former Yugoslavia. A conservative estimate of that spent on the 1988–96 "lobby-related" activities of the Albanian American diaspora (political lobbying, PR-media work, and political campaign contributions) probably exceeds $9–$11 million. Big-name congressmen had taken the issue under their wing. One resolution followed another. In the House, the Albanians' staunchest backer, Rep. Eliot Engel of New York, created the Albanian Issues Caucus. The Albanian Americans also had able congressional insiders such as aides Ilir Zherka and Mira Barata (a Croatian American) working in the offices of key committee members. In late 1996 Zherka and others, many of whom had broken from the Civic League, founded the National Albanian American Council (NAAC), which, through Zherka, maintained regular access to the Clinton White House and its foreign policy team.

U.S. policy makers had been made aware that a concerned Albanian constituency was out there, something the Bosnian Muslims, for example, could never demonstrate. Certainly, through diaspora efforts, Kosovo's plight had gained international profile. It was important, too, that Kosovo was no longer deemed a purely "internal affair" of Serbia. International NGOs and human rights groups were on the ground in Kosovo. In 1996 the U.S. government set up an information office in Pristina.

But the "powerful Albanian lobby" had not made a dent on the issue that mattered most to Kosovar Albanians. Regarding national independence, the very essence of their struggle, the Kosovar Albanians were no closer to their ultimate goal. Despite their new legion of "friends in Congress," U.S. policy had not budged on Kosovo's status, present or future: Kosovo was and would remain a constituent part of Serbia. The ethnic Albanians deserved wide-ranging autonomy and full human rights, but only within Yugoslavia. The Kosovars stuck adamantly to their insistence on full independence, while the international community bluntly insisted it would never happen. Until something dramatic happened, the Kosovo issue was at an impasse.

The restless post-Dayton climate failed to shake President Rugova and the LDK apparatus from their somnolence. The elected custodians of the Kosovar cause displayed no new energy or incentives. At the grassroots, signs of growing restiveness were percolating. The Kosovar students' and women's groups pushed for the resumption of demonstrations. (The last demonstration had been in 1992.) Ever more disaffected voices called for hunger strikes, reconvening the parliament and reoccupying the schools and universities. But Rugova, backed fully by the West, suffocated stirrings of a more dynamic civil opposition voicing the usual objections. There were rumblings in Kosovo of a coup against the president, or at least calls for new elections. That said, much of the population seemed resigned to the status quo and the lackluster leadership of the LDK. Certainly starting a war against Serbia was not considered a reasonable alternative.

The inability of either the homeland or the diaspora leadership to present a new strategy for the Kosovar Albanians played directly into the hands of Kosovo's most radical factions. As early as 1993 armed elements in Kosovo had begun ambushing Serb policemen. The assassins declined to announce themselves until three years later when a hitherto unknown group, called the Kosovo Liberation Army, claimed credit for the attacks in the radical émigré newspapers published in Switzerland—and declared that more attacks would follow.[1] Masked men toting automatic weapons and grenades strapped to their belts intensified the violence, launching strikes against Serb police stations, border patrols, and ethnic Albanian "collaborators." In 1996 Serb officials counted thirty-one attacks. They were well planned and professionally executed, the authorities noted. At the time of the KLA's emergence, Rugova insisted that the new force on the scene was a creation of the Serb security services. He probably even believed that was true.

It was not until November 28, 1997, that Kosovo's guerrilla army unveiled its face to the public. At the funeral of a slain Kosovar schoolteacher, three KLA fighters presented themselves to the twenty thousand mourners: "Serbia is massacring Albanians," one of them declared. "The KLA is the only force that is fighting for the liberation and national unity of Kosovo! We shall continue to fight!" That evening every television set in Kosovo showed images of the men in black ski masks, signaling that a new chapter had begun in the Albanian struggle in Kosovo.

It was not a coincidence that the KLA first declared its existence in the pages of the Swiss-based organ of the Popular Movement for Kosovo, *Zëri i Kosovës* (The Voice of Kosovo). The publication had served as the radicals' mouthpiece since the early 1980s, back when the pro-Albania Marxist-Leninist party called itself the Popular Movement for the Republic of Kosovo. Its veteran activists, many Macedonian Albanians among them, such as Fazli Veliu, Ali Ahmeti, and Bardhyl Mahmuti, had emigrated in the aftermath of the 1981 crackdown.[2] A younger generation included the future KLA commander Hasim Thaçi and the spokesperson for Germany Sabri Kiçmari. The professional revolutionaries' fleeting cooperation with the LDK and republican structures on military matters in 1990–93 ended in discord and rancor. The Popular Movement had given up on Rugova and Bukoshi years before the KLA fired its first shot. Even before the LDK came along, the Popular Movement's cultish adoration of Enver Hoxha never attracted more than a thousand activists between Stockholm and Milan.[3] The 1997 report of Germany's Verfassungschutz (Bureau for the Protection of the Constitution) estimated that the group's members in the country numbered a paltry three hundred. This amounted to less than 1 percent of the LDK members in Germany at the time.

This tiny band of toughs–cum–liberation fighters fit the paradigm of Babylonian exile as accurately as did the Croat émigré Gojko Šušak and his fellow diaspora agitators. Banished from the homeland and told never to return, they lived in a half-fictional world of guns, spies, and national heroes. Their chimera was not just to overthrow Serb rule in Kosovo but to liberate all the Albanian populated parts of western Macedonia, Montenegro, southern Serbia, and northern Greece—one step at a time. Nor did their pipe dreams stop there. They planned to correct the faulty hand of history and join these Albanian lands with Mother Albania, as they believed the Great Powers should have done in 1913. It takes a moment to digest these preposterous fantasies. Did this tiny grouping of powerless dreamers really believe that it could throw all southeastern Europe into a war, and win it? It seems so. And, like their Croat counterparts, they never gave up on these far-flung ideas, despite all logic to the contrary. One immediate obstacle was that almost no one took them seriously. Like the Croat "revolutionaries" in Canada, the Popular Movement extremists in Switzerland spoke for a minuscule sliver of the diaspora. Writer Tim Judah refers to them as the "loony fringe." They hid in the crevices of Swiss society, refusing to learn its ways or master its languages, much as generations of gastarbeiter before them had done. In Switzerland they lived in one of the world's most successful multiethnic democracies. But nothing of this experience sunk in. Even though they officially scuppered their ideological commitment to "Enverism" in the 1990s, their conspiratorial ways and political disposition reflected the doctrine they had preached for a decade.

These extremist factions also emerged from obscurity at a moment when crisis flashed, one they helped to create, just as Šušak had done when he fired the Ambrust rockets into Borovo Selo. At a moment of desperation, when institutions of democracy were nearly nonexistent, they linked up with a like-minded marginal element in the homeland. A similar radicalization that transformed Croatia in 1990–91 happened in Kosovo in 1997–98. Only in this way could these fringe diaspora groups win the influence that they did.

This marginal element in the homeland lived in rural Kosovo in the sturdy-walled compounds called *kulla* that house multiple generations of

Kosovo's clan families. The stone-and-mortar walls are usually twelve to fifteen inches thick and stand more than seven feet in height. The kullas are practically fortified villages with their garden plots and livestock, family dwellings and communal spaces. The kullas and the independent-minded clans of central Kosovo's Drenica region had long been the stuff of Kosovar legend. When these extended families were not battling invaders, such as Serbs, they fought out blood feuds with one another. Smuggling of some kind was part of the profile. One such Drenica family, the Jasharis, was led by paterfamilias Adem, a brigand wanted by the Serb authorities on charges of murdering a police officer. The authorities, however, were certain that any attempt to arrest Adem Jashari would be resisted, so at first they steered clear.

Drenica's clan families defied the political categories of Kosovo's urban population. Their horizons stretched no further than the hills they could see over the walls of their kullas. These hills, though, belonged to them—not Yugoslavia, not Serbia, and not the local Serb police. Clans such as the Jasharis had greeted Kosovo's declaration of independence in 1991 and had even briefly cooperated with the LDK. Adem Jashari had participated in the republic's first military formations in the early 1990s. The Serbs' raid on the Kosovars' covert defense and interior operations may have crippled the republic's embryonic military structures, but it did not touch clans like the Jasharis.

The nucleus of the KLA emerged when the Popular Movement operatives in Switzerland closed ranks with the armigerous clans. This strategy resembled the plans of diaspora revolutionaries before them, like the U.S.–backed Albanian commandos of the 1950s and the Croat Bugojnici of the 1970s: first infiltrate the occupied homeland, hook up with the domestic resistance, and deliver arms. Then spark a revolt. The local insurgency will catch like a brush fire, igniting a wider popular uprising that will return the exiles to power.

The Popular Movement leadership set up a four-man council to begin recruiting for the KLA. One of the four was Xhavit Haliti, whose connection to Albanian secret services would surely expedite the work. A second figure was the twenty-eight-year-old Thaçi, a graduate student at the University of Zurich.

The stumbling block in this early phase was access to money and weaponry. But two events would eradicate those deficits almost overnight. In March 1997 the neighboring state of Albania imploded. The collapse of a rigged investment scheme cost thousands of Albanian citizens their life savings and unleashed waves of fierce rioting across the country. The revolt not only brought down the government of Albania's president Sali Berisha, it decimated the fragile structures of Europe's poorest state. As the nation plunged into anarchy, rioters looted army depots and police stations, relieving the state of hundreds of thousands of automatic weapons. The flood of small arms into the region turned Albania into a floating arms bazaar, offering merchandise at rock-bottom prices. A standard issue Kalashnikov sold for a mere ten to twenty dollars. The well-tread mule routes over the Albanian mountains into Kosovo made gunrunning a cinch.

Albania's meltdown lost a crucial ally to Kosovo's prime minister in exile. When the Albanian socialists returned to power, replacing Berisha, Bukoshi no longer had a friend in Tirana. This realignment would cost him dearly, removing him even further from Kosovo's borders.

The second catalyst came a year later in the form of the March 1998 massacre at the Jashari compound. By 1998 the KLA units in Kosovo had stepped up their attacks on Serb targets, dispelling any doubt that the KLA meant business and that a low-intensity guerrilla war was on in Kosovo. The Serb police struck back against the Drenica families with resounding force. In a first offensive the Serb units killed more than twenty Kosovar Albanians in central Kosovo before they pushed on to their real target, the Jashari compound in the village of Prekaz. After a prolonged firefight, the police units rolled out artillery and proceeded, Bosnia-style, to shell the compound to rubble. Fifty-eight of the clan, including women and children, perished in the battle. In Kosovo Adem Jashari overnight became a martyr and national hero. Prekaz was the rallying cry that would radicalize the Albanian population in Kosovo and the diaspora. It also signaled that their new army had to turn itself into a serious fighting force if it was to withstand the wrath of Serbia's military might.

Like a long, shrill primal scream, the Drenica massacres released the pent-up fury and humiliation that had accumulated over the course of the 1990s. In Kosovo mourners defied Serb authorities to march in funeral processions for the Drenica victims. In Europe and the United States protesters descended on the Yugoslav embassies and missions, and in New York on the UN. In late March coordinated demonstrations in Europe's capitals and eight U.S. cities brought more than one hundred thousand people onto the streets. "20,000 in D.C. Demonstrate for Tougher Action by the U.S." ran the headline in a special issue of *Illyria*. The protesters in Lafayette Park carried signs that read "Stop the Killing!" "USA Free Kosova!" "Independence = Freedom, Autonomy = Slavery." A long line of the Albanian Americans' favorite congresspeople took the podium to promise their constituency that they were on the case. There would be no more business as usual, they said. The energized Albanian lobby groups would keep them to their word.

It was at these emotional demonstrations that most Kosovars first learned of Vendlindja Thërret, or Homeland Calling, a "foundation" that purported to represent the KLA. In the crowds its representatives circulated appeals for contributions. This money was not going to schools, health clinics, or U.S. congressmen, they said plainly, but to Kosovo's army. The same people distributed the first sign-up lists for young men to fight in the homeland.

Homeland Calling was not born in 1998 nor was it, strictly speaking, a foundation. It was a network of bank accounts that the Popular Movement leadership in Geneva had set up three years earlier. Until Drenica, the numbers of Homeland Calling's accounts—in Switzerland, Germany, Australia, the United States, Austria, Norway, Denmark, France, Sweden, Italy, Belgium, and Canada—could be found in the back pages of *Zëri i Kosovës*. The central account in Geneva was overseen by the Popular Movement's Jashar Salihu, a former schoolteacher from Kosovo. From Geneva the funds went to Tirana, where the KLA's chief logistics officer, Haliti, had established the KLA headquarters, in a building provided by Albania's Ministry of Defense.

The Popular Movement operatives promoted the fund as they stumped through the gastarbeiter clubs and refugee communities in Germany and Switzerland, railing against Bukoshi, Rugova, and the "LDK traitors." "Passive resistance has brought us nothing!" they cried. "These people are doing the Serbs' bidding." "Serb bastards!" they shouted, referring to Rugova and Bukoshi. The radicals' supreme goal may have been to overthrow Serb rule in Kosovo, but to do so they first had to dislodge Rugova and the LDK from power. The KLA was meant to do both. Bukoshi's bank accounts would be part of the bounty. The Popular Movement operatives spoke openly about their guerrilla army and its ongoing preparations for war. But until the KLA's coming out in 1997 and then Drenica, the reception was tempered. These guys had been talking much the same line for almost 20 years.

All at once, in the diaspora, Homeland Calling was on everyone's lips. Most diaspora Kosovars did not immediately associate it with the shadowy Popular Movement. "I didn't tag it at first," admits Joe DioGuardi, who quickly jumped on the bandwagon to promote the KLA. He and his wife clashed with the Popular Movement's U.S. point man regarding who would speak in the name of the KLA. "By then," says DioGuardi, "we could say that we were all KLA. It was the legitimate expression of the Kosovar Albanians."

"People were confused," says the former LDK diaspora spokesperson Donika Gërvalla, who immediately recognized the faces behind Homeland Calling from her own distant past. She suspected that some of the figures in the Popular Movement had been involved in her father's murder in 1982. "Lots of people thought the LDK was really behind it," she says, referring to Homeland Calling. Many surmised that Rugova was denying knowledge of the KLA for tactical purposes, because he had to, Gërvalla says. "They wondered whether they should pay into Homeland Calling or not. Should they stop paying into the Three Percent Fund? Or should they pay into both?" The diaspora Kosovars didn't want one cause with two or three heads. These internal divisions smacked to them of "politics," something at odds with the greater good of Kosovo. Symptomatic of diasporas, they drifted toward the voice that screamed the loudest.

The arrival of the KLA and Homeland Calling reshuffled the deck in the Albanian diaspora. Top LDK people, and even Bukoshi's Information Minister, Xhafer Shatri, defected to the new force. Homeland Calling's representatives took over some of the LDK offices, and other LDK branches voluntarily threw themselves behind the campaign. In New York the LDK office in the Bronx, one of the world's biggest, raised money simultaneously for the LDK, Bukoshi, and the KLA. On Arthur Avenue the offices of the Albanian Yellow Pages became a communications hub for the movement. Diaspora Kosovars, removed from the political in-fighting, were prepared to support the struggle in any way they could. To them, Drenica was an open declaration of war against their people, and they were not going to sit idly by.

The diaspora was flush with war fever, much more so than in the homeland. Observers who traveled frequently between Kosovo and abroad noted a distinct discrepancy between the mood in the homeland at the time and that in the diaspora. The appearance of the KLA electrified the ethnic Albanians in Kosovo, too. But most ordinary Kosovars did not want war. There was no rush to pick up arms for the KLA, for example. The man on the street was scared, concerned for his family's welfare. Surprisingly few volunteered for the new guerrilla army. Despite the rumblings, Rugova still had broad popular support, and the arguments the LDK leadership used against armed struggle in the early 1990s still held water: the Yugoslav army and the Serb paramilitary forces had overwhelming military superiority over the Kosovar Albanians' lightly armed insurgents. An uprising at this point, if unabetted by the West or regional allies, would, at best, turn into a protracted guerrilla war fought by the Kosovars from the mountains. A full-blown conflict could destabilize the entire region, with the severest consequences for ethnic Albanians in neighboring states. The West and NATO had not saved the Muslims of Srebrenica, why would they come to Kosovo's rescue after all these years?

Nevertheless the KLA's numbers burgeoned after Drenica and morale soared, drowning out the voices that preached caution. In central Kosovo roaming KLA units boasted at having "liberated" large swaths of territory. But in the summer of 1998 the Serbs struck back with a counteroffensive that easily routed the KLA from their checkpoints and village strongholds. The retreat of the KLA left their villages easy prey for the Serb forces, which scorched the earth behind them as they marauded through the Kosovar countryside. By August more than two hundred thousand Kosovars had been displaced by the fighting. Almost two thousand a month were streaming into Germany alone.

The tragic scenes of women and children sleeping under the stars and the landscape of charred villages did not deter the KLA. Part of the KLA strategy entailed provoking the Serbs, getting them to lash back with predictable ferocity and thus forcing a Western military response. The more cruel the repression, the more vivid the message that Albanians could not live under Serb domination. The KLA was fishing for Western sympathy, just as Rugova had done in a different way. The Bosnian Muslims had played the victim card for years—before the West stepped in and partitioned their country. Why the KLA leadership thought that the West would intervene on its behalf, when it had not done so for the Bosnians, is hard to fathom.

It was a high-risk strategy that panned out only because of the extraordinary sequence of events that ultimately led to the NATO military action against Yugoslavia. The scenes on the television news of refugee convoys, mutilated corpses, and Serb paramilitary units on the rampage awakened the international community to the fact that Bosnia could happen again, in Kosovo, just as the Kosovars had been warning for ten years. Drenica and the Serb offensive shifted international diplomacy into high gear. But the U.S. negotiators, led by Richard Holbrooke, sought a negotiated compromise to the conflict, one along similar lines to those suggested in the past: some far-reaching autonomy or "third republic" status for Kosovo within Yugoslavia. Western diplomats, dutifully following their superiors' orders, sought every avenue available to bring a peaceful settlement to Kosovo. Aiding the Kosovar Albanians' liberation war with Stealth bombers was not an option under discussion. In fact, the Kosovars were not even included in the first round of negotiations.

The West would exhaust all other options before reluctantly taking military action. In late 1998, acting under the threat of air strikes, Milošević allowed an Organization for Security and Cooperation in Europe verification mission into Kosovo to monitor Serb and Albanian compliance with the ongoing negotiations. In early 1999 the warring parties and brokers in the international community met in the French chateau of Rambouillet, outside Paris, to work out a negotiated deal. There were numerous real chances for the Serbs to stave off intervention. Contrary to the Kosovars' calculations, the Western alliance was not spoiling for a fight. The United States was as wary as ever about intervening in the faraway, unpredictable Balkans, where its interests were poorly defined. Key allies such as Germany felt profoundly uncomfortable about going to war with another sovereign state. Russia and China, both members of the UN Security Council, openly opposed any military intervention in Kosovo. The NATO campaign in the spring of 1999 was anything but inevitable.

The KLA may have been hoping to draw the West in, but it was not counting on help from anyone. The Kosovars had only just begun to fight their war of liberation. If the West would not step in, Kosovar Albanians in the West would. The KLA was financed from Europe, largely from the Kosovar bastions in Switzerland, such as the cantons of Zurich, Geneva, Vaud, and Berne, and the Western German states of Bavaria, Baden-Württemberg, Berlin, Hesse, and North Rhine–Westphalia. In 1998 the number of Kosovars in Germany and Switzerland had swelled to around five hundred thousand. In Switzerland, unlike in Germany, refugees had the right to work, thus enabling the diaspora there to generate as much money, if not more, than the numerically superior diaspora in Germany.

An old diaspora institution, the gastarbeiter club, reinvented itself in the new circumstances. When the clubs reopened their doors, full again for the first time since the early 1980s, the shuttered rooms still reeked of the cigarettes of thousands of gastarbeiter. Refugees flocked to the clubs or to Albanian cultural centers to watch the news reports from the front.

In Berlin, the temporary residence of twenty thousand Kosovo Albanians, the Bajram Curri Club filled up early in the evening for the television news from Tirana. (Bajram Curri had been an Albanian anti-monarchist guerrilla leader, killed in 1925.) The 6:30 P.M. satellite news from Tirana was an institution in the diaspora, a critical one for the diaspora politicians who influenced it. More so than the Internet or the newspapers, the satellite news informed and defined the Kosovars' European diaspora. When the reform communist (socialist) party in Albania returned to power in 1997, ousting the LDK-ally Berisha, Bukoshi and Rugova lost their hold on the satellite programming, breaking their most vital communication link to the diaspora. Bukoshi had paid $3 million for the satellite channel and for extensive improvements at TV Shqiptar, an investment that had repaid itself many times over. But when the Berisha government fell in Albania, Bukoshi's most valued propaganda instrument was no longer under his control. Representatives of the Popular Movement, with old friendships among the Albanian socialists, moved in and took over diaspora programming. At the Bajram Curri Club, with a beer or heavily sugared tea, one could also read the new diaspora-wide daily newspaper out of Zurich, *Bota Sot*. It, too, carried the KLA line.

Regular "information sessions" packed the clubs and cultural halls. The KLA's frontmen, such as Ibrahim Kelmendi, leader of the Popular Movement satellite in Germany, the Democratic Union of Albanians in Germany (DVAD), insisted that now was the time to liberate Kosovo. Those who could not go and fight should pay into Homeland Calling. On the walls at the Bajram Curri, like elsewhere, donor lists were posted for all to see. Those who did not contribute, it was said, could not expect their villages to be protected. "It's *your* families we're defending!" In April 1998 alone, claimed the DVAD, Homeland Calling collected $3.5 million in Germany. The German authorities gave it all a wink and a nod. There's nothing illegal going on here, they assured journalists.

The organizers of Homeland Calling had picked up a few tricks from the Three Percent Fund, such as the idea of an international network of bank accounts. But the parallels stopped there. Homeland Calling was a front: for the Popular Movement and for a guerrilla army. The DVAD, for example, was created to mask Homeland Calling's origins in the militant scene, while insuring that all the KLA funding ran through Popular Movement channels. It was not only among the rank-and-file diaspora that the Popular Movement had an unsavory reputation. In Germany authorities had branded it an organization "with aims that threaten state security."[4] In addition, the proximity of the Popular Movement figures to the criminal underworld, including drug trafficking, put officials on guard.

In Germany, as in Switzerland and elsewhere in Europe, the law discourages private organizations from funding armed movements abroad. Moreover, the UN arms embargo against the former Yugoslavia explicitly included Kosovo. Although Homeland Calling registered itself as a humanitarian organization, it was no secret that it financed all of the KLA's "logistics needs." To dispel any lingering doubt about that, one could simply log on to the DVAD website and see Adem Jashari and his fellow gunmen staring back from the screen. Or, at the DVAD offices in Bonn, one did not have to ask twice to receive bombastic KLA posters. With cell phones beeping like a small orchestra, the offices were in constant contact with the KLA commanders in the field. This, too, was top-secret, unless you inquired about it politely. But, as with the arming of Croatia, neither U.S. nor European officials appeared eager to dig deeply enough to find out. They looked the other way. Certainly the German officials did not go after Homeland Calling as it had the accounts of the militant Kurdish Workers Party (PKK) in the 1980s.

"What we sent was for potatoes, socks, uniforms," says Dino Asanaj, a New York City contractor and the political liaison for the KLA in America, referring to the $5 million[5] he claims Homeland Calling raised in the United States. "And if they [the KLA] wanted something else with it, well, that wasn't our understanding," he says in a sing-song voice, obviously meaning that his words are not to be taken at face value.

Asanaj's contacts with the Popular Movement in Europe were strong, and his trust in Haliti, his childhood friend from Peć, still vibrant. In the 1980s

Asanaj had moved in the circles around the Jusuf Gërvalla Association, the U.S. equivalent of the Popular Movement. But he waves off the old leftist jargon. One way or another, he says, Albanians all want to live in one state. Brawny and gruff, he says that the mistake the Kosovar Albanians made was to wait too long. "When Croatia and Bosnia were at war, that was the time for us to make war on Serbia. We had to open up the southern front, start two or three wars at once." He should know, he says. Asanaj studied military science in Belgrade and served for years as an officer in the JNA. "Sure," he admits, "you lose more people, maybe we would have had more victims than in Bosnia, but at least at Dayton we would have been a player." The breakup of Yugoslavia, he insists, would have had one act and not two.

In the United States men such as Florin Krasniqi, another founder of Homeland Callings U.S. branch, were profoundly uncomfortable with the leaders of the KLA from the "Class of '81." Krasniqi wanted to finance Kosovo's guerrilla army, not the private businesses of the Popular Movement's heavies. Homeland Calling and the KLA, explains the owner of Triangle Roofing, were much more than the Popular Movement. Krasniqi claims that his brother, Adrian, was the first KLA soldier to fall in battle, on October 15, 1997. In total, nineteen of his brothers and cousins died in the field during the 1990s.

Through his brother, the KLA was in contact with Krasniqi as early as 1996. "At first I was suspicious because they were so young," he says in a luncheon diner next to his Brooklyn office. "But Rugova was a joke, and I saw these people really mean business. So I got totally involved."

Krasniqi is a chatty and likable guy, thirty-something, a dark blue Triangle Roofing T-shirt stretched over his chest. His business office is in a small white house in Flatbush, with a screen door like every other on the street. Before we begin talking he takes me down to the cellar and pulls out a crate of gleaming brass 50-mm nitroglycerin bullets. "Just in case," he says, with a big and white toothy smile. "If they had had these in Tuzla [a Bosnian city] things would have looked different."

Although Krasniqi was in with the KLA from Day One, he didn't trust the characters associated with the Popular Movement, those on the other end of the line in Tirana. Political parties of all kinds, Krasniqi argues, should keep their noses out of the diaspora. "Homeland Calling was the KLA fund," he stresses, "and we were all KLA." He suspected that the millions being collected in the United States for the KLA were not getting to the front but were winding up in someone's pockets. Krasniqi insisted that the "merchandise" be bought and personally delivered into Albania, circumventing the shady middleman. "I insisted on this," he says. But it didn't go down well with Haliti and friends. "Every time I went to Tirana we almost ended up killing each other about this. They wanted cash. I said,

'What the fuck do you need cash for?' They said they were buying guns cheaper. Yeah, buying shitty guns. I'll bring you uniforms, radios, guns, food, everything. You can't bring thousands of young people over the borders [to fight] and give them these crummy weapons to get killed with. That's what they did."

Krasniqi's supplies came from the warehouses of U.S. weapons dealers, transported in privately chartered planes. "With money you can do anything," he tells me, and smiles his Pepsodent smile. "The Second Amendment is a lovely amendment. It's the best." The guns that fired the 50-mm rounds in his cellar were purchased over the counter in stores in Pennsylvania.

Despite his tiffs with the Popular Movement reps, Krasniqi gives Haliti his due: "He did a very dirty job in a dirty place at a dirty time. No one could have done the job the way he did. He was in charge of organizing everything—with Europe, with the Albanian government, with the Albanian secret services. I couldn't have done that."

In contrast to the Bukoshi fund, Homeland Calling was a seat-of-the-pants operation. There were no receipts, no records, and cash was readily accepted. The Popular Movement/DVAD representatives distributed "collector cards" to trusted members that enabled them to solicit funds on Homeland Calling's behalf. When it came to depositing the proceeds, the honor system was in effect. Understandably rumors of misappropriated funds were rampant, and charges of fraud circulated long after the end of the war. The secret of the total that Homeland Calling collected was probably lost forever when its banker, Jashar Salihu, died in 2000.[6] The means employed to fill the coffers also differed from Bukoshi's. The reps went door to door leaning on people to cough up donations. The spokespeople for the fund declared a mandatory 1,000–German mark ($500) "special tax" on all working members of the Kosovar diaspora.[7] Those who did not pay could expect to receive visits in the night.

Two other issues dogged the KLA: its proximity to organized crime, particularly drug trafficking, and the involvement of Middle Eastern Islamic fundamentalists in its campaign. European narcotics experts had traced drug running operations to Kosovo as early as the 1980s. But it was the collapse of communism, and the wars in Bosnia and Croatia, that turned Kosovo and northern Albania into a conduit for heroin smuggling. High-grade opium traveled from its source in Afghanistan and Pakistan through the processing plants in Turkey into the Balkans. A short speedboat trip over the Adriatic landed the booty in Italy. From there it flooded the Western European market, which Albanian criminal gangs had cornered in several countries by the early 1990s. Between 1990 and 1992 more than one thousand Kosovar Albanians had been imprisoned in Switzerland for running drugs and arms.[8] Drug busts in Albania and Macedonia seized hundreds of kilograms of processed heroin. By 2000 Interpol estimated that Kosovar Albanians controlled 40 percent of the European heroin trade.[9] Law-enforcement officials also confirmed that the drug money was buying weapons headed for the Balkans.

The extent to which drug barons bankrolled the KLA is another question, and is nearly impossible to answer. The Serb media labeled Kosovar Albanian activists of all stripes as "separatist narco-terrorists." Evidence certainly pointed to links between the Popular Movement/KLA commanders and Switzerland's drug lords and crime bosses. Individual commanders in the field also had their private connections to underworld money. That said, the predominant source of the KLA's guns and money was not big-time criminals but the enormous disenfranchised diaspora population spawned by Milošević's policies. The contributions for KLA weaponry came from the same migrants who had deposited hundreds of millions of German marks into Bukoshi's accounts for the shadow state. A portion of the KLA's funding may have been dirty money, but it did not explain the KLA.

The charges of Islamic sponsorship are even less valid. Although the majority of Kosovar Albanians are Muslim, only a small fraction practices the religion. Islamic relief agencies, fronts for Al Qaeda and others, may have operated in Albania during the war and even tried to gain a foothold in the KLA, as they had in the Bosnian army. But the Popular Movement's old Enverists had nothing in common with Islamic radicals, and the latter probably learned this quickly. As I toured the Albanian diaspora, I kept an eye open for signs of such sympathies. But where one might have expected a star and crescent, there were portraits of Skanderbeg and Mother Theresa (a Macedonian-born Albanian). Aware of its political implications, the Kosovars consciously kept their distance from Islam, to the extent that Rugova at one point favored a countrywide conversion to Catholicism. The idea was quickly abandoned.

It was not Arabic-speaking muhajedin that the KLA command wanted on the front lines but rather fit, capable young Kosovar men. The diaspora was teeming with them. The Atlantic Brigade may have been window dressing, but substantial numbers, probably more than a third, of the KLA troops originated from the diaspora. (Estimates of the number of KLA troops on the ground in early 1999 range from six thousand to twenty thousand, with the true figure probably closer to the lower end. It is thus conceivable that nearly half that number came from the European diaspora.) At first glance it seems unlikely that a home-grown guerrilla army would need reinforcements from the diaspora. At the time hundreds of thousands of refugees were streaming out of Kosovo into Albanian and Macedonian refugee camps. The men could be conscripted immediately. But the refugees were often badly traumatized and in poor health. For most of them, the paramount concern was the daily survival of their families, now homeless and destitute. They may have been angry, but they did not make the best soldiers.

The diaspora Kosovars had a different profile. A World Bank assessment of the Kosovar diaspora in Germany and Switzerland reports that by the late 1990s the deluge of diaspora newcomers was overwhelmingly young, male, and single. More than half the diaspora population was between eighteen and thirty-five years of age. Two-thirds had been displaced from rural areas. In Germany Kosovars were mostly jobless, drifting in a semi-legal gray zone, many without proper papers. Their meager education had been in the parallel schools. The conflict and "dispersion experiences," writes the World Bank report, had taken a heavy toll on the Kosovars' traditional family structures. Their dire situations often led the young men into the world of crime and drugs. It was these Kosovars who had earned the name "the lost generation."

One of the best seats from which to observe the various dramas of Kosovar exile politics in the 1990s was the twenty-first floor of the Deutsche Welle in Cologne, in the Albanian section of Germany's worldwide television and radio service. The section's program director, Adelheid Fielcke-Tiemann, only a quick subway trip from Bonn, saw quite a bit of Bukoshi, the LDK, the Popular Movement diaspora reps, and the swollen ranks of Kosovar refugees, tens of thousands lodged thick in Cologne's immediate vicinity. By the late 1990s the situation in the diaspora, she says, was a ticking time bomb:

> While the war refugees from Bosnia were mostly women, old people, and children, this massive influx of Kosovars was the opposite: military-aged men—without wives or women here. Often it was the eldest sons who were expected to make money and send it back, but that wasn't usually possible. In fact, they faced deportation at any moment. So there was a lot of aggressive potential in this community. They found themselves in a nasty vicious circle that led to a political radicalization. They were made-to-order for the KLA.

These young men didn't need to have their arms twisted when the KLA general command, via satellite TV, called for volunteers. In Germany alone an estimated fifty thousand volunteered at recruitment centers such as the Aleksandër Moisiu Albanian Club for the Visual Arts and Theater in Stuttgart and the Casanova Disco in Solingen, although only a fraction of that number ever suited up, much less arrived at the front. Blaring march tunes and a lot of patriotic hoopla accompanied the sign-up and send-off ceremonies, all covered thoroughly by the German media. With the cry "Freedom or death!" the recruits filed into rented charter buses and headed off to Italy. From there, by ship, they headed for the Albanian port of Durrës, where the volunteers from across Western Europe arrived. Their destination after Durrës was, like the Atlantic Brigade, the training camps in northern Albania, and then to the front.

Bukoshi was neither dormant nor forgotten during the emergence of the KLA and the buildup to war in Kosovo. Unlike Rugova, he did not deny the KLA's existence or attribute it to Serb security forces. He would finally act, taking decisions between 1997 and 1999 that would turn him into a figure more divisive and, in some circles, more maligned than Rugova, the symbol of Kosovo's failed Ghandiism. In fact, it was these decisions that would land his name on a KLA hit list on his return to Kosovo and stunt his political career for years to come. Bukoshi would not be remembered for funding Kosovo's shadow state for eight years but as the man who sold out the KLA as it liberated Kosovo from Serb rule.

In the spring of 1997 Bukoshi reactivated the Republic of Kosovo's defense and security portfolios. The post of minister of defense had been vacant since 1992, and the Kosovars' underground paramilitary network had been defunct since the Serb clampdown in 1993. Bukoshi took the initiative reluctantly, he claims, without President Rugova's go-ahead, which he felt he required. Nevertheless, he insisted that he could not wait any longer. Kosovo was poised to blow and, when it did, the Kosovar Albanians could not be left defenseless. As it happened, he had already waited too long.

Bukoshi organized a series of secret meetings in Bavaria with ethnic Albanian officers who had previously served in the JNA. In the cities of Augsburg and Würtzburg, the defense specialists convened to discuss the resumption of military preparations on behalf of the Republic of Kosovo. Some of the officers had served in the Slovenian, Bosnian, or Croatian armies or were doing so at the time. In contrast to the KLA figures, these men were qualified military professionals, former officers with specialized experience in tank warfare, artillery, counter-terrorism, and strategic planning. The group chose as its commander Ahmet Krasniqi, a former Yugoslav officer and veteran of the 1991 war in Croatia, who was then living in semi-retirement on the Dalmatian coast. Krasniqi's patriotic credentials were stellar: he hailed from an opposition family and had done time in Serb jails for sedition. Krasniqi, who had had contact with the Bukoshi government since its days of Slovenian exile, was waiting for the call. In the fall of 1997 Bukoshi named him the new minister of defense and sent Krasniqi to Albania with the mandate to build a Kosovar army, the Armed Forces of the Republic of Kosovo, or FARK.

Bukoshi's critics charge that by establishing FARK he financed a parallel army, a rival to the KLA, and thus split the Kosovar ranks. But as early as

1997 the KLA was not an army. It numbered several hundred fighters, most of them in central Kosovo employing hit-and-run tactics against the Serb forces. Its larger strategy was as opaque as the nature of its leadership or the source of its funding. Krasniqi's mandate was to prepare the structures for a professional army capable of waging a protracted war against Serbia. At the very least, a Kosovar militia had to be prepared to defend Albanians against Serbia's irregular paramilitary units, such as those that had conducted the ethnic cleansing and massacres in Bosnia.

According to Bukoshi, FARK was not designed to undermine the KLA but to help organize its fighters into a combat-ready force. The strikes against Serb policemen may have raised cheers from frustrated Kosovars, but it neither dented the Serbs' armor nor damaged their morale. If it provoked Serb retaliation, such as the expulsion of the Kosovar Albanians from Kosovo, the KLA command had no counter-strategy, just patriotic sloganeering about a bloody battle to the finish. In contrast, Bukoshi and Krasniqi thought of a guerrilla army primarily as a long-term option, should it come to all-out war. After years of imploring the West to take note of Kosovo's plight, Bukoshi was skeptical that a strategy of provoking atrocities would garner the desired result. This, he felt, was just what the Serbs wanted in order to cleanse Kosovo of its ethnic Albanians forever.

But attempts to reconcile and merge the KLA and FARK never got off the ground. Both commands had headquarters in Tirana: the KLA's in official Albanian government offices, FARK in private housing. The socialist government in the Albanian capital impeded FARK step by step, says Bukoshi and former FARK volunteers. FARK officers and soldiers, for example, could not walk around Tirana armed. Krasniqi made monthly payoffs to local chieftains in northern Albania for access to roads and mafia-controlled territories. One late payment resulted in his abduction. Tensions between the KLA and FARK often spilled over into violence, both in Tirana and in northern Albania where both had training camps. Observers spoke of a civil war erupting between rival Kosovar factions in Albania. Soldiers with FARK insignia dared not enter the districts of Tirana that the KLA controlled, and vice versa. Bukoshi's forces boasted more funding, higher-quality weapons, and professional officers. But the KLA ruled the Kosovar countryside, and there lay the loyalties of the clan families.

The chances for FARK to mount a credible fighting force were snuffed out on the night of September 21, 1998. Krasniqi and several of his officers and their body guards were returning from dinner when Albanian police disarmed them at a road block. This kind of mistreatment was nothing new. But two armed men with pistols were lying in wait for the entourage outside the FARK headquarters, which was also Krasniqi's residence. They commanded the twelve men to step out of their cars and kneel on the ground with their hands behind their heads. They demanded to know which one was Krasniqi and proceeded to execute him at point-blank range.

Despite the recriminations over Krasniqi's murder, negotiations over the cooperation between, and possible merger of, FARK and the KLA continued. Bukoshi insisted that the KLA units come under FARK command, since FARK was the legitimate military of the Kosovar government. Haliti and Thaçi, Bukoshi's negotiating partners, refused to relinquish control of their units. For them, the issue on the table was money. The KLA command did not need FARK troops or want their officers. Bukoshi's refusal to give in infuriated the KLA leaders. In New York, at a seven-hour meeting in the Waldorf Astoria, Asanaj tried to get Bukoshi to fork over the republic funds: "I told him to give us the money for arms. It was happening, I told him, see what is coming. But they didn't believe in fighting for freedom. Bukoshi didn't believe in his own people's will."

Bukoshi's financial resources exceeded those of the KLA/Homeland Calling. In addition to the Three Percent Fund, in 1997 Bukoshi established a separate fund exclusively for military-related purposes. The London-based Everything for an Independent Kosovo Fund collected $30 million during its two-year run, another extraordinary figure. At rallies and meetings in the United States and Western Europe Bukoshi stated explicitly that this was a war chest—and money flowed in. This is Bukoshi's side of the story:

> They [Haliti, Asanaj, and Thaçi] told us [the government] that they had always wanted the war option, so keep your mouth shut and give us the money to wage war. I rejected this logic. We tried for ten years to get the world to recognize Kosovo as a problem, to make it sensitive to our concerns, and we did. This was also a battle but one without weapons. Ultimately it didn't bear fruit, as Kosovo was never recognized as an independent country. So now the people have chosen another path. We [the Kosovar government] respect that, and I'm further available to follow this path myself. I will organize our country's self-defense through Kosovo's legitimate institutions. We have to respect the rules in wartime, too, not go about it as a gang would.

This is vintage Bukoshi: by the book, even as full-scale war threatened the very existence of his people. His refusal to dispense *all* the funds (he eventually gave them $4 million) incensed not only the KLA leaders but many ordinary Kosovars. Bukoshi maintained that he was not about to hand over the Kosovar taxpayers' money to a bunch of gangsters. Like his dispute with Rugova in the early 1990s, Bukoshi had legitimate points, but he was unwilling—or unable—to pose a viable alternative from the diaspora. He wound up sitting on the fence, criticizing those on the ground without risking anything himself. The KLA leadership was a corrupt lot, and millions of dollars surely went astray there. Its strategy was reckless and short-sighted, but it had conviction and acted on it with determination. It did what Bukoshi would not do: go for broke, against all odds, and in the face of all the rules.

I first met Bukoshi in April 1999, at the peak of fighting, five weeks into the NATO bombing campaign. He was alone in his Bonn office, sleeves rolled up, preparing a press release. By this time the KLA leaders had displaced him as prime minister, a move he declared illegal. This made him one of two self-declared prime ministers of a self-declared country, half of whose population was living in refugee camps outside its borders. In other words, Bukoshi was as dead as a politician could be. Like exiled leaders before him, his office had degenerated into an empty title, devoid of legal or popular legitimacy. At the very least he could have joined FARK's scattered units on the ground in Albania or delivered aid to the refugees in Macedonia or Albania. But he chose his exile domain, Bonn, where he clung stubbornly to his title and the diaspora bank accounts.

Whatever his perceived errors, one could also argue that Bukoshi played a shrewd hand to the very end. Even as a political outcast, he returned defiantly to Kosovo in June 1999 with $30 million in diaspora funds. He refused to transfer the monies to the provisional government or to Kosovo's UN administrators, earning him yet another set of enemies. Instead, he set up a charitable organization in the name of the Kosovar people that doled out the monies for rebuilding schools and other worthy projects. Though not as an elected official, he remained a player, one above the brutal political fray in Kosovo. In doing so, he kept his options open for a political career down the road. In the spring of 2002 he broke with the LDK and formed his own party, the New Party for Kosovo, which would contest local and parliamentary elections in the future.

News of the Serbs' surrender reached the camp of the Atlantic Brigade soldiers on June 11, 1999. NATO's sustained bombing of military and civilian targets in Belgrade and other major Serbian cities had crippled Serbia's infrastructure. More destruction was too high a price for Milošević. For the Atlantic Brigade, it was all over even before it had really begun. Operation Arrow had pushed the Serb forces off Mount Paštrik in four days of heavy fighting. Eight Albanian Americans had been wounded, several seriously, but the Atlantic Brigade escaped without a single battlefield casualty.

As the Serb columns withdrew northward in the direction of Serbia proper, the Atlantic Brigade soldiers charged down into the Dukagjin Valley, stopping first in Prizren before heading on to Pristina. They were the first KLA soldiers to enter Kosovo's empty capital, which resembled a ghost town. The Albanian residents who stayed there during the war expressed shocked disbelief that the Serb forces had actually left. The Atlantic soldiers jumped out of the back of a truck to the shouts and cheering of the locals. It was probably the first time Pristina's inhabitants had seen live members of their own army. People hugged them. Women wept. "It was like something out of a movie," says Florim.

The Atlantic Brigade experienced the heroes' welcome, the made-for-Hollywood ending that émigrés fantasize about late into the night in their private diaspora clubs, sipping strong cups of coffee. This is probably the way Croatia's Bugojnici imagined their triumphant march into Zagreb, or how the Albanian émigrés, those who did the CIA's bidding in the 1950s, pictured their liberation of Tirana. But they ended up dead. Taking nothing away from their bravery, the stars lined up for the Kosovar Albanians in 1999. That it all could have ended much differently is irrelevant today. The Kosovar Albanians are not scattered across the region like the unhappy Kurds nor are they confined to miserable occupied ghettos like the Palestinians. Kosovo is not independent yet, but it lives under the benevolent tutelage of the United Nations.

At the Atlantic Brigade Association on Arthur Avenue in the Bronx, just across the hall from the Albanian Yellow Pages, the guys still meet to relive their once-in-a-lifetime adventure. The windowless rooms sport an impressive collection of KLA paraphernalia and lots of blurry snapshots of soldiers and mountains. The veterans roll up their sleeves to show off their KLA tattoos, insignia that mean nothing to their coworkers and fellow students. Florim is a graduate student in international relations at George Washington University in Washington, D.C. Fadil is the dinner-shift manager at Michael Jordan's New York City Steak House in Grand Central Station. The stories become more embellished with each telling, as war stories do. But who cares? Even Haxhi Dervisholli, who lost his left leg on Mount Paštrik, beams with pride at the memories. "Any regrets?" I ask him. "Of course not," he says, smiling broadly. "Kosovo is free."

Conclusion

D
o Bukoshi, Šušak, and Djordjevich occupy a place in the annals of exile politics next to the likes of Mazzini, Lenin, and Herzen? Certainly they belong to a determined tradition of diaspora activism, one that has unjustly become faded in the historical record. The concept of diaspora was born in antiquity, and ever since geographically dispersed peoples have united, dreamed, and mobilized. Long-distance nationalism can be traced back to the early days of the nation-state, a relationship so symbiotic that one of its nineteenth-century critics would call exile "the nursery of nationality."[1] The political impact of its multifarious incarnations, not always labeled diaspora, shaped contemporary Europe as well as North America. By no means limited to Europeans or to Jews, during the last decade the Chechen, Tamil, Armenian, Indian, and Chinese diasporas, among many others, have mounted vigorous campaigns in their peoples' names.

Though not new, the nature of diaspora engagement in home affairs, and in those of their adopted countries, has changed radically since transatlantic ships transported Albanian tutors to the Massachusetts konaks. The imported instructors from Europe's exiled Albanian communities taught the forefathers of the gastarbeiter how to read, availing them of the indispensble vehicle of modern nationalism, a technology called print media. This enabled the first Albanian Americans to participate, albeit belatedly, in Europe's national revolutions. More recently, just over the past decades, diasporas and their relationship to their homelands have again been dramatically transformed by state-of-the-art technological advances in communications and transportation. The facsimile and e-mail, the cell phone and the Internet, compress the time and space between those living in the heimat and those displaced from it. Diasporas have come a long way since the 1970s, when Ayatullah Khomeini's taped sermons circulated in the bazaars of Isfahan and Tehran. In the Balkans, satellite communications had an enormous impact on marshaling diaspora cohesion and defining the cause. Whether it was Bukoshi or Milošević, he who ruled the satellite programming commanded the loyalty of the greater diaspora. Literacy was no longer a requirement.

The speed and affordability of air travel has also shrunk the size of the world. There is a fluidness of exchange between diaspora and home county that blurs their dichotomy. Simply put, as the planet gets smaller, the distance and barriers between diaspora and homeland break down. Rather than two worlds there is one: a transnational community inhabited by all the nation's members, regardless of their addresses. Globalization has turned the world into a single integrated economy in which the exchange of goods and services, capital flows, as well as ideas, information, and images pay no heed to the frontiers of state.

The explosion of transnational phenomena, from websites to multinational corporations, facilitates the business of diasporas. Many of the strategies employed by the Balkan diasporas in the 1990s would have been unthinkable only a decade earlier. When Šušak sent out his famous letter beseeching the diaspora to arm Croatia, he used a couple of fax machines imported from Canada, technology nonexistent in Yugoslavia only a couple of years earlier. In a few short hours his office had blanketed the world's Croat community centers, sports clubs, Catholic churches, newspapers, radio stations, and folk dancing societies. The Kosovar Albanians' Three Percent Fund relied on the latest telecommunications and Internet services to push its fund-raising appeals, transnational banking networks to collect donations, and international businesses to deliver the money in Kosovo. On their cell phones, the KLA's arms suppliers manning the money fronts in Germany, Switzerland, and the United States stayed in instantaneous contact with the guerrilla commanders in the frontline trenches. Direct Mail replaced requisition forms. While NATO allies directed the air war over the trenches from war rooms in Brussels and Washington, the Kosovar exiles supplied the ground troops from Stuttgart and Geneva. In the Balkans, as in the Middle East and elsewhere, regional ethnic struggles are now global conflicts, unintelligible without examining their interconnected, cross-border components.

Another factor empowering today's transnational communities is the mind-boggling movement of peoples around the globe. The sheer numbers surging across national frontiers provides raw material for enriching diasporas or inventing them anew. These migrations and the modern-day migrant tend to look different from the Cold War variety. Though millions still flee from war, famine, poverty, and natural catastrophe, the Babylonian exile of the postwar era is a dying breed. Many more people than in the past elect to reside outside the country where they were born, while refusing to leave it behind entirely. Globalization's multinational jet-set follows the flow of capital, bringing their cultural identities with them. In Europe the two hundred million working members of the European Union may take advantage of a single job market that stretches from Stockholm to Athens. They do so as Irish, Portuguese, or whatever nationality, confident of their purpose and place in the transnational world.

In the Balkan diasporas, the category of political exile has lost its meaning. Men such as Michael Djordjevich or the Atlantic Brigade's Fadil Idrizi could resettle in their lands of birth now that pluralist democracies have begun to take root there. But they live in America, as respected Americans, and engage in the affairs of their mother countries as Serbs and Albanians, keeping a foot in both worlds. The émigrés note with a chuckle that when they travel from North America to the homeland they speak English with one another at the airport and as they board the flight. Somewhere over the Atlantic an unconscious shift occurs, and by the time the plane lands in Belgrade or Sarajevo everyone is chatting away in Serbian and Bosnian. Sipping their morning coffee in Chicago, émigrés can follow their favorite homeland soccer team on its web page; when visiting the Old World, the box score of the previous evening's Cubs or White Sox game is only as far away as the next Internet café. The same applies to their chosen pop groups, religious interests, and political affiliates. These hybrid, transnational identities are accepted on both sides of the Atlantic in an unprecedented way. This Croatian president Franjo Tudjman learned only when his "exiled Croatia" declined to return to liberated Croatia by the tens of thousands. Today these peoples' identities straddle the two societies as does their sense of responsibility. In the absence of conflict, diaspora activists will need to redefine these responsibilities, which will now be all the greater given the vast opportunities the new epoch offers.

These opportunities are loaded with both promise and disquiet. Despite the worldly pretensions of transnationalism, it has failed to eradicate some fundamental ingredients that can make diasporas obstructive players in world affairs. On the one hand, the centrifugal forces of globalization erode the cornerstones of the classic nation-state: its cherished sovereignty, solid national borders, the requirement of undivided loyalty, and exclusive political participation. Logically it would seem that as the traditional nation-state wanes in significance, so, too, should old-fashioned patriotism and nationalist passions lose their appeal. Yet, contrary to reason, this is not the case. In the transnational world, devotion to patria (one or more) remains a vital symptom of our age. One explanation suggests that the anonymity and homogenizing effects of globalization have driven its frightened children back into the embrace of the nation to find meaning and security.

Nor have the exigencies of transnational life entirely closed the gap between diaspora and homeland. As sophisticated as communications have become, diaspora communities inevitably become detached from the mundane developments in the homeland. Without the accumulation of the countless minor details of everyday life, the émigrés' idea of the homeland becomes disembodied and reconstructed by memory and imagination. Their view tends to move apart from that of the homelanders, however closely the émigrés try to stay in touch. Theoretically satellite television broadcasts should keep the diaspora updated on all aspects of life in the homeland. But when state-run news agencies function as the mouthpiece of regimes, the diaspora is inculcated with misinformation that further skews its perspective. To compound this disjuncture, it lacks the corrective that is provided by opposition media or home-grown independent culture—from graffiti to pop music. Rather than a mirror of the homeland, the diaspora becomes its alter ego.

Moreover, no number of visits or phone calls, Christmas presents or re-mittance transfers, alleviates the nagging guilt of not being there, not en-during the same hardships as close relatives and friends are subject to. Dias-poras overcompensate for their physical absence, and for the hypocrisy of being patriots who forfeit life in the patria. The men in the Atlantic Brigade would die for Kosovo, but they were not prepared to live there. Nor have the Balkan diasporas come to terms with the liberal requirement of sharing the homeland's territory with other ethnic peoples, even if they somehow manage to cohabit in Toronto and Frankfurt. Obviously they lack the daily experience of shoulder-to-shoulder living with the other ethnic peoples in the region. But there is more to it. These other peoples, by definition, do not belong to their ethnic nation. Diasporas are ethnically homogeneous entities, in a way that no country in the world is. A democratic state is the sum of all its varied citizens; the diaspora is a selection from just one volk.

Lastly, for all its merits, transnationalism does not render diasporas one iota more accountable for their projects than before. The means for diaspo-ras to participate in the political, economic, and cultural life of the home countries has never been greater. But émigrés still do not live the conse-quences of their undertakings, which are often motivated by high-minded ideals rather than pragmatism. The Balkan diasporas sprang to the defense of their nations in time of war, spending millions for arms, but have proved frugal and uninspired when it comes to postwar economic initiatives and building the institutions of their young democracies.[2] Too often their faulty vision—or self-interest—cause them to act contrary to the interests of the people they profess to love so deeply. Even in an age when dual nationality is becoming more commonplace, most émigrés do not vote, pay taxes, or hold elected positions in the homeland; they act, but without the responsi-bilities of citizenship or office.

In the West diasporas have taken full advantage of the forums of democ-racy to promote homeland agendas. The political leverage that diasporas wield in foreign policy, particularly in the United States, Canada, and Aus-tralia, has soared. Changing attitudes about "ethnic politics" have opened new vistas for diasporas to influence international policy toward their native regions. One reason for this is that the old ideal of the ethnic melting pot no longer demands that immigrants shed their Old World affinities in order to become "good citizens." Today's multicultural democracies allow ethnic groups considerably more leeway to maintain their cultural traditions and to pursue political agendas without raising suspicions of disloyalty. The official multicultural policies of Canada and Australia, even more than those in the United States, champion ethnic diversity and fund its expressions. When Serbian Americans demonstrated in the nation's capital against the U.S.–led NATO bombing of Yugoslavia, screaming at the top of their lungs that President Clinton was a Nazi and a murderer, no one batted an eye. Older German and Japanese Americans must have shaken their heads in disbelief.

The "ethnic factor" has become so much a part of U.S. politics that every candidate or elected politician has staff assigned to court America's diasporic communities. They are a plentiful source of money and votes, and they offer their resources to both major parties. This phenomenon is not entirely novel. In the past, though, it was predominantly right-wing Republicans who wooed the Eastern European émigrés by playing up to their anticommunism. George Kennan noted the role that Serbian American and Croatian American groups played in torpedoing his efforts to normalize relations with Tito's Yugoslavia in the early 1960s. But today these constituencies cut across party lines, and they are solicited, engaged, and promised action on a scale as never before. President Clinton's 1996 presidential reelection campaign had a particularly active ethnic outreach office, whose director, coincidentally, was Ilir Zherka, one of the Albanian Americans' top advocates. Zherka pointedly reminded the president of the strong ethnic vote when the White House grappled with the question of deploying air power against Milošević's Yugoslavia in 1998 and 1999.

Diasporas are nothing without their institutions, and these, too, have matured since the end of the Cold War. Professional lobby groups such as the Serbian Unity Congress and the Albanian American Civic League, to name only two, boast canny insider knowledge of how Washington works. Back in the 1950s or 1960s the leaders of the old-school émigré organizations felt flattered to have their pictures snapped next to a congressman in Washington. Today the lobby groups demand much more from the politicians whose campaigns they help to fund. They expect a role as players in the foreign-policy making process. The operations of the Balkan diasporas still pale in comparison, for example, with those of Jewish or Cuban Americans. But the Balkan groups, as well as other diasporas, emulate those lobbies and strive to attain a fraction of their influence. (Waiting their turn, Cuban Americans may have studied the Eastern European returnees as they entered the political fray in their freshly post-communist countries.)

The verdict is mixed on whether the ethnicization of foreign policy contributes to a more coherent international order. In *Marketing the American Creed Abroad*,[3] political scientist Yossi Shain argues that ethnic involvement in U.S. foreign affairs provides disenfranchised groups with an entry ticket into American society and politics. Their input legitimately reflects America's ethnic mosaic and offers a useful corrective to foreign policy-as-usual conducted by U.S. elites. He maintains that to win a voice in U.S. foreign affairs, diaspora groups must demonstrate a convincing commitment to democratic values, and to exporting them abroad. These ethnic activists become emissaries of American values and "the moral conscience of new democracies or newly established states in their homelands." As the selfless advocates of democracy and human rights, diaspora activists will nudge the United States to adhere to these noble principles, even when doing so contradicts Washington's short-term geostrategic interests.

If only it were so. During the 1990s the Balkans' diasporic groups—from the churches to PACs—lobbied blindly in the name of their people's national aspirations. They invoked democracy and human rights primarily as a strategic ploy to gain purchase and win concessions. Much to their discredit, the diasporas often promoted agendas even more nationalistic than those backed by the majority in the homeland. They failed dismally to act as the "moral conscience" of their young democracies, as indeed they should have after decades in Western societies. Dissenters found themselves branded as "traitors" and effectively excluded from the groups that claimed to speak on their behalf. One of the greatest disappointments was the Kosovar Albanians, whose legitimate grievances over human rights violations attracted broad sympathy and ultimately prompted NATO's intervention. But the moment they gained the upper hand in Kosovo, the Albanians turned on the newly defenseless Kosovar Serbs with repellent fury. Even the Bronx's Atlantic Brigade partook in torching the homes of resident non-Albanians as they marched victoriously toward the capital.[4]

The project remains of turning the considerable resources and energies of southeastern Europe's diasporas into constructive forces that foster democracy, prosperity, and stability in the Balkans. It is not utopian. The diasporas could start with the reform of their own organizations, remaking them as accountable, democratic institutions with less parochial visions. The diaspora-host country relationship must also be a two-way street. U.S. policy makers have had some success winning over diaspora representatives on select issues and using them to send pointed messages to leaders in the homeland. It took some arm-twisting, for example, to get the Albanian Americans to explicitly disavow the goal of a Greater Albania. But they did, for the most part, and the diaspora organizations helped to turn around opinion in the region. The financial resources of diasporas can also be put to much better use. From the United States alone, $30 billion every year is transferred from immigrant workers to homeland relatives.[5] These transfers keep families alive and prop up depressed regions around the world, as they do in the Balkans. Economists estimate that $375–$425 million a year in remittances entered Kosovo in the late 1990s.[6] But all too rare are examples of serious investment with long-term vision focused on stimulating productive economic activity in the region. Further, the fraud and manipulation of diaspora donations during the 1990s has left many interested parties understandably gun-shy about new financing schemes.

The tragedy of September 11, 2001, and the unnerving revelations about the breadth of the Al Qaeda organization, brought into stark relief the sinister potential of international networks, transnational undergrounds, and the abuse of democracy's freedoms. It is questionable indeed whether this new light will illuminate or distort the process of understanding our increasingly transnational societies. One hopes that the discourse will not revert to the invidious categories of the not-so-distant past when carriers of dual allegiances bore the stigma of "the enemy within." The challenge of extracting the tremendous potential from diasporas lies before us.

Notes

INTRODUCTION

1. See Loring M. Danforth, *The Macedonian Conflict: Ethnic Nationalism in a Transnational World* (Princeton, N.J.: Princeton University Press, 1995).

2. See, for example, *Diaspora: A Journal of Transnational Studies* (Toronto), initiated in 1991; also see Robin Cohen, *Global Diasporas: An Introduction* (Seattle: University of Washington Press, 1997).

3. Edward Said, *Reflections on Exile and Other Essays* (Cambridge, Mass.: Harvard University Press, 2001), xxxv.

4. The U.S.–backed Assembly of Captive Nations included Albania, Bulgaria, Czechoslovakia, Estonia, Hungary, Latvia, Lithuania, Poland, and Romania. Neither Yugoslavia nor any of its constituent nationalities belonged to the Assembly, a consequence of Tito's 1948 split with Stalin and the congenial relations between Yugoslavia and the West.

5. Eva Hoffman, "The New Nomads," in *Letters of Transit: Reflections on Exile, Identity, Language, and Loss,* ed. Andre Aciman (New York: New Press, 1999), 63.

CHAPTER 1. PICNIC IN MISSISSAUGA

1. *Večernji List,* May 5, 1998, 1.

2. Ibid.

3. "Tudjman je od Haaga spasila smrt!" *Dani,* April 21, 2001.

4. The Western press and diplomat corps also bought into the greatly embellished stories that Šušak spread about his past. In *Origins of a Catastrophe* (New York: Times Books, 1996), the former U.S. ambassador to Yugoslavia Warren Zimmermann refers to Šušak as a "pizza millionaire" from Canada (154). (Zimmermann also unfairly brands Šušak as an anti-Semite.) The European special envoy to former Yugoslavia, David Owen, claims that Šušak ran "a highly successful chain of restaurants in Canada" (*Balkan Odyssey* [New York: Harcourt, Brace, New York, 1995], 138). In fact, Tops Pizza was a take-out pizza shop in a roadside strip mall outside Ottawa. Šušak reportedly sold it at a loss.

5. *Globus,* December 3, 1999, 164–67; December 10, 1999, 168–72; December 31, 1999, 66–71.

6. Manolić interview, June 12, 2000; *Globus,* December 10, 1999, 68–73.

7. Ivana Djurić shows that the orientation of the Croatian Fraternal Union's publication, *The Federalist,* during the 1990s was anything but nonpolitical ("The Croatian Diaspora in North America and Nation-State Building Process in Croatia," M.A. thesis, Central European University, 1999). The organization and its periodical weighed in heavily on behalf of Croatian independence and other political issues. However, it never endorsed Tudjman as a candidate or the HDZ as a party.

8. Ivan Čizmić, Ivan Miletić, and George J. Pripić, *From the Adriatic to Lake Erie: A History of Croatians in Greater Cleveland* (Zagreb: Institute of Social Sciences Ivo Pillar, 2000), 416.

9. Ante Beljo, *YU-Genocide: Bleiburg, Death Marches, UDBA (Yugoslav Secret Police)* (Toronto: Northern Tribune Publishing, 1995).

10. Mark Aarons and John Loftus, *Unholy Trinity: The Vatican, the Nazis, and the Swiss Banks* (New York: St. Martin's Griffin, 1998).

11. Ibid., 120–39.

12. Hubert Butler, *The Sub-prefect Should Have Held His Tongue, and Other Essays* (New York: Penguin, 1985), 275–76, 288–89.

13. Croatian journalists, such as *Nacional's* star reporter Jasna Babić, have questioned much of Šušak's self-propagated life history. They claim that Šušak's father was never in the Ustashe and that Šušak's house was never burned down. See Babić's articles in *Globus*, July, 29, 1994; July 22, 1994.

14. Butler, *The Sub-Prefect*, 287–90. Today the center is a home for retired Croat priests.

15. Stella Alexander, *Church and State in Yugoslavia since 1945* (Cambridge: Cambridge University Press, 1979), 29.

16. Mart Bax, *Medjugorje: Religion, Politics, and Violence in Rural Bosnia* (Amsterdam: VU Uitgeverij, 1995), xvii.

17. Čizmić, Miletić, and Pripić, *From the Adriatic to Lake Erie*, 454–55.

CHAPTER 2. RECONCILING CROATIA

1. *Otpor,* no. 5 (1987): 24–28.

2. *The Fraternalist*, October 28, 1987. Translated by I. Djurić.

3. Dubravko Horvatić and Stjepan Šešlj, *Hrvatsko Slovo*, December 27, 1996.

4. Laura Silber and Allan Little, *The Death of Yugoslavia* (London: Penguin, 1996), 85.

5. Dona Kolar-Panov, *Video, War and the Diasporic Imagination* (London: Routledge, 1997), 104, 110–12.

6. Mark Thompson, *A Paper House: The Ending of Yugoslavia* (New York: Pantheon, 1992), 269.

7. Silber and Little, *Death*, 144.

CHAPTER 3. THE AVENGERS OF BLEIBURG

1. Richard West, *Tito and the Rise and Fall of Yugoslavia* (London: Sinclair-Stevenson, 1994), 302.

2. *Verfassungsschutzbericht 1972* (Bonn: Bundesministerium des Innern, 1973), 139. All the mercenaries save one, a seventeen-year-old minor, were killed in battle or executed. The survivor served nineteen years in prison, winning his freedom in 1991 with Croatia's independence. According to Nikola Stedul, who was at the Ministry of Defense at the time, the released prisoner left immediately for the front only to die in mysterious circumstances one week later.

3. "Mord und Terror im Exil," *Süddeutsche Zeitung*, May 4, 1972.

4. John R. Lampe, *Yugoslavia as History: Twice There Was a Country* (Cambridge: Cambridge University Press, 1996), 289.

5. "Emigranten: Starke Hand," *Der Spiegel*, October 5, 1970.

6. John B. Allcock, *Explaining Yugoslavia* (London: Hurst, 2000), 88.

7. Lampe, *Yugoslavia as History*, 273.

8. *Hrvatska Država*, no. 183 (May/June 1970).

9. *Stern*, June 6, 1971, 22–26.

10. See *Globus*, January 28, 2000, 91–95.

11. Ian Buruma, *Bad Elements: Chinese Rebels from Los Angeles to Beijing* (New York: Random House, 2001), 12.

12. *New York Times*, June 26, 1981, A10; May 16, 1982, A2.

13. *The Ottawa Citizen*, November 30, 1979, 29; "Protest Piglet Rescued," *The Ottawa Journal*, December 1, 1979, 5–6.

14. *Večernji List*, May 5, 1998, 1.

15. The handful of self-acclaimed "Muslim Croats" was an exception. Their affinity to the Croat diaspora was solely political.

16. The Vatican eventually recognized the Norval parish in 1987.

CHAPTER 4. MAKING BABY MIGS

1. President Tudjman was forced to withdraw Rojnića's nomination for the post. This, however, did not stop Rojnića, a textile businessman, from using his close relationship with the

1989–99 president of Argentina Carlos Menem to smuggle arms to Croatia. He also set up a recruiting and training operation in Argentina for mercenaries who wanted to fight in Croatia (*New York Times*, June 27, 1993). There are an estimated one hundred thousand ethnic Croats in Argentina.

2. Mark Wyman, *DPs: Europe's Displaced Persons, 1945–1951* (Ithaca, N.Y.: Cornell University Press, 1998), 9, 13.

3. After the HDZ government was voted out of power in early 2000 Maruna stepped back into his former position at the Croatian Heritage Foundation. He appointed the former *Nova Hrvatska* editor Jakša Kučan as his deputy.

4. *Nacional*, December 23, 1999.

5. *Globus*, November 2, 1992.

6. *Nacional*, March 15, 2000, 8–9.

7. Ibid., September 15, 2000.

8. Misha Glenny, *The Fall of Yugoslavia: The Third Balkan War* (New York: Penguin, 1996), 283.

9. *Nacional*, February 21, 2001.

10. Ibid.

11. Ibid., December 23, 1999.

12. *Washington Post*, August 13, 1991, A10. The report notes that the group's Otpor had already been linked to extortionist letters demanding up to $5,000 from wealthy Croatian Americans for the purchase of arms.

13. *Toronto Star*, February 9, 1987, A6.

14. Ibid., November 30, 1991, A17.

15. Warren Zimmerman, *Origins of a Catastrophe* (New York: Random House, 1996), 181.

16. Roger Cohen, *Hearts Grown Brutal: Sagas of Sarajevo* (New York: Random House, 1998), 304.

17. *Jane's Intelligence Review*, March 1, 1997, 102.

18. *The Guardian*, March 18, 1996, 8.

19. Tudjman's turn on the Bosnian Muslims sparked a rash of defections from his party and from his administration, and in the diaspora. Both Nikola Stedul and Boris Maruna expressed their objections personally to the president. Stedul stepped down from his position in protest. Maruna was elbowed out of his.

20. *New York Times*, October 28, 1995, A1.

21. "Privatizing War," *The Nation*, August 4, 1997, 11–17; *Newsweek*, August 27, 2001, 30–31.

22. When the International Tribunal for Crimes in the former Yugoslavia indicted several top Croat generals, such as Ante Gotovina, they cried foul, maintaining that the United States had cooperated in the planning of Operation Storm every step of the way.

23. On the same train journey, Tudjman reiterated his commitment to repatriating "exiled Croatia" to the homeland, an option all the more feasible with the Croatian Serbs gone: "Another promise is to return thousands, tens and hundreds of thousands, of Croatian people from all continents of the world. We must return them to the hearths of their ancestors. I make a pledge to myself and to all of you, to the entire Croatia, the authorities and to all people to do this, to ensure that as many of them return as possible." *Transition*, September 22, 1995, 60.

24. Cohen, *Hearts*, 438.

25. *Nacional*, June 1, 2000.

CHAPTER 5. WHITE EAGLES OVER CHICAGO

1. Milošević was elected president of the Federal Republic of Yugoslavia in July 1997. He served two elected terms as the president of the Republic of Serbia from 1990 to 1997.

2. *Washington Post*, April 25, 1999, H1.

3. Another exception was the Parisian businessman Boris Vukobrat, the figure behind one honorable little NGO called the Foundation for Peace and Crisis Management.

4. Historian Miranda Vickers claims that a concerted strategy existed on behalf of the Kosovar Albanians, supported financially from the diaspora, to buy up Serb-owned land in Kosovo. She implies that some of that funding was linked to drug smuggling (Miranda Vickers, *Between Serb and Albanian: A History of Kosovo* [London: Hurst, 1998], 225).

5. Official U.S. sources close to the émigré scene at the time strongly suspected that the killing was the result of rivalries within the Serb émigré community.

6. George Kennan, *Memoirs*, vol. 2: *1950–1963* (Boston: Little, Brown, 1972), 314.

7. *New York Times*, October 21, 1963, A1. Much mystery still surrounds this incident. The nationality of the two intruders remains a source of contention between Croat and Serb émigré groups, both proudly claiming the two intruders, or as they say "hitmen," as their own. According to author Richard Reeves, they were Croats, both former Yugoslav spies who were working in the hotel (*President Kennedy: Profile of Power* [New York: Simon and Schuster, 1993], 633). Knowledgeable Serb émigrés vehemently deny this. Croat émigré leader Martin Meštrović says that, after the incident, he met one of the men, Aleksander Karilanović. The young man told him that the communists had killed his parents and that he was trying to intercede on behalf of persecuted relatives. A rumor spread through the Croat community later that both men had been murdered.

8. See *Patriarch German's VIOLATIONS of the Holy Canons: Rules and Regulations of the Orthodox Church in Tito's Yugoslavia*, prepared by the Ret. Rev. Bishop Dionisije (Libertyville, 1965). This document includes Dionisije's attack against the Belgrade Patriarch and his rebuttal of the charges against him. It contains the official list of accusations against him for "conduct not becoming the priestly rank and profession." They include the charge "that he committed many disgraceful and shameful acts with the female set, among which included his public scandal with Miss Rada Milentijevich. She came as a student from Yugoslavia to be married, but this was spoiled by Bishop Dionisije; that bought an automobile for Rada Milentijevich and gave her money to open a hotel in Paris" (179). Dionisije calls this a "complete lie" (181).

9. *Washington Post*, February 22, 1997, H1.

10. "Izveštaj o korišćenju sredstava po osnovu zajma za privredni razvoj Srbije," Komisiji Vlade Republike Srbije za ispitivanje zloupotreba u oblasti privrede I finansijskog (Belgrade, April 2001).

CHAPTER 6. THE NEW LINGUA FRANCA

1. Daniele Conversi, "Moral Relativism and Moral Equidistance in British Attitudes to the War in the Former Yugoslavia," in *This Time We Knew: Western Responses to Genocide in Bosnia*, ed. Thomas Cushman and Stjepan Meštrović (New York: New York University Press, 1996), 259.

2. George Kennan, *Memoirs*, vol. 2: *1950–1963* (Boston: Little, Brown, 1972), 287. Perhaps the irony should be noted that Kennan, the author of the famous 1946 Long Telegram that helped set the confrontational tone of East-West relations that defined the Cold War, was brought down by the same kind of irrational anticommunism that his historic cable had played a part in bringing to life.

3. The SUC and SerbNet were just two of the dozens of pro-Serb groups around the world that together comprised the international Serb lobby. As nasty as their rivalries could be, the groups often overlapped in terms of membership and even board members. Their political objectives were virtually identical. Some of the groups were fronts for or subsets of organizations that already existed, formed for tax purposes or to make the lobby as a whole look more powerful than it really was.

Among the dozens of associations were the Serbian American Voters Alliance (Los Angeles), the Lord Byron Foundation for Balkan Studies (London), the Vuk Karadžić–Brothers Grimm Society (Berlin), the Serbian American Affairs Office (Washington, D.C.), the North American News Analysis Network (California, an SUC off-shoot), Serbian American Media Center, Serbian Information Initiative (a U.S.–based electronic newsgroup), the Serbian American Coalition for Peace (North American–church supported), and L'Association pour la Defense des droits et Interets du Peuple Serbe (Paris). Many of the pro-Serb associations were linked to Orthodox Churches.

4. At the 1964 Republican Party Convention in Chicago, presidential candidate Goldwater indirectly acknowledged Djordjevich's role in helping him win California. He said: "You Illinoisans are the witness of our policies to bribe our friends. Communist Yugoslavia has obtained two billion, three hundred million dollars in aid from America since 1948. The purpose of this aid was to bribe Tito not to follow the Communist path. What have we achieved? We have strengthened dictatorship and a government which has close ties with Moscow. Encouraged by our aid, secure in our leniency, Communist Tito now attempts to take control over the property of the Serbian Orthodox Church in America. The Bishop of the Serbian Orthodox–Canadian Diocese has already been assailed by the communist-controlled church in Yugoslavia" (quoted in Stanimir Spasovic, *The History of the Serbian Orthodox Church in America and Canada, 1941–1991* (Belgrade: n.p., 1998), 132.

5. SerbNet engaged the firms of David Keene and Associates and McDermott O'Neill. In Great Britain Ian Greer Associates represented the Serbs. The latter was paid, however, not by the United Kingdom Serb lobby but directly by Belgrade for a total of $160,000. See David Leigh and Ed Vulliamy, *Sleaze: The Corruption of Parliament* (London: Fourth Estate Limited, 1997), 110.

6. See Takis Michas, *Unholy Alliance: Greece and Milošević's Serbia* (College Station, Tex.: Texas A&M University Press, 2002).

7. www.suc.org/politics/media_watch.

8. *San Francisco Chronicle,* April 7, 1990, A16.

9. *The Path of Orthodoxy,* December 1995, 1.

10. Brad Blitz, "The Serbian Unity Congress and the Serbian Lobby: A Study of Contemporary Revisionism and Denial," www.freeserbia.net/Documents/Lobby.html. For an undiluted Serb rendition of the Balkan wars, see Danielle S. Sremac, *War of Words: Washington Tackles the Yugoslav Conflict* (Westport, Conn.: Praeger, 1999).

11. See Carole Hodge, *The Serb Lobby in the United Kingdom,* Donald W. Treadgold Papers, no. 22 (September 1995); and Brendan Simms, *Unfinest Hour: Britain and the Destruction of Bosnia* (London: Penguin, 2000).

12. Blitz, "The Serbian Unity Congress and the Serbian Lobby," 212–13. See Blitz's extensive analysis of the SUC's lobbying activities in his "Serbia's War Lobby: Diaspora Groups and Western Elites," in Cushman and Meštrović, *This Time We Knew,* 187–243.

13. In fact, individual Greek and Serb PACs accounted for 35 percent of the total donations Hamilton received in the first half of 1993. In the first half of 1995, contributions from Balkan diaspora sources totaled nearly 40 percent of the itemized contributions made by congressmen.

14. Blitz, *Serbia's War Lobby,* 215.

15. The former congressman Hamilton declined to be interviewed for this book. As of 2002 he is the director of the Washington, D.C.–based Woodrow Wilson International Center for Scholars.

16. Hodge, *The Serb Lobby in the United Kingdom,* 28.

CHAPTER 7. TURNING ON SLOBO

1. Louise Brandon and Dusko Doder, *Milosevic: Portrait of a Tyrant* (New York: Free Press, 1999), 146. In chapter 7, "The Unquiet American," the authors provide a thorough account of Panić's term in office.

2. In fact, former Congresswoman Helen Delich Bentley claims that she secured Milošević's promise to resign two months earlier. It was Panić, she implies, who sabotaged the deal.

3. David Owen, *Balkan Odyssey* (New York: Harcourt Brace, 1995), 25.

4. Brad Blitz, "Serbia's War Lobby: Diaspora Groups and Western Elites," in *This Time We Knew: Western Responses to Genocide in Bosnia,* ed. Thomas Cushman and Stjepan Meštrović (New York: New York University Press, 1996), 219.

5. Manojlo Vukotić, *Srpski San Milana Paniča,* trans. D. Krivokapić (Belgrade: n.p., 1994).

CHAPTER 8. SKANDERBEG'S WAY

1. Shkëlzen Maliqi, *Separate Worlds: Reflections, Analyses 1989–1998* (Pristina: Dukagjini, 1998), 108.

2. Denisa Kostovičová, "Parallel Worlds: Response of Kosovo Albanians to Loss of Autonomy in Serbia, 1989–1996," Keele European Research Center, Southeast Europe series, Research Paper 2 (Keele, U.K: Keele University, 1996), 35.

3. Maliqi, *Separate Worlds*, 98.

4. There are no official German statistics for the numbers of ethnic Albanians, from Kosovo or elsewhere, in Germany during the 1990s. At the time Kosovar Albanians were counted simply as citizens of Yugoslavia. Also, many Macedonian Albanians, Albanians from Albania, and other peoples, such as gypsies, claimed to be Kosovar Albanians in order to receive refugee status, which would distort even the best of estimates. It should be noted that diasporas' own figures for their size always err to the higher end of those estimates.

5. Tim Judah, *Kosovo: War and Revenge* (New Haven, Conn.: Yale University Press, 2000), 65–66.

6. In 1991 Albania's parliament issued a declaration requesting that the government recognize Kosovo as a state. This was a proclamation by legislators, not formal and internationally binding recognition. The Kosovar diaspora put Albania's politicans under no little pressure to take the cause of Kosovo to heart. In 1992, Kosovar emigres contributed money and technical help (like fax machines and computers) to the campaign of the opposition leader of the Democratic Party, Sali Berisha, whose grandstanding on the issue had raised Kosovar hopes that Albania would come to their rescue. Berisha's party won the March 1992 vote, but, under pressure from Washington, the new president backed down from his calls for a state union of Kosovo and Albania.

7. Nicholas Bethell, *Betrayed* (New York: Times Books, 1984).

8. "Gewalt," *Kölnische Rundschau*, January 20, 1982.

9. "Die Jugoslawen halten sich nicht an Geheimabsprache," *Stuttgarter Nachrichten*, January 19, 1982.

CHAPTER 9. BIRTH OF A LOBBY

1. This is the figure DioGuardi uses. Most estimates for the number of people with ethnic Albanian ancestry in the United States run from 300,000 to 450,000. When DioGuardi and others speak of a seven million–strong Albanian diaspora, they include the estimated five million ethnic Albanians who live in Turkey.

2. When it came to Albanian issues, the Greek American organizations were more than just pinch-hitting for their regional allies and Orthodox brothers, the Serbs. A history of sour relations between Greeks and Albanians, stemming primarily from rival territorial claims, explains the mistrust on both sides. Ultimately the Greeks fear that an empowerment of the Albanian people in the Balkans would pose a security threat to Greece.

3. *The Albanians: Europe's Forgotten Survivors* (Boulder, Colo.: Westview, 1977).

4. Howard Clark, *Civil Resistance in Kosovo* (London: Pluto, 2000), 83.

CHAPTER 10. EXILE ON KÖNIGSTRASSE

1. Michael Reisman, "Governments-in-Exile: Notes Toward a Theory of Formation and Operation," in *Governments-in-Exile in Contemporary World Politics*, ed. Yossi Shain (London: Routledge, 1991), 238.

2. Ibid.

3. Hivzi Islami, "Kosovo's Demographic Ethnic Reality and the Targets of Serbian Hegemony," as quoted in Miranda Vickers, *Between Serb and Albanian: A History of Kosovo* (London: Hurst, 1998), 272.

4. "Conflict and Change in Kosovo: Impact on Institutions and Society," ECSSD Working Paper, no. 31 (2001), 65.

5. See "Fjala e Kryeministrit të Republikës së Kosovës dr. Bujar Bukoshi, me rastin e Raport mbi Punën Qeverisë për perivdhën tetor 1991–dhjetor 1999," January 30, 2000. In the report, Bukoshi states that 44 percent of total contributions to the Three Percent Fund came from Germany and 40 percent from Switzerland.

6. Yossi Shain, "Governments-in-Exile and International Legitimation," in Shain, *Governments-in-Exile*, 221.

7. Direct remittances to family members from the diaspora dwarfed even the impressive numbers of the Three Percent Fund. The Kosovar Institute for Development Research (Riinvest) reports that total remittances from the Kosovar Albanian diaspora during the late 1990s averaged $375–$425 million annually, thus three times more each year than the total amount collected by the Three Percent Fund over seven years. The remittances were taxed by the parallel system in Kosovo, thus making diaspora monies in toto responsible for the vast share of the shadow state's revenues ("War Consequences on Family Economies and Businesses," survey, December 1999).

8. Howard Clark, *Civil Resistance in Kosovo* (London: Pluto Press), 117.

9. Vickers, *Between Serb and Albanian*, 283.

10. Shain, *Governments-in-Exile*, 32.

11. Fabian Schmidt, "Show Trials in Kosovo," in *Transitions*, November 3, 1993.

CHAPTER 11. FRANKIE GOES TO KOSOVO

1. See Tim Judah's thorough account of the history of the KLA and the Popular Movement's origins in Switzerland in *Kosovo: War and Revenge* (New Haven, Conn.: Yale University Press, 2000) as well as his "History of the Kosovo Liberation Army," in *Kosovo: Contending Voices on Balkan Interventions*, ed. William Joseph Buckley (Grand Rapids, Mich.: Eerdmans, 2000), 108–16. See also Chris Hedges, "Kosovo's Next Masters?" *Foreign Affairs* 78, no. 3 (1999): 24–42.

2. After the 1999 war in Kosovo the Macedonian Albanians moved their operation to the predominantly Albanian-populated villages in western Macedonia. The National Liberation Army, or NLA, was the Macedonian Albanian successor to the KLA and relied on the same sources for funds. In June 2001 U.S. authorities froze all U.S. bank accounts connected with the group, proof that officials could act against diaspora money-raising activities when they chose to. Swiss and German authorities followed suit.

3. The Popular Movement for Kosovo split its ranks in the early 1990s, spawning two rival organizations, the National Movement for the Liberation of Kosovo (LKCK) and the Albanian Revolutionary Party (PRSH).

4. *Verfassungsschutzbericht 1998* (Bonn: Bundesministerium des Innern, 1998), 174.

5. Florin Krasniqi maintains that the total figure was $20 million. Two-thirds of that was raised in the New York–New Jersey area, and the rest from elsewhere in the United States and Canada.

6. The estimate of the Washington-based think tank, International Crisis Group, of $30–$50 million collected by Homeland Calling is a decent ballpark figure.

7. *Berliner Zeitung*, July 9, 1998, 3.

8. *San Francisco Chronicle*, December 18, 1992, A1.

9. *Boston Globe*, June 3, 2001, A14.

CONCLUSION

1. Benedict Anderson, *The Spectre of Comparisons: Nationalism, Southeast Asia, and the World* (London: Verso, 1998), 59. The quote is from Lord Acton.

2. A disheartening World Bank report concluded that post-conflict regions with proportionately large diasporas have been proven to pose a significantly greater risk of renewed conflict during the five years after war than societies with small diasporas. Diasporas, it states, "appeared to be major additional risk factors in post-conflict societies." One reasonable way to

discourage these kinds of diaspora-supported conflicts, it argued, would be to collectively criminalize the financing of rebel movements by diaspora organizations (Paul Collier, "Policy for Post-conflict Societies Reducing the Risks of Renewed Conflict," World Bank Group paper, 2000).

3. Yossi Shain, *Marketing the American Creed Abroad* (Cambridge: Cambridge University Press, 1999).

4. *New York Times Magazine*, December 9, 1999, 108.

5. *New York Times*, November 12, 2002, 1.

6. "War Consequences on Family Economies and Businesses," *Riinvest Survey Report*, December 1999.

Selected Bibliography

CROATIA

Bennett, Christopher. *Yugoslavia's Bloody Collapse: Causes, Course, and Consequences.* New York: New York University Press, 1995.

Busic, Julienne Eden. *Lovers and Madmen: A True Story of Passion, Politics, and Air Piracy.* New York: Writers Club Press, 2000.

Čizmić, Ivan. *Povijest Hrvatske Bratske Zajednice, 1894–1994.* Zagreb: Golden Marketing, 1994.

Djilas, Aleksa. *The Contested Country: Yugoslav Unity and Communist Revolution, 1919–1953.* Cambridge, Mass.: Harvard University Press, 1991.

Djurić, Ivana. "Croatian Diaspora in North America: Identity, Ethnic Solidarity, and the Foundation of a Transnational Community." *Spaces of Identity,* no. 3 (October 2001).

Goldstein, Ivo. *Croatia: A History.* London: Hurst, 1999.

Goni, Uki. *The Real Odessa: How Peron Brought the Nazi War Criminals to Argentina.* London: Granta, 2002.

Haberl, Othmar Nikola. *Die Abwanderung von Arbeitskräften aus Jugoslawien. Zur Problematik ihrer Auslandsbeschäftigung und Rückführung.* Munich: R. Oldenburg Verlag,1978.

Hudelist, Darko. "Gojko Šušak: Crne Rupe u Političkoj Biografiji." *Globus,* nos. 468–80 (November 1999–February 2000).

Jurčevic, Josip, Vlado Sakić, and Marin Sopta. *Budučnost Iseljene Hrvatske.* Zagreb: Institute Ivo Pilar, 1998.

Jurdana, Srećko. *Stupovi Društva.* Zagreb: Media Press, 1997.

Kučan, Jakša. *Bitka za Novu Hrvatska.* Rijeka: Otokar Keršovani, 2000.

Krizman, Bogdan. *Pavelić u Bjekstvu.* Zagreb: Globus, 1986.

Maletić, Franjo, ed. *Who Is Who in Croatia.* Zagreb: Golden Marketing, 1993.

Mesić, Stipe. *Der Verfall Jugoslawiens.* Zagreb: Mislav Press, 1994.

Mursalo, T. A. *In Search of a Better Life: A Story of Croatian Settlers in Southern Africa.* Epping, Cape: Printpak, 1981.

Rotim, Karlo. *Široki Brijeg.* Široki Brijeg, 1994.

Skrbiš, Zlatko. *Long-Distance Nationalism: Diasporas, Homelands, and Identities.* Sydney: Ashgate, 1999.

Slany, William. "Supplement to the Preliminary Study on U.S. and Allied Efforts to Recover and Restore Gold and Other Assets Stolen or Hidden during World War II." Report. Washington, D. C.: U.S. Department of Economic, Business, and Agricultural Affairs, 1998.

Sopta, Marin, and Gabriele Scardellato. *Unknown Journey: A History of Croatians in Canada.* Downsview, Ontario: Polyphony, 1994.

Steinberg, Jonathon. "Types of Genocide? Croatians, Serbs, and Jews, 1941–45." In *The Final Solution: Origins and Implementation*, edited by David Cesarani. London: Routledge, 1994.

Tudjman, Franjo. *Horrors of War: Historical Reality and Philosophy*. New York: Evans, 1996.

Tanner, Marcus. *Croatia: A Nation Forged in War*. New Haven, Conn.: Yale University Press, 1997.

Winland, Daphne N. " 'We Are Now an Actual Nation': The Impact of National Independence on the Croatian Diaspora in Canada." *Diaspora: A Journal of Transnational Studies* 4, no. 1 (1995): 3–29.

SERBIA

Djukić, Slavoljub. *Milošević und die Macht: Serbiens Weg in den Abgrund*. Bad Vilbel: Nidda Verlag, 2000.

Gakovich, Robert P., and Milan M. Radovich. *Serbs in the United States and Canada*. Minneapolis: Immigration History Research Center, University of Minnesota Press, 1976.

Gutman, Roy. *A Witness to Genocide: The 1993 Pulitzer Prize–Winning Dispatches on the "Ethnic Cleansing" of Bosnia*. New York: Macmillan, 1993.

Judah, Tim. *The Serbs: History, Myth, and the Destruction of Yugoslavia*. New Haven, Conn.: Yale University Press, 1997.

Kavaja, Nikola. *Sinovi izdate Srbije*. Belgrade: Odjek, 2001.

Kisslinger, Jerome. *The Serbian Americans*. New York: Chelsea House, 1990.

Krazich, Thomas, ed. *Serbs in Australia: History and Development of the Free Serbian Orthodox Church Diocese for Australia and New Zealand*. Canberra: Monastery Press, 1971.

Libal, Wolfgang. *Die Serben: Blüte, Wahn und Katastrophe*. Vienna: Europaverlag, 1996.

Lopusina, Marko. *Srbi u Americi*. Belgrade: Evro, 2000.

Pavlowitch, Stevan. *Serbia: The History of an Idea*. New York: New York University Press, 2002.

Popovich, Milan. *The Serbian Orthodox Church through 750 Years*. Cleveland: n.p., 1969.

Prochter, Nicholas. *Serbian Australians in the Shadow of the Balkan Wars*. Sydney: Ashgate, 2000.

Slijepchevich, Djoko. *The Transgressions of Bishop Dionisije*. Chicago: n.p., 1965.

Thomas, Robert. *Serbia under Milošević: Politics in the 1990s*. London: Hurst, 1999.

Vrga, Djuro J., and Frank J. Fahey. *Changes and Socio-Religious Conflict in an Ethnic Minority Group: The Serbian Orthodox Church in America*. San Francisco: R and E Research Associates, 1975.

KOSOVO

Blaku, Rifat. *Hintergründe der Auswanderung von Albanern aus Kosova in die Westeuropäischen Staaten*. Vienna: Norbertus, 1995.

Brand, Marcus. "Kosovo under International Administration: Statehood, Constitutionalism, and Human Rights." Ph.D. diss., University of Vienna, 2002.

Buckley, William, ed. *Kosovo: Contending Voices on Balkan Interventions*. Grand Rapids, Mich.: Eerdmans, 2000.

Drezov, Kyril, et al., eds. *Kosovo: The Politics of Delusion*. London: Frank Cass, 2001.

Duijzings, Ger, Dušan Janjić, and Shkëlzen Maliqi. *Kosovo-Kosova: Confrontation or Coexistence*. Nijmegen: Peace Research Centre, 1996.

Elsie, Robert, ed. *Kosovo: In the Heart of the Powder Keg*. New York: Columbia University Press, 1997.

Gashi, Dardan, and Ingrid Steiner. *Albanien: Archaisch, Orientalisch, Europäisch*. Vienna: Promedia, 1997.

Hamzaj, Bardh. *A Narrative about War and Freedom: Dialog with the Commander Ramush Haradinaj*. Pristina: Zëri, 2000.

Kaser, Karl, Robert Pichler, and Stephanie Schwander-Sievers, eds. *Die Weite Welt und das Dorf: Albanische Emigration am Ende des 20. Jahrhunderts*. Vienna: Böhlau Verlag, 2002.

Kopani, Arthur, and Naim Dedushaj. *LDK në SHBA: Historia e një lëvizjeje*. New York: n.p., 2000.

Lamaj, Idriz. *Komiteti Kombëtar "Shqipëria e Lirë" 1949–1956*. New York: n.p., 2000.

Lipsius, Stephan. Series of articles on Kosovo's radical underground parties in the journal *Südost* (Munich), 1999–2001.

Malcolm, Noel. *Kosovo: A Short History*. London: Macmillan, 1998.

Mertus, Julie A. *Kosovo: How Myths and Truths Started a War*. Berkeley: University of California Press, 1999.

Pettifer, James, and Miranda Vickers. *Albania: From Anarchy to a Balkan Identity*. New York: New York University Press, 1997.

Royse, M. W., ed. *The Albanian Struggle: In the Old World and New*. Boston: The Writer, Inc., 1939.

"Wag the Dog: The Mobilization and Demobilization of the Kosovo Liberation Army." Brief 20, Bonn International Center for Conversion, 2001.

Index